W9-BRZ-257

SYNTAX and SEMANTICS

VOLUME 11

EDITORIAL BOARD

A list of the contents of previous volumes appears at the end of this book.

SYNTAX and SEMANTICS

VOLUME 11

Presupposition

Edited by

CHOON-KYU OH

DAVID A. DINNEEN

Department of Linguistics
University of Kansas
Lawrence, Kansas

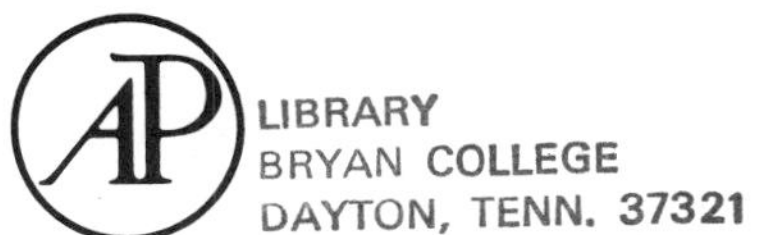

ACADEMIC PRESS *New York San Francisco London*

A Subsidiary of Harcourt Brace Jovanovich, Publishers

ACADEMIC PRESS, INC.
111 Fifth Avenue, New York, New York 10003

United Kingdom Edition published by
ACADEMIC PRESS, INC. (LONDON) LTD.
24/28 Oval Road, London NW1 7DX

LIBRARY OF CONGRESS CATALOG CARD NUMBER: 72–9423

ISBN 0–12–613511–8

PRINTED IN THE UNITED STATES OF AMERICA

79 80 81 82 9 8 7 6 5 4 3 2 1

CONTENTS

LIST OF CONTRIBUTORS

Numbers in parentheses indicate the pages on which the authors' contributions begin.

JAY DAVID ATLAS (265), *Department of Philosophy and Intercollegiate Linguistics Program, Pomona College, Claremont, California 91711 and Wolfson College, Oxford OX2 6UD, England*

DEREK BICKERTON (235), *Department of Linguistics, University of Hawaii, Honolulu, Hawaii 96822*

JANET DEAN FODOR (199), *Department of Linguistics, University of Connecticut, Storrs, Connecticut 06268*

GERALD GAZDAR (57), *School of Social Sciences, University of Sussex, Brighton, BN1 9QG England*

KURT GODDEN (225), *Department of Linguistics, University of Kansas at Lawrence, Lawrence, Kansas 66045*

LAURI KARTTUNEN (1), *Department of Linguistics, University of Texas at Austin, Austin, Texas 78712*

JERROLD J. KATZ (91), *City University Graduate Center, City University of New York, New York, New York 10036*

RUTH M. KEMPSON (283), *School of Oriental and African Studies, University of London, London, England*

S.-Y. KURODA (183), *Department of Linguistics, University of California, San Diego, La Jolla, California 92093*

JAMES D. McCAWLEY (371), *Department of Linguistics, University of Chicago, Chicago, Illinois 60637*

CHOON-KYU OH (225), *Department of Linguistics, University of Kansas at Lawrence, Lawrence, Kansas 66045*

STANLEY PETERS (1), *Department of Linguistics, University of Texas at Austin, Austin, Texas 78712*

PHILIP L. PETERSON (325), *Department of Philosophy, Syracuse University, Syracuse, New York 13210*

ELLEN F. PRINCE (389), *University of Pennsylvania, Philadelphia, Pennsylvania 19104*

IVAN A. SAG (389), *Department of Linguistics, Stanford University, Stanford, California 94305*

TRAUGOTT SCHIEBE (127), *University of Stockholm and Salagatan 5A, S-753 30 Uppsala, Sweden*

DAN SPERBER (299), *CNRS and Université de Paris X, Nanterre, France and 33, Rue Croulebarbe, 75013 Paris, France*

S. K. THOMASON (357), *Department of Mathematics, Simon Fraser University, Burnaby, British Columbia V5A 1S6 Canada*

JOHAN VAN DER AUWERA (249), *Germaanse–Linguistiek, University of Antwerp, Universiteitsplein 1, B-2610 Wilrijk, Belgium*

RALPH M. WEISCHEDEL (155), *Department of Computer and Information Sciences, University of Delaware, Newark, Delaware 19711*

DEIRDRE WILSON (299), *Department of Phonetics and Linguistics, University College of London, Gower Street, London WCIE 6BT, England*

PREFACE

Although PRESUPPOSITION may not be accepted by all readers of—or even all contributors to—this volume as the proper term for referring to the full range of phenomena discussed herein, one could observe at the conference held at the University of Kansas in April, 1977, that leading figures and newcomers alike found it the most nearly acceptable cover term. At a conference, of course, one can take advantage of opportunities to clarify definitions and to reach a common (though often temporary) understanding of the terms used by the speakers and discussants. The editors recognize the impossibility of re-creating that situation on paper but hope that the arrangement of the papers and the brief comments in this preface will help make the reading of these papers as fruitful as the conference was.

It should be noted immediately that, although this volume includes many of the papers given at the conference (Numbers 1, 10, 11, and 14–16)—some extensively revised in the light of discussions at Lawrence—it also includes papers from colleagues who could not be present but whose contributions were felt to be essential. There were a number of papers given at the conference that could not be included due to space constraints or to prior publishing commitments. Those papers and the scholars who gave them contributed much to the success of the conference and, indirectly, to the shape of this volume.

The contributors to this study are linguists, philosophers, mathematicians, and computer scientists, all of whom appear to share some or all of the following assumptions: Sentences in natural languages may contain linguistic structures (words, expressions, or syntactic forms–ordering) that reflect a presupposition on the part of the speaker/hearer/third party; to state fully the meaning of a sentence containing such a structure, the analyst must include the "presuppositions," whatever he may call them or however he may subclassify them; there are limits to the application or effect of presuppositions in nonsimplex sentences; and although intuition may lead one to discover presuppositions, formal tests are necessary to establish their presence.

With the motive of being of service to the readers, we decided to take the risk of presuming to impose an order on the papers and to group them in a sequence that we find most suitable.

The Karttunen–Peters paper seemed an obvious lead article, among other reasons because it contains excellent and authoritative background information. More importantly, Karttunen and Peters propose formal criteria for distinguishing among various distinct phenomena indiscriminately called PRESUPPOSITION in recent literature. They then proceed to present a projection system based on Montague's model theoretic semantics, extending it to include conventional implicature. (The reader may profitably return to this section of the paper after reading the subsequent articles.)

The following four papers constitute a natural follow-up to the Karttunen–Peters paper. Gazdar, as do many of the contributors to this volume, refers to earlier Karttunen papers, giving an excellent summary of arguments and proposing a solution to the projection problem that is essentially a cumulative hypothesis very similar to the original Langendoen–Savin projection system but additionally equipped with an ingenious cancellation device of some potential implicatures and presuppositions just in case they create an inconsistency. Katz also offers a solution that, on the lexical level, marks each argument position for a predicate item with respect to referentiality on the basis of the relative simplicity of predicting semantic properties and relations and, on the level of complex constituents, provides the projection rule that may install or remove "heavy parentheses" (Katz uses his heavy parenthesis notation to mark referentiality), thereby modifying the referentiality configuration thus far established.

In the same set, Schiebe returns the reader to a pragmatic concept of presuppositions, with a definition that involves specifically the "context of the MOMENT of the utterance" and with the introduction of the notion of various "worlds" (overall contexts) to which the sentence in question may be related. According to Schiebe, one does not project the presuppositions of a complex sentence from the presuppositions of component sentences but, rather, accounts for the ways in which higher predicates modify or "dye" the truth-levels of the presuppositions involved.

We conclude this section with Weischedel's paper, in which, although recognizing the absence of a universally accepted definition of presupposition and the heterogeneity of examples of presupposition in the literature, he argues quite convincingly that one can compute the presuppositions of a sentence while parsing that sentence, regardless of the complexity of, or the kinds of predicates used in, the sentence. Weischedel presents a particular parser with its associated lexicon that encompasses most, if not all, examples of presupposition.

While reading presupposition literature, one cannot help observing that intuition has infected presupposition theory almost as much as it has transformational theory. The papers in the second set may best be characterized as attempts to differentiate diverse phenomena lumped together under the cover term PRESUPPOSITION and to supply some sort of strategy for justifying the classification of each of these phenomena. Kuroda, for instance, argues that ENTAILMENT, PRAGMATIC PRESUPPOSITION OF THE INTERROGATIVE, and what he calls SEMANTIC$_2$ PRESUPPOSITION are grounded on various levels of reason, whereas the justification of semantic presupposition as conceived by the presuppositionist semanticists is based solely on the investigator's intuition, which is "a product of various competence and performance factors." Fodor, on the other hand, attempts—with a good deal of success, in our judgment—to spell out some principles that underlie various intuitions, especially those on the truth-value gap. In doing so, she introduces a valuable subclassification of relations expressed by natural language predicates on the basis of whether or not it is required that all arguments of a predicate have a point of reference in the same world.

Oh and Godden are primarily concerned with supplying an explanation for various recent observations on presupposition projection in terms of some natural governing principles. According to them, a PRESUPPOSITION is one of the propositions that constitute a given discourse context, which is reflected in the choice of lexical items and syntactic constructs. They handle the projection problem by introducing a set of general principles governing the efficiency of speech acts. Presupposition failure may arise on these two distinct levels. Bickerton also lists a set of principles that characterize the behavior of presuppositions, especially those that govern the conjoinability of sentences that bear certain entailment relations.

We close this third section with Van der Auwera's paper, in which he characterizes PRAGMATIC PRESUPPOSITION as irrefutable meaning or the "kernel meaning that is necessary and sufficient for an expression to qualify as an assertion." Van der Auwera explains various presuppositional behaviors in terms of the interaction between contextual structures and what he calls the "principle of inertia." An irrefutable meaning gets reduced or simplified in a variety of ways, depending on the contextual structure in which a speech act is performed.

We introduce the final set with Atlas's paper, which is written in the framework of an attempt to bring linguists and philosophers together in their study of presupposition theory. Atlas argues in favor of the ANTI-REALIST THEORY OF MEANING, specifically objecting to postulating an ambiguity between so-called internal (or choice) negation and external (or exclusion) negation. Attacking a similar problem, Kempson argues against the ambiguity analysis of natural language negation. But, unlike Atlas, Kempson supports an approach based on intensional logic and takes sides with Montague. Kempson uses the thesis of the nonexistence of internal–external negation ambiguity to argue against the presuppositionists' hypothesis.

Wilson and Sperber attack both semantically based and pragmatically based presuppositionist positions but go beyond just a negative criticism and propose a semantic account of presuppositional behavior. In their approach, a sentence is analyzed semantically into a set of entailments while the syntactic, lexical, or phonological form imposes an ordering on the entailments, thus pushing some of them into the background. (Compare Gazdar's treatment of the rank-ordering of various meaning components.)

Peterson's paper is concerned with the analysis and comparison of referential presuppositions, especially on the event level, and with factive presuppositions. He also provides syntactic and semantic tests to distinguish among events, facts, and propositions and includes an appendix on the implications of his observations for Montague grammar.

Thomason discusses a mathematical model that is rich enough to account for "the most famous examples" of presuppositions without utilizing "any artifices" such as supervaluations, intermediate truth values, and possible worlds or individuals. He contrasts what he calls a METALANGUAGE MODEL and an OBJECT LANGUAGE MODEL. The concept of presupposition is defined in the former, but it is the latter, Thomason argues, that displays "perspicuously some properties of that notion."

We conclude this final section and the collection with McCawley's lucid discussion of context and contextual domain. The parallel he draws between the two is especially fruitful in that he is able to resolve the problem of discourse reference on independently justified grounds.

ACKNOWLEDGMENTS

The editors wish to acknowledge, with thanks, the support and encouragement of their colleagues and students at the University of Kansas and, in particular, the Office of Academic Affairs, the College of Liberal Arts and Sciences, the Bureau of Child Research, the Applied English Center, and the Department of Linguistics for contributing to the support of the conference held in April, 1977. Special thanks are also due to the staff at the Raymond Nichols Space Technology Center for their kindness in allowing us to use their excellent conference area.

CONVENTIONAL IMPLICATURE[1]

LAURI KARTTUNEN AND STANLEY PETERS
University of Texas at Austin

1. INTRODUCTION

The term PRESUPPOSITION is an honorable one, with a respectable, if controversial, history in philosophy and philosophical logic. Such important figures as Frege and Strawson have found it essential to make presupposition a basic notion in their theories. In view of this fact, it is not surprising that linguists should have fastened on the concept when they began to describe those aspects of sentences which seem to be preconditions for successful use or functioning of the sentences in speaking. Beginning with Paul and Carol Kiparsky, a number of linguists have isolated features of sentences that contain certain lexical items or syntactic constructions and identified them as presuppositions of the sentences, propositions which the sentences are not primarily about but which have to be established prior to utterances of the sentences in order for communication to go smoothly. The central theme that runs through the abundant literature on this topic is that presuppositions constitute an aspect of meaning distinct from the kind of semantic content that is the subject matter of ordinary truth-conditional semantics.

[1] This work was supported by the National Science Foundation under grant BNS 76-20307. An earlier version of the first part of the chapter was presented at the Third Annual Meeting of the Berkeley Linguistics Society in February 1977.

Syntax and Semantics, Volume 11: Presupposition

ISBN 0-12-613511-8

We have no quarrel with the idea of recognizing non-truth-conditional aspects of meaning; on the contrary, we are convinced that this is inevitable. But we do take issue with the view that all so called presuppositions are instances of the same phenomenon. We believe that a wide range of different things have been lumped together under this single label and that this fact is, more than anything else, responsible for the continuing controversy about how to analyze presuppositions.[2] To resolve it, we propose to do the sensible thing, namely to divide up this heterogeneous collection and to put the particular cases into other categories of phenomena, such as particularized and generalized conversational implicatures (Grice, 1975), preparatory conditions on speech acts (Searle, 1969), and conventional implicatures.[3] Since something is already known about the nature of these other phenomena, in this way we may actually be able to explain some of the diverse behavior of different things that various linguists have at one time or another called presuppositions.

We begin by giving an example of so called presupposition that we think is a case of particularized conversational implicature, that is, an inference which arises from considerations involving (*a*) what the sen-

[2] This same point has been made in many recent works on the topic, for example, Wilson (1975), Kempson (1975), Boër and Lycan (1976). There is disagreement, however, on what conclusion should be drawn from this. Boër and Lycan take the pessimistic view that the notion of presupposition is entirely misguided. Wilson and Kempson are willing to recognize only very few cases of real "presuppositional phenomena," such as the particle *even*.

[3] An IMPLICATURE in Gricean terms means the following. If the uttering of a sentence ϕ in a given context licenses the inference that p even though the proposition p is something over and above what the speaker actually says, then he has IMPLICATED that p and p is an IMPLICATURE (or IMPLICATUM) of the utterance of ϕ. Grice discusses two kinds of implicatures: CONVERSATIONAL and CONVENTIONAL. The former sort is ultimately connected with his notion of cooperative conversation, in which the participants observe certain conversational maxims. Conversational implicatures can be divided further into PARTICULARIZED and GENERALIZED conversational implicatures on the basis of how closely they depend on a particular context of utterance. CONVENTIONAL implicatures arise not from the interplay of what is said with conversational maxims, but from the conventional meanings of words and grammatical constructions that occur in the sentence. One typical characteristic of conventional implicatures is that they are DETACHABLE, that is, there is another way of saying the same thing which does not give rise to the implicature. Conversational implicatures, on the other hand, are harder to detach because they depend more on the content of what is said and less on how it is expressed. Another difference is that conventional implicatures are NOT CANCELABLE; it is contradictory for the speaker to deny something that is conventionally implicated by the sentence he has uttered. Conversational implicatures can always be prevented from arising by being explicitly disavowed. See Grice (1975) for examples and discussion.

tence actually says, that is, its truth conditions, (*b*) the particular situation in which it is uttered, and (*c*) Gricean maxims of conversational interaction. In such cases the ordinary truth-conditional account of sentence meaning is in fact perfectly satisfactory and it is misguided to think that the phenomenon in question is evidence for, or to be explained by, some added non-truth-conditional aspect of sentence meaning.

Next we will take up a case of what Grice calls generalized conversational implicature. We show that the so called presupposition can be explained in terms of truth conditions, preparatory conditions on speech acts, and conversational principles. What makes it a generalized rather than a particularized conversational implicature is that the inference in question is not dependent on characteristics peculiar only to certain contexts of utterance.

In both of these cases we argue that the previous analyses, which attribute the phenomenon in question to some special component of sentence meaning called presupposition, are mistaken. Our next step is then to turn to a class of so called presuppositions which we regard as genuine instances of a phenomenon that cannot be accounted for in terms of ordinary truth-conditional semantics and general pragmatic considerations. This class seems to us to fall under Grice's notion of conventional implicature. By way of introduction, we point out some of the differences between conversational and conventional implicatures and discuss the relationship between implicature and felicity. The main objective of our chapter is to show how model-theoretic methods of semantic interpretation can be extended to account for both truth-conditional and conventionally implicated meanings of sentences.

The system that we present here was first outlined in our 1975 Berkeley paper (Karttunen and Peters, 1975) and we have made use of it in our 1976 Chicago paper (Karttunen and Peters, 1976) on indirect questions and in a number of other studies. It is an extension of the system of semantic interpretation developed by Montague in his "Proper Treatment of Quantification in Ordinary English" (henceforth PTQ). In the present chapter, we give a brief summary of its main principles and descriptive apparatus, and then apply it to a number of examples to show how the system can describe some typical cases of conventional implicature that have been called presuppositions. We do not have space to discuss more than a few examples, but we have included in an appendix our complete revised version of Montague's PTQ rules.

2. PRESUPPOSITIONS DISBANDED

Let us now turn to a case of so called presupposition that is not a case of conventional implicature and does not provide any clear evidence for the existence of a non-truth-conditional aspect of sentence meaning. It has been said (e.g., in Lakoff, 1970) that subjunctive conditionals, also known as counterfactual conditionals, presuppose the falsity of their antecedent clauses. For example, Sentence (1)

(1) *If it were raining outside, the drumming on the roof would drown out our voices.*

presupposes that it is not raining outside.

It is indeed true that in most conversational situations the hearer is entitled to assume, upon hearing (1), that the speaker regards the antecedent clause as false. However, it is a mistake to jump from this observation to the conclusion that this fact must somehow be recorded in the semantic description of this particular sentence and that there must be a rule of grammar which accomplishes that. One need not appeal to a counterfactual presupposition in order to explain how the sentence indicates that the speaker believes the antecedent to be false. Note, to begin with, that whenever Sentence (1) is asserted, it will be readily apparent to any listener who understands the sentence that the consequent clause is false. Just by hearing the words clearly, the addressee will immediately recognize that the speaker's voice is not being drowned out. The falsity of the antecedent clause then follows straightforwardly, assuming that the conditional sentence is true. For it is clear, even without going into details about the truth conditions of subjunctive conditionals, that such a sentence cannot be true under conditions where its antecedent clause is true and its consequent clause false. For this reason, the speaker of (1), by overtly committing himself to the truth of what he says, implicitly indicates his belief that his surroundings are free of rain just by choosing such an obviously false consequent clause to utter.

A second important fact about the subjunctive conditional construction is that, besides it being unnecessary to postulate a counterfactual presupposition for a sentence such as (1), it would be incorrect to postulate a general rule to the effect that a subjunctive conditional sentence presupposes that its antecedent clause is false. As a case in point, consider

(2) *If Mary were allergic to penicillin, she would have exactly the symptoms she is showing.*

This sentence would, if anything, normally tend to suggest that its antecedent clause is true, in contravention of any principle that this construction carries a counterfactual presupposition.

We will shortly come to other examples which can suggest that the antecedent clause is true, and these examples together with Sentence (2) clearly show that subjunctive conditionals do not as a rule presuppose that their antecedent is false, in any sense of presupposing that can be formalized as a part of grammatical theory. Before taking up these other examples though, let us briefly note why Sentence (2) suggests that its antecedent is true. Unlike Sentence (1), (2) has a consequent clause which is obviously true. Therefore the falsity of the consequent clause does not prevent (2) and its antecedent clause from both being true. Moreover, subjunctive conditional sentences are well fitted by virtue of their truth conditions to proposing explanations of known facts, to explaining them on the grounds that the fact stated as the consequent clause follows from the hypothesis stated in the antecedent clause. Of course the known fact is explained only if the hypothesis from which it follows is also true. Therefore, if Sentence (2) is offered as a conjecture as to why Mary has exactly the symptoms she is showing, this has to indicate that at least the speaker does not know the antecedent to be untrue.

Let us now consider some subjunctive conditional sentences whose consequent clauses are neither as blatantly false as that of (1) nor as obviously true as that of (2). For instance, consider

(3) *If Shakespeare were the author of Macbeth, there would be proof in the Globe Theater's records for the year 1605.*

Certainly it is possible to indicate one's belief that Shakespeare did not write Macbeth by uttering this sentence in a context where the Globe Theater's records for the year 1605 have just been searched and found to lack any evidence of Shakespeare's authorship. The existence of this possibility can be explained in a fashion parallel to the explanation we gave of why (1) normally indicates that the antecedent is false. But Sentence (3) does not as a rule indicate that Shakespeare is not the author of Macbeth. Such indication occurs only when the sentence is uttered in a particular kind of setting, one where there is reason to believe that the consequent of (3) is false. In a different sort of context, the sentence may indicate that its antecedent could well be true. For example, if Sentence (3) is uttered in the course of speculating about how the authorship of Macbeth could be established, where it is not known that the antecedent is false, the sentence indicates that the speaker does not know whether or not Shakespeare did write Macbeth. In such a context, this sentence behaves somewhat like Sentence (2). Note that the latter sort of context should not be confused with one where it is already agreed that Shakespeare did not write Macbeth, and Sentence (3) is uttered as a way of suggesting how further evidence could be gathered to support this agreed upon proposition. In this sort of context, it is not the uttering of (3) which indicates that Shakespeare did not write Macbeth. Rather, that proposition has been agreed to before Sentence (3) is produced, and so this kind of context provides no evidence for saying that (3) requires the presupposition that Shakespeare did not write Macbeth.

The now-you-see-it-now-you-don't behavior of the supposed counterfactual presupposition is reminiscent of another kind of phenomenon which is by now familiar from the work of Grice—namely, conversational implicature. In the cases where an utterance of a subjunctive conditional sentence indicates that the antecedent clause is false, this conclusion on the hearer's part is necessitated by the need to reconcile the fact, evident in the context of utterance, that the consequent clause is false with the assumption that the speaker is observing Gricean maxims of conversation—in particular the maxim, "Speak the truth!" On the other hand, in the cases where uttering the subjunctive conditional sentence in a given context indicates the speaker's belief that the antecedent might be true, that conclusion is required if the hearer is to reconcile the assumption that the speaker is observing the Gricean maxim, "Be relevant!" with what is known about the truth of the consequent clause of the sentence uttered.

Now certain further consequences flow from our tentative conclusion that no rule associates with the subjunctive conditional sentences a presupposition that the antecedent is false, or for that matter that it is possibly true. Instead the utterance of such sentences conversationally implicates in some contexts that the antecedent is false and in other contexts that the antecedent could be true. Since particularized conversational implicatures like these are highly context dependent, it should be possible to make them come and go by working alterations in the context surrounding the utterance of the sentence. In some cases, these conversational implicatures can be made to disappear by explicitly disavowing them. For instance, a doctor who elaborates on (2) by saying,

(4) *If Mary were allergic to penicillin, she would have exactly the symptoms she is showing. But we know that she is not allergic to penicillin.*

does not implicate that Mary is, or even might be, allergic to penicillin. The doctor's disavowal of that proposition makes it clear that uttering the subjunctive conditional is simply part of running through the possible causes of Mary's symptoms, not an explanation of them. Likewise, a person who expanded on (3) by saying

(5) *If Shakespeare were the author of Macbeth, there would be proof in the Globe Theater's records for 1605. Let's go through them once more to make sure we didn't overlook that proof.*

makes it clear that he is not willing to accept that the consequent clause of the subjunctive conditional clause is false, and in that way cancels what might otherwise have been implicated.

Moreover, if a subjunctive conditional clause is embedded as the complement of a higher verb, then even if that higher verb is what Karttunen (1973, 1974) has called a hole to presuppositions the erstwhile counterfactual implicature may be canceled. If I say, for instance,

(6) *It is unlikely that, if it were raining outside, the drumming on the roof would drown out our voices.*

I in no way suggest that I think it is not raining outside. But the context *It is unlikely that* ______ is a hole to presuppositions. For instance,

(7) *It is unlikely that Mary realizes that John is here.*

presupposes that John is here just as much as

(8) *Mary realizes that John is here.*

does. In the case of the subjunctive conditional sentence, the reason for the disappearance of the counterfactual implicature in this context is, of course, that the speaker can perfectly well be speaking the truth despite the obvious falsehood of the consequent clause of the embedded conditional sentence. This is so even if the antecedent clause is true, since Sentence (6) does not commit the speaker to the embedded conditional being true.

In summary then, the supposed counterfactual presupposition of subjunctive conditionals is neither present with all subjunctive conditional sentences—for example, (2)—nor does it follow the same laws for projecting presuppositions to complex sentences as the so called factive presupposition of (8) does. The supposed counterfactual presupposition cannot, therefore, be classified in the same group with all the other presuppositions. However, it behaves exactly as we expect a particularized conversational implicature to behave, which we therefore conclude that it is.

Before leaving the topic of subjunctive conditionals, let us say one further thing to avoid a possible misunderstanding. There is a distinct difference between

(9) *If John were going our way, he would give us a ride.*

and the indicative,

(10) *If John is going our way, he will give us a ride.*

This could conceivably be due to something like a presupposition contributed by the subjunctive mood, though whatever that presupposition is, it is not that the antecedent is false. Perhaps the difference is also due to some characteristic of indicative conditionals lacking in their subjunctive counterparts. By saying (10) I indicate that I think there is a reasonable chance the antecedent might turn out to be true, that is, that there is no good reason to think John is not going our way. In a situation where it is agreed upon or evident that the antecedent clause is false, only the subjunctive conditional can be used. Correspondingly, in a situation where it is evident or agreed upon that the antecedent clause is true, only the indicative conditional is acceptable. If we have already accepted the hypothesis that John is going our way, then we must use the indicative conditional (10) rather than the subjunctive conditional (9) to lay out further consequences of that hypothesis. This suggests to us that indicative and subjunctive conditionals are related to each other in the manner shown in (11).[4]

(11) "If A then B" conventionally implicates:
 a. Indicative mood[5]
  "It is epistemically possible that A"
 b. Subjunctive mood
  "It is epistemically possible that $\neg$A"

[4] By "epistemically possible" we mean "possible in relation to what is known." A proposition p is epistemically possible just in case its negation does not logically follow from the set of propositions which are regarded as true. In the case that p itself is assumed to be true, p is of course also epistemically possible, while $\neg p$ is epistemically impossible.

[5] In our view this principle is not in conflict with the fact that indicative conditionals can be used in so-called "indirect proofs," that is, in arguments of the form *If ϕ then ψ. But ψ is false. Therefore, not ϕ.* In most cases, of course, a person who puts forth such an argument is well aware in advance that ϕ is false and, therefore, the subjunctive conditional should properly be used. We are forced to say that indirect proofs with an indicative conditional as the key premise involve some pretense or temporary suspension of

In addition, it may well be the case, as Lewis (1973) has argued, that the two kinds of conditionals also have different truth conditions, but that is another matter which we cannot go into here.

We will now turn to another well-known case of so called presupposition, where the analysis originally offered seems as unsatisfactory to us as in the case of subjunctive conditionals. Fillmore (1972), in his paper on verbs of judging, discusses presuppositions associated with a class of evaluative verbs that can be used for reporting what a person said or thought about some situation. In order to save time, we will discuss only one of these verbs, namely *criticize*, and leave it up to the reader to apply similar treatment to the others.

According to Fillmore, a person who says,

(12) *John criticized Harry for writing the letter.*

presupposes

(13) *Harry is responsible for writing the letter.*

As evidence he cites that

(14) *John didn't criticize Harry for writing the letter.*

presupposes Harry's having written the letter, as the affirmative sentence does. As was the case with subjunctive conditionals, the presupposition of a sentence like (12) is not so firmly attached to the sentence that it cannot be canceled. One need only think about sentence sequences like

(15) *John criticized Harry for writing the letter. Since the letter was actually written by Mary, it was quite unfair of John.*

---

belief "for the sake of the argument." Perhaps there is a real rhetorical advantage in doing so, but most likely it is just a matter of dialectic convention. In arguing that a particular proposition is contrary to fact it is customary to start from the supposition that it could be true and, so to speak, "discover" its falsehood only at the end. This is a case of exploiting the conventional implicature that accompanies the indicative conditional, not a counterexample to (11a).

The formula of an indirect proof can itself be further exploited for sarcastic effect, as in *If that is so then I'm a monkey's uncle* (*the Queen of Sheba*, or whatever bizarre). The effect of sarcasm is in part produced by the implicature that the antecedent proposition is epistemically possible when in fact the truth of the whole conditional obviously requires that it be false. Note that the feeling of sarcasm disappears if the subjunctive is used instead (*If that were so, then I would be a monkey's uncle*).

Although it is difficult to give any general principle by which one could distinguish true counterexamples from instances where a principle is exploited or flouted, we are convinced that the cases discussed above are of the latter sort as far as (11a) is concerned.

to realize that this presupposition too has the feature of cancelability so characteristic of conversational implicatures. In the case of verbs of judging we want to argue that the so-called presupposition is in fact a generalized conversational implicature, not a particularized one as with the subjunctive conditionals. We will see shortly why this makes a difference.

How might this generalized conversational implicature arise? To answer that question one needs to know what kind of speech act criticizing is, namely the kind that Searle (1975) calls expressive. The essential condition for the performance of an act of criticizing is that the speaker's utterance count as an expression of disapproval of the addressee's involvement in a certain situation. Illocutionary acts of this kind have in general the preparatory condition that the thing towards which the speaker is expressing an attitude must in fact be the case. So, in particular, the act reported by (12) has as a preparatory condition that Harry wrote the letter.

Now the verb *criticize* has a meaning such that the verb is useful for reporting speech acts of just this kind. Unlike some other verbs of judging, it cannot be used performatively for making speech acts of the same kind that it can be used to report; this is merely an idiosyncracy of the lexical item *criticize*. Now how does it come about that when we report a speech act such as John performed—he may have said to Harry, perhaps in a disapproving tone of voice, "You wrote the letter"—that we usually indicate that Harry did in fact write the letter. The explanation is to be found in what Lewis (1969) has described as a convention of truthfulness and trust prevailing among speakers of a language. Roughly, this says that speakers ought to perform only such illocutionary acts as meet all conditions of felicity and that listeners can trust speakers generally to obey this injunction. Assuming that this convention prevails in a community of speakers, if I report John's speech act by saying (12), then in the absence of further qualification the principle of trust justifies the assumption on the part of my addressee that John's speech act was felicitous. And if it was felicitous, then its preparatory condition had to have been met, that is, the object of John's criticism had to have been responsible for the situation of which John was expressing disapproval. Thus my utterance of Sentence (12) will usually convey that Harry did write the letter.

Of course the convention of truthfulness and trust can be violated on occasion. If I know that John did violate it, even inadvertently and unintentionally, by criticizing Harry for something Harry was not responsible for or which never in fact happened, then to conform to the convention of truthfulness and trust it is incumbent on me to add that

John's criticism was misplaced, lest you, by trusting me, derive a mistaken impression that John's criticism was justified. As a general matter, therefore, you can take it from my saying (12) that Harry wrote the letter, unless I clearly indicate otherwise.

The generation of this conversational implicature is not dependent on particular characteristics peculiar to certain contexts of utterance, as the counterfactual implicatures of subjunctive conditionals were. That is what makes this one a generalized rather than a particularized conversational implicature. It exhibits another feature too that one would expect of a generalized conversational implicature, namely nondetachability. Other verbs that report speech acts differing from that reported by *criticize* just in the strength of disapproval expressed, to wit *chide* and *condemn,* also give rise to the same generalized conversational implicature as *criticize.*[6]

3. CONVENTIONAL IMPLICATURE

Let us now proceed to the second topic of this chapter. A large set of cases that have been called presupposition are really instances of conventional implicature. The most obvious examples are those associated with particles like *too, either, also, even, only,* and so on. This class also includes the presuppositions of certain factive verbs, such as *forget, realize, take into account,* and so on, and those that accompany implicative verbs like *manage* and *fail.* Presuppositions of cleft and pseudocleft constructions also seem to be genuine examples of conventional implicature. These are just a few examples; the list could be made much longer. In these cases the notion of there being a rule of the language that associates a presupposition with a morpheme or grammatical construction was on the right track.

As a typical example, let us look at the word *even* in Sentence (16).

(16) *Even Bill likes Mary.*

There are a number of reasons for thinking with Stalnaker (1974) that

[6] One remaining problem is to explain that Fillmore's observation that *John didn't criticize Harry for writing the letter* presupposes just as much as its affirmative counterpart (12) does that Harry is responsible for the letter. The same seems to be true of *Did John criticize Harry for writing the letter?, John may have criticized Harry for writing the letter,* and *If John criticized Harry for writing the letter, then Harry is likely to be angry.* In all of these cases, the so called presupposition is cancelable, just as it is in the case of Sentence (12). This leads us to conjecture that we are dealing with a generalized conversational implicature in these cases too, but we are presently unable to explain how it arises. See Rogers (1978) for further discussion.

the word *even* in this sentence plays no role in determining its truth conditions, that the sentence is true in case Bill likes Mary and false otherwise. To say it still another way, as far as the truth-conditional aspects of meaning are concerned, (16) and (17) are equivalent; they express the same proposition.

(17) *Bill likes Mary.*

It is clear, of course, that the presence of *even* in (16) contributes something to the meaning of the sentence. One is entitled to infer from (16) not just that Bill likes Mary but also what is expressed by the sentences in (18).

(18) a. *Other people besides Bill like Mary.*
b. *Of the people under consideration, Bill is the least likely to like Mary.*

By asserting (16) the speaker commits himself to (18a) and (18b) just as much as to (17). If it should happen that (18a) or (18b) is false while (17) is true, the speaker can justly be criticized for having a wrong idea of how things are. Interestingly enough, though, such criticism would normally be rather mild, usually crediting the speaker with saying something that is partially correct. A response to (16) in such circumstances might run *Well yes, he does like her; but that is just as one should expect.* In the contrasting situation, where (17) is false, partial credit would not normally be given even if (18a) and (18b) were true. One would hardly reply to an assertion of (16) in this situation with *Yes, you wouldn't expect Bill to like Mary; as a matter of fact, he doesn't like her.* Stronger criticism is called for because the speaker's principal commitment, which is to the truth of (17), has run afoul of the facts. The milder criticism is warranted only when the principal commitment accords with the facts and the speaker's error concerns one of his subsidiary commitments, to (18a) and (18b). (See Peters, 1977b, for further discussion.)

The disparity just pointed out indicates that the truth of what (16) actually SAYS depends solely on whether Bill likes Mary. Following Grice, we interpret these facts to mean that the propositions expressed in (18) are IMPLICATED by sentence (16), not asserted. Furthermore, these implicatures are CONVENTIONAL in nature. They cannot be attributed to general conversational principles in conjunction with the peculiarities common to certain contexts of utterances; they simply arise from the presence of the word *even*. One indication of the conventional nature of these implicatures is that they cannot be canceled or disassociated from the sentence. A speaker who utters (19), for instance, commits himself to a contradiction.

(19) *Even Bill likes Mary but no one else does.*

The distinction between the two aspects of meaning in (16) can be brought out even more clearly by considering the meaning of complex sentences such as (20), which contains (16) in an embedded position.

(20) *I just noticed that even Bill likes Mary.*

Sentence (20) says that the speaker has just noticed that Bill likes Mary. It does not mean that he has just noticed that other people like Mary or just noticed that Bill is the least likely person to do so. In (20), the meaning of *notice* applies only to the proposition that constitutes the truth conditions of (16)—that is, to the one expressed by (17)—not to (18a) or (18b) or to the conjunction of (17) and (18).

Another important fact about the meaning of (20) is that it commits the speaker to the view that (18a) and (18b) are true just as strongly as does Sentence (16). The conventional implicature associated with the complement sentence in (20) is "inherited," so to speak, by the larger construction in an unchanged form. This example illustrates an important difference in the roles that the truth-conditional part of the meaning and the meaning conventionally implicated play in determining the meanings of larger constructions.

The same point can also be illustrated with examples like (21).

(21) *If even Bill likes Mary, then all is well.*

It is clear that (21) does not commit the speaker to (17); on the contrary, the conditional suggests that he is unsure of whether (17) is true. In this respect, the meanings of (16) and (21) differ. At the same time, (21) commits the speaker to (18a) and (18b) just as much as (16) does. As in the previous case, the truth-conditional aspect of meaning and the meaning conventionally implicated by (16) have to be distinguished and treated differently by rules that specify the meaning of a complex construction.

This distinction is also important for a pragmatic theory that deals with the ordering of sentences in a discourse. To see why this is so, let us first introduce the notion of COMMON GROUND.

Imagine a group of people engaged in an exchange of talk. At each point in their conversation there is a set of propositions that any participant is rationally justified in taking for granted, for example, by virtue of what has been said in the conversation up to that point, what all the participants are in a position to perceive as true, whatever else they mutually know, assume, and so on. This set of propositions is what we call the common ground or the common set of presumptions (see the definition of "presupposition set" in Stalnaker, 1974). In the course of the conversation these presumptions may change. Indeed, if the purpose of the conversation is to exchange information, enlarging the common ground may be thought of as one of the participants' goals. When a participant says something, thereby advancing the conversation to a new point, the new set of common presumptions reflects the change from the preceding set in terms of adjunction, replacement, or excision of propositions, depending on the exact relation of what was said to the previous common ground.

It has often been observed that what we here call conventional implicatures play a role in determining the felicity or appropriateness of utterances in conversational settings. As a general rule, in cooperative conversation a sentence ought to be uttered only if it does not conventionally implicate anything that is subject to controversy at that point in the conversation. Since the least controversial propositions of all are those in the common ground, which all participants already accept, ideally every conventional implicature ought to belong to the common set of presumptions that the utterance of the sentence is intended to increment. This observation lies at the heart of many of the definitions of "pragmatic presupposition" found in the literature (e.g., Karttunen, 1973, 1974; Gazdar, 1976).

We believe that the import of conventional implicatures to the pragmatics of discourse arises from the fact that conventional implicatures are not set apart so they can be challenged in a direct way. Challenging them necessitates a digression away from what was actually said. It brings about a disruption in the flow of the discourse, which all parties in a cooperative conversation have an interest in avoiding. For example, consider the case of (16), *Even Bill likes Mary.* Any direct response, such as *No, that's not so! Really? I don't believe it,* will be seen as pertaining only to the proposition that Bill likes Mary, which constitutes the truth conditions of (16). Furthermore, such simple challenges signal tacit acceptance of what the sentence conventionally implicates. If one wishes to take issue with one of the conventionally implicated propositions, one has to spell it out explicitly: *Yes, but no one else does, No, but it would not be at all surprising if he did.* There is no simple way to indicate just the rejection of something that is conventionally implicated. This phenomenon is particularly striking in the case of questions. For example, if the speaker asks *Does even Bill like Mary?* either one of the two casual answers indicates that the answerer is in agreement with what is being implicated. To disassociate himself from these propositions he has to digress from answering the question.

In short, we believe that the well-known connection between conventional implicature and felicity is a phenomenon that can be explained on the basis of the theory we are proposing and further refinement of Grice's COOPERATIVE PRINCIPLE. The main difference between our present approach and the direction taken in most discussions of pragmatic presupposition in earlier literature is that we are content to accept the notion of conventional implicature as primitive and do not attempt to define it in terms of felicity or appropriateness, notions which themselves need clarification. At present we have no answer to questions like "Why is it that there are conventional implicatures?" and "Why are there words like *even* which mean something but which have no effect on truth conditions?" In this chapter we concentrate on presenting an account of HOW this aspect of meaning can be described in an explicit way.

4. DESCRIPTIVE APPARATUS

In order to give an explicit and precise account of the meaning of *even*, and of other elements of language which give rise to conventional implicatures, we need a formal method of semantic description. The most satisfactory one developed so far is Montague's version of model theory. However, it only describes what we have called the truth-conditional aspect of meaning; it is not designed to give any account of conventional implicature. We will explain in a moment how we intend to improve on it after we first say a few words about Montague grammar in general.

One advantage that Montague-style syntactic description has over transformational descriptions is that it makes possible a fairly straightforward technique of semantic interpretation. Each syntactic category (common noun, noun phrase, intransitive verb phrase, etc.) consists of phrases that are either listed in the lexicon (basic phrases) or generated by syntactic rules (derived phrases). A meaning is listed for each basic phrase, and each syntactic rule is accompanied by a semantic rule which assigns to each resulting derived phrase an appropriate meaning constructed from the meanings of its constituent phrases. Montague's semantics is based on the principle of compositionality: The meanings of complex phrases are determined by the meanings of their parts and the particular syntactic rule by which they are derived.

In PTQ (Montague, 1974) meanings are represented by logical expressions. Each phrase of PTQ English has a translation, a corresponding expression of interpreted intensional logic. By "interpreted" we mean that the logical expressions, and hence the English phrases whose meaning they represent, are systematically related to nonlinguistic objects, such as individuals, truth values, sets, properties, propositions, and the like, in accordance with the principles of model theory. As we mentioned earlier, Montague treated only the truth-conditional aspect of meaning; his system does not give any account of conventional implicature.

To describe the twin aspects of meaning we are concerned with here, we extend Montague's system in the following way. Each English phrase is associated with two expressions of intensional logic. One of these, which we will call the extension expression, is identical to the single translation that Montague would provide. This expression stands for what logicians would call the denotation of the phrase, roughly the things of which the phrase is true. Its sense is the meaning EXPRESSED by the phrase. The second one, the implicature expression, signifies what the phrase conventionally IMPLICATES (if it is a sentence), what it contributes (if it is smaller than a sentence) to the conventional implicatures of sentences having it as a part.[7]

For each basic phrase, the appropriate extension and implicature expression are listed in the lexicon with the phrase. To each phrase derived by means of a syntactic rule, the paired semantic rule (called a translation rule) assigns an extension expression and an implicature expression as a function of the extension and implicature expressions of the phrases from which it is derived. To aid in grasping further details, we will make use of a simple example.

Sentence (17) is derived in the fragment of English Montague described in PTQ from the three basic phrases—*Mary, Bill,* and *like*—by means of two syntactic rules, the verb + object rule and the sub-

[7] In translating each English phrase to an ordered pair of formulas, ⟨extension expression; implicature expression⟩, we arrive at a system which is very similar in concept to H. Herzberger's (1973) "two dimensional logic." In Herzberger's semantics each formula is paired with two binary semantic values: a correspondence value and a bivalence value. The former dimension plays the same role as extension expressions in our system; notions like logical consequence and validity are defined solely in terms of correspondence values. Herzberger leaves the semantics of the bivalence dimension quite open. We could think of the bivalence value as being the truth value of our implicature expression. Herzberger's four "composite" semantic values, T, F, t, and f, which represent the four possible combinations of correspondence and bivalence values, would therefore correspond to the four possible cases in our system: (*a*) what the sentence says is true and what it conventionally implicates is true (T); (*b*) what the sentence says is false but what it conventionally implicates is true (F); (*c*) what the sentence says is true but what it conventionally implicates is false (t); and (*d*) what the sentence says is false and what it conventionally implicates is also false (f).

ject + predicate rule. The sentence's syntactic structure is displayed as

(22)

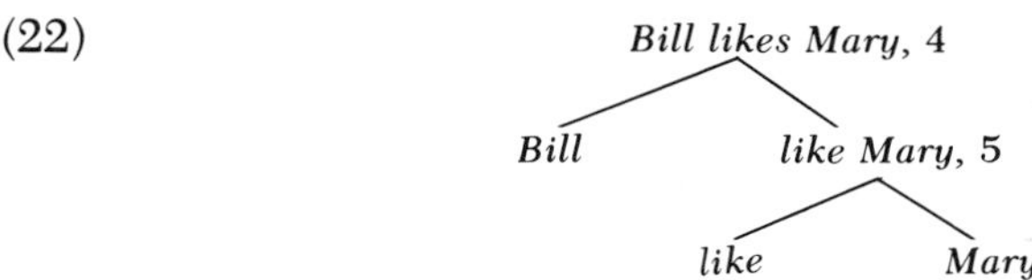

(See Montague, 1974, or Partee, 1975, for detailed discussion.)

In explaining how the translation rules function, we shall abbreviate the extension expression assigned to a phrase α as α^e and the implicature expression assigned to the same phrase as α^i. The translation rule correlated with the derivation of *like Mary* from *like* and *Mary*, then, must say how to construct $\boldsymbol{like\text{–}Mary}^e$ and $\boldsymbol{like\text{–}Mary}^i$ from $\boldsymbol{like}^e$, $\boldsymbol{like}^i$, $\boldsymbol{Mary}^e$, and $\boldsymbol{Mary}^i$.

The extension expression of *like Mary* is compounded only of $\boldsymbol{like}^e$ and $\boldsymbol{Mary}^e$; it does not involve the implicatures associated with the two constituent phrases. This is, in fact, a feature of most translation rules, though not of all. Following Montague, we will simply set $\boldsymbol{like\text{–}Mary}^e$ equal to $\boldsymbol{like}^e({}^\wedge\boldsymbol{Mary}^e)$; that is, we fill one argument position of the relation $\boldsymbol{like}^e$ with the intension expressed by the noun phrase *Mary* (in intensional logic ${}^\wedge\boldsymbol{Mary}^e$ denotes the intension of $\boldsymbol{Mary}^e$).

Turning to the implicatures, it may not be obvious that sentence (17) implicates anything. For the sake of discussion, though, let us suppose that it implicates three things, arising from the three basic phrases it contains: that Bill is male, that he is acquainted with Mary, and that Mary is female. (This is purely an expository device; we are not really proposing that these are the conventional implicatures introduced by *Mary, Bill,* and *like*.)

The conventional implicatures associated with the verb phrase *like Mary* are a slightly more complicated matter than the extension of the phrase. They include on the one hand whatever implicature is introduced by the verb *like;* we are supposing it to be that the affected individual is acquainted with the object of his affection. Another implicature arises from the object noun phrase *Mary;* of this more shortly. But first note that the implicature introduced in Sentence (17) by the verb *like* relates Bill to the extension of the object noun phrase, rather than to what the phrase *Mary* conventionally implicates; Bill is supposed to be acquainted with Mary herself, not merely with her sex. Utilizing our abbreviation $\boldsymbol{like}^i$ for the implicature expression of *like* we can, thus, symbolize this part of the verb phrase's conventional implicatures with the expression $\boldsymbol{like}^i({}^\wedge\boldsymbol{Mary}^e)$.

It may seem that all we need do now is conjoin this implicature with the one, symbolized $\boldsymbol{Mary}^{i}$, arising from the object noun phrase to obtain the conventional implicatures of *like Mary*. Such a maneuver could only be adequate for simple examples such as this one, though; so in the interest of generality we introduce at this point a complication which will not be motivated until after discussion of the present example is completed. We associate with the verb *like* a third expression $\boldsymbol{like}^{h}$(besides $\boldsymbol{like}^{e}$ and $\boldsymbol{like}^{i}$) of intensional logic, which we allow to act on the sense of what the object noun phrase implicates before adding the result to the implicature stemming from the verb. That is, we conjoin $\boldsymbol{like}^{h}({}^{\wedge}\boldsymbol{Mary}^{i})$, rather than $\boldsymbol{Mary}^{i}$, with the expression $\boldsymbol{like}^{i}({}^{\wedge}\boldsymbol{Mary}^{e})$ obtained in the preceding paragraph.

Thus we want to write something on the order of $\boldsymbol{like}^{i}({}^{\wedge}\boldsymbol{Mary}^{e}) \wedge \boldsymbol{like}^{h}({}^{\wedge}\boldsymbol{Mary}^{i})$ as the implicature expression of *like Mary*. For technical reasons, though, this expression is not well-formed. So we use a variable $\boldsymbol{x}$ in order to conjoin the two parts of the expression, and set $\boldsymbol{like\text{–}Mary}^{i}$ equal to

$$\hat{\boldsymbol{x}}[\boldsymbol{like}^{i}(\boldsymbol{x}, {}^{\wedge}\boldsymbol{Mary}^{e}) \wedge \boldsymbol{like}^{h}(\boldsymbol{x}, {}^{\wedge}\boldsymbol{Mary}^{i})].$$

This expresses the property characteristic of precisely those individuals that stand to Mary in the relation conventionally implicated by *like* given that whatever conventional implicature the phrase *Mary* introduces is true.

It is now easy to see how the rule should be stated which assigns the ordered pair $\langle \boldsymbol{like\text{–}Mary}^{e}, \boldsymbol{like\text{–}Mary}^{i} \rangle$ as the translation of the verb phrase *like Mary*. In fact let us state both the syntactic rule (numbered 5 by Montague in PTQ) which generates the verb phrase from its constituent phrases, and the associated translation rule.

(23) If α is a transitive verb (Montague's Category TV) and β is a noun phrase (Montague's Category T), then $\alpha\bar{\beta}$ is a verb phrase (Montague's Category IV), where $\bar{\beta}$ is the accusative form of β.
Translation: $\langle \alpha^{e}({}^{\wedge}\beta^{e});\ \ \hat{x}[\alpha^{i}(x, {}^{\wedge}\beta^{e}) \wedge \alpha^{h}(x, {}^{\wedge}\beta^{i})] \rangle$

Tree (22) records an application of this syntactic rule for the case of α = *like* and β = *Mary*. The translation rule assigns to the phrase generated in this case exactly the extension expression and implicature expression that we argued it should have.

Montague's Rule 4 of PTQ (reproduced here in the Appendix, where we reformulate all his translation rules to take care of conventional implicature as well as truth-conditional aspects of meaning) completes the derivation of Sentence (17), *Bill likes Mary* from the noun phrase *Bill* and the verb phrase *like Mary*—see (22). The associated translation rule (in our revision) assigns the extension expression and the implicature expression shown in (24).

(24) a. $\textbf{Bill–likes–Mary}^{e} = \textbf{Bill}^{e}({}^{\wedge}\textbf{like}^{e}({}^{\wedge}\textbf{Mary}^{e}))$
b. $\textbf{Bill–likes–Mary}^{i} = [\textbf{Bill}^{i}({}^{\wedge}\textbf{like}^{e}({}^{\wedge}\textbf{Mary}^{e})) \wedge \textbf{Bill}^{h}(\hat{x}[\textbf{like}^{i}(x, {}^{\wedge}\textbf{Mary}^{e}) \wedge \textbf{like}^{h}(x, {}^{\wedge}\textbf{Mary}^{i})])]$

The rule which produces this translation parallels the translation rule just discussed. The extension expression of sentence (17) is compounded of the extension expressions of its subject and verb phrase. From the sentence's extension expression, $\textbf{Bill}^{e}({}^{\wedge}\textbf{like}^{e}({}^{\wedge}\textbf{Mary}^{e}))$, it can be seen that the subject noun phrase functions semantically to predicate something of the verb phrase. (See Cooper, 1977, for the motivation of Montague's treatment of noun phrase semantics.) Accordingly, the second conjunct of the implicature expression (24b) shows the conventional implicatures associated with the verb phrase as being inherited by the sentence under the effect of the third expression, $\textbf{Bill}^{h}$, associated with the subject. The first conjunct of the implicature expression represents the conventional implicature contributed by the subject noun phrase *Bill* by predicating that noun phrase's implicature expression of the sense of the verb phrase's extension expression.

Consideration of the interpretation assigned to the logical expressions in (24) would show that the extension expression $\textbf{Bill–likes–Mary}^{e}$ is equivalent to $\textbf{like}^{e}_{*}(b, m)$, which more closely resembles the familiar predicate calculus symbolization of sentence (17). Similar consideration would show that, under our expository assumptions (see the Appendix for a formal statement of them), $\textbf{Bill–likes–Mary}^{i}$ is equivalent to $\textbf{male}^{e}_{*}(b) \wedge \textbf{be–acquainted–with}^{e}_{*}(b, m) \wedge \textbf{female}^{e}_{*}(m)$.

Now that we have shown how a common variety of translation rule functions to assign extension and implicature expressions to syntactically derived phrases, let us turn to motivating the third expressions such as $\textbf{like}^{h}$ and $\textbf{Bill}^{h}$, which were used in constructing the implicature expressions of derived phrases. When one of several phrases that combine to form a larger one functions semantically as a predicate or operator on the meanings of the other phrases (the way a transitive verb does to its object or a sentence-embedding verb does to its complement), then the conventional implicatures associated with those other phrases will in general be inherited by the derived phrase under a transformation that is determined by the predicate or operator. Note that sentences (26a–c), which embed the cleft sentence (25) under different verbs, vary in the mode in which they implicate that someone tapped Mary's phone, the most salient conventional implicature of (25).

(25) *It wasn't Bill who tapped Mary's phone.*

(26) a. *John forgot that it wasn't Bill who tapped Mary's phone.*
b. *John hoped that it wasn't Bill who tapped Mary's phone.*
c. *John told Sue that it wasn't Bill who tapped Mary's phone.*

Sentence (26a) conventionally implicates everything that sentence (25) does; in particular it commits the speaker to the view that Mary's phone was tapped. In this respect *forget* is similar to verbs like *realize, point out, discover,* etc. Sentence (26b), in contrast, conventionally implicates only that John believed someone tapped Mary's phone; the speaker of this sentence does not commit himself to the belief's being correct, but only to John's having had it. Besides *hope,* this class includes verbs like *believe, suspect,* and *fear.* Finally, sentence (26c) is noncommital about whether Mary's phone was tapped; it reports only that John told Sue a certain thing, not necessarily the truth.[8] Similar examples with verbs like *say, report, claim,* etc., are equally noncommital with respect to the conventional implicatures of the complement sentence.

To deal with such facts, we introduce a heritage function h which takes as its arguments the extension and implicature expressions of the predicate or operator phrase α and yields as the corresponding value $h(\alpha^e, \alpha^i)$ the appropriate transformation (which we have written α^h for short) to apply to the conventional implicatures of the other

[8] In saying that the conventional implicatures of (25) are not inherited in their original form by (26b) and (26c), we do not mean to deny the fact that in many contexts the utterance of (26b) and (26c) would suggest to the hearer that Mary's phone was tapped. In contrast to (26a), however, this implicature is clearly cancelable in connection with (26b) and (26c); that is, it is a conversational implicature, not a conventional one. In the case of (26c) it arises from the same principle of truthfulness and trust that we discussed earlier in connection with *criticize* (page 10). As far as (26b) is concerned, it conventionally implicates only that John believes that Mary's phone was tapped. If the speaker should know that this belief is false and that the audience is not aware of it, it would be incumbent upon him, by Grice's Cooperative Principle, to indicate how things actually are. If the speaker fails to comment on the matter in a situation where a correction would be in order, the audience can justifiably infer that Mary's phone actually was tapped. A clear sign of the conversational nature of this implicature is the fact that a sentence like *John mistakenly believed that Mary's phone was tapped and he hoped that it wasn't Bill who tapped it* does not give rise to it.

phrases constructed with α. Thus ***forget***^{h}(=h(***forget***^{e}, ***forget***^{i})) is something like the identity transformation, ***hope***^{h} transforms a proposition into an ascription of belief in it, and ***tell***^{h} transforms every proposition into a trivial one (a truism that requires no commitments).

Referring back to the translation displayed in (24) of the sentence *Bill likes Mary,* note that the verb functions semantically to predicate something of the direct object, as one can see from the extension expression (24a); accordingly it is the verb that, in the implicature expression (24b), determines how to transform the conventional implicatures associated with the object noun phrase into the form appropriate for inheritance by the resulting verb phrase. (We alluded earlier to the fact that the verb *like* occasions no alterations in the implicatures arising from its object; thus ***like***^{h} is something like the identity transformation.) As we pointed out earlier, the subject noun phrase can be seen in (24a) to predicate something of the verb phrase. Thus the subject is the phrase which determines, via ***Bill***^{h} in (24b), how to transform the implicatures of the other phrase into the appropriate form; ***Bill***^{h} specifies, in particular, that it is Bill who is to have the property implicated by the verb phrase (e.g., of being acquainted with Mary). Thus the two heritage expressions ***like***^{h} and ***Bill***^{h} in our illustrative example play precisely the role that such expressions play in general.

We will proceed shortly to give a formal description of the conventional implicatures arising from the word *even,* but first let us examine briefly how we could describe the conventional implicatures associated with implicative verbs like *manage* and *fail* with the apparatus under our control. The facts to be described are twofold. For one thing, sentence (27a) is true under exactly the same conditions as (27b); likewise (28a) and (28b).

(27) a. *Mary failed to arrive.*
b. *Mary didn't arrive.*
c. *Mary was expected to arrive.*

(28) a. *John managed to sit through a Chinese opera.*
b. *John sat through a Chinese opera.*
c. *Sitting through a Chinese opera requires some effort for John.*

Secondly, asserting (27a) or (28a) commits the speaker to something like (27c) or (28c), respectively, by way of conventionally implicating the latter. One can tell that the (c) sentences are conventionally implicated through considerations like the ones we applied with *even.* Sentence (29a) commits the speaker to (29b) but not to (29c).

(29) a. *I just discovered that Mary failed to arrive.*
b. *I just discovered that Mary didn't arrive.*
c. *I just discovered that Mary was expected to arrive.*

Similarly, (30) does not commit the speaker to (28b), but does commit him to (28c) just as much as (28a) does.

(30) *If John managed to sit through a Chinese opera, he deserves a medal.*

Let us borrow Montague's syntactic rule from PTQ, which generates verb phrases like *fail to arrive* and *manage to sit through a Chinese opera* by combining a verb that takes a special verb phrase complement (*fail to* or *manage to*) with a verb phrase (*arrive* or *sit through a Chinese opera*). This rule is stated in the Appendix (Rule 8), along with our revised version of the associated translation rule. It and the other rules we have just discussed generate the sentence *Mary fails to arrive* with the structural description (31).

(31)

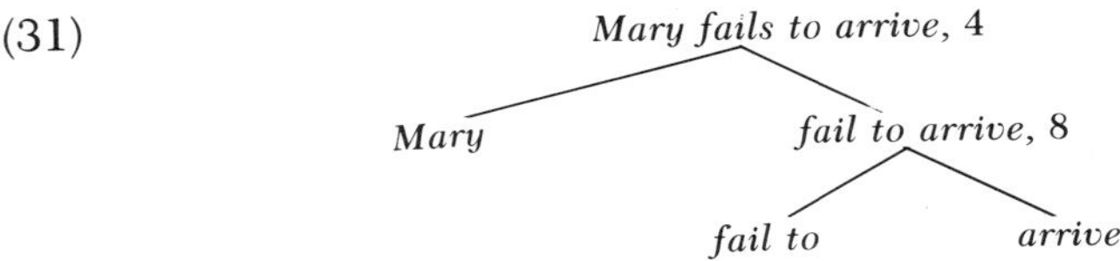

The translation rules operating in the fashion we have described assign this structure the following extension and implicature expressions.

(32) $\textbf{\textit{Mary–fails–to–arrive}}^{e} = \textbf{\textit{Mary}}^{e}(\hat{}\,\textbf{\textit{fail–to}}^{e}(\hat{}\,\textbf{\textit{arrive}}^{e}))$
$\textbf{\textit{Mary–fails–to–arrive}}^{i} = [\textbf{\textit{Mary}}^{i}(\hat{}\,\textbf{\textit{fail–to}}^{e}(\hat{}\,\textbf{\textit{arrive}}^{e}))$
$\wedge\, \textbf{\textit{Mary}}^{h}(\hat{x}[\textbf{\textit{fail–to}}^{i}(x, \hat{}\,\textbf{\textit{arrive}}^{e}) \wedge \textbf{\textit{fail–to}}^{h}(x, \hat{}\,\textbf{\textit{arrive}}^{i})])]$

If we require (as a meaning postulate in the Appendix does) that $\textbf{\textit{fail–to}}^{e}$ be assigned the interpretation essentially of negation, then $\textbf{\textit{Mary}}^{e}(\hat{}\,\textbf{\textit{fail–to}}^{e}(\hat{}\,\textbf{\textit{arrive}}^{e}))$ comes out equivalent to $\neg\textbf{\textit{arrive}}^{e}_{*}(m)$, and sentence (27a) is true just in case (27b) is. A further assumption concerning the interpretation of $\textbf{\textit{fail–to}}^{i}$ (the meaning postulate is stated in the Appendix) makes the second conjunct of the implicature expression in (32) imply $\textbf{\textit{try–to}}^{e}(\hat{}\,m, \hat{}\,\textbf{\textit{arrive}}^{e})\ \hat{}\vee y\ \textbf{\textit{expect–that}}^{e}(y, \hat{}\,W\ \textbf{\textit{arrive}}^{e}(\hat{}\,m))$. The improbability of this formula's first disjunct, which says that Mary tries to arrive, suggests that the second alternative is the one that obtains. Thus (27a) conventionally implicates (27c), while

My son failed to lift our piano instead implicates that my son tried to lift the piano.

A similar treatment handles the facts about *manage*. We adopt the meaning postulate $\hat{}\,\boldsymbol{manage\text{–}to}^{\mathrm{e}} = \hat{}\,\lambda P\,\check{}\,P$ governing the interpretation of *manage to*'s extension expression; this makes *manage to* vacuous as far as truth conditions go. And we adopt the meaning postulate $\hat{}\,\boldsymbol{manage\text{–}to}^{\mathrm{i}} = \hat{}\,\lambda P \hat{x} \neg \boldsymbol{easy}^{\mathrm{e}}(\hat{}\,P\{x\})$ governing the interpretation of the implicature expression; this makes (28a) conventionally implicate that for John to sit through a Chinese opera wasn't easy.[9]

Let us close our discussion of these verbs by pointing out that our analysis predicts an interesting peculiarity of sentence (33).

(33) *Bill managed to catch a fish.*

The feature of particular interest is the specificity or nonspecificity of the indefinite noun phrase *a fish*. The fish which (33) asserts to have been caught—because its truth conditions are just those of *Bill caught a fish*—certainly has to be a specific one. At the same time, there is an ambiguity in what (33) conventionally implicates (roughly: for Bill to catch a fish was not easy). The implicature can either be about a specific fish Bill was angling for, or about fish in general and not any one in particular. The two essentially different ways in which our analysis generates (33), one of them Montague's "quantifying in," correspond to exactly these two meanings. Thus we predict the correct ambiguity in (33), in particular, the interesting fact that the indefinite NP can be specific as far as truth conditions are concerned and at the same time nonspecific for purposes of conventional implicature.[10]

5. ANALYSIS OF *EVEN*

To show how our descriptive apparatus can be adapted to solve a fairly complicated problem, let us return to the word *even*. The analysis we present was first developed in Karttunen and Karttunen (1977), and the insights on which it is based are mostly drawn from the sub-

[9] In many cases of conventional implicature it is difficult to express precisely what is being implicated. Our meaning postulates for $\boldsymbol{manage}^{\mathrm{i}}$ and $\boldsymbol{fail}^{\mathrm{i}}$ are reasonably good approximations but they can undoubtedly be improved with further work. See Coleman (1975) for an interesting discussion. She argues that the implicature associated with *manage* is less specific than what we here take it to be and gives a number of examples which are intended to show that *manage* can implicate a number of things ranging from trying and difficulty to mere unlikelihood.

[10] We are indebted to David Dowty for pointing this out to us.

stantial previous literature on the topic, most notably from Horn (1969), Fraser (1971), Anderson (1972), Heringer (1973), Epstein (1974), Kempson (1975), Fauconnier (1975), and Altmann (1976). These works contain a wealth of observations about the intricacies of this particle. Since it would take too much space to present a formal analysis that would account for all the uses of *even,* we will limit our discussion to a subset of *even* sentences. However, we will also outline how this analysis could be extended to cover the remaining data. The most important limitation is that we only consider cases where *even* "focuses" on a noun phrase—in the sense explained shortly—and where the NP is interpreted *de re* with respect to the particle. That is, we will concentrate on sentences like those in (34). (To highlight the intended reading, we use capitals to mark the focused constituent.)

(34) a. *Even BILL likes Mary.*
b. *Bill likes even MARY.* (≡Bill even likes MARY.)

For the moment we leave out of consideration examples of the sort given in (35), where *even* focuses on a constituent that belongs to some other syntactic category, such as verb, verb phrase, adjective, and if-clause.

(35) a. *Mary even ADMIRES Bill.* [TV-focus]
b. *Bill even DRINKS BEER.* [VP-focus]
c. *Even INFERIOR coffee is expensive.* [ADJ-focus]
d. *Even IF SHE DOESN'T COME, there will be too many people.* [ADV-focus]

We will return to cases of this sort briefly later on, after we first spell out the details of our analysis for sentences where *even* has NP focus.

Another self-imposed limitation is that we will only consider cases where *even* immediately precedes its focus. In reality *even* can sometimes follow its focus, as in (36a). In case the focused constituent is located inside a verb phrase, *even* typically occurs in the beginning of the verb phrase, as in examples (36b) and (36c). In spoken English, the intended focus of *even* can be marked by stress to reduce ambiguity.

(36) a. *BILL, even, likes Mary.*
b. *Mary even wants to go out with BILL.*
c. *John even talked about NIXON in his commencement address.*

Except for the syntactic complications, sentences of this sort are not problematical for our analysis, and we have no need to consider them here. In the following we therefore adopt the convenient fiction that *even* always occurs in front of the constituent it focuses on.

Before we get down to the formal details of our analysis, it is perhaps useful to discuss the main idea in informal terms. We contend that the implicature associated with *even* in a particular sentence depends on two things: the FOCUS and the SCOPE of the particle. The first of these terms refers to the particular constituent in the sentence with which *even* is associated. The need for this concept can be seen by considering examples (34a) and (34b). *Even BILL likes Mary* implicates, among other things, that some people other than Bill like Mary; *Bill likes even MARY* implicates, among other things, that Bill likes other people besides Mary. In both cases, this "existential" implicature contributed by *even* can be represented roughly as in (37).

(37) *There are other x under consideration besides*
a such that $\underbrace{\ldots x \ldots}_{\text{SCOPE}}$
FOCUS

In (37), *a* stands for what we call the FOCUS of *even: Bill* in (34a) and *Mary* in (34b). As these examples show, the choice of *even* focus restricts the range of the existential quantifier that implicitly is associated with the particle. By the SCOPE of *even* we mean the open sentence, . . . *x* . . . in (37), which is bound by that quantifier. In the examples at hand, this scope sentence can be obtained by deleting the particle and replacing the focused constituent by a variable. Thus in (34a) the scope of *even* is *x likes Mary;* in (34b) *even* has scope over *Bill likes x.* In simple sentences like these, the scope of *even* is determined trivially by the choice of focus. In more complex examples, however, there may be alternative scope assignments with the same focus. For example consider Sentence (38).

(38) *It is hard for me to believe that Bill can understand*
even SYNTACTIC STRUCTURES.

Although *even* here unambiguously focuses on *Syntactic Structures,* the sentence has two readings, which differ with respect to the understood scope of *even.* On one reading the sentence implicates, among other things, that there are other books about which it is hard for me to believe that Bill can understand them. On this reading *even* has the scope given in (39a). The second reading of (38) gives us the implicature that there are other books that Bill can understand besides *Syntactic Structures.* This interpretation is based on the scope assignment (39b).

(39) a. *It is hard for me to believe that Bill can understand x.*
b. *Bill can understand x.*

Although there undoubtedly is a tendency to interpret *even* with the narrowest possible scope, examples like (38) show clearly that the choice of the focus does not always completely determine the scope of the particle. Therefore we must deal with these matters separately, in spite of the fact that many earlier writers have not done so. (One outstanding exception is Heringer, 1973.)

So far we have discussed only the first of the two implicatures associated with *even,* namely that *there are other x under consideration besides a such that . . . x . . . .* By making use of the concepts of focus and scope, we can now characterize the remaining implicature in an equally general way, although it is a bit harder to put in plain English. Intuitively, (34a) *Even BILL likes Mary* implicates that Bill is an "extreme case," less likely to have the property of liking Mary than any other individual under consideration. Correspondingly, (34b) gives rise to the implicature that Mary is the least likely of those under consideration to be the object of Bill's affection. Schematically this "scalar" implicature of *even* can be represented roughly as in (40).

(40) *For all x under consideration besides a, the likelihood that . . . x . . . is greater than the likelihood that . . . a . . .*

Here . . . *x* . . . is the open sentence which constitutes the scope of *even;* . . . *a* . . . is the sentence obtained from it by substituting *a* for *x*. As before, *a* stands for the focus of the particle; in cases such as (34), . . . *a* . . . is simply the original sentence without *even.*

As a final illustration of how the existential and scalar implicatures contributed by *even* depend on the focus and the scope of the particle, we sketch our analysis for example (34b):

(41) *Bill likes even MARY.*
Focus of *even: Mary*
Scope of *even: Bill likes x*
Existential implicature: *There are other x under consideration besides Mary such that Bill likes x.*
Scalar implicature: *For all x under consideration besides Mary, the likelihood that Bill likes x is greater than the likelihood that Bill likes Mary.*

It is interesting to consider the scalar implicature of *even* in connection with examples such as (38). In a case like this, alternative scope assignments—such as (39)—produce a striking contrast in what the focused constituent is supposed to be an extreme case of. The two contrasting scalar implications are given in (42).

(42) a. *For all x under consideration besides* Syntactic Structures, *the likelihood that it is hard for me to believe that Bill can understand x is greater than the likelihood that it is hard for me to believe that Bill can understand* Syntactic Structures.

b. *For all x under consideration besides* Syntactic Structures, *the likelihood that Bill can understand x is greater than the likelihood that Bill can understand* Syntactic Structures.

In order to bring out the import of these cumbersome phrases, let us consider the matter in less formal terms. On the wide scope reading of *even*, (38) suggests that *Syntactic Structures* is an easy book to understand; as (42a) says, it is least likely to make me doubt Bill's ability to understand it. The narrow scope reading of *even* in (38) gives us an implicature which suggests exactly the opposite. If *Syntactic Structures* is the least likely work for Bill to understand, as (42b) says, then it probably is a difficult book. The possibility of alternative scope assignments in (38) thus explains the curious phenomenon that this sentence can be understood to implicate what seem like completely opposite things (compare Heringer, 1973).

In the previous section we discussed the conventionally implicated meaning of *even* sentences. We contend, for the reasons explained in Section 3, that this particle makes no contribution to the truth conditions of these sentences: *Even Bill likes Mary* expresses the same proposition as *Bill likes Mary*. Let us now consider the question of how this account of the meaning of *even* can be stated in terms of our formal apparatus.

In order to determine the implicature associated with the particle, we need to know what constituent it focuses on and what scope it has. Here we make the simplifying assumption that the focused constituent is a noun phrase and that it immediately follows the particle. The scope of *even* is an open sentence with a subscripted pronoun (a free variable). Given these assumptions, the natural way to generate *even* sentences in Montague's syntax is by a rule of quantification similar to Montague's Rule 14 in PTQ. The main effect of the rule is to prefix *even* to the focus NP and to substitute the result for the subscripted pronoun in the scope sentence. Let us call this rule the EVEN RULE. (A complete statement of the rule can be found in the Appendix.) As an example of its application, consider the analysis tree (43).

(43)

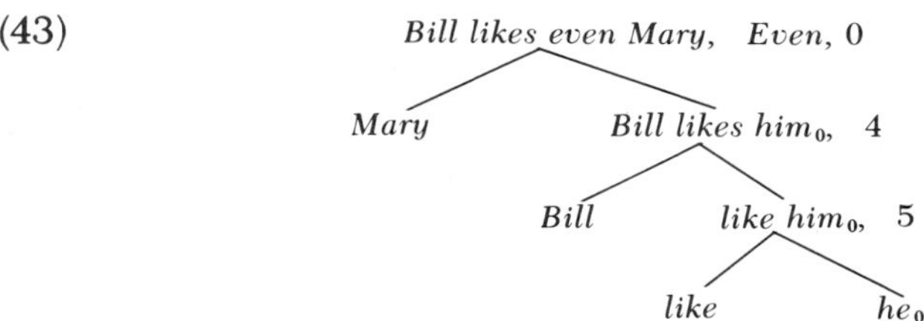

As (43) shows, we treat the particle syncategorematically: The word *even* by itself is not assigned to any syntactic category (see the treatment of *every, the, a,* and *not* in Montague's PTQ). Furthermore the phrase *even Mary* is not considered to be a constituent phrase either. Given the simplifying assumptions made here, it would of course be possible to let *even* combine with the noun phrase *Mary* to form a derived noun phrase, but this alternative has little to recommend it, considering that in general *even* need not be adjacent to its focus.

Let us now turn to the question of what the corresponding translation rule ought to be. How do we define ⟨***Bill–likes–even–Mary***^{e}; ***Bill–likes–even–Mary***^{i}⟩ given the translations of *Mary* and *Bill likes him*$_0$? As far as the truth-conditional aspect of meaning is concerned, the matter is simple. Since *even* has no effect on truth conditions and the EVEN RULE is essentially a rule of quantification, this part of the translation rule should have the same effect as Montague's T14 in PTQ. For this reason, we have formulated it to give us the result shown in (44).

(44) ***Bill–likes–even–Mary***^{e} = ***Mary***$^{e}(\hat{x}_0$ ***Bill–likes–him***$^{e}_{0})$ ≡ ***Bill–likes–Mary***^{e} ≡ ***like***$^{e}_{*}(b, m)$

As for the implicature expression, ***Bill–likes–even–Mary***^{i}, we need first of all to make sure that the conventional implicatures of the focus NP and the scope sentence get inherited in the proper form. This is accomplished by generating the conjunction [***Mary***$^{i}(\hat{x}_0$ ***Bill–likes–him***$^{e}_{0}) \wedge$ ***Mary***$^{h}(\hat{x}_0$ ***Bill–likes–him***$^{i}_{0})$] as part of ***Bill–likes–even–Mary***^{i}. [This is equivalent to ***Bill–likes–Mary***^{i}, as shown in (24b).] To complete our task we only need to augment it with a formula representing the existential and scalar implicatures that arise from the particle itself. For this purpose we introduce in the translation rule a special constant ***even***^{i}, for which we give a meaning postulate in the Appendix. This constant enables us to express the desired implicatures in an optimally concise way, namely as $\boldsymbol{even}^{i}({}^{\wedge}\boldsymbol{Mary}^{e}, \hat{x}_0 \boldsymbol{Bill\text{–}likes\text{–}him}^{e}_{0})$. The complete implicature expression for *Bill likes even Mary* generated by our translation rules is shown in (45).

(45) $$\boldsymbol{Bill\text{–}likes\text{–}even\text{–}Mary}^{i} = [[\boldsymbol{Mary}^{i}(\hat{x}_0\, \boldsymbol{Bill\text{–}likes\text{–}him}^{e}_{0}) \wedge \boldsymbol{Mary}^{h}(\hat{x}_0\, \boldsymbol{Bill\text{–}likes\text{–}him}^{i}_{0})] \wedge \boldsymbol{even}^{i}({}^{\wedge}\boldsymbol{Mary}^{e}, \hat{x}_0\, \boldsymbol{Bill\text{–}likes\text{–}him}^{e}_{0})]$$

Here $\boldsymbol{even}^{i}$ expresses a certain—rather complicated—relation that holds between the sense of *Mary* and the property of being an individual that Bill likes. By virtue of the meaning postulate for $\boldsymbol{even}^{i}$ (see the Appendix), the last conjunct of (45) is equivalent to the formula given in (46).

(46) $$\boldsymbol{even}^{i}({}^{\wedge}\boldsymbol{Mary}^{e}, \hat{x}_0\, \boldsymbol{Bill\text{–}likes\text{–}him}^{e}_{0}) \equiv [\bigvee x[{*}\{{}^{\vee}x\} \wedge \neg[{}^{\vee}x = m] \wedge \boldsymbol{like}^{e}_{*}(b, {}^{\vee}x)] \wedge \bigwedge x[[{*}\{x\} \wedge \neg[{}^{\vee}x = m]] \longrightarrow \boldsymbol{exceed}^{e}(\boldsymbol{likelihood}^{e}({}^{\wedge}\boldsymbol{like}^{e}_{*}(b, x)), \boldsymbol{likelihood}^{e}({}^{\wedge}\boldsymbol{like}^{e}_{*}(b, m)))]]$$ [11]

The complexity of the right side of (46) reflects the difficulty of expressing precisely what *even* implicates. The easiest way to understand what this formula is designed to say is to compare it with its semi-English paraphrase in (41). The first conjunct expresses the proposition that there are some other individuals under consideration besides Mary whom Bill likes; the second conjunct says that Mary is the least likely individual of those under consideration to be the object of Bill's affection.

As the formulas in (44) and (45) indicate, the translation part of the EVEN RULE correctly accounts for the intuitive meaning of examples like *Bill likes even Mary*. This sentence comes to have the same truth conditions as *Bill likes Mary* and the same conventional implicatures except for the additional implicature which is determined by the focus and the scope of the particle. The same holds for the example *Even Bill likes Mary*, whose derivation and the resulting translation is shown in (47).

[11] Here * is a constant (of type $\langle s, \langle\langle s, e\rangle, t\rangle\rangle$) which represents the contextual restriction on things that are being quantified over; it picks out the set of individuals that are "under consideration" on a given occasion. The constant $\boldsymbol{likelihood}^{e}$ denotes a (context-dependent) function from propositions to real numbers from 0 to 1; $\boldsymbol{exceed}^{e}$ is to be interpreted in the obvious way. The last two constants are used to represent the scalar implicature associated with *even*.

(47) a.

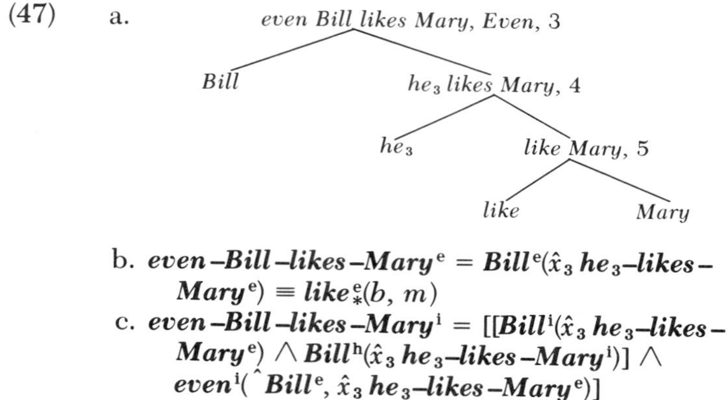

b. $\textbf{\textit{even-Bill-likes-Mary}}^{e} = \textbf{\textit{Bill}}^{e}(\hat{x}_3\, \textbf{\textit{he}}_3\textbf{\textit{-likes-Mary}}^{e}) \equiv \textbf{\textit{like}}^{e}_{*}(b, m)$

c. $\textbf{\textit{even-Bill-likes-Mary}}^{i} = [[\textbf{\textit{Bill}}^{i}(\hat{x}_3\, \textbf{\textit{he}}_3\textbf{\textit{-likes-Mary}}^{e}) \wedge \textbf{\textit{Bill}}^{h}(\hat{x}_3\, \textbf{\textit{he}}_3\textbf{\textit{-likes-Mary}}^{i})] \wedge \textbf{\textit{even}}^{i}(\hat{\ }\textbf{\textit{Bill}}^{e}, \hat{x}_3\, \textbf{\textit{he}}_3\textbf{\textit{-likes-Mary}}^{e})]$

The last conjunct of (47c) says, in effect, that other people like Mary besides Bill, and Bill is the least likely to do so. This is as it should be.

The fact that the analysis also accounts for negative *even* sentences provides additional support for it. Consider the derivation and translation of *Even Bill doesn't like Mary* in (48).

(48) a.

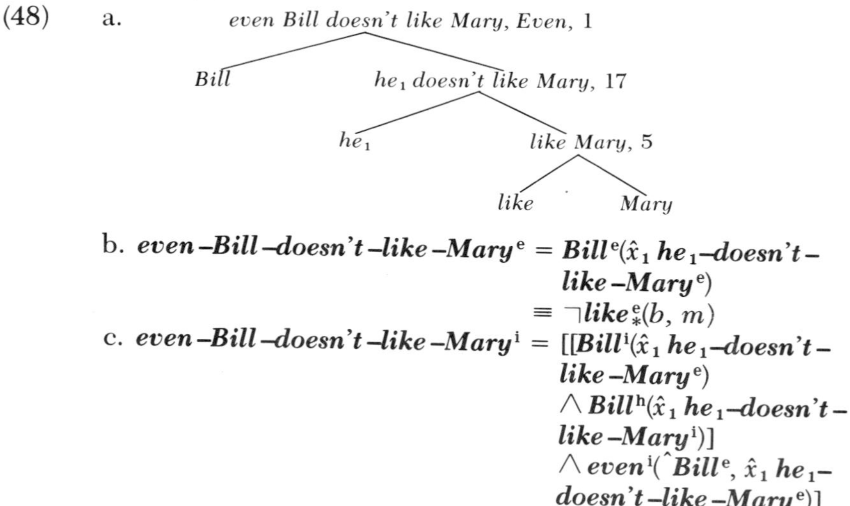

b. $\textbf{\textit{even-Bill-doesn't-like-Mary}}^{e} = \textbf{\textit{Bill}}^{e}(\hat{x}_1\, \textbf{\textit{he}}_1\textbf{\textit{-doesn't-like-Mary}}^{e}) \equiv \neg \textbf{\textit{like}}^{e}_{*}(b, m)$

c. $\textbf{\textit{even-Bill-doesn't-like-Mary}}^{i} = [[\textbf{\textit{Bill}}^{i}(\hat{x}_1\, \textbf{\textit{he}}_1\textbf{\textit{-doesn't-like-Mary}}^{e}) \wedge \textbf{\textit{Bill}}^{h}(\hat{x}_1\, \textbf{\textit{he}}_1\textbf{\textit{-doesn't-like-Mary}}^{i})] \wedge \textbf{\textit{even}}^{i}(\hat{\ }\textbf{\textit{Bill}}^{e}, \hat{x}_1\, \textbf{\textit{he}}_1\textbf{\textit{-doesn't-like-Mary}}^{e})]$

As (48b) shows, this sentence comes to have the same truth conditions as *Bill doesn't like Mary*. Because our version of Montague's T17 (see the Appendix) applies negation only to the extension expression, not to the implicatures arising from the constituent phrases, the first conjunct of (48c) is equivalent to the corresponding part of (47c) and hence to $\textbf{\textit{Bill-likes-Mary}}^{i}$. Consequently ***even-Bill-doesn't-like-***

Mary[i] entails, as it should, that Bill is acquainted with Mary. The striking difference in what is conventionally implicated by the two sentences is entirely due to the fact that in (47) *even* has scope over an affirmative sentence, in (48) over the corresponding negative sentence. Given our meaning postulate for the particle, $\boldsymbol{even}^{i}({}^{\wedge}\boldsymbol{Bill}^{e}, \hat{x}_1\ \boldsymbol{he}_1\text{–}\boldsymbol{doesn't}\text{–}\boldsymbol{like}\text{–}\boldsymbol{Mary}^{e})$ says, in effect, that there are other people besides Bill who don't like Mary and that Bill would be the most likely person to feel affection toward her (that is, the least likely not to like Mary). Thus (47) and (48) implicate opposite things about Bill.[12] This is reminiscent of Example (38), where a similar phenomenon results from scope ambiguity, from the possibility of applying the EVEN RULE at different points in the derivation of the sentence. (For more examples of this sort, see Heringer, 1973, and F. and L. Karttunen, 1977.)

As we mentioned earlier in connection with the examples in (35), the present treatment of *even* is incomplete because it deals only with cases where the particle has NP focus. In fact *even* can focus on constituents of many other syntactic categories. For example, in (35c) *Even INFERIOR coffee is expensive, even* focuses on the adjective *inferior*. This inadequacy can be corrected without changing any essential features of our analysis. Nothing prevents us from generalizing the EVEN RULE in such a way that phrases of other syntactic categories can be in the focus of the particle. We will not pursue the matter here, however, because the reformulation would require modifications in

[12] It is important to note that this correct outcome is in part due to the way negation is treated in the PTQ syntax. As (48a) illustrates, Rule 17 forms a negative sentence as it combines a subject NP with a verb phrase. In PTQ there is no other way of forming negative sentences, in particular, no rule for adding negation to an affirmative sentence. Since we introduce *even* syntactically by means of a quantification rule that inserts the focus NP into an open sentence, it follows that the existential and universal quantifiers which implicitly are associated with the particle are guaranteed to have wider scope with respect to negation in the same clause. Although this produces the desired outcome in the case at hand, there are examples that show that some rule of "sentential negation" may be needed in Montague's system. For instance, consider a sentence like

(i) *I hope we don't have to work even on Sundays.*

This obviously expresses the same proposition as *I hope we don't have to work on Sundays*. On the most plausible reading of the sentence, *even* gives rise to the implicature that the speaker considers Sunday to be the least likely day of the week for us to have to work. For this implicature to be generated correctly by our present rules *even* must take scope over the sentence *we have to work on x*. Negation will have to be added by a later rule after *even* and *Sundays* have been quantified in. Note that having *even* take scope over "we don't have to work on x" produces the pragmatically rather implausible implicature that Sunday is the least likely day for us not to have to work.

the PTQ syntax which are too extensive for our present concerns. For example, we would need to introduce proforms for each of the syntactic categories listed in (35). For instance, to derive Example (35c) we would need some proadjective, say *such* $_0$, for which a real adjective is substituted by a generalized version of the EVEN RULE. This is illustrated in (49).[13]

(49)

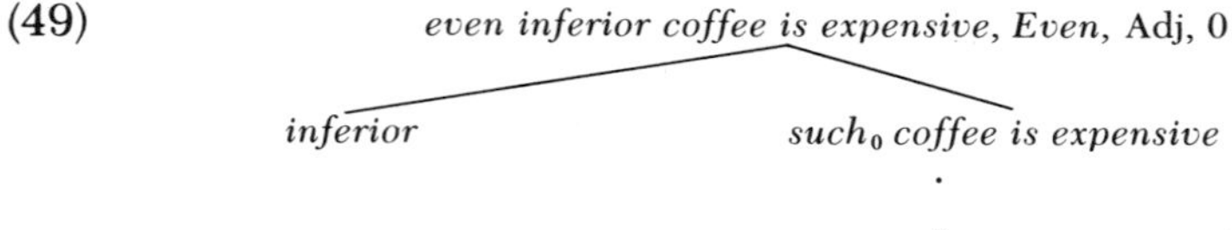

The resulting extension expression would be equivalent to that of *Inferior coffee is expensive,* and the implicature expression would entail that other kinds of coffee are expensive and that the inferior kind is less likely to be expensive than any of the others. Note that the general form of the implicature remains the same no matter to what syntactic category the focus constituent belongs.

As we mentioned earlier, there are a number of other particles besides *even* which give rise to conventional implicatures but apparently contribute nothing to the truth conditions of sentences in which they occur. The particles *also, too,* and *either* are similar to *even* in their meaning as well; they give rise to the same kind of existential implicature we have described. Their syntax and semantics can be described with minor modifications of what we just have proposed for *even.* The case of *only* is more complicated, although it also involves a distinction between focus and scope. The same is true of cleft and pseudocleft constructions (see Halvorsen, 1977).

In order to have a particularly simple example of conventional implicature to use in connection with compound sentences, which is our next topic, we close this section with a brief discussion of the particle *too.* Given all that we have said about *even,* it should be readily obvious what our analysis of *too* will look like. The NP-focused reading of (50), which conventionally implicates that there are others who drink besides John, is generated in the manner shown in (51a). The TOO RULE inserts a focus NP in an affirmative scope sentence (compare *ei-*

[13] The generalized EVEN RULE must "know" not only the subscript of the proform that is bound by the rule but its syntactic category as well, hence the marking "*Even,* Adj, 0" on the top line of (49). This information is needed to make the translation rule work properly. In this case we are quantifying over possible adjective intensions, not over individuals as in most of our examples.

ther) and adds a sentence final *too*. In other respects it is similar to our EVEN RULE. (See the Appendix.)

(50) *JOHN drinks too.*

(51) a.

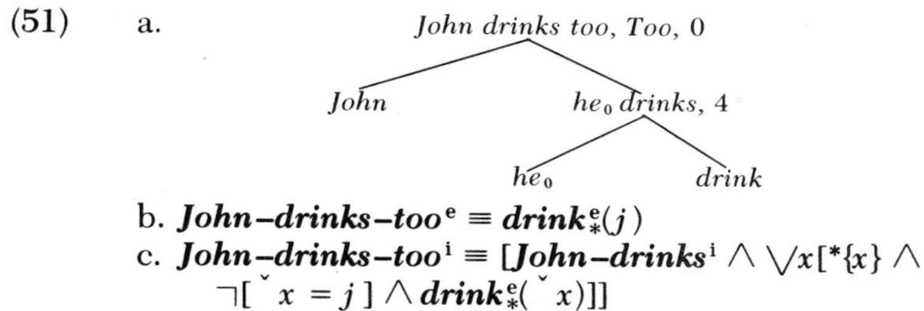

b. $\boldsymbol{John\text{–}drinks\text{–}too}^{e} \equiv \boldsymbol{drink}^{e}_{*}(j)$

c. $\boldsymbol{John\text{–}drinks\text{–}too}^{i} \equiv [\boldsymbol{John\text{–}drinks}^{i} \wedge \bigvee x[{}^{*}\{x\} \wedge \neg[{}^{\vee}x = j] \wedge \boldsymbol{drink}^{e}_{*}({}^{\vee}x)]]$

As far as truth conditions go, (50) is equivalent to *John drinks;* this result is expressed in (51b). The implicature brought in by the particle shows up in (51c); ***John –drinks –too***^{i} entails that there is someone else under consideration besides John who drinks. We will return to this example in the next section.

6. COMPOUND SENTENCES

One striking characteristic of conventional implicatures is the manner in which they are inherited by complex sentences from subordinate clauses. Since Langendoen and Savin's 1971 paper several people have given serious study to the rules of inheritance (for example, Karttunen, 1973, 1974; Morgan, 1973; Liberman, 1973; Reis, 1974; Wilson, 1975; Schiebe, 1975; Peters, 1975, 1977a; Soames, 1976; Gazdar, 1976; Hausser, 1976). We have already discussed this problem in Section 4 with regard to embedded sentential and infinitival complements. As we observed, their conventional implicatures are either inherited as such (*know, point out, discover,* and so on), transformed into implicatures about the beliefs of the subject (*hope, believe, fear,* and so on), or blocked entirely (*report, say, claim,* and so on), depending on the kind of verb the complement is embedded under. In our system, this is accounted for in terms of the heritage function, which assigns to every functor phrase a suitable heritage expression that determines what happens to the implicatures of its argument phrases. In the following we discuss compound sentences, sentences formed with connectives such as *and, or,* and *if . . . then.* We explain how we propose to account for their conventional implicatures in the framework of our revised PTQ grammar. Those who are familiar with the earlier literature on the topic will notice that the rules in question (see Rules

11–13 in the Appendix) incorporate the same inheritance principles for compound sentences that can be found—in different disguise—in Karttunen (1974) and Peters (1975, 1977a).

Before we embark on this project, let us first review the derivation of compound sentences in PTQ. Montague treats the connectives *and* and *or* syncategorematically: They are not considered to belong to the basic lexicon; instead they are introduced by syntactic rules which form conjoined and disjoined sentences (Rule 11), and verb phrases (Rule 12), and disjoined noun phrases (Rule 13). This feature of PTQ is in itself of no importance—it would be easy enough to do things otherwise—but it has some technical consequences. Since the word *and* by itself has no translation in the system, the heritage function plays no part in determining how the conventional implicatures of a compound sentence like *Bill is an alcoholic and John drinks too* depend on the translations of its component clauses; this is determined solely by the rule that conjoins the two clauses (i.e., Rule 11). Another minor detail, this one a slight inconvenience, is that the original PTQ grammar does not generate conditional sentences at all. Since conditionals are as interesting for us in this connection as conjunctions and disjunctions, we will introduce a new rule that generates sentence adverbials of the form *if* ϕ; these can then be combined by Montague's Rule 9 with a sentence ψ to form the compound *if* $\phi\psi$. For expository convenience, though, we do not introduce this new rule immediately, but proceed at first as if Montague's Rule 11 generated sentences of the form *if* ϕ *then* ψ along with ϕ *and* ψ and ϕ *or* ψ.

The question that faces us, then, is this: How are the truth conditions and the conventional implicatures of *if* ϕ *then* ψ, of ϕ *and* ψ, and of ϕ *or* ψ related to those of ϕ and of ψ? For the truth conditions, we tentatively adopt the traditional position that identifies these English connectives with their standard logical counterparts. Thus we will assign the extension expressions in (52).

(52) a. $\textbf{\textit{if}}\text{–}\phi\text{–}\textbf{\textit{then}}\text{–}\psi^{e} = [\phi^{e} \longrightarrow \psi^{e}]$
b. $\phi\text{–}\textbf{\textit{and}}\text{–}\psi^{e} = [\phi^{e} \wedge \psi^{e}]$
c. $\phi\text{–}\textbf{\textit{or}}\text{–}\psi^{e} = [\phi^{e} \vee \psi^{e}]$

Classical two-valued logic gives us no guidance, however, in deciding what the corresponding implicature expressions ought to look like. This we need to justify by appealing to intuitive judgments alone. Let us first take up the case of *if . . . then*. The simplest examples of the relevant sort are sentences such as those in (53).

(53) a. *If JOHN drinks too, then the bottle is empty.*
b. *If the bottle is empty, then JOHN drinks too.*
c. *If Bill is not a teetotaler, then JOHN drinks too.*

We pointed out on page 8 that indicative conditional sentences, such as these are, seem to conventionally implicate that their antecedent clause is not known to be false. This implicature is introduced, of course, by virtue of the conditionals being in the indicative mood; it is not inherited from either the antecedent or the consequent clause.

To see what implicatures are inherited, recall that (50) *JOHN drinks too*, where *too* focuses on *John*, conventionally implicates that there is someone else who drinks besides John. Sentence (53a) clearly commits the speaker to this proposition just as much as (50) does. This is a consequence of what appears to be the general rule that a conditional sentence inherits all the conventional implicatures of its antecedent clause. (More examples of this sort can be found in the papers referred to at the beginning of this section.) As a rule, then, we want to make ***if*–ϕ–*then*–ψ^i** entail ϕ^i.

Sentences (53b) and (53c) show that the matter is not as simple regarding conventional implicatures that originate in the consequent clause of a conditional. The former sentence seems to suggest that there is someone other than John who drinks; however, (53c) does not implicate this. The difference is obviously due in some way to the fact that in (53c) the proposition implicated by the consequent is entailed by the antecedent clause. The facts deserve a somewhat closer examination and it would be helpful if we had some way of sharpening our raw intuition about what commitments are made in asserting a sentence. One rather good method for assessing what a sentence conventionally implicates is to consider what it would take to assure one that the conventional implicatures of the sentence are true. Karttunen (1973, 1974) considered a wide variety of examples relevant to the inheritance of conventional implicatures (there called pragmatic presuppositions) from the consequent clause of conditionals, and he showed that the antecedent clause can help to assure that the consequent clause's conventional implicatures are true. The generalization that emerged from his study was that a set S of hypotheses (such, for example, as those which constitute the common ground—page 13 above) assure the truth of the conventional implicatures of *if* ϕ *then* ψ just in case (*i*) S assures that the conventional implicatures of ϕ are true and (*ii*) $S \cup \{\phi\}$ assures that the conventional implicatures of ψ are true. [Condition (*i*) is what requires that a conditional sentence implicate everything its antecedent does—see Peters (1975, 1977a) for different formulations of the same generalization.] The locution $S \cup \{\phi\}$ *assures that the conventional implicatures of* ψ *are true* is just another way of saying that, whenever ϕ and every sentence in S is true, then all conventional implicatures of ψ are true—that is, S together with ϕ entails each and every conventional implicature of ψ. Since ϕ is true just in case ϕ^e is, and since the conventional implicatures of ψ add up to ψ^i, clause (*ii*) just says that $S \cup \{\phi^e\}$ entails ψ^i. Given the logical properties of entailment and of the material conditional, this is equivalent to saying that S entails $[\phi^e \longrightarrow \psi^i]$. So Karttunen's generalization boils down to this: S entails ***if*–ϕ–*then*–ψ^i** just in case (*i*) S entails ϕ^i and (*ii*) S entails $[\phi^e \longrightarrow \psi^i]$, which in turn clearly holds just in case S entails $[\phi^i \wedge [\phi^e \longrightarrow \psi^i]]$. What this means is that we can equate the conventional implicature of ***if*** ϕ ***then*** ψ with $[\phi^i \wedge [\phi^e \longrightarrow \psi^i]]$. Adding to this the implicature of epistemic possibility discussed on page 8, we have (54).[14]

(54) $$\textbf{\textit{if}}\text{–}\phi\text{–}\textbf{\textit{then}}\text{–}\psi^i = [\neg \mathbf{K} \neg \phi^e \wedge \phi^i \wedge [\phi^e \longrightarrow \psi^i]]$$

Reverting to plain English, what we have seen is that the conventional implicatures of the consequent clause are inherited as conditional propositions by a conditional sentence. In particular, the implicature contributed to (53b) by its consequent clause is

(55) *If the bottle is empty, then there is someone other than John who drinks*

and the implicature which the same consequent clause contributes to (53c) is

(56) *If Bill is not a teetotaler, then there is someone other than John who drinks.*

How does this conclusion jibe with our first intuition about what (53b) and (53c) conventionally implicate? In the case of the latter sentence, our naive feeling was that the implicature brought in by *too* disappeared completely from the list of implicatures of the conditional sentence; this is fully in accord with our formal conclusion that the implicature of the consequent clause is transformed into the proposition expressed by (56). The proposition in question is trivially true (given that Bill and John are different people), and therefore committing oneself to its truth is no commitment at all. Indeed, any conven-

[14] As we pointed out in connection with (11), indicative and subjunctive conditionals differ in what they implicate about the epistemic possibility of the antecedent clause. We do not have the means yet to account for this difference formally.

tional implicature of a consequent clause which is entailed by the antecedent clause will be "filtered out" in this manner, the conditional proposition into which it is transformed being necessarily true.[15] It is important to realize that this "filtering" is caused by the semantic relation between the antecedent clause and the implicature of the consequent clause, not by the mere appearance in (53c) of the name *Bill* in the antecedent. Note, for example, that (57) is like (53b) in suggesting that there is someone other than John who drinks.

(57) *If Bill is not present, then JOHN drinks too.*[16]

What of our feeling that (53b) indicates that John is not the only drinker? Does our technical conclusion that (53b) conventionally implicates the proposition expressed by (55) agree with this intuition? The answer seems to us affirmative. We believe that the naive feeling that (53b) conventionally implicates that someone else besides John drinks is partly illusory, stemming from the tendency to assess what commitments inhere in a sentence by the method of imagining the sentence asserted in various contexts. Let us examine more closely what commitments a speaker actually does make by asserting the indicative conditional sentence (53b). One of those commitments is to have adequate grounds for believing the conventional implicatures of (53b) to be true, which according to our analysis includes having adequate grounds for believing that, if the facts should turn out to be such that the antecedent clause is true, then the conventional implicatures of the consequent clause will also be true. What could those grounds be? One conceivable ground might be that the speaker knows that the antecedent clause is false, and knows therefore that this obligation is

[15] We should point out that committing oneself to the truth of a triviality by conventionally implicating it differs in an important way from making that commitment by asserting a trivially true sentence. Because an assertion of a trivial kind may seem utterly pointless at first blush, it can generate conversational implicatures by means of the maxims of conversation—along lines sketched in Grice (1975). Conventionally implicating a triviality while asserting a contingently true sentence, however, will often have a perfectly clear point; the speaker may just wish to avoid incidentally committing himself to any possibly controversial proposition. Therefore, conventionally implicating a triviality will not usually give rise to conversational implicatures in the same way that asserting a triviality will.

[16] Examples of this sort may sound a bit strange in isolation. It requires some mental effort to imagine a situation where it would make sense to say something like (57). Suppose that it has been established that some of the prospective guests at a party use alcohol and the hostess wants to know what to expect of John. In that context, if one knew that John generally drinks but never in the presence of his boss, (57) would be a natural thing to say.

an empty one. This is eliminated as a possibility, however, by the fact that the speaker of (53b) commits himself to not knowing the antecedent clause to be false. It follows, then, that the speaker must allow for the possibility that the antecedent clause could turn out to be true and must have adequate reasons for thinking that, if it does, then the conventional implicatures of the consequent will likewise be true. We can divide this possibility into two cases:

I The speaker has reasons independent of what the antecedent clause says for thinking that the consequent's conventional implicatures are true.

II The speaker knows enough about facts attending the particular occasion of utterance to be morally certain that, for the various ways in which the antecedent might turn out to be true (i.e., ways consistent with everything the speaker knows), all of them would also make the conventional implicatures of the consequent clause true.

Case II might obtain, for example, on a typical occasion when Sentence (58a) is asserted.

(58) a. *If Tommy can name at least three colors, he can name a NONPRIMARY color too.*
b. *If Tommy can name at least three colors, then he can name a primary color.*

Anyone who holds the widespread belief that the first color terms learned tend to be names of primary colors is unlikely to take the speaker of (58a) to be implicating that Tommy can name a primary color, despite the fact that its consequent clause clearly does conventionally implicate this proposition. Rather, he would likely assent to the conventional implicature (58b) of (58a) without regard to how many colors Tommy can name. Another example of the same sort is (59a).

(59) a. *If there is a depression, THE PRESIDENT OF GENERAL MOTORS will lose his job too.*
b. *If there is a depression, someone other than the president of G.M. will lose his job.*

Given our factual knowledge about the effects of depression on employment, (59b) is an obvious truth. Its very triviality accounts for the subjective impression which many people have that the implicature contributed by *too* in (59a) disappears completely.

For many sentences, though, including Sentence (53b), it is highly implausible that the speaker could have the kind of knowledge which

Case II requires; then the only way he could be meeting his obligations in speaking is to have adequate grounds for believing the conventional implicatures of the consequent clause to be true, independently of the truth or falsity of the antecedent clause. It is this fact which leads one to feel that (53b) implicates not the proposition expressed by (55), but the stronger proposition that someone else besides John drinks. Thus the rule that produces (54) is evidently the correct one.[17]

[17] If the implicatures of the antecedent clause are inherited in an unchanged form, as we claimed above, conditional sentences exhibit a kind of asymmetry with respect to the inheritance phenomenon. There has been much discussion of this issue in the literature. Karttunen 1973, which was the first paper to address this question, claimed that this asymmetry was characteristic of all compound sentences; that is, in *if* ϕ *then* ψ, ϕ *and* ψ, and ϕ *or* ψ the presuppositions of ϕ were inherited by the compound in an unchanged form while those originating in ψ were 'filtered' (in effect, changed to conditionals with ϕ^e or $\neg\phi^e$ as the antecedent). Counterexamples to asymmetric filtering conditions have been presented, for example, in Liberman 1973 (with respect to *or*), Reis 1974 (with respect to *and*), Wilson 1975 (with respect to all connectives), and Soames 1976. Karttunen 1974 acknowledged that *or* was most likely symmetric but retained asymmetry for *if . . . then* and *and*. We take the same position here because we find the counterarguments inconclusive. But contrary to Wilson (1975, p. 37), asymmetry is not "the most important claim" of our theory. It would be a simple matter to replace (54) by

(i) $$\textit{if-}\phi\textit{-then-}\psi^i = [\psi^e \longrightarrow \phi^i] \wedge [\phi^e \longrightarrow \psi^i].$$

This would make the conventional implicatures of ϕ undergo a similar change to those originating in ψ and this would account for Wilson's judgments (which we disagree with) about sentences like "If all of Bill's friends have encouraged him, he must have friends." Opting for this alternative would obligate us to find a new explanation for the fact that sentences like (53a) intuitively seem to implicate everything that their antecedent clauses implicate, not something weaker, that is, $[\psi^e \longrightarrow \phi^i]$, as (i) stipulates.

There is one problematic type of example that in fact has made us consider adopting (i) or something else like it in place of (54). Consider sentence (ii).

(ii) *I'll leave if YOU leave too.*

This sentence can clearly be used in a situation which involves only two people: the speaker and his addressee. In that case one would not understand (ii) as implicating that the speaker will leave. Under these circumstances (ii) has approximately the force of *I'll leave if you leave with me.* Note that if *too* in (ii) is interpreted as having scope over *x leaves*, then *YOU leave too* implicates that someone other than you is leaving, and so our analysis predicts that (ii) as a whole will implicate this. But as we just observed, no such implication is present in the situation we described. This apparent insufficiency of our treatment could easily be remedied by replacing (54) by (i), in which case the implicature contributed by *too* under the above analysis would be transformed into a triviality (*If I leave then there is someone other than you who leaves*). We do not regard this as desirable, because we think that there is a genuine ambiguity in (ii) with regard to conventional implicature. The preferred reading of (ii) (or at least something close to it) is obtained in our present system by letting *too* take scope over *I'll leave if x leaves*, which

Having discussed the inheritance rules for conditionals at such length, we can deal with conjunctions and disjunctions more quickly. The inheritance rule for conjunctions is stated as (60)—cf. (54).

(60) $$\phi\text{-}\mathbf{\mathit{and}}\text{-}\psi^{i} = [\phi^{i} \wedge [\phi^{e} \longrightarrow \psi^{i}]]$$

As far as the inheritance of conventional implicatures is concerned, conjunctions behave exactly like conditionals. This can be seen from the examples in (61).

(61) a. *JOHN drinks too and Mary doesn't like it.*
b. *Bill is not present and JOHN drinks too.*
c. *Bill indulges in booze and JOHN drinks too.*

Sentence (61a) obviously commits the speaker to every proposition conventionally implicated by the first conjunct. Examples (61b) and (61c) differ just as the corresponding sentences in (53) do. Note that, although (61c) does commit the speaker to the proposition that there is someone other than John who drinks, it does so because of its truth conditions, that is, by virtue of what the first conjunct—*Bill indulges in booze*—says, not because of *too* in the second conjunct. This can be

---

gives rise to the implicature that there is some y other than you (viz. the speaker himself) such that the speaker leaves if y does. Since this is an obvious truth the analysis does account for the fact that on this reading *too* in (ii) gives rise to no absolute commitment by the speaker to leave.

In order to avoid possible misunderstandings we emphasize, however, that we are not rigidly committed to (54) or any other such detail of our theory. What is important to us is that the right inheritance principle, whatever it is, be expressible in our general framework.

One interesting consequence of the asymmetry of 'filtering' of conventional implicatures, depending on whether they originate in the antecedent or the consequent clause of a conditional, is that the rule of contraposition fails to preserve meaning. Clearly

(iii) *If John is at home, then Bill will realize that John is at home*

and

(iv) *If Bill won't realize that John is at home, then John isn't at home*

do not mean the same thing although they do have exactly the same truth-conditions, according to our analysis. Because "filtering" of conventional implicatures is asymmetric, (iv) implicates that John is at home and thus commits its speaker to the proposition that Bill will realize that John is at home; that is, (iv) is a perverse way of saying what *Bill will realize that John is at home* expresses concisely. [Sentence (iv) may have another meaning—reading it as containing "external" negations—which is the same as the meaning of (iii).] Sentence (iii), on the other hand, does not implicate that John is at home, because that implicature of (iii)'s consequent clause is "filtered out"; therefore (iii) means something different than (iv), something which (iii) is in fact quite a concise way of saying. (We are indebted to John Searle for bringing these facts to our attention.)

shown conclusively by embedding (61c) in a suitable larger sentence that differentiates between these two aspects of meaning. For example, consider (62)

(62) *If Bill indulges in booze and JOHN drinks too, then I will be amazed.*

As we observed earlier, a conditional sentence inherits all of the conventional implicatures of the antecedent clause. Since (62) obviously does not commit the speaker to the view that there is someone other than John who drinks, it shows that this aspect of the meaning of (61c) is not a matter of conventional implicature. What is conventionally implicated by (61c) is the conditional in (63).

(63) *If Bill indulges in booze then there is someone other than John who drinks.*

Since (63) is an obvious truth, the word *too* in (61c) and (62) does not give rise to any substantive commitment on the part of the speaker.

In stating the inheritance rules for conditionals and conjunctions, that is, (54) and (60), we have postulated a left-to-right asymmetry: The conventional implicatures of the first member of the pair are inherited by the compound sentence in an unchanged form; those of the second member are transformed into conditionals. Contrary to what was proposed in Karttunen (1973), such an asymmetry does not seem to hold for sentences of the form (*either*) ϕ *or* ψ—see Liberman (1973), Karttunen (1974), Wilson (1975). Consequently, our inheritance rule for disjunctions is symmetric.

(64) $$\phi\text{-}\boldsymbol{or}\text{-}\psi^{i} = [[\phi^{i} \vee \psi^{e}] \wedge [\phi^{e} \vee \psi^{i}]].$$

This rule is supported by examples such as those in (65).

(65) a. *Either JOHN drinks too or I will lose my bet.*
b. *Either I will lose my bet or JOHN drinks too.*
c. *Either JOHN drinks too or Bill doesn't use any liquor.*
d. *Either Bill doesn't use any liquor or JOHN drinks too.*

Examples (65a) and (65b) both suggest that there is someone other than John who drinks. According to (64), they conventionally implicate (66).

(66) *Either I will lose my bet or there is someone other than John who drinks.*

That this is the correct conventional implicature to assign can be shown by means of an argument similar to the one given on pages 37–39 for inheritance from the consequent clause of a conditional sentence. Rather than repeat that argument here, we will simply note that the proposition expressed by (68) seems clearly to be the correct conventional implicature for sentences (67a) and (67b).

(67) a. *Either Tommy can name at most two colors or he can name a NONPRIMARY color too.*
b. *Either Tommy can name a NONPRIMARY color too or he can name at most two colors.*

(68) *Either Tommy can name at most two colors or he can name a primary color.*

In contrast to (65a) and (65b), (65c) and (65d) are clearly noncommital as to whether anybody drinks. According to (64) they conventionally implicate (69)

(69) *Either Bill doesn't use any liquor or there is someone other than John who drinks.*

Since (69) expresses a trivially true proposition, the particle *too* gives rise to no substantive commitments in these examples.

In concluding this section we would like to emphasize once more that the rules which we have given for generating the implicature expressions of compound sentences[18] are equivalent to the admittance

[18] The implicature expressions of conjoined and disjoined sentences—(60) and (64)—are assigned by Rule 11 of the Appendix, which generates these two forms of sentence. Since that rule does not really generate conditional sentences, we need to make good now on our promise to state the rule generating *if*-clauses as sentence adverbials. Recall that these will be combined with other sentences by Rule 9 of the Appendix to make conditional sentences. The rule we need is stated as (i).

(i) If α is a subordinating conjunction (Montague would assign it category ((t/t)/t) and ϕ is a sentence (Montague's category t), then $\alpha\phi$ is a sentence adverbial (Montague's category t/t).

Translation: $\langle \alpha^{e}(\hat{}\,\phi^{e});\ \lambda q[\alpha^{i}(\hat{}\,\phi^{e})(q) \wedge \alpha^{h}(\hat{}\,\phi^{i})(q)]\rangle$

This rule together with those in the Appendix generates "If Bill is not a teetotaler JOHN drinks too" in the manner shown in (iia), and assigns it the extension expression (iib) and implicature expression (iic).

(ii) a. if Bill is not a teetotaler John drinks too, 9

If Bill is not a teetotaler, (i) John drinks too

if Bill is not a teetotaler

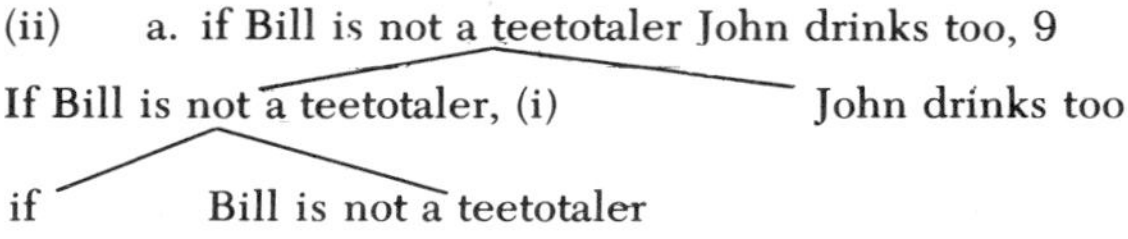

principles in Karttunen (1974), which was an attempt to develop a pragmatic theory of presupposition. In this connection, it is worth noting that the uncomprehending critique of Karttunen's theory in Katz and Langendoen (1976) is completely incorrect in concluding that no formal theory is possible of how presuppositions of compound sentences are "contextually filtered." The syntactic and semantic rules of our Appendix (and Footnote 18) assign precisely the conditional sort of "presuppositions" that are needed to account for "context-dependent filtering," as we have argued in the preceding pages, with no need for the hand-waving about linguistic performance which Katz and Langendoen indulge in.[19]

---

b. $\textit{\textbf{if–Bill–is–not–a–teetotaler–John–drinks–too}}^{e}$
$= \textit{\textbf{if}}^{e}\,({}^{\wedge}\textit{\textbf{Bill–is–not–a–teetotaler}}^{e})$
$({}^{\wedge}\textit{\textbf{John–drinks–too}}^{e})$

c. $\textit{\textbf{if–Bill–is–not–a–teetotaler–John–drinks–too}}^{i}$
$= [\lambda q[\textit{\textbf{if}}^{i}\,({}^{\wedge}\textit{\textbf{Bill–is–not–a–teetotaler}}^{e})(q)$
$\wedge\, \textit{\textbf{if}}^{h}\,({}^{\wedge}\textit{\textbf{Bill–is–not–a–teetotaler}}^{i})(q)]$
$({}^{\wedge}\textit{\textbf{John–drinks–too}}^{e})$
$\wedge\, \textit{\textbf{if–Bill–is–not–a–teetotaler}}^{h}$
$({}^{\wedge}\textit{\textbf{John–drinks–too}}^{i})]$

To obtain equivalence with the extension expression (52a) and the implicature expression (54), we need only adopt the meaning postulates (iii) and require that the heritage function h have the values shown in (iv) on *if* and on *if*-clauses, as we clearly are able to do.

(iii) a. $\Box[\textit{\textbf{if}}^{e}\,(p)(q) \longleftrightarrow [{}^{\vee}p \longrightarrow {}^{\vee}q]]$
b. $[\textit{\textbf{if}}^{i}\,(p)(q) \longleftrightarrow \neg K \neg {}^{\vee}p]$

(iv) a. $h(\textit{\textbf{if}}^{e}, \textit{\textbf{if}}^{i}) = \lambda p\, \lambda q\ {}^{\vee}p$
b. $h(\textit{\textbf{if}}–\phi^{e}, \textit{\textbf{if}}–\phi^{i}) = \lambda q[\phi^{e} \longrightarrow {}^{\vee}q]$

[19] It is not only in their critical remarks that Katz and Langendoen fall seriously into error. For instance, contrary to their claims the account they present does not explain the 'filtering' of the consequent clause's factive presupposition in

(i) *If Nixon appoints J. Edgar Hoover to the cabinet, he will regret having appointed a homosexual.*

For in the sentence *If Nixon appoints J. Edgar Hoover—who, as we all know, is a homosexual—to the cabinet, he will regret having appointed a homosexual,* into which Katz and Langendoen contend Sentence (i) is somehow pragmatically interpreted, the appositive relative clause does not fall within the scope of the conditional's "hypotheticality" but rather its truth is entailed; thus it will not trigger Katz's heavy parenthesis wipe-out rule. In contrast to their ad hoc and unsuccessful treatment, our rules assign to the original sentence the conventional implicature expressed by *If Nixon appoints J. Edgar Hoover to the cabinet, he will have appointed a homosexual;* this implicature is true if Hoover is a homosexual (and is appointed by Nixon), if Nixon appoints some homosexual—not Hoover—to the cabinet, and under many other conditions as well.

Exactly the principles we have formalized here can also be incorporated in a "classical" semantic theory of presupposition by defining the truth tables for *and, or,* and *if . . . then* in a suitable way, as was shown in Peters (1977a). So far as their empirical consequences are concerned, the differences between these two competing approaches are actually more elusive than most people, including the present authors, have assumed. We should briefly point out, in this connection, how close the so-called "strong projection method" incorporated in Kleene's three-valued truth tables is to the treatment of connectives in Karttunen (1974) and in this paper. Unfortunately, the far-reaching similarities have eluded most people who have written on this topic (e.g., Hausser, 1976).

Kleene's three-valued truth tables (reproduced from Hausser, 1976) are given in (70) ("#" stands for the third, "indeterminate" truth value).

(70)

ϕ	$\neg\phi$
1	0
0	1
#	#

$\longrightarrow$	1	0	#
1	1	0	#
0	1	1	1
#	①	#	#

$\wedge$	1	0	#
1	1	0	#
0	0	0	0
#	#	⓪	#

$\vee$	1	0	#
1	1	1	1
0	1	0	#
#	①	#	#

(The truth tables in Peters, 1977a, are identical to these except that the circled values are all #s.)[20]

By the usual semantic definition of presupposition, sentence ϕ presupposes ψ if ψ is true whenever ϕ is bivalent (either true or false). One interesting consequence of this definition is that every sentence presupposes the disjunction of itself and its negation. This can be seen from the table in (71). (Sentence ϕ has 1 or 0 as its value just in case $[\phi \vee \neg\phi]$ has the value 1.)

Thus our rules succeed in capturing the variable ways in which the "presupposition" of (i) can be satisfied.

Moreover, it is far from clear that Katz and Langendoen's device of heavy parentheses can represent the sort of "presuppositions" associated with implicative verbs such as *manage* and *fail,* particles like *even* and *too,* or in fact anything other than existential and factive presuppositions. Yet the former kinds of "presupposition" are filtered in just the same way as the latter, which strongly indicates that they ought to be treated within the same theory of presupposition inheritance. See Gazdar 1978 for other cogent criticisms of Katz and Langendoen's position.

[20] Peters (1977a) took Karttunen (1974) to be proposing asymmetric filtering of presuppositions with *or* as well as with *and* and *if . . . then,* unlike the interpretation we give here to Karttunen (1974).

(71)

ϕ	$\neg\phi$	$\phi \vee \neg\phi$
1	0	1
0	1	1
#	#	#

Furthermore, $[\phi \vee \neg\phi]$ is the "maximal presupposition" of ϕ since it entails every other presupposition of ϕ and is entailed by the sum of all the other presuppositions. Using ϕ^p to abbreviate the maximal presupposition $[\phi \vee \neg\phi]$ of ϕ, for any sentence ϕ, we have in particular (72).

(72)
a. $[\phi \longrightarrow \psi]^p \equiv [\phi \longrightarrow \psi] \vee \neg[\phi \longrightarrow \psi]$
b. $[\phi \wedge \psi]^p \equiv [\phi \wedge \psi] \vee \neg[\phi \wedge \psi]$
c. $[\phi \vee \psi]^p \equiv [\phi \vee \psi] \vee \neg[\phi \vee \psi]$

The formulas on the right side of (72) are equivalent in Kleene's system to their counterparts in (73). (This can be shown easily by making use of familiar rules of inference that hold in this system as well as in classical two-valued logic: De Morgan's Laws, interdefinability of $\longrightarrow$ and $\vee$, distributivity of $\wedge$ over $\vee$, and vice versa, associativity and commutativity of $\wedge$ and $\vee$.)

(73)
a. $[\phi \longrightarrow \psi]^p \equiv [\neg\psi \longrightarrow [\phi \vee \neg\phi]] \wedge [\phi \longrightarrow [\psi \vee \neg\psi]]$
b. $[\phi \wedge \phi]^p \equiv [\psi \longrightarrow [\phi \vee \neg\phi]] \wedge [\phi \longrightarrow [\psi \vee \neg\psi]]$
c. $[\phi \vee \psi]^p \equiv [\neg\psi \longrightarrow [\phi \vee \neg\phi]] \wedge [\neg\phi \longrightarrow [\psi \vee \neg\psi]]$

Since $[\phi \vee \neg\phi]$ and $[\psi \vee \neg\psi]$ are abbreviated ϕ^p and ψ^p, respectively, the formulas in (73) merely express the equivalences (74).

(74)
a. $[\phi \longrightarrow \psi]^p \equiv [\neg\psi \longrightarrow \phi^p] \wedge [\phi \longrightarrow \psi^p]$
b. $[\phi \wedge \psi]^p \equiv [\psi \longrightarrow \phi^p] \wedge [\phi \longrightarrow \psi^p]$
c. $[\phi \vee \psi]^p \equiv [\neg\psi \longrightarrow \phi^p] \wedge [\neg\phi \longrightarrow \psi^p]$

This should make transparent the connection between Kleene's three-valued truth tables and the present treatment using conventional implicature. The equivalences in (74) correspond to our (54), (60), and (64). (The maximal presupposition ϕ^p is analogous to our implicature expression ϕ^i, the sentence ϕ to our extension expression ϕ^e.) Rule (64) matches exactly with (74c), because of the interdefinability of $\longrightarrow$ and $\vee$. In the other cases there is a difference due to the fact that Kleene's truth tables "filter" symmetrically in conditionals and conjunctions (where we do not) as well as in disjunctions (where we do). To make the semantic projection method filter asymmetrically where we do, one would have to replace the circled values by "#" in the tables for $\longrightarrow$ and $\dot{\wedge}$ in (70). While linguistic intuition supports asymmetrical filtering, this move would destroy some of the beauty of Kleene's system by doing away with many of the classical equivalences that he carried over from two-valued logic. Nevertheless, we believe that sentences such as

(75) *If John drinks too, then Bill doesn't drink*

and

(76) *John drinks too and Bill isn't a teetotaler either*

show that we are right not to "filter" the presupposition which *too* contributes to these sentences, and that the Kleene "strong projection method" is not empirically adequate as Hausser (1976) contends.

There has been much controversy in the literature about the inheritance of conventional implicatures (presuppositions) under negation. In our discussion—and in restating Montague's Rule 17 (see the Appendix)—we have assumed that a negative sentence shares all the conventional implicatures of its affirmative counterpart. However, in some instances negation seems to block off the implicatures of the sentence it has scope over. This is evidenced by the fact that discourses such as the following are not perceived as self-contradictory, although in each the second sentence explicitly denies what the first would implicate if its conventional implicatures were unaffected by negation.

(77) a. *John didn't fail to arrive. He wasn't supposed to come at all.*
b. *Bill hasn't already forgotten that today is Friday, because today is Thursday.*
c. *Mary isn't sick too. Nobody else is sick besides her.*

The traditional solution to this problem is to recognize two kinds of negation. In the context of three-valued logic this can be accomplished in the manner shown below.

(78) a.

	ϕ	$\neg\phi$
INTERNAL	1	0
NEGATION	0	1
	#	#

b.

	ϕ	$\neg\phi$
EXTERNAL	1	0
NEGATION	0	1
	#	1

Ordinary negation—the "internal" negation—of ϕ has the third, indeterminate truth value whenever ϕ is indeterminate; thus ϕ and $\neg\phi$ have the same semantic presuppositions. The "external" negation of ϕ, which might be rendered in English as *it is not true that* ϕ, never has the indeterminate truth value; consequently, it has no falsifiable presuppositions at all. On this view, the lack of contradiction in (77) can be explained by interpreting the negation in the first sentence of each example as a case of external negation.

We think that there is ample justification of a pragmatic, semantic, syntactic, and even phonological kind for regarding the negation in (77) as something other than ordinary negation. But since our logic is bivalent, we of course will not characterize this difference in the manner of (78). Negative sentences of the sort in (77) have a special function in discourse. They contradict something that the addressee has just said, implied, or implicitly accepted. One indication of their role is that they tend to be produced with a distinctive intonation contour (Liberman and Sag, 1974). Another characteristic property of this kind of negation is that it does not affect the distribution of polarity items—note the appearance of *already* in (77b) and *too* in (77c).

We think that contradiction negation differs semantically from ordinary negation only by virtue of having a broader target. As we see it, ordinary negation pertains just to the proposition expressed by the corresponding affirmative sentence; it does not affect conventional implicatures. Contradiction negation, on the other hand, pertains to the total meaning of its target sentence, ignoring the distinction between truth conditions and conventional implicatures. Letting ϕ be an affirmative sentence whose meaning we represent as $\langle \phi^e; \phi^i \rangle$, the two negations of ϕ in our system have the translations shown in (79).

(79) a. ORDINARY NEGATION OF ϕ: $\langle \neg\phi^e; \phi^i \rangle$
b. CONTRADICTION NEGATION OF ϕ: $\langle \neg[\phi^e \wedge \phi^i]; [\phi^i \vee \neg\phi^i] \rangle$

A sentence with contradiction negation is by itself non-specific (in the absence of contrastive intonation) in regard to what it is that the speaker is objecting to. Although the discourse fragments in (77) were intentionally designed so as to show that the speaker was objecting to something that had been conventionally implicated, this is not a necessary feature of contradiction negation—compare (77b) with *Bill hasn't already forgotten that today is Friday. I know for sure that he still remembers it.*

From what we have said earlier, it follows that there should be a separate rule, in addition to Montague's Rule 17, for forming sentences with contradiction negation. We have not included such a rule in the Appendix, mainly because we do not know how to represent their prosodic characteristics in the present framework. Another unsolved problem of formalization concerns the contextual linkage of such sentences. How to capture the fact that the contradiction negation of ϕ seems to require that the addressee has just indicated his acceptance of ϕ^e and ϕ^i requires further research. (This could conceivably be an instance of Searle's preparatory conditions on felicitous assertion.)

7. FINAL REMARKS

In this chapter we have attempted to do two things. First of all we have tried to show that so-called presuppositions are not instances of a single phenomenon. We believe that this fact is in part responsible for the continuing controversy about how to analyze presuppositions. The two examples of so-called presupposition that we have examined in detail—subjunctive conditionals and the particle *even*—are at extreme ends of the spectrum. In the first case it is simply a mistake to think that the phenomenon in question is to be described in terms of some separate presuppositional component of sentence meaning. In the second case such an analysis is clearly on the right track. These two examples seem to constitute paradigm cases of what Grice has called PARTICULARIZED CONVERSATIONAL and CONVENTIONAL implicatures, respectively.

We have not attempted to do a complete inventory of so-called presuppositions but we think that many of the genuine cases involve conventional implicatures, including the so-called existential presuppositions that accompany quantifiers like *all, every,* and the definite article. In some cases we are not sure what the correct analysis is; aspectual verbs like *stop* and *begin* are a case in point. As we point out in our discussion of *criticize,* the distinction between generalized conversational implicatures and conventional implicatures is sometimes hard to draw. We hope that these outstanding problems can be solved by extending and deepening the theory we have outlined here.

Our second objective has been to show how model-theoretic methods of semantic interpretation can be extended to account both for truth-conditional and conventionally implicated meaning. By presenting a detailed analysis of *even* and by discussing the problems posed by compound sentences we hope to have shown that the insights obtained in previous studies can be incorporated in our framework.

APPENDIX: REVISED PTQ RULES

RULE 2. If ζ is a CN-phrase, then $F_0(\zeta)$, $F_1(\zeta)$, and $F_2(\zeta)$ are T-phrases, where $F_0(\zeta)$ is *every* ζ, $F_1(\zeta)$ is *the* ζ, and $F_2(\zeta)$ is *a* ζ or *an* ζ according as the first word of ζ takes *a* or *an*.

Translation of $F_0(\zeta)$: $\langle \hat{P} \bigwedge x[\zeta^e(x) \longrightarrow P\{x\}];\ \hat{P} \bigvee x[\zeta^e(x) \wedge \zeta^i(x)]\rangle$
$F_1(\zeta)$: $\langle \hat{P} \bigvee y[\bigwedge x[\zeta^e(x) \longleftrightarrow x = y] \wedge P\{y\}];$
$\hat{P} \bigvee y[\bigwedge x[\zeta^e(x) \longleftrightarrow x = y] \wedge \zeta^i(y)]\rangle$
$F_2(\zeta)$: $\langle \hat{P} \bigvee x[\zeta^e(x) \wedge P\{x\}];\ \hat{P} \bigvee x \zeta^i(x)\rangle$

Value of h on translation of

$F_0(\zeta)$: $\hat{P} \bigwedge x[\zeta^e(x) \longrightarrow P\{x\}]$
$F_1(\zeta)$: $\hat{P} \bigvee y[\bigwedge x[\zeta^e(x) \longleftrightarrow x = y] \wedge P\{y\}]$
$F_2(\zeta)$: $\hat{P} \bigvee x[\zeta^e(x) \wedge P\{x\}]$

NOTE: What we have written after "Translation" in Rule 2 is shorthand for "If ζ is a CN-phrase and ζ translates to $\langle \zeta^e; \zeta^i\rangle$, then $F_0(\zeta)$ translates to $\langle \hat{P} \bigwedge x[\zeta^e(x) \longrightarrow P\{x\}];\ \hat{P} \bigvee x[\zeta^e(x) \wedge \zeta^i(x)]\rangle$, $F_1(\zeta)$ translates to . . ." We will follow the same convention throughout. At some point we have to specify what value the heritage function h takes on pairs of expressions of INTENSIONAL LOGIC. It is convenient to do this as we go along in the translation rules for the pairs of expressions where the value of h will matter.

RULE 3. If ζ is a CN-phrase and ϕ is a t-phrase, then ζ *such that* $\phi^{(n)}$ is a CN-Phrase, where $\phi^{(n)}$ comes from ϕ by replacing each occurrence of he_n or him_n by

$\left\{\begin{matrix} he \\ she \\ it \end{matrix}\right\}$ or $\left\{\begin{matrix} him \\ her \\ it \end{matrix}\right\}$,

respectively, according as the first basic CN in ζ is of

$\left\{\begin{matrix} \text{masc.} \\ \text{fem.} \\ \text{neut.} \end{matrix}\right\}$

gender.

Translation: $\langle \hat{x}[\zeta^e(x) \wedge [\lambda x_n \phi^e](x)];\ \hat{x}[\zeta^i(x) \wedge [\lambda x_n \phi^i](x)]\rangle$

RULE 4. If α is a t/IV-phrase and δ is an IV-phrase, then $\alpha\delta'$ is a t-phrase, where δ' is the result of replacing the first verb in δ by its third person singular present.

Translation: $\langle \alpha^e(\hat{\ }\delta^e);\ [\alpha^i(\hat{\ }\delta^e) \wedge \alpha^h(\hat{\ }\delta^i)]\rangle$

NOTE: In translation Rule 4 we have written α^{h} as shorthand for h $(\langle\alpha^{e}; \alpha^{i}\rangle)$, the value of the heritage function h on the argument $\langle\alpha^{e}; \alpha^{i}\rangle$. We will adhere to this convention throughout.

RULE 5. If δ is an IV/T-phrase and β is a T-phrase, then $F_5(\delta, \beta)$ is an IV-phrase, where $F_5(\delta, \beta)$ is $\delta\beta$ if β does not have the form he_n and $F_5(\delta, he_n)$ is $\delta\ him_n$.

Translation: $\langle \delta^{e}(\hat{\ }\beta^{e}); \hat{x}[\delta^{i}(\hat{\ }\beta^{e})(x) \wedge \delta^{h}(\hat{\ }\beta^{i})(x)]\rangle$

RULE 6. If δ is an IAV/T-phrase and β is a T-phrase, then $F_5(\delta, \beta)$ is an IAV-phrase.

Translation: $\langle \delta^{e}(\hat{\ }\beta^{e}); \lambda P\ \hat{x}[\delta^{i}(\hat{\ }\beta^{e})(P)(x) \wedge \delta^{h}(\hat{\ }\beta^{i})(P)(x)]\rangle$

Value of h on translation: $\lambda P\ \hat{x}P\{x\}$

RULE 7. If δ is an IV/t-phrase and β is a t-phrase, then $\delta\beta$ is an IV-phrase.

Translation: $\langle \delta^{e}(\hat{\ }\beta^{e}); \hat{x}[\delta^{i}(\hat{\ }\beta^{e})(x) \wedge \delta^{h}(\hat{\ }\beta^{i})(x)]\rangle$

RULE 8. If δ is an IV//IV-phrase and β is an IV-phrase, then $\delta\beta$ is an IV-phrase.

Translation: $\langle \delta^{e}(\hat{\ }\beta^{e}); \hat{x}[\delta^{i}(\hat{\ }\beta^{e})(x) \wedge \delta^{h}(\hat{\ }\beta^{i})(x)]\rangle$

RULE 9. If δ is a t/t-phrase and β is a t-phrase, then $\delta\beta$ is a t-phrase.

Translation: $\langle \delta^{e}(\hat{\ }\beta^{e}); [\delta^{i}(\hat{\ }\beta^{e}) \wedge \delta^{h}(\hat{\ }\beta^{i})]\rangle$

RULE 10. If δ is an IV/IV-phrase and β is an IV-phrase, then $\beta\delta$ is an IV-phrase.

Translation: $\langle \delta^{e}(\hat{\ }\beta^{e}); \hat{x}[\delta^{i}(\hat{\ }\beta^{e})(x) \wedge \delta^{h}(\hat{\ }\beta^{i})(x)]\rangle$

RULE 11. If ϕ and ψ are t-phrases, then ϕ *and* ψ and ϕ *or* ψ are t-phrases.

Translation of ϕ *and* ψ: $\langle[\phi^{e} \wedge \psi^{e}]; [\phi^{i} \wedge [\phi^{e} \longrightarrow \psi^{i}]]\rangle$
ϕ *or* ψ: $\langle[\phi^{e} \vee \psi^{e}]; [[\phi^{i} \vee \psi^{e}] \wedge [\phi^{e} \vee \psi^{i}]]\rangle$

RULE 12. If γ and δ are IV-phrases, then γ *and* δ and γ *or* δ are IV-phrases.

Translation of γ *and* δ: $\langle \hat{x}[\gamma^e(x) \wedge \delta^e(x)];$
$\hat{x}[\gamma^i(x) \wedge [\gamma^e(x) \longrightarrow \delta^i(x)]]\rangle$
γ *or* δ: $\langle \hat{x}[\gamma^e(x) \vee \delta^e(x)]; \hat{x}[[\gamma^i(x) \vee \delta^e(x)] \wedge [\gamma^e(x) \vee \delta^i(x)]]\rangle$

RULE 13. If α and β are T-phrases, then α *or* β is a T-phrase.

Translation: $\langle \hat{P}[\alpha^e(P) \vee \beta^e(P)]; \hat{P}\ [[\alpha^i(P) \vee \beta^e(P)] \wedge [\alpha^e(P) \vee \beta^i(P)]]\rangle$

Value of h on translation: $\hat{P}[\alpha^e(P) \vee \beta^e(P)]$

RULE 14. If α is a T-phrase and ϕ is a t-phrase, then $F_{10,n}(\alpha,\phi)$ is a t-phrase, where either (a) α does not have the form he_k and $F_{10,n}(\alpha,\phi)$ comes from ϕ by replacing the first occurrence of he_n or him_n by α and all other occurrences of he_n or him_n by

$$\begin{Bmatrix} he \\ she \\ it \end{Bmatrix} \text{ or } \begin{Bmatrix} him \\ her \\ it \end{Bmatrix},$$

respectively, according as the gender of the first basic CN or T in α is

$$\begin{Bmatrix} \text{masc.} \\ \text{fem.} \\ \text{neut.} \end{Bmatrix},$$

or (b) α is he_k and $F_{10,n}(\alpha,\phi)$ comes from ϕ by replacing all occurrences of he_n or him_n by he_k or him_k, respectively.

Translation: $\langle \alpha^e(\hat{x}_n\phi^e); [\alpha^i(\hat{x}_n\phi^e) \wedge \alpha^h(\hat{x}_n\phi^i)]\rangle$

RULE 15. If α is a T-phrase and ζ is a CN-phrase, then $F_{10,n}(\alpha, \zeta)$ is a CN-phrase.

Translation: $\langle \hat{y}\ \alpha^e(\hat{x}_n\zeta^e(y)); \hat{y}\ [\alpha^i(\hat{x}_n\zeta^e(y)) \wedge \alpha^h(\hat{x}_n\zeta^i(y))]\rangle$

RULE 16. If α is a T-phrase and δ is an IV-phrase, then $F_{10,n}(\alpha, \delta)$ is an IV-phrase.

Translation: $\langle \hat{y}\ \alpha^e(\hat{x}_n\delta^e(y)); \hat{y}\ [\alpha^i(\hat{x}_n\delta^e(y)) \wedge \alpha^h(\hat{x}_n\delta^i(y))]\rangle$

RULE 17. If α is a T-phrase and δ is an IV-phrase, then $F_{11}(\alpha, \delta)$, $F_{12}(\alpha, \delta)$, $F_{13}(\alpha, \delta)$, $F_{14}(\alpha, \delta)$, and $F_{15}(\alpha, \delta)$ are t-phrases, where as in PTQ $F_{11}(\alpha, \delta)$ is the negation, $F_{12}(\alpha, \delta)$ the future, $F_{13}(\alpha, \delta)$ the negative future, $F_{14}(\alpha, \delta)$ the present perfect, and $F_{15}(\alpha, \delta)$ the negative present perfect of $F_4(\alpha, \delta)$.

Translation of $F_{11}(\alpha, \delta)$: $\langle \neg\alpha^{e}({}^{\wedge}\delta^{e}); [\alpha^{i}({}^{\wedge}\delta^{e}) \wedge \alpha^{h}({}^{\wedge}\delta^{i})]\rangle$
$F_{12}(\alpha, \delta)$: $\langle W\alpha^{e}({}^{\wedge}\delta^{e}); W[\alpha^{i}({}^{\wedge}\delta^{e}) \wedge \alpha^{h}({}^{\wedge}\delta^{i})]\rangle$
$F_{13}(\alpha, \delta)$: $\langle \neg W\alpha^{e}({}^{\wedge}\delta^{e}); W[\alpha^{i}({}^{\wedge}\delta^{e}) \wedge \alpha^{h}({}^{\wedge}\delta^{i})]\rangle$
$F_{14}(\alpha, \delta)$: $\langle H\alpha^{e}({}^{\wedge}\delta^{e}); H[\alpha^{i}({}^{\wedge}\delta^{e}) \wedge \alpha^{h}({}^{\wedge}\delta^{i})]\rangle$
$F_{15}(\alpha, \delta)$: $\langle \neg H\alpha^{e}({}^{\wedge}\delta^{e}); H[\alpha^{i}({}^{\wedge}\delta^{e}) \wedge \alpha^{h}({}^{\wedge}\delta^{i})]\rangle$

EVEN RULE. If α is a T-phrase and ϕ is a t-phrase containing an occurrence of HE_n (*he*$_n$, *him*$_n$, or *his*$_n$), then $F_{\text{even},n}(\alpha, \phi)$ is a t-phrase and is derived from ϕ by replacing the first occurrence of HE_n by *even* α and each of its subsequent occurrences by the corresponding unsubscripted pronoun whose gender matches the gender of α.

Translation: $\langle \alpha^{e}(\hat{x}_n\phi^{e}); [[\alpha^{i}(\hat{x}_n\phi^{e}) \wedge \alpha^{h}(\hat{x}_n\phi^{i})] \wedge even^{i}({}^{\wedge}\alpha^{e}, \hat{x}_n\phi^{e})]\rangle$

Basic Expressions

Expression	Category	Translation	Value of h
Bill	T	$\langle \hat{P}\, P\{{}^{\wedge}b\}; \hat{P}\, \mathbf{male}^{e}({}^{\wedge}b)\rangle$	$\hat{P}\, P\{{}^{\wedge}b\}$
Mary	T	$\langle \hat{P}\, P\{{}^{\wedge}m\}; \hat{P}\, \mathbf{female}^{e}({}^{\wedge}m)\rangle$	$\hat{P}\, P\{{}^{\wedge}m\}$
he$_0$	T	$\langle \hat{P}\, P\{x_0\}; \hat{P}\, x_0 = x_0\rangle$	$\hat{P}\, P\{x_0\}$
be	TV	$\langle \lambda\mathcal{P}\, \hat{x}\mathcal{P}\{\hat{y}[{}^{\vee}y = {}^{\vee}x]\}; \mathbf{be}^{i}\rangle$	$\lambda\mathcal{P}$ $\hat{x}\bigvee P\mathcal{P}\{P\}$
necessarily	t/t	$\langle \hat{p}\Box{}^{\vee}p; \hat{p}\, p = p\rangle$	$\hat{p}\ {}^{\vee}p$
like	TV	$\langle \mathbf{like}^{e}; \mathbf{like}^{i}\rangle$	$\mathbf{like}^{h}$
		where $\mathbf{like}^{e}$, $\mathbf{like}^{i}$, and $\mathbf{like}^{h}$ are constants of INTENSIONAL LOGIC of type f(TV)—as ***love'*** is in PTQ—and similarly for the other basic expressions of PTQ which Montague translates there as constants.	

Meaning Postulates

${}^{\wedge}\mathbf{like}^{i} = {}^{\wedge}\lambda\mathcal{P}\, \hat{x}\mathcal{P}\{\hat{y}\ \mathbf{be\text{-}acquainted\text{-}with}^{e}_{*}({}^{\vee}x, {}^{\vee}y)\}$
${}^{\wedge}\mathbf{like}^{h} = {}^{\wedge}\lambda\mathcal{P}\, \hat{x}\bigvee P\mathcal{P}\{P\}$
${}^{\wedge}\mathbf{assert\text{-}that}^{h} = {}^{\wedge}\lambda p\, \hat{x}p = p$
${}^{\wedge}\mathbf{hope\text{-}that}^{h} = {}^{\wedge}\lambda p\, \hat{x}\ \mathbf{believe\text{-}that}^{e}(x, p)$
${}^{\wedge}\mathbf{forget\text{-}that}^{h} = {}^{\wedge}\lambda p\, \hat{x}[{}^{\vee}p]$
${}^{\wedge}\mathbf{fail\text{-}to}^{e} = {}^{\wedge}\lambda P\, \hat{x}\neg P\{x\}$
${}^{\wedge}\mathbf{fail\text{-}to}^{i} = {}^{\wedge}\lambda P\, \hat{x}[\mathbf{try\text{-}to}^{e}(x, P) \vee \bigvee y\ \mathbf{expect\text{-}that}^{e}(y, {}^{\wedge}WP\{x\})]$

$$\hat{}\,\textit{fail-to}^{\mathrm{h}} = \hat{}\,\lambda P\, \hat{x} P\{x\}$$
$$\hat{}\,\textit{forget-that}^{\mathrm{i}} = \hat{}\,\lambda p\, \hat{x}[\check{}\,p \wedge H\textit{know-that}^{\mathrm{e}}(x, p)]$$
$$\hat{}\,\textit{even}^{\mathrm{i}} = \hat{}\,\lambda \mathscr{P}\, \hat{Q} \mathscr{P}\{\hat{y}[\bigvee x[*\{x\} \wedge \neg[\check{}\,x = \check{}\,y] \wedge Q\{x\}] \wedge \bigwedge x[[*\{x\} \wedge \neg[\check{}\,x = \check{}\,y]] \longrightarrow \textit{exceed}^{\mathrm{e}}(\textit{likelihood}^{\mathrm{e}}(\hat{}\,Q\{x\}), \textit{likelihood}^{\mathrm{e}}(\hat{}\,Q\{y\}))]]\}$$

Note

NOTE: One problem with these rules is that they do not assign the correct conventional implicatures to sentences such as *Someone managed to succeed George V on the throne of England.* What the rules given here predict is (correctly) that this sentence is true iff someone succeeded George V to the throne and (incorrectly) that it conventionally implicates that it was difficult for someone to do that. This is unsatisfactory because the implicature just stated is true (you or I would have found it extremely difficult), but the sentence is in fact an odd thing to say precisely because it conventionally implicates a falsehood—namely that George V's successor had difficulty ascending to the throne. What our rules as stated lack is any way of linking the choice of a person who is implicated to have difficulty to the choice of a person who is asserted to have succeeded. We expect that this deficiency will be remedied through further research, but we note here that this task is not a trivial one. If we simply changed our rules so that the sentence above would conventionally implicate that someone who succeeded to the throne had difficulty in doing so, then we would predict incorrectly that *If someone managed to succeed George V on the throne of England, then that country is still a monarchy* and *Did someone manage to succeed George V on the throne of England?* both conventionally implicate the same proposition, and therefore conventionally implicate that someone did succeed to the throne.

While the problem of giving a correct account of the conventional implicatures of sentences containing expressions with indefinite reference (including indefinite reference by past or future tenses) is quite a challenging one, it is not peculiar to the formal framework we present here for describing those implicatures. Instead the problem arises directly from the decision to separate what is communicated in uttering a sentence into two propositions. In particular, it exists in connection with the notion of conversational implicature and also with any theory of presupposition that separates these from truth conditions (i.e., does not treat them simply as conditions for having a determinate truth value).

REFERENCES

Altmann, H. *Die Gradpartikeln im Deutschen. Untersuchungen zu ihrer Syntax, Semantik und Pragmatik.* Tübingen, Germany: Niemeyer, 1976.

Anderson, S. R. How to get *even*. *Language,* 1972, *48,* 893–906.

Boër, S. E. and Lycan, W. C. The myth of semantic presupposition. *OSU Working Papers in Linguistics,* Vol. 21. Columbus, Ohio: Ohio State University, 1976.

Coleman, L. The case of the vanishing presupposition. In *BLS 1: Proceedings of the First Annual Meeting of the Berkeley Linguistics Society.* Berkeley, California, 1975.

Cooper, R. Review of R. H. Thomason (Ed.), *Formal Philosophy, Selected Papers of Richard Montague. Language,* 1977, *53,* 895–910.

Epstein, S. A study of *even*. Unpublished paper. Department of Linguistics, University of California, San Diego, 1974.

Fauconnier, G. Polarity and the scale principle. In *CLS 11: Papers from the Eleventh Regional Meeting.* Chicago: Chicago Linguistic Society, 1975. Pp. 188–199.

Fillmore, C. (1972) Verbs of judging: An exercise in semantic description. In C. J. Fillmore and D. T. Langendoen (Eds.), *Studies in linguistic semantics.* New York: Holt, 1972. Pp. 273–289.

Fraser, Bruce (1971) An analysis of *even* in English. In C. J. Fillmore and D. T. Langendoen (Eds.), *Studies in Linguistic Semantics.* New York: Holt, 1972. Pp. 151–180.

Frege, Gottlob (1879) On sense and reference. In P. Geach and M. Black (Eds.), *Translations from the philosophical writings of Gottlob Frege.* Oxford: Basil Blackwell, 1966. Pp. 56–78.

Gazdar, G. (1976) Formal pragmatics for natural language. Implicature, presupposition and logical form. Unpublished doctoral dissertation. University of Reading, Reading, England.

Gazdar, G. Heavy parenthesis wipe-out rules, okay? *Linguistics and Philosophy* 1978, *2,* 281–289.

Grice, H. P. Logic and conversation. In D. Davidson and G. Harman (Eds.), *The logic of grammar.* Encino, California: Dickenson, 1975. Pp. 64–75.

Halvorsen, P.-K. (1977) Syntax and semantics of cleft constructions. Unpublished doctoral dissertation. University of Texas at Austin.

Hausser, R. R. Presupposition in Montague grammar. *Theoretical Linguistics,* 1976, *3*(3), 245–280.

Heringer, J. T. *Even* and negative polarity. Unpublished paper, 1973. [Abstract in the Meeting Handbook for the 1973 Summer LSA Meeting.]

Herzberger, H. G. Dimensions of truth. *Journal of Philosophical Logic,* 1973, *2*(4), 535–556.

Horn, L. A presuppositional analysis of *only* and *even*. In *CLS 5: Papers from the Fifth Regional Meeting.* Chicago: Chicago Linguistic Society, 1969. Pp. 98–107.

Karttunen, F. and Karttunen, L. *Even* questions. In *NELS 7: Proceedings of the Seventh Annual Meeting of the North Eastern Linguistic Society,* 1977. Pp. 115–134.

Karttunen, L. Presuppositions of compound sentences. *Linguistic Inquiry,* 1973, *4,* 169–193.

Karttunen, L. Presupposition and linguistic context. *Theoretical Linguistics,* 1974, *1,* 181–194.

Karttunen, L. and Peters, S. Conventional Implicature in Montague grammar. In *BLS 1: Proceedings of the First Annual Meeting of the Berkeley Linguistics Society.* Berkeley, California, 1975. Pp. 266–278.

Karttunen, L. and Peters, S. What indirect questions conventionally implicate. In *CLS 12: Papers from the Twelfth Regional Meeting.* Chicago: Chicago Linguistic Society, 1976, Pp. 351–368.

Katz, J. and Langendoen, T. Pragmatics and presupposition, *Language,* 1976, *52,* 1–17.

Kempson, R. M. *Presupposition and the delimitation of semantics.* Cambridge, England: Cambridge University Press, 1975.

Kiparsky, P. and Kiparsky, C. Fact. In D. Steinberg and L. Jakobovits (Eds.), *Semantics. An Interdisciplinary Reader.* Cambridge, England: Cambridge University Press, 1971.

Lakoff, G. Linguistics and Natural Logic. *Synthese,* 1970, *22,* 151–271.

Langendoen, D. T. and Savin, H. B. The projection problem for presuppositions. In C. J. Fillmore and D. T. Langendoen (Eds.), *Studies in linguistic semantics.* New York: Holt, 1971, Pp. 55–60.

Lewis, D. *Convention: A philosophical study.* Cambridge, Massachusetts: Harvard University Press, 1969.

Lewis, D. *Counterfactuals.* Cambridge, Massachusetts: Harvard University Press, 1973.

Liberman, M. Alternatives. In *CLS 9: Papers from the Ninth Regional Meeting.* Chicago: Chicago Linguistic Society, 1973. Pp. 346–355.

Liberman, Mark and Ivan Sag. Prosodic Form and Discourse Function. In *CLS 10: Papers from the Tenth Regional Meeting.* Chicago: Chicago Linguistic Society, 1974, Pp. 402–415.

Montague, R. The proper treatment of quantification in ordinary English. In R. H. Thomason (Ed.), *Formal Philosophy. Selected Papers of Richard Montague.* New Haven: Yale University Press, 1974.

Morgan, J. *Presupposition and the representation of meaning. Prolegomena.* Unpublished doctoral dissertation, University of Chicago, 1973.

Partee, B. Montague grammar and transformational grammar. *Linguistic Inquiry,* 1975, *6,* 203–300.

Peters, S. Presuppositions and conversation. In *Texas Linguistic Forum 2.* Department of Linguistics, University of Texas at Austin, 1975, Pp. 122–133.

Peters, S. A truthconditional formulation of Karttunen's account of presupposition. In *Texas Linguistic Forum 6.* Department of Linguistics, University of Texas at Austin, 1977. Pp. 137–149. (a)

Peters, S. In consequence of speaking. In R. Butts and J. Hintikka (Eds.), *Basic problems in methodology and linguistics.* Dordrecht: Reidel, 1977. Pp. 283–297. (b)

Prince, E. On the function of existential presupposition in discourse. In *CLS 14, Papers from the 14th regional meeting.* Chicago: Chicago Linguistic Society, 1978.

Reis, M. *Präsuppositionen und Syntax. Eine Vorstudie.* Habil.-Schrift. University of Münich, Germany, 1974.

Rogers, A. On generalized conversational implicature and preparatory conditions. *Texas Linguistic Forum,* 1978, *10,* 72–75.

Schiebe, T. *Uber Präsuppositionen zusammengesetzer Sätze im Deutschen.* Stockholm, Sweden: Almqvist and Wiksell, 1975.

Searle, J. R. *Speech acts.* Cambridge, England: Cambridge University Press, 1969.

Searle, J. R. A classification of illocutionary acts. In A. Rogers, B. Wall, and J. P. Murphy (Eds.), *Proceedings of the Texas Conference on Performatives, Presuppositions and Implicatures.* Arlington, Va: Center for Applied Linguistics, 1977. Pp. 27–45.

Soames, S. A critical examination of Frege's theory of presupposition and Contemporary Alternatives. Unpublished doctoral dissertation. MIT, Cambridge, Massachusetts.

Stalnaker, R. Pragmatic presuppositions. In M. K. Munitz and P. K. Unger (Eds.), *Semantics and Philosophy*. New York: New York University Press, 1974. Pp. 197–214.
Strawson, P. F. Identifying reference and truth-values. *Theoria*, 1964, *30*, 96–118.
Wilson, D. Presupposition, assertion and lexical items, *Linguistic Inquiry*, 1975, *6*, 95–114.

A SOLUTION TO THE PROJECTION PROBLEM

GERALD GAZDAR
School of Social Sciences
University of Sussex

1. THE PROJECTION PROBLEM

> Assume that, for each noncompound sentence, we can list its presuppositions. What we need in addition is some recursive procedure for doing the same for compound sentences. This is the notorious "projection problem" [Karttunen, 1973b, 1].

Langendoen and Savin (1971) proposed the following solution: "Presuppositions of a subordinate clause . . . stand as presuppositions of the complex sentence in which they occur [p. 57]." Morgan (1969) and subsequent writers have drawn attention to numerous examples, many of which are given in Section 6, which show this solution to be unworkable. Trivalent or supervalent presupposition logics induce distinct partial solutions to the projection problem depending on how negation and the sentential connectives are defined. As Wilson (1975) and others have demonstrated, these solutions also fail to account for the data of natural language.

In his original solution to the problem Karttunen (1973a, b, 1974a) divides items that can combine with a sentence or sentences to form complex sentences into three classes. The first class, "holes," lets through all the presuppositions of their component sentences and includes such complementizable predicates as factive verbs (e.g., *re-*

Syntax and Semantics, Volume 11: Presupposition

ISBN 0-12-613511-8

gret), aspectual verbs (e.g., *begin*) and implicatives (e.g., *manage*). The second class is that of "plugs," which includes verbs of saying (e.g., *ask, promise, warn,* etc.), which according to Karttunen block the presuppositions of their complements EXCEPT when used in the first person simple present tense or when the complement is an indirect question. Most of the theoretical interest of Karttunen's system lies in the treatment of his third class, the "filters," which contains just the expressions *if . . . then . . . , and* and *either . . . or . . . .* These block the presuppositions of one clause whenever certain complex conditions relating to the entailments of the other clause, taken together with the context, are met.

Hausser (1973), Liberman (1973), Reis (1974), Wilson (1975), and Karttunen have drawn attention to a number of examples which show that the original filtration theory did not provide a satisfactory solution to the projection problem. Subsequent modifications (Karttunen, 1974b, and this volume) have taken care of some of these examples [though not others; see, for example, (57), (105), (114), (117), (130), (151), and (152) which follow] but only at the cost of considerably weakening the overall theory: Genuine presuppositions whose source lies in a "plugged" complement, in a disjunct, or in the consequent of a conditional, have to be rescued from near cancellation by informal and ad hoc auxiliary hypotheses about contextual assumptions and conversational implicatures (see Gazdar, in press, for a full discussion). The clue to the historical reason why Karttunen's "plugs, holes and filters" system is inadequate to the data is given in the name of the system itself: It started off as a sophisticated, but essentially ad hoc, attempt to patch up the even more inadequate semantic system. It works as well as it does because the filters partially synthesize the cancellation effects which the quantity implicatures of the compound sentences are actually responsible for (the force of this remark will become apparent in Section 6). In other words, Karttunen's system captures, or is equivalent to, a fragment of the more general apparatus set out in subsequent sections of this chapter. But it functions without reference to quantity implicatures and in doing so forces extra apparatus into one's pragmatics for a language, namely, special constraints to read off presuppositions correctly in addition to the apparatus required in any case for reading off implicatures. The system to be defined, then, is to be preferred, not just on the grounds of simplicity and an increased capacity to predict the data, but also on the grounds of generality and explanatory adequacy. Karttunen's answer to the question "Why do compound sentences not have certain presuppositions?" can only be "Because those presuppositions have been filtered out by my filter conditions." The answer given in this chapter is that the presuppositions do not appear because they would be inconsistent with the already established implicatures of the sentence.

2. POTENTIAL IMPLICATURES

In this section two functions are defined which, taken together, yield for any sentence the set of potential quantity implicatures that that sentence could have. That is, they give us all the implicatures which the sentence could possibly have prior to contextual cancellation. I shall call these potential implicatures IM-PLICATURES and in Section 4 another function will be defined which, given a sentence context pair, will yield as value the appropriate postcancellation subset of these im-plicatures, which subset will be referred to as the "implicatures" of the sentence in that context. The im-plicature functions are defined as relations between SENTENCES and SETS OF SENTENCES.

The only previous attempt I know of to formalize such a function for Grice's (1975) quantity maxim is due to Horn (1972), and I shall em-correct. It is worth noting that the explanatory purpose of Horn's definition is somewhat different from my own; his is largely to explain the distributional facts about the lexical incorporation of negative elements whereas mine is largely to explain the facts of presupposition cancellation. We have here a case where one independently motivated generalization (Grice's maxim of quantity) serves to explain two additional classes of phenomena.

To assist in the following discussion, I provide a couple of abbreviatory definitions.

(I) A sentence φ is SIMPLE WITH RESPECT TO AN OCCURRENCE OF A COMPONENT EXPRESSION α iff φ contains no logical functors having wider scope than α.[1]

The set of logical functors includes (but is, perhaps, not exhausted by) negation, quantifiers, connectives, and modal operators.

(II) Sentences φ_α and φ_β are EXPRESSION ALTERNATIVES WITH RESPECT TO α and β iff φ_α is identical

[1] A SENTENCE is to be understood here as any member of the set of well-formed strings defined by the formation rules of the language employed for semantic representation. An EXPRESSION is any substring of a well-formed string. One cannot really be more precise than this without specifying the grammar of semantic representation, a task which is outside our present brief.

to φ_β except that in ONE place where φ_α has α, φ_β has β.

Horn does not define his notion "quantitative scale" although it is easy to gather ostensively the kind of thing he has in mind. Definition is not easy because of the requirement that the items in a scale be qualitatively similar in addition to being quantitatively ordered. One way of capturing qualitative similarity is by reference to the notion of SORTAL CORRECTNESS for which a formal semantic treatment is available in Thomason (1972). It would take us too far afield to explore this topic here so I shall restrict myself to pointing out that to say of two expressions α and β that they have the same DOMAIN OF SORTAL APPLICABILITY is much the same as saying that they impose or are subject to exactly the same set of "selectional restrictions." The notion DOMAIN OF SORTAL APPLICABILITY can be defined straightforwardly in Thomason's system.

(III)[2] An n-tuple Q of expressions is a quantitative SCALE iff
i. $Q = \langle \alpha_0, \alpha_1, \ldots \alpha_{n-1} \rangle$ where $n > 1$ and each member of Q has the same domain of sortal applicability as every other member.
ii.[3] $[\varphi_{\alpha_i}] \subset [\varphi_{\alpha_{i+1}}]$ where φ_{α_i} and $\varphi_{\alpha_{i+1}}$ are any pair of simple expression alternatives with respect to $\alpha_i, \alpha_{i+1} \in Q$.

For detailed discussion of, and criteria for setting up, one such scale see Caton (1966).

We may define a function of f_s which, given a sentence ψ as argument, will return a set of scalar quantity im-plicatures as its value:

(IV)[4] $f_s(\psi) = \{\chi\colon \chi = K\neg\varphi_{\alpha_i}\}$ for all φ_{α_i} such that for some Q, $\alpha_i, \alpha_{i+1} \in Q$.

[2] This definition is inadequate to the extent that it allows couples like ⟨*John, someone*⟩ to count as quantitative scales, but it will suffice for the purpose at hand (i.e., solving the projection problem). See Gazdar (in press) for further discussion of the inadequacy.

[3] The symbol [ ] is a function from sentences into propositions, $[\varphi]$ is the proposition (i.e. set of possible worlds) denoted by the sentence φ. We can say that φ ENTAILS ψ if and only if $[\varphi] \subseteq [\psi]$. See Section 4.

[4] Unsubscripted K is used as an abbreviation for the string *speaker knows that.* Unsubscripted P is used as an abbreviation for the string *for all the speaker knows* and for *it is compatible with all the speaker knows that.* It is assumed that K and P have exactly the properties ascribed to them in Hintikka (1962), thus for example, $K\varphi \longleftrightarrow \neg P\neg\varphi$ is assumed to hold for all values of φ. Formal proofs involving K and P will be done in the same way that Hintikka does them and reference to Hintikka (1962) will be necessary if the proofs are to be checked. Hintikka's logic may be regarded, to all intents and purposes, as a notational variant of Lewis's S4.

i. $\psi = \overbrace{X\ \varphi_{\alpha_{i+1}}\ Y}$, where X and Y are any expressions, possibly null.
ii. $[\psi] \subseteq [\varphi_{\alpha_{i+1}}]$.

This definition generates im-plicatures such as those shown in the following examples where the (b) sentence is the im-plicature of the corresponding (a) sentence and the boldface words are the scalar expressions involved.

(1) a. ***Some of the*** *boys were at the party.*
b. $K\neg$(***All of the*** *boys were at the party.*)

(2) a. ***Possibly*** *prices will rise.*
b. $K\neg$(***Necessarily*** *prices will rise.*)

(3) a. *Osmosis* ***may*** *involve porosity.*
b. $K\neg$(*Osmosis* ***must*** *involve porosity.*)

(4) a. *Mary* ***tried*** *to cash a check.*
b. $K\neg$(*Mary* ***succeeded*** *in cashing a check.*)

(5) a. *He* ***believes*** *he is ill.*
b. $K\neg$(*He* ***knows*** *he is ill.*)

Surprisingly, perhaps, (IV) not only gives us im-plicatures from expressions like those in boldface in (1)–(5) but also from logical connectives since the couple $\langle\wedge, \vee\rangle$ is a quantitative scale under (III). Thus $\varphi \vee \psi$ potentially implicates $K\neg(\varphi \wedge \psi)$, which explains why disjunctions are commonly heard as exclusive given the deduction shown in (6).

(6) 1. $\varphi \vee \psi$.
2. $\neg(\varphi \wedge \psi)$, entailed by im-plicature of 1.
3. $\varphi\ \overline{\vee}\ \psi$, materially equivalent to conjunction of 1 and 2.

Scalar im-plicatures are not, however, the only quantity im-plicatures that arise in compound sentences. Let us define a function f_c which, given a compound sentence φ as argument, will return a set of CLAUSAL QUANTITY IM-PLICATURES as its value:

(V) $f_c(\varphi) = \{\chi : \chi \in \{P\psi, P\neg\psi\}\}$ for all sentences ψ such that
i. $\varphi = \overbrace{X\ \psi\ Y}$, where X and Y are any expressions, possibly null.
ii. $[\varphi] \not\subseteq [\psi]$.
iii. $[\varphi] \not\subseteq [\neg\psi]$.
iv. φ has some expression alternative φ_α with re-

spect to ψ and α, where α is an arbitrary sentence such that

a. $\alpha \neq \psi$.
b.[5] $K\alpha \notin f_p(\varphi_\alpha)$.
c. $K\neg\alpha \notin f_p(\varphi_\alpha)$.

Any such set $f_c(\varphi)$ is consistent if every constituent sentence ψ in φ is itself consistent. This definition gives us, for example, the following im-plicatures:

(7) a. *If John sees me he will call the police.*
b′. $P\neg$(***John will see me.***)
b″. $P\neg$(***John will call the police.***)

(8) a. *My sister is in the bathroom or she is in the kitchen.*
b′. $P\neg$(***My sister is in the bathroom.***)
b″. $P\neg$(***My sister is in the kitchen.***)

More formally it follows that the set of this class of im-plicatures for otherwise simple disjunctions and conditionals (of whatever type) whose constituents meet the conditions of (V) is as given in (9):

(9) $f_c(\varphi \textbf{ or } \psi) = f_c(\textbf{if } \varphi \textbf{ then } \psi) = \{P\varphi, P\psi, P\neg\varphi, P\neg\psi\}$.

Condition iv of (V) deserves some explanation: This ensures that the im-plicatures are not read off from clauses which are already pre-supposed (under the definition of f_p given in Section 3. If this condition were not present then every pre-supposition which was not also an entailment would automatically get canceled by the system defined in Section 4. When a sentence has the same clause in TWO places, one in a pre-suppositional environment and the other not in such an environment, then, assuming the other three conditions apply, this condition generates the relevant im-plicatures despite the presence of the pre-suppositional context. Thus (10) im-plicates (7b′) but (11) does not im-plicate (7b′):

(10) *If John sees me he will regret seeing me.*

(11) *If John tells Margaret he will regret seeing me.*

The Gricean argument for the im-plicatures generated by this definition goes as follows: If one utters a compound or complex sentence having a constituent which is not itself entailed or pre-supposed by the matrix sentence and whose negation is likewise neither entailed nor pre-supposed, then one would be in breach of the maxim of quan-

[5] For the definition of f_p see (VI) in Section 3.

tity if one knew that sentence to be true or false, but was not known to so know, since one could have been more informative by producing a complex sentence having the constituent concerned, or its negation, as an entailment or a presupposition. It follows that, ceteris paribus, the utterance of such a complex sentence implicates that both the constituent sentence and its negation are compatible with what the speaker knows.

This Gricean argument relies on the fact that natural languages provide their users with pairs of sentences of ROUGHLY EQUIVALENT BREVITY which differ only in that in one, one or more constituent clauses are not entailed. This means that strict adherence to the maxim of quantity does not involve violation of the maxim of manner (BE BRIEF). If one is in a position to, then one can always utter the stronger and more informative sentence without increasing the length of one's utterance. Here are some examples:

(12) ***Since** John was there we can assume that Mary was too.*

(13) ***If** John was there we can assume that Mary was too.*

(14) *We **know** that John was there.*

(15) *We **think** that John was there.*

(16) *John was there **and** Mary was absent.*

(17) *John was there **or** Mary was absent.*

f_c and f_s typically give us several im-plicatures, even from quite simple sentences. Thus (18) im-plicates (19) in virtue of (IV) and im-plicates (20) and (21) in virtue of (V):

(18) *John believes Margaret to be unfaithful.*

(19) $K\neg$(***John knows Margaret to be unfaithful.***)

(20) P(***Margaret is unfaithful.***)

(21) $P\neg$(***Margaret is unfaithful.***)

The class of verbs that give rise to im-plicatures like (20) and (21) approximates to those called "plugs" in Karttunen (1973a) and it includes many verbs of propositional attitude (*believe, think, hope, dream,* etc.) and verbs of saying (*ask, say, tell,* etc.) which have in common that they neither entail nor pre-suppose their complements. This "coincidence" will be shown to have some explanatory consequences for Karttunen's own examples in Section 6. This type of implicature was first noted by Sacks (1968), who gives the following example (which I have abbreviated) from a newspaper report:

(22) David Searles returned to the street with his girl and found the car was missing. At first he thought it had been stolen. Then he realized it had been towed away by the police [New York Times 2 Nov. 1967].

Sacks comments that "'he realized' stands in opposition to 'he thought', by reference to the fact that 'thought' would be used were it the case that it turned out he was wrong [p. 1]."

3. POTENTIAL PRESUPPOSITIONS

I wish now to introduce a piece of technical terminology, peculiar to the present enterprise, namely PRE-SUPPOSITION. A pre-supposition is a POTENTIAL presupposition. Sets of them are assigned to sentences in a completely mechanical way. They are what the presuppositions would be if there was no projection problem, no "ambiguity" in negative sentences and no context sensitivity. A compound sentence has all the pre-suppositions of its components but may not, of course, presuppose all its pre-suppositions. Even if a given sentence can NEVER on any occasion of use actually presuppose one of its pre-suppositions, this fact in no sense makes the assignment of that pre-supposition to the sentence incorrect: Pre-suppositions are notional entities whose only role is a technical one in the process of assigning actual presuppositions to utterances.

f_p is to be defined as a function taking a SENTENCE as argument and yielding a SET OF SENTENCES as value, this set being the set of pre-suppositions. The function is assumed to apply to the sentences of the semantic representation, as in the case of the im-plicature functions. In defining f_p I take the notions "noun phrase" and "sentence" for granted and assume that they are well defined on whatever formal language is employed for the semantic representation.

Let F be a set of cardinality n where n is some small finite number and where F is to be regarded as the set of all the subfunctions required to tap the various sources of sentential pre-suppositions. Among the members of F will be f_1, f_2, f_3 defined as follows:[6]

[6] I am not seriously proposing that sentences of semantic representation contain items like *that, there,* and *is*. They appear in the definitions partly to increase perspicuity and partly because it is not obvious to me what should stand in their place.

(23) $f_1(\varphi) = \{\psi : \psi = K\chi \cdot \varphi = X \frown v \frown \textit{that} \frown \chi \frown Y\}$[7]
where v is a factive or semifactive verb, φ and χ are sentences, and X and Y are any strings, possibly null.

(24) $f_2(\varphi) = \{\psi : \psi = K\chi \cdot \varphi = X \frown \textit{the} \frown \alpha \frown Y \cdot \chi = \textit{there is } \textit{a} \frown \alpha\}$,
where $\textit{the} \frown \alpha$ is the longest string, having that occurrence of ***the*** as its initial element, which is of the category noun phrase, φ and χ are sentences, and X and Y are any strings, possibly null.

(25) $f_3(\varphi) = \{\psi : \psi = K\chi \cdot \varphi = X \frown \textit{before} \frown \chi \frown Y\}$,
where φ and χ are sentences and X and Y are any strings, possibly null.

Obviously one can go on and define f_4, f_5, f_6, and so on, for all the other sources of pre-suppositions but I do not propose to pursue this task here. Given a definition for every $f \in F$ we may now define f_p as follows:

(VI) $$f_p(\varphi) = \bigcup_{f \in F} f(\varphi) \qquad \text{for any sentence } \varphi.$$

This definition requires no additional projection clause for the pre-suppositions of compound or embedded sentences because the individual functions in F operate without respect to the complexity of the sentences they apply to.

The formulation of the members of F involves certain assumptions about the nature of the semantic representation and it may be that some versions of the latter would permit a more economical f_p in which certain potentially distinct members of F collapse. One hypothetical example would be that of aspectual verbs like *stop* which, on a lexical decomposition analysis, might well turn out to have *before* as the operative constituent component in semantic representation. Other good candidates for a single collapsed rule are clefts, pseudo-clefts, and *wh*-questions, all of which share a pre-supposition which is arrived at, more or less, by extracting the *wh*-clause and substituting the appropriate existentially quantified phrase for the *wh*-phrase within it.

[7] This is insufficient since most factives also pre-suppose that the subject of the matrix sentence knows the complement to be true.

4. PROJECTION

This section presents the formal system which, given an utterance, tells us what that utterance implicates and presupposes.

A presupposition and implicature assignment device Π is a 6-tuple:

(VII) $$\Pi = \langle f_c, f_s, f_p, D, W, [\![\ ]\!] \rangle.$$

where f_c, f_s, and f_p are the im-plicature and pre-supposition functions defined in Sections 2 and 3, respectively, D is the set of all sentences of the semantic representation of English, and W is the set of all possible worlds on which we define the set J of propositions, as follows:

(VIII) $$J = \mathcal{P}W.$$

In (VII) $[\![\ ]\!]$ is a function from D into J and is to be understood as the semantic interpretation function for the language D, which assigns to each sentence a proposition, namely, the set of possible worlds in which that sentence is true. Such functions are available for the semantic representations of various fragments of English (see, e.g., those in Montague, 1974 and Partee, 1976).

We define a consistency predicate, con, on sets of propositions as follows:

(IX) $$\text{con } X \text{ iff } \cap X \neq \Lambda.$$

and we will adopt the convention of writing inc$X$ for $\neg$con$X$. Next we define a set M of contexts:

(X) $$M = \{X : X \subseteq J \cdot \text{con } X\}.$$

Contexts, thus, are sets of propositions constrained only by consistency.

We are now in a position to define a set E of possible utterances as follows:

(XI) $$E = N \times D \times M,$$

where N is the set of nonnegative integers, where for all $e \in E$, $e = \langle n, d, m\rangle$ whose members will be referred to as e_0, e_1, and e_2, respectively, and which may also, on occasion, be superscripted with the number of the utterance, that is, $e_0^n = n$.[8] This notational procedure is due to Hamblin (1971). Each utterance, then, is a triple consisting of the sen-

[8] This superscript convention will be used both for the utterance number given by e_0 and also, as a notational convenience, for the example number used in the text to index the sentence. In the latter case, of course, (XVIII) will not apply.

tence uttered (e_1), the sequential position (e_0) at which it occurred, and some set of propositions representing the context (e_2).

We adopt the following abbreviatory definitions to give us, for each utterance in E, the sets of propositions corresponding to the sets of clausal and scalar im-plicatures and pre-suppositions deriving from the sentence uttered:

(XII) $e_c = \{x : x = [\varphi] \cdot \varphi \in f_c(e_1)\}$ for all $e \in E$.

(XIII) $e_s = \{x : x = [\varphi] \cdot \varphi \in f_s(e_1)\}$ for all $e \in E$.

(XIV) $e_p = \{x : x = [\varphi] \cdot \varphi \in f_p(e_1)\}$ for all $e \in E$.

When a speaker asserts a sentence φ he is, in effect, committed to KNOWING THAT φ under Grice's maxim of quality (see Gazdar, in press, for defense of this assumption). We can capture this fact by defining a new context of utterance (e_u) which consists of the union of the old context (e_2) and the speaker's knowledge of the sentence uttered (Ke_1):

(XV) $e_u = e_2 \cup \{[Ke_1]\}$ for all $e \in E$.

We move now to the single most important definition in the present theory: It can be usefully glossed as a formal rendition of the slogan "all the news that fits."

(XVI) The satisfiable incrementation of a set of propositions X by a set of propositions Y ($X \cup! Y$) is defined as follows (for all X, $Y \subseteq J$): $X \cup! Y = X \cup \{y : y \in Y. (Z \subseteq X \cup Y)[\text{con}(\{y\} \cup Z) \longleftrightarrow \text{con } Z]\}$.

If the definitions which follow are to be properly understood then the reader will need a good intuitive grasp of what (XVI) does. $X \cup! Y$ is the union of X with a set which consists of all those members of Y which can be added to X without ANY RISK of an inconsistency arising. Any member of Y which is a necessary component of some inconsistent subset of $X \cup Y$ is excluded from $X \cup! Y$. Here are some examples of the way $\cup!$ operates:

(26) $\{[\varphi], [\psi]\} \cup! \{[\chi]\} = \{[\varphi], [\psi], [\chi]\}$.

(27) $\{[\varphi], [\psi]\} \cup! \{[\neg\varphi], [\chi]\} = \{[\varphi], [\psi], [\chi]\}$.

(28) $\{[\varphi], [\psi]\} \cup! \{[\varphi \longrightarrow \neg\psi], [\chi]\} = \{[\varphi], [\psi], [\chi]\}$.

(29) $\{[\varphi], [\psi]\} \cup! \{[\varphi \longrightarrow \neg\chi], [\chi]\} = \{[\varphi], [\psi]\}$.

(30) $\{[\varphi], [\psi]\} \cup! \{[\varphi \longrightarrow \pi], [\chi], [\neg\pi]\} = \{[\varphi], [\psi], [\chi]\}$.

The notion of SATISFIABLE INCREMENTATION allows us to capture formally the context sensitivity of both implicature and presupposition. ONLY those im-plicatures and pre-suppositions which are satisfiable in the context of utterance actually emerge as the implicatures and presuppositions of the utterance. The "process" is complicated by the fact that the incrementation is ORDERED: That is, clausal im-plicatures are added to the context first, then scalar im-plicatures, and, finally, pre-suppositions. This ordering plays a part in the explanation of the data discussed below, but it is not itself explained. We define the new context e_U which results from utterance of a sentence e_1, as follows:

(XVII) $e_U = ((e_u \cup! e_c) \cup! e_s) \cup! e_p$ for all $e \in E$.

The initial context is, for all intents and purposes, taken as primitive in the apparatus given earlier but we can provide a recursive clause for giving us the context for each successive utterance after the first:

(XVIII) $e_2^{n+1} = e_U^n$

Formal pragmatic definitions for quantity implicature and presupposition follow straightforwardly from (XVII):

(XIX) A proposition x is a QUANTITY IMPLICATURE of an utterance e iff $x \in e_U \cap (e_c \cup e_s)$.

(XX)[9] A proposition x is a PRESUPPOSITION of an utterance e iff $x \in e_U \cap e_p$.

5. IMPLICATURES

(31) *Some of the boys were there.*
(32) *Not all of the boys were there.*
(33) *Some of the boys, in fact all of them, were there.*

Sentences (31) and (33) both im-plicate *K*32, but utterance of (33), unlike (31), can never implicate [*K*32].[10] That (31) and (33) im-plicate *K*32 follows straightforwardly from the definition of f_s given in (IV). The formal explanation for the behavior of utterances of (33) is marginally more complex, so I present in (34) an abbreviated proof:

(34) *i.* [*K*32] $\in e_S^{33}$ by (IV) and (XIII).
ii. inc{[32], [33]} by inspection.
iii. inc{[*K*32], [*K*33]} from ii.

[9] I shall refer, indifferently, to a pre-supposition φ as having been CANCELED, SUSPENDED, or FILTERED OUT when $\varphi \in e_p$ but $[\varphi] \notin e_U$ for some e—analogously with im-plicatures.

iv. $[K33] \in e_{\mathrm{u}}^{33}$ by (XV).
v. $[K32] \notin e_{\mathrm{U}}^{33}$ by (XVI) and (XVII) from iii.

Since the proof just given is quite independent of the value of e_2^{33} it follows that e_1^{33} can never implicate [*K*32].

A similar proof can be given for Grice's own example of intrasentential im-plicature cancellation, shown as (35):

(35) *I saw Mrs. Smith trying to cash a check at the bank at noon today, and I have not the slightest doubt that she succeeded.*

The fact that clausal im-plicatures get added to the context before scalar im-plicatures has an interesting consequence for a certain class of sentences. Consider (36)–(38):

(36) *John did it or Mary did it.*

(37) *John did it or Mary did it or both of them did it.*

(38) *John did it and Mary did it.*

Although (36) and (37) are truthfunctionally equivalent, it is only (36) which can have the pragmatic exclusive disjunction interpretation induced by the scalar im-plicature $K\neg(38)$ in the manner discussed in Section 2 [see (6)]. Example (37) never has this interpretation because the scalar im-plicature $K\neg(38)$ is inconsistent with the clausal im-plicature $P(38)$ arising from the final clause under definition (V). Definition (XVII) has the effect of excluding the scalar im-plicature in favor

---

[10] Note the following conventions respecting example numbers:

(20) *Caesar lives.*

(21) *Brutus dies.*

In addition to the standard use of (20) to refer to the sentence *Caesar lives*, we employ a number of abbreviatory conventions:

$\neg20$ or $\neg(20)$ for *Caesar does not live.*
*K*20 for *Speaker knows that Caesar lives.*
*P*20 for *For all the speaker knows, Caesar lives.*
[20] for [*Caesar lives*].

These conventions are generative and compound expressions like $[K\neg P20]$ occur frequently in Section 6. Although [20] always denotes the proposition that Caesar lives, expressions like (20) and *K*20 are sometimes used with systematic utterance–sentence–proposition ambiguity: Thus, **(20) neither pre-supposes nor presupposes *K*21** abbreviates **It is not the case either that the sentence (20) pre-supposes the sentence *K*21 or that utterance of (20) ever presupposes the proposition [*K*21].**

of the clausal one. The same intrasentential cancellation is involved in (40):

(39) *Some of the students were there.*

(40) *Some, if not all, of the students were there.*

(41) *All of the students were there.*

Sentences (39) and (40) have the same truth conditions but (40), unlike (39), will not carry the scalar implicature [$K\neg$(41)] because this is inconsistent with the clausal implicature [$P\neg\neg$(41)], induced by the antecedent of the conditional under (V). Predictably (42) and (43) behave in a similar fashion:

(42) *John or Mary did it, if not both.*

(43) *Some, or all, of the students were there.*

The preceding paragraph shows, in a rather striking manner, that the CONVERSATIONAL CONTRIBUTION of two materially equivalent sentences, uttered in the same context, may be quite different. Of course we all know this intuitively but the system just defined explains, for a restricted range of data, how this comes to be the case. Note that I am assuming, both here and elsewhere in this chapter, that sentences like (43) decompose into something like (44) in semantic representation:

(44) *Some of the students were there or all of the students were there.*

This assumption is not critical but it makes the formulation of the definitions a great deal less complicated than if some contrary assumption were made.

So far we have only considered cases where an im-plicature is prevented from becoming an implicature because it is inconsistent with either an entailment of the sentence or an implicature of the utterance. There are also cases where im-plicatures are prevented from being implicatures by the previously established context. This is most readily shown using preceding discourse as the context, as in the following examples:

(45)		
	a. *All of the cats talk.*	assumption
	b. *If some of the cats talk then dogs are unhappy.*	assumption
	c. *Some of the cats talk.*	from (45a)
	d. ∴ *Dogs are unhappy.*	modus ponens from (45b), (45c)

Sentence (45c) im-plicates that the speaker knows that not all of the cats talk (by IV) but this im-plicature is canceled by its inconsistency with the context which, at (45c), includes [K(45a)], this having been registered in the context initially by reference to (XV) and then retained in it by the recursive clause (XVIII). The following example is analogous:

(46)		
	a. *Cats talk but dogs don't.*	assumption
	b. *If either cats or dogs talk then I'll eat my hat.*	assumption
	c. *Cats talk.*	from (46a)
	d. *Cats or dogs talk.*	from (46c)
	e. ∴ *I'll eat my hat.*	modus ponens from (46b), (46d)

Here (46d) im-plicates (inter alia) that it is compatible with all the speaker knows that dogs talk, but this im-plicature is canceled by the preceding context established initially by (46a). These examples may seem artificial but the principles involved are completely general. Consider (47):

(47) *Mrs. Smith has three children.*

Now (47) im-plicates that the speaker knows that Mrs. Smith does not have more than three children (any number greater than three will precede three on the quantitative scale in which three appears) but there are plausible situations in which this im-plicature will get contextually canceled. Imagine that we are discussing the elegibility of each of a group of women for welfare benefits and that we know of each how many children she has (Mrs. Smith, for example, has five): If one of the welfare benefit eligibility criteria is having three children then one could utter (47) in such a discussion without having been heard as implicating that Mrs. Smith did not have more than three children. Lakoff (1975) discusses a similar example to (47) in terms of his notion of "context-dependent entailment" but his treatment does little more than relabel the phenomenon, whereas ours offers a well defined account of the im-plicature cancellation process.

6. PRESUPPOSITION

In what follows I shall apply the apparatus developed above to a very large number of examples, a lot of them culled from the "presupposition" literature and many of them ones which constitute problems for, or counterexamples to, existing treatments of presupposition. It should be noted that, except where the discussion makes it obvious that the assumption has been suspended, I shall assume that the context is neutral with respect to cancellation. Thus when it is claimed that some pre-supposition is also a presupposition, this claim should be understood as being qualified by an implicit claim to the effect that this is so just in case there is nothing in the context to prevent it. The same ceteris paribus clause is in operation when I treat some im-plicature as being an implicature in order to show its role in pre-supposition suspension.

It seems appropriate to begin with an example of the operation of the pre-supposition function f_p:

(48) *The Prince of Wales didn't regret (washing his hands before the King of Buganda washed his)* [the parentheses are simply to remove the structural ambiguity otherwise allowed by the sentence].

(49) $f_p(e_1)$ = {**K(*There is a Prince of Wales*), K(*There is a King of Buganda*), K(*The King of Buganda washed his hands*), K(*The Prince of Wales washed his hands before the King of Buganda washed his*)**}, when e_1 = (48).

The relation of (48) to (49) is deliberately based on the three subfunctions of f_p given in Section 3: There are probably additional pre-suppositions that should be taken into consideration, for example, that the dramatis personae actually have hands, and that the Prince of Wales knew that he had washed his hands before the King of Buganda. Pre-suppositions are all-pervasive, if the reader needs convincing then it is suggested that he pick a sentence at random from the present text and make a list.

Consider Example (50). I shall discuss the pre-supposition cancellation involved in this example in considerable detail so that it can stand as an illustration of the way this treatment of presupposition works. It will also assist the reader in becoming familiar with the mechanics of the approach and enable him to test whether putative counterexamples to the theory really are counterexamples. Subsequent examples will be dealt with more cursorily, that is less formally, but in every case a similar detailed formal argument can be constructed to prove the point at issue.

(50) *John doesn't regret killing his mother because he didn't kill her.*

(51) *John killed his mother.*

We have that:

(52)	a. [50] $\subseteq$ [$\neg$51].	*because* clauses are entailed
	b. [K51] $\in e_{\mathrm{p}}^{50}$.	by (VI) and (XIV)
	c. [K50] $\in e_{\mathrm{u}}^{50}$.	by (XV)
	d. inc{[50], [51]}.	from a.
	e. inc{[K50], [K51]}.	from d.
	f. [K51] $\notin e_{\mathrm{U}}^{50}$.	from e. by (XVII)
	g. [K51] $\notin e_{\mathrm{U}}^{50} \cap e_{\mathrm{p}}^{50}$.	from f.
	h. ∴Utterance of (50) does not presuppose [K51].	from g. by (XX)

A very similar proof can be given for why (53) does not presuppose [K54],[11] only here we need to know that *passing the exam* entails *not failing the exam:*

(53) *John doesn't regret failing the exam because, in fact, he passed.*

(54) *John failed the exam.*

The affirmative sentences corresponding to (50) and (53) entail their factive complements which are thus not cancelable by (XVII). This predictably leads to the anomaly found in (55):

(55) **John regrets failing the exam because, in fact, he passed.*

Consider examples (56) and (57):

(56) **For all I know Oedipus regrets killing his father although, in fact, he didn't kill him.*

(57) *For all I know Oedipus regrets killing his father although, in fact, I don't know that he killed him.*

(58) *Oedipus killed his father.*

For (56) we may reason as follows:

(59)	a. [K56] $\subseteq$ [56] $\subseteq$ [P58].	first conjunct entailment
	b. [K56] $\subseteq$ [$K\neg$58] $\subseteq$ [$\neg P$58].	second conjunct entailment
	c. inc{[$\neg P$58], [P58]}.	

[11] Any locutions of the form **sentence φ does not presuppose x** are to be understood as elliptical for **no utterance of φ can presuppose x.** See Footnote 10 for exposition of the systematic sentence–proposition ambiguity to be found in certain other locutions.

d. $[K56] = \Lambda$. from a., b., and c.
e. $[K56] \in e_u^{56}$. by (XV)
f. inc e_u^{56}. from e. and d.

The inconsistency inherent in e_u^{56} produces the anomaly. The second clause in (57) is of the form $\neg K58$ and this, unlike the form $\neg 58$ found in (56), does not lead to an inconsistency with the first clause. Thus (57) is not heard as anomalous.

(60) *The Queen asked the Prime Minister to be more polite to the Duke of Edinburgh.*

(61) *There is a Duke of Edinburgh.*

(62) *Lord Avon said that Churchill regretted resigning.*

(63) *Churchill resigned.*

These pairs of examples are predicted to be related presuppositionally by the system defined since there are no grounds for cancellation. This prediction is contrary to that given by Karttunen's system and so I leave it to the intuitions of the reader to decide which is right. On the other hand, while (64) pre-supposes (65), it does not PRESUPPOSE it in most contexts since in most contexts it is known that there is no King of France:[12]

(64) *Strawson said that Russell was wrong about the King of France.*

(65) *There is a King of France.*

The proof is as follows:

(66) a. $[K65] \in e_p^{64}$. by(VI) and (XIV)

[12] It will be apparent that the present theory offers a straightforward solution to the problem posed by sentences like (i) (discussed by, e.g., Biggs, 1976, p. 203):

(i) *The King of France does not exist.*

On a Strawsonian view of presupposition this sentence should appear paradoxical: It asserts the denial of its own presupposition. But (i) is not paradoxical or anomalous and the present account gives us no reason to think that it should be: (i) does indeed pre-suppose that there is a King of France but it can never presuppose that there is a King of France. The pre-supposition is invariably canceled in the light of its inconsistency with the sentence itself. We thus have no reason to suppose that the logical form of (i) is any different from the logical form of (ii):

(ii) *The King of France does not sing.*

See Kneale and Moore (1936).

b. $[K\neg 65] \in e_2^{64}$.	usual contextual assumption
c. $[K\neg 65] \in e_u^{64}$.	by(XV) from b.
d. inc{[*K*65], [*K*¬65]}.	
e. $[K65] \notin e_U^{64}$.	from d. by (XVII)
f. $[K65] \notin e_U^{64} \cap e_p^{64}$.	from e.
g. ∴Utterance of (64) does not presuppose [*K*65].	from f. by (XX)

The following examples constitute counterexamples to any account of presupposition that does not allow cancellation:[13]

(67) *He doesn't know that she's a secretary.*

(68) *I don't know that she's a secretary.*

(69) *Speaker knows that she's a secretary.*

Given that *know* is a factive verb both (67) and (68) must pre-suppose (69). On the system defined above, (67) also presupposes [69] since con{[*K*67], [69]}, but (68) cannot presuppose it because inc{[*K*68], [69]} and cancellation is thus forced by (XVII). Semantic accounts of presupposition would presumably claim that both (67) and (68) were potentially ambiguous because of the two types of negation, but that only the nonpresuppositional reading was found in (68). Those pragmatic accounts which do not have two kinds of negation to play with and which do not allow cancellation could only claim that there were two senses of *know* involved, one of them exclusive to first person negative sentences.

Unfortunately for any proponents of the later position, exactly the same phenomenon appears in Examples (70)–(72):

(70) *She is not aware that she is allowed to use that area.*

(72) *I am not aware that she is allowed to use that area.*

(72) *Speaker knows that she is allowed to use that area.*

This is readily explained on the present account if we allow that *A knows that* φ entails that *A is aware that* φ. Modus tollens gives us (73) from (71) and cancellation of [72] follows automatically.

(73) *I do not know that she is allowed to use that area.*

A rather more complex example is (74):[14]

[13] See Kiparsky and Kiparsky (1970: 249, Footnote a).

[14] I am indebted to Colin Biggs for this example.

(74) *Nobody has yet discovered that protons are (in any way) influenced by the CIA.*

(75) *Protons are influenced by the CIA.*

(76) *Nobody knows that protons are influenced by the CIA.*

If we allow that *Nobody has discovered that* φ entails *Nobody knows that* φ, as all but the most ardent proponents of innate ideas or revelatory knowledge must, then (74) entails (76) but (76) entails that the SPEAKER does not know that (75), by universal instantiation, so we have:

(77) a. $[K74] \subseteq [74] \subseteq [76] \subseteq [\neg K75]$.
b. $[K75] \in e_{\mathrm{P}}^{74}$. by (VI) and (XIV)
c. $\mathrm{inc}\{[\neg K75], [K75]\}$.
d. $[K75] \notin e_{\mathrm{U}}^{74}$. and is thus not presupposed

Intuitions may vary with this example, partly because of the epistemologic assumption necessary for the suspension, but largely because the quantifier *nobody* is usually used indexically to range over only some limited domain, for example, a domain that excludes speaker and addressee, or a domain restricted to students as in (78):

(78) *Nobody has yet discovered that all the questions in paper II are about Quine.*

In the event that either of the doubtful entailments assumed in (77a) fail then no suspension takes place and (74) will presuppose [*K*75]. For another example involving the verb *discover*, see (152).

We have seen above that appended clauses entailing the negation of a pre-supposition of a preceding part of the sentence have the effect of suspending it. This is also true of cases of lexical presupposition as in the following examples (given in Stalnaker, 1974):[15]

(79) *My cousins aren't boys anymore, they've had sex-change operations.*

(80) *My cousins aren't boys anymore, they've grown into fine young men.*

In (79) the first clause entails that the cousins used to be boys and hence that they used to be male. The second clause, taken together

[15] The examples originate in Langendoen (1971, p. 343).

with the entailment that they used to be male, itself entails that they are now female. This entailment is inconsistent with the pre-supposition (due to *boy*) that they are male and the latter is consequently suspended. In (80), of course, no such inconsistency arises. Examples (81) and (82) behave in a similar fashion:

(81) *Hilary isn't a widow,* ***he's*** *a widower.*

(82) *Hilary isn't a widow, she's* ***divorced.***

The cases of pre-supposition suspension that have attracted most attention in the literature are those involving logical connectives where it appears to be partly dependent on the connective involved whether or not cancellation takes place. The behavior of such examples is quite straightforwardly predicted by the apparatus developed above in which the implicatures of the sentence suspend the pre-suppositions of the sentence just in case the latter are inconsistent with the former. Consider the examples (83) and (84), which are similar to those discussed in Karttunen (1973a):

(83) *If he was crying then he regrets killing his father.*

(84) *If he killed his father then he regrets it (=killing his father).*

(85) *He killed his father.*

(86) *He was crying.*

Under (VI), *K*85 is a pre-supposition of both (83) and (84) but it is only a presupposition in the case of (83). The relevant difference between them lies in the implicatures deriving from the antecedent. Under (V), (83) will implicate [*P*¬86] whereas (84) will implicate [*P*¬85]. The former implicature is consistent with the pre-supposition (i.e., con{[*P*¬86], [*K*85]}) but the latter is not (i.e., inc{[*P*¬85][*K*85]}) and so the presupposition is canceled by (XVII) in (84) but not in (83). The same proof applies to the suspension of the existence pre-supposition with definite descriptions:

(87) *If he pulled the Fort Knox job then the Godfather must be a very rich man.*

(88) *If there is such a man then the Godfather must be a very rich man.*

(89) *There is a Godfather.*

A similar argument can be made in the case of disjunctions like (90) and (91):

(90) *Either he wasn't crying or he regrets killing his father.*

(91) *Either he didn't kill his father or he regrets killing him.*

Karttunen is forced to give a separate rule for disjunctions but in the present approach (V) enables a uniform treatment of disjunctions and conditionals [cf. (9) in Section 2].

Our analysis correctly predicts the presuppositional behavior of example (92) which Lakoff (1975) discusses informally in terms of Karttunen's "filters" and his own notion of implicatures as context-dependent entailment.

(92) *If Sam asks Professor Snurd to write him a recommendation to graduate school, and Professor Snurd writes the recommendation, saying only that Sam has nice handwriting, then Sam will regret that Professor Snurd wrote him a bad recommendation.*

(93) *Professor Snurd will write Sam a bad recommendation.*

(94) *Professor Snurd will write Sam a recommendation.*

Under (V), (92) will implicate [$P\neg 94$] but this is inconsistent with the pre-supposition that $K93$, so the latter will be canceled by (XVII). Since this alternative account is available it can be seen that example (92) fails to provide, pace Lakoff, supporting evidence for a theory that equates implicature with entailment. Needless to say, in simple conjunctions there are no implicatures of this kind since both conjuncts are entailed by the sentence as a whole. In more complex cases of logical compounding (V) still gives us the implicatures required to cancel pre-suppositions in accord with our intuitions. The following examples are due to Karttunen (1974a):

(95) *If John is married and still living with his wife, then he is probably not interested in becoming your roommate.*

(96) *If no one has come out of that room, then either John never went in or we all know that he is still in there.*

(97) *John has a wife.*

(98) *John was in there.*

Example (95) pre-supposes *K*97 but does not presuppose it, likewise (96) pre-supposes but does not presuppose *K*98. Example (95) implicates that, for all the speaker knows, John is not married under (V) and this is inconsistent with [*K*97] so the latter cannot be presupposed. An analogous argument applies for (96) and [*K*98]. On Karttunen's account, suspension in these examples is the result of a highly complex filtered summation of the presuppositions and entailments of the various component sentences, but on the account presented here they are as simply explained as (84). Because Karttunen's (1973a) account of *or* was asymmetrical it made incorrect predictions in respect of the following examples:

(99) *Either all Bill's friends are keeping very quiet or he has no friends.*

(100) *Bill has friends.*

(101) *Either all of Jack's letters have been held up or he has not written any.*

(102) *Jack's letters exist.*

(103) *If Nixon knows the war is over, the war is over.*

(104) *The war is over.*

Sentences (99), (101), and (103) pre-suppose, but do not presuppose, *K*100, *K*102, and *K*104, respectively. Karttunen's (1973a) filters incorrectly predicted that the presupposition was maintained in each case. (101) is due to Karttunen (1973a), (99) and (103) are due to Wilson (1975). Because (V) generates im-plicatures from the nonentailed clauses of compound sentences without reference to their position in the sentence, the system given here correctly predicts the pre-supposition suspension that takes place. Proof is along the lines of that given for (84). Another counterexample to Karttunen's filters, (105), due to Wilson (1975), is equally susceptible to the present treatment although proof is a little more complicated:

(105) *If all Bill's friends have encouraged him, he must have friends.*

(106) *Bill must have friends.*

(107) *Bill has friends.*

Example (105) pre-supposes but does not presuppose $K107$ contrary to Karttunen's predictions. If we accept Karttunen's (1972) arguments that *must* in sentences like (105) amounts to an epistemic necessity operator (i.e., K) then we have that $[106] = [K107]$. Under (V) we will that $[P\neg 106]$ is an implicature of (105), but, given the equivalence just noted, this implicature is equivalent to $[P\neg K107]$. Although $K107$ is pre-supposed by (105), this pre-supposition is inconsistent with the implicature just established (i.e., inc$\{[P\neg K107], [K107]\}$) and so it is canceled by (*X*VII).[16]

There is a class of examples which involve compound sentences having contradictory pre-suppositions where both should be suspended. These were noted in Hausser (1973) and Wilson (1975).

(108) *Either John has stopped beating his wife or he hasn't begun beating her.*

(109) *John has beaten his wife.*

(110) *John has not beaten his wife.*

Example (108) pre-supposes, but does not presuppose, either $K109$ or $K110$. We have that inc$\{[K109], [K110]\}$, so, under the definition of $\cup!$, NEITHER pre-supposition will be allowed into $e_{\cup}^{108}$. An identical analysis applies to example (111), which is due to Wilson (1975:73), and the relation it bears to (112) and (113):

(111) *Your teacher will be either a bachelor or a spinster.*

(112) *Your teacher will be male.*

(113) *Your teacher will be female.*

Likewise Wilson's (1975:75) example, given as (114), causes no embarrassment to the present theory:

(114) *If Sartre knows that Chomsky is alive, I'll be surprised, but if he knows that Chomsky is dead, I'll be amazed.*

Consider the following examples (which are due to Liberman, 1973):

(115) *Maybe John used to beat his wife but has now stopped doing so.*

[16]

(1)	$P\neg Kx \in \mu$	assumption
(2)	$Kx \in \mu$	counterassumption
(3)	$\neg Kx \in \mu^*$	from (1) by C.P.*
(4)	$Kx \in \mu^*$	from (2) by C.KK*

(116) *John used to beat his wife.*

Example (115) pre-supposes, but does not presuppose, *K*116. Sentence (115) contains an occurrence of (116) but this is not entailed by the matrix sentence so under (V) we have $[P\neg 116]$ as an implicature. This implicature is inconsistent with the pre-supposition *K*116 and the latter is thus canceled. Exactly the same explanatory principle applies to (117) and (118) in respect of their canceled pre-supposition given in (119):

(117) *Perhaps John has no children, but perhaps his children are away on vacation.*

(118) *It is more likely that John has no children than that his children are away on vacation.*

(119) ***K(John has children).***

The system developed in this chapter makes the correct predictions about sentences of arbitrary complexity. We can illustrate this with the following example (suggested to me by Lauri Karttunen):

(120) *If Bill is married then his wife comes from a rich family and Bill hopes to profit from his wife's rich relatives.*

This sentence has the structure shown schematically in (121):

(121) $$A \longrightarrow (B \wedge C).$$

Among its many pre-suppositions, (120) gives rise to that shown in (122), thanks to the complex definite description, *his wife's rich relatives,* found in clause C:

(122) $$K(A \wedge B)$$

But (120) also gives rise to the following set of clausal im-plicatures:

(123) $\{PA,\ PB,\ PC,\ P\neg A,\ P\neg B,\ P\neg C,\ P(B \wedge C),\ P\neg(B \wedge C)\}$

and we have that

(124) $\mathrm{inc}(\{[K(A \wedge B)]\} \cup \{[PA], [PB], [PC], [P\neg A], [P\neg B], [P\neg C], [P(B \wedge C)], [P\neg(B \wedge C)]\})$.

Thus, the pre-supposition that the speaker knows that Bill has a wife with rich relatives is canceled. And this is intuitively correct.

Consider the following examples (due to Thomason but given in Karttunen, 1974a):

(125) *Some member of the Harvard Philosophy Department has stopped beating his wife* (take the nonspecific interpretation of *some member*).

(126) *Either Quine has stopped beating his wife, or Putnam has stopped beating his wife, or Rawls has stopped beating his wife . . .* (and so on, until we have enumerated every member of the HPD).

The interesting thing about these is that they have exactly the same truth conditions but they can have different presuppositions.[17] Thus (125) will presuppose [*K*127] but only (126) can presuppose [*K*128]:[18]

(127) *Some member of the HPD used to beat his wife.*

(128) *Quine used to beat his wife, Putnam used to beat his wife, Rawls used to beat his wife, ...* (that is, **every** member of the HPD used to beat his wife).

This is correctly predicted by both the system developed previously and by Karttunen's filters; however Karttunen used to think that presuppositions had something to do with truth conditions and so he could not accept the DIFFERENCE in presuppositions in view of the fact that (125) and (126) have the SAME truth conditions. He argued (in Karttunen 1974a) that (126) was ambiguous between a reading which does presuppose [*K*128] and a "cleft" reading, glossed in (129), which does not presuppose [*K*128] but does presuppose [*K*127].

(129) *Either it is Quine who has stopped beating his wife, or it is Putnam who . . . .*

On my account there is no need to postulate an ambiguity since in most contexts of use [$P\neg 128$] will be assumed and the pre-supposition will get canceled anyway. [*K*128] could only emerge uncanceled among conversationalists who had a very low opinion of philosophers or of Harvard or both.

Keenan (1971) gives a somewhat similar example involving iterated cleft sentences which constitutes a counterexample to the semantic account of presupposition:

[17] I am grateful to Hans Kamp for showing me that an early formulation of (XVI) foundered on these examples.

[18] Note that both (125) and (126) entail (127). Strictly speaking (126) does not presuppose [*K*128] but rather a set of propositions whose intersection is [*K*128].

(130) *You say that someone in this room loves Mary. Well maybe so. But it certainly isn't Fred who loves Mary. And it certainly isn't John* . . . . (We continue in this way until we have enumerated all the people in the room.) . . . *Therefore no one in this room loves Mary.*

Because of the cleft construction, the third, fourth, and subsequent sentences (except the last) pre-suppose *K*131 but clearly the text does not have this as a presupposition.

(131) *Someone in this room loves Mary.*

Under (V) the first sentences implicates [*P*¬131] and once this has entered the context it will suffice to suspend the pre-supposition of *K*131 of subsequent sentences as it is carried along by the recursive context clause (XVIII). Interestingly enough, since Keenan presumably did not invent his example with my system in mind, the second sentence implicates [*K*¬*K*131] according to (IV) since *maybe* will appear on a quantitative scale of epistemic qualifiers after *must be*, and we have already noted above that *must* can be equated with epistemic necessity. Thus the presence of either the first OR the second sentence is sufficient to cancel the cleft pre-supposition throughout the subsequent text.

Compound sentences which contain verbs of propositional attitude like *think*, *dream*, or *believe* caused problems for Karttunen's (1973a) system which could not handle (132), for example.

(132) *Bill believed that Fred had been beating his wife and Harry hoped that Fred would stop beating her.*

(133) *Fred had been beating his wife.*

Under (V) we will have [*P*¬133] as an implicature of (132) since (*a*) (133) occurs in (132); (*b*) (133) is not entailed by (132); (*c*) its negation is not entailed by (132); and (*d*) if an arbitrary sentence is substituted for its occurrence then that sentence is not pre-supposed by (132). This implicature cancels the pre-supposition *K*133. The same explanation is available for the cancellation of *K*135 from (134), an example which is originally due to Morgan (1969):

(134) *I dreamt that I was a German and that I regretted being a German.*

(135) *I was a German.*

So far we have mostly considered cases where the entailments of the sentence itself, or its implicatures, or both, suspend one of its pre-suppositions; but (130) shows that the context itself can suspend pre-suppositions. Heinämäki (1972) gives many examples where the context suspends the pre-supposition arising from sentences containing the word *before*. Although she has no formal solution to the problem this creates, her discussion is wide ranging and thorough and will not be paraphrased here. It will suffice to give a couple of examples and show how the formal system proposed above correctly predicts their presuppositional behavior.

(136) *Max reread his diaries before he finished his autobiography.*

(137) *Max died before he finished his autobiography.*

(138) ***Max finished his autobiography*** (at time $t + 1$).

(139) ***Max died*** (at time t).

The pre-supposition function f_p tells us that K138 is a pre-supposition of both (136) and (137) and yet clearly it is a presupposition of only (136), but (137) has no relevant implicatures which could be involved in the suspension, nor is the first clause inconsistent with the second (i.e., con{[139], [138]}). However if we assume that the contexts in which (136) and (137) are produced and evaluated contain a general principle or law of nature like (140) then we may derive the inconsistency required to suspend the pre-supposition.

(140) *Nobody does anything after they have died.*

We now have that [140], [K137] $\in e_u^{137}$ and [K138] $\in e_p^{137}$ but since inc{[K138], [K137], [K140]} we may infer that [K138] $\notin e_U^{137}$ and thus that [K138] is not presupposed by (137). In contexts, such as a seance, in which (140) is not assumed then (137) WILL presuppose [K138] unless there is some other contextual proposition operative (e.g., an assumption that spirits cannot write or that they have total amnesia in respect of their earthly existence). Contextual components can REVERSE the most natural suspension pattern for sentences like (136) and (137), as the following examples show:

(141) A: *Why didn't Max complete his autobiography?*
B: *Because he made the mistake of rereading his diaries before he finished it.*

(142) A: *What was it about the completion of Max's autobiography that finally made you believe in life after death?*
B: *The fact that Max died* ***before*** *he finished it.*

Now that we have established that extralinguistic context is a partial determinant of pre-supposition suspension we can move to a type of example, apparently first noted by J. D. McCawley, which has long haunted the presupposition literature. Compare (143) and (144):

(143) *If Carter invites Governor Wallace's wife to the White House, then the president will regret having invited a black militant to his residence.*

(144) *If Carter invites Angela Davis to the White House, then the president will regret having invited a black militant to his residence.*

(145) *The president will have invited a black militant to his residence.*

Clearly, while *K*145 is a pre-supposition of both (143) and (144), it is a presupposition only of the former. (143) and (144) have among their implicatures [*P*¬146] and [*P*¬147], respectively:

(146) *Carter will invite Governor Wallace's wife to the White House.*

(147) *Carter will invite Angela Davis to the White House.*

Now given a context containing real-world knowledge to the effect that Carter is the president and that the White House is his residence, we may deduce [*P*¬148] and [*P*¬149] from [*P*¬146] and [*P*¬147], respectively:

(148) *The president will invite Governor Wallace's wife to his residence.*

(149) *The president will invite Angela Davis to his residence.*

To prove the inconsistency necessary for suspension in (144) we need, in addition, contextually given propositions regarding the respective skin color and militancy of Governor Wallace's wife and Angela Davis, and a rule of anaphora for *a*.[19] It is no part of the present enterprise to privide such a rule but clearly it will have to provide for the fact that (143) is an acceptable sentence even though *a black militant* cannot "refer" to Governor Wallace's wife, whereas the ceteris paribus interpretation of (144) is one in which *a black militant* does "refer" to

[19] See Hawkins (1974) for one formulation of such a rule.

Angela Davis. Given such a rule, the inconsistency required for pre-supposition suspension is derivable from the context and (144) but not from the context and (143). Note that *a black militant* does not HAVE TO "refer" to Angela Davis in (144) as (150) demonstrates:

(150) *It's all very well for him to invite Huey Newton over but if Carter invites Angela Davis to the White House, then the president will regret having invited a black militant to his residence. Having more than one black militant about always causes trouble.*

In this case *a black militant* can "refer" to Huey Newton and if it does then no pre-suppositional inconsistency will arise. The data presented in (136)–(150) prove, if it still needs proving, that presupposition is a pragmatic and not a semantic phenomenon.

Stalnaker (1974) pointed out that Karttunen's (1971) distinction between two types of factive verb (FACTIVES including *regret, forget, resent*, etc., and SEMIFACTIVES including *realize, see, discover*, etc.), and his consequent need to distinguish two types of presupposition relation, is rendered otiose by the kind of pragmatic account provided in this chapter. We assumed this implicitly in considering examples (74) and (78). What follows is a demonstration that Stalnaker's informal findings can be proven within the formal framework defined here. Consider the following examples (due Karttunen, 1971):

(151) *If I realize later that I have not told the truth then I will confess it to everyone.*

(152) *If I discover later that I have not told the truth then I will confess it to everyone.*

(153) *If I regret later that I have not told the truth then I will confess it to everyone.*

(154) *I have not told the truth.*

Whereas (151)–(153) all pre-suppose *K*154, only (153) retains it as a presupposition. I take it that the following entailments hold by virtue of the meaning of the words involved:[20]

(155) [A ***knows that*** φ] $\subseteq$ [A ***has realized that*** φ].

(156) [A ***knows that*** φ] $\subseteq$ [A ***has discovered that*** φ].

Note however that there is no entailment in (157):

[20] See the discussion of example (74).

(157) [A *knows that* φ] $\not\subseteq$ [A *has regretted that* φ].

From (155) and (156), (158) and (159) follow respectively by contraposition:

(158) [A *has not realized that* φ] $\subseteq$ [A *does not know that* φ].

(159) [A *has not discovered that* φ] $\subseteq$ [A *does not know that* φ].

Examples (151) and (152) will implicate [*P*160] and [*P*161], respectively:

(160) *I will not realize later that I have not told the truth.*

(161) *I will not discover later that I have not told the truth.*

(162) *I do not know that I have not told the truth.*

From either of these implicatures we may infer [*P*162] in virtue of the entailments given in (158) and (159).[21] Further we have that inc{[*K*154], [*P*162]} so the pre-supposition gets canceled in examples (151) and (152) but not in example (153) where no such inconsistency is provable by reference to (157).

ACKNOWLEDGMENTS

I am very grateful to Hans Kamp and Edward Keenan, without whose supervision the work reported herein would not have been, and to Lauri Karttunen, whose benign criticism made me aware of the sophistry and misrepresentation present in the first draft of this chapter. The theory of presupposition described in this chapter was first presented, albeit incoherently, in a paper called "Presupposition: An Epistemic Approach" at a seminar in Cambridge in 1973. A radically revised version was subsequently distributed in 1975 as a mimeo under the title "Implicature and Presupposition." In 1975–1976, the theory was revised yet again and the definitions given in this chapter are those given in my 1976 doctoral dissertation.

REFERENCES

Biggs, C. Reference, and its role in grammars of natural language. Unpublished doctoral dissertation, University of Cambridge, 1976.

[21] This inference fudges the tense issue but not to do so would make the proof even longer and more unwieldy than it is. For details of the complex interplay of presupposition and temporal matters see Givon (1972).

Caton, C. Epistemic qualification of things said in English. *Foundations of Language*, 1966, *2*, 37–66.

Fillmore, C. J., and Langendoen, D. T. *Studies in linguistic semantics*. New York: Holt, 1971.

Gazdar, G. J. M. *Pragmatics*. New York: Academic Press, in press.

Givon, T. Forward implications, backward presuppositions and the time-axis of verbs. In J. P. Kimball (Ed.), *Syntax and semantics I*. New York: Academic Press, 1972. Pp. 29–50.

Grice, H. P. Logic and conversation. In P. Cole and J. Morgan (Eds.), *Syntax and semantics 3: Speech acts*. New York: Academic Press, 1975. Pp. 41–58.

Hamblin, C. L. Mathematical models of dialogue. *Theoria*, 1971, *37*, 130–155.

Hausser, R. R. Presuppositions and quantifiers. In *Papers from the 9th Regional Meeting*. Chicago Linguistic Society, 1973. Pp. 192–204.

Hawkins, J. A. Definiteness and indefiniteness. Unpublished doctoral dissertation, University of Cambridge, 1974.

Heinämäki, O. Before. In *Papers from the 8th Regional Meeting*. Chicago: Chicago Linguistic Society, 1972. Pp. 139–51.

Hintikka, J. *Knowledge and belief*. Ithaca, New York: Cornell University Press, 1962.

Horn, L. R. On the semantic properties of logical operators in English. Unpublished doctoral dissertation, University of California, Los Angeles, 1972.

Karttunen, L. Some Observations on Factivity. *Papers in Linguistics*, 1971, *4*, 55–70.

Karttunen, L. Possible and Must. In J. P. Kimball (Ed.). *Syntax and semantics I*. New York: Academic Press, 1972. Pp. 1–20.

Karttunen, L. Presuppositions of Compound Sentences. *Linguistic Inquiry*, 1973, *4*, 169–193(a).

Karttunen, L. The last word. Princeton, New Jersey: Mathematical Social Sciences Board. Mimeo, 1973(b).

Karttunen, L. Remarks on presuppositions. Austin: University of Texas, Mimeo, 1974(a).

Karttunen, L. Presupposition and linguistic context. *Theoretical Linguistics*, 1974, *1*, 181–194(b).

Karttunen, L., and Peters, P. S. Conventional Implicature in Montague Grammar. *Proceedings of the 1st Annual Meeting of the Berkeley Linguistic Society*, 1975, Pp. 266–278.

Karttunen, L., and Peters, P. S. What indirect questions conventionally implicate. In *Papers from the 12th Regional Meeting*. Chicago: Chicago Linguistic Society, 1976. Pp. 351–368.

Keenan, E. L. Two kinds of presupposition in natural language. In C. J. Fillmore and D. T. Langendoen (Eds.), *Studies in linguistic semantics*. New York: Holt, 1971. Pp. 45–54.

Kiparsky, P. Fact. In D. D. Steinberg and L. A. Jakobovits (Eds.). *Semantics*. Cambridge: Cambridge University Press, 1970. Pp. 345–369.

Kneale, W., and Moore, G. E. Is existence a predicate? *Aristotelian Society Supplementary Volume 15*, 1936, 154–188.

Lakoff, G. Pragmatics in Natural Logic. In E. L. Keenan, *Formal Semantics of Natural Language*. Cambridge: Cambridge University Press, 1975. Pp. 253–286.

Langendoen, D. T., and Savin, H. B. The projection problem for presuppositions. C. J. Fillmore and D. T. Langendoen (Eds.), *Studies in linguistic semantics*. New York: Holt, 1971. Pp. 55–62.

Liberman, M. Alternatives. In *Papers from the 9th Regional Meeting*. Chicago: Chicago Linguistic Society, 1973. Pp. 356–368.

Montague, R. *Formal philosophy: Selected papers* (edited by R. H. Thomason). New Haven: Yale University Press, 1974.

Morgan, J. L. (1969) On the treatment of presupposition in tranformational grammar. *Papers from the 5th Regional Meeting.* Chicago: Chicago Linguistic Society, 1969. Pp. 167–177.

Partee, B. H. (Ed.). *Montague grammar.* New York: Academic Press, 1976.

Reis, M. Further *and's* and *but's* about conjunction. *Papers from the 10th Regional Meeting.* Chicago: Chicago Linguistic Society, 1974. Pp. 539–550.

Sacks, H. Lecture, May 29th. University of California at Irvine. Mimeo, 1968.

Stalnaker, R. C. Pragmatic presuppositions. In M. K. Munitz and P. K. Unger, *Semantics and philosophy.* New York: New York University Press, 1974. Pp. 197–213.

Thomason, R. H. A semantic theory of sortal correctness. *Journal of Philosophical Logic,* 1972, *1,* 209–258.

Wilson, D. M. *Presupposition and non-truth-conditional semantics.* New York: Academic Press, 1975.

A SOLUTION TO THE PROJECTION PROBLEM FOR PRESUPPOSITION[1]

JERROLD J. KATZ
Graduate Center, City University of New York

1. INTRODUCTORY REMARKS

The projection problem for presupposition (first called this by Langendoen and Savin, 1971) is the problem of explaining "how the presuppositions and assertions of a complex sentence are related to the presuppositions and assertions of the clauses it contains." If the notion of presupposition is taken, as Langendoen, Savin, and I take it, to be semantic, this problem is obviously a component of the broader problem of explaining the compositionality of sentence meaning.[2] The broader problem is how the meaning (and hence the semantic properties and relations) of full sentences is determined by the meaning of their lowest order syntactic parts and by the syntactic structure of the sentences. The narrower problem arises in the particular form that Langendoen and Savin formulated when presupposition is identified as one of the semantic properties and relations of sentences.

In this chapter, we shall describe the general solution to the nar-

[1] Some of the material in this essay is a revised version of the discussion of presupposition in Katz (1977a, pp. 91–117).

[2] The notion of a semantic presupposition (as opposed to a contextual presupposition) is that of one whose content is a function of the grammatical structure of a sentence type (see Katz and D. T. Langendoen, 1976).

Syntax and Semantics, Volume 11: Presupposition

ISBN 0–12–613511–8

rower problem within the context of the theory developed so far as a partial solution to the broader one (Katz, 1972, 1977). This is to say, our general solution to the projection problem for presupposition will take the following form. FIRST, there will be two definitions of "presupposition of the sentence *S* (on a sense)." One definition specifies the presupposition of a particular sentence on the basis of its semantic representation; the other explains the logical status of presupposition. SECOND, there will be an account of how presuppositional information is formally specified in the semantic representations of lexical items. THIRD, there will be a statement of the projection principles that operate on the semantic representations of the lexical items in a sentence and combine them in accord with its syntactic structure to form semantic representations for the sentence. These principles have to form semantic representations that predict the presupposition of each sense of a sentence on the basis of the definitions of presupposition.

2. THE NATURE AND JUSTIFICATION OF SEMANTIC PRESUPPOSITION

What one can say about the nature of a notion depends on the justification one has used to introduce the notion into the theory. Inadequate attention to this methodological principle is responsible for the confusing variety of notions in linguistics referred to as "presupposition." I have argued elsewhere that Chomsky's justification for introducing his notions of focus and presupposition is that they are required to define the rhetorical or stylistic relation of "natural answer" and consequently these are not the sort of notions that can be used, as he uses them, to argue against the thesis that SEMANTIC rules apply exclusively to underlying phrase markers (Katz, 1972, to appear). Chomsky's failure to attend to the fact that natural answer restrictions are a matter of use rather than meaning is responsible for yet another notion in linguistics labeled "presupposition" but having little to do with the traditional notion. This has confused the issue of whether transformational rules contribute to the meaning of sentences.

In conformity with this methodological principle, my exposition of the semantic notion of presupposition will concentrate initially on the justification for introducing this notion into the set of semantic properties and relations (the set of notions that semantic theory has to explain). I will take the standards of justification to be those of traditional philosophical discussions: A justification of presupposition answers the question whether theories of the logical structure of sentences should make a provision for presuppositions or follow Russell in not doing so. I will not use far looser standards that prevail in many recent linguistic discussions of presupposition because too many of the alleged justifications of presupposition in these discussions are too weak to overcome obvious Russellian replies.

The concept of presupposition that I proposed in *Semantic Theory* (Katz, 1972, pp. 414–441) as a further semantic property comes down to us from two highly influential philosophical discussions of presupposition, one in Frege's (1952) "On Sense and Reference" and one in Strawson's (1950) "On Referring." However, the particular concept that I proposed departs in important ways from theirs. The following two are the main divergences. In Frege's case, the divergence is a function of the difference in attitude toward natural language. Frege's attitude was that natural languages are very imperfect instruments for thinking, full of all sorts of logical pitfalls (e.g., ambiguities, vagueness, and perhaps even incoherence) and should be replaced, as far as possible, by artificial languages that are more suitable instruments for thinking. My attitude is the opposite. It is that natural languages are not imperfect and need no such rational reconstruction, but only more carefully and theoretically informed study; it is a corollary of this that artificial languages, though useful in mathematics, computer sciences, and so on, are either parasitic on a natural language or else too expressively weak to be useful for thinking. Therefore, I reject Frege's notion that presuppositional failure is an imperfection of language and abandon his goal of a rational reconstruction in terms of "A logically perfect language [which satisfies] the conditions that every expression grammatically well constructed as a proper name out of signs already introduced shall in fact designate an object, and that no new sign shall be introduced as a proper name without being secured a reference [Frege, 1952, p. 70]."

In Strawson's case, the divergence is, principally, a matter of different conceptions of meaning that form the framework within which presupposition is to be understood. I take meaning to have to do with language rather than its use. This is not to deny that there is such a thing as utterance meaning but to say that utterance meaning IS sentence meaning (Katz, 1977a, pp. 18–19). Accordingly, I reject his use account of meaning on which the significance or meaningfulness of a sentence consists in "the fact that the sentence COULD be used, in certain circumstances, to say something true or false" and the significance or meaningfulness of an expression consists in the fact that "the expression COULD be used, in certain circumstances, to mention a particular person [etc.][Strawson, 1950/1971, p. 184]."

I should also point out here that, though I agree with Strawson the defender of presupposition, I do not agree with his defense itself. Indeed, I had in mind arguments of this kind when I said that many alleged justifications of presupposition are too weak to overcome obvious Russellian replies. Strawson says, ". . . . suppose someone were in fact to say to you with a perfectly serious air: 'The king of France is wise'. Would you say, 'That's untrue'? I think it is quite certain that you would not" (Ibid., p. 183). Strawson thinks that such a response would not be made because, insofar as no king of France exists, the question of his wisdom does not arise. Strawson thinks that his presuppositional treatment of *The king of France is wise* can explain why the response "That's untrue" would not be made and Russell's treatment cannot. But, in fact, Russell's treatment can explain it. Russell can say that his analysis of this sentence together with pragmatic considerations (independently needed in the theory of language and its use) imply the inappropriateness of replying "That's untrue." On Russell's analysis, the sentence makes three assertions: first, that a king of France exists; second, that there is no more than one such; and third, that everything that is king of France is wise. If we suppose, along with Grice, that there is a pragmatic principle requiring that speakers make their contributions as informative as required, then, in the circumstance, saying simply, "That's untrue" will be inappropriate because the response gives less information than required. It is like my asserting that roses are red, violets are blue, and sugar is sweet; and your replying "That's untrue." Do you mean that roses are not red, that violets are not blue, that sugar is not sweet, or what? If the hypothetical respondent said instead, "No king of France exists, so that's untrue," the situational inappropriateness would not arise, but, then, it is not at all clear that a real respondent would not say this.

Frege mistakenly attributes to language what is, in fact, a matter of limitations on our knowledge of the world.[3] Strawson's use account of meaning leads to disastrous consequences in connection with presupposition. His account of the meaningfulness of expressions has the obviously false consequence that neither the subject of a sentence like (1) nor the sentence itself is meaningful, since the subject

[3] Frege's claim that the existence of expressions that fail to designate an object is an "imperfection of language" is on a par with a misguided claim such as that cars are imperfect because they can be driven off cliffs and into trucks. Expressions that fail to designate exist for two reasons, first, the grammatical rules of a natural language enable it to freely construct expressions in accord only with grammatical selectional relations, and second, the world lacks various and sundry possible objects, for example, a present king of France. The only imperfections I can see in this connection are imperfections in our stock of beliefs about the world (not our language) which cause us to think some objects exist which do not. See my discussion of Frege's claim in Katz (1971, pp. 13–14, Footnote 10; see also Katz, 1978).

(1) *The least convergent series is infinite.*

of (1) cannot be used to refer and, as a consequence, (1) cannot be used to assert something true or false.

My concept of presupposition may be explained as follows: The property of having a presupposition applies to senses of declarative sentences. These senses are assertive propositions.[4] Such propositions have a sequence of terms that pick out the objects or sets of objects that the proposition is about. Such propositions also have a predicate (or predicates) that expresses the assertion that the proposition makes about the objects or sets of objects on a literal use of the sentence to make a statement. A sentence makes a statement when each of the terms in the proposition it expresses successfully refers. When the objects or sets of objects to which these terms refer satisfy the predicate (or predicates), the proposition makes a true statement. When each of the terms in a proposition successfully refers and the objects or sets of objects to which they refer does not satisfy the predicate (or predicates), the proposition makes a false statement. The theory of presupposition explains the logical status of a proposition when some of its terms do not successfully refer.

Russellian accounts of logical form claim that no special explanation is necessary. They say that such a proposition makes a false statement. It makes a statement because the sentence expressing it is meaningful and the statement is false because it asserts the existence of an object or set of objects that does not exist (Russell, 1919, pp. 162–180). In contrast, presuppositional accounts of logical form say that, in cases of the failure of a term to refer, the proposition makes no statement at all. Since the proposition is about nothing, there is nothing of which something true or false can be asserted. (Russell's account avoids the counterintuitive claim that an assertion can be false even though it is about nothing by making the equally counter-intuitive claim that an assertion of a sentence like "The king of France is wise" is about everything—ships, shoes, sealing wax, number, etc.) On our account, as opposed to Russell's, the necessary and sufficient condition for the statementhood of a proposition is successful reference of each referring term in the proposition. This is its presupposition. For Russell, any meaningful sentence (any sentence that expresses a proposition) is ipso facto a statement, that is, either true or false. Frege and Strawson impose the stronger condition of statementhood, viz., over and

[4] I discuss presupposition in connection with nonassertive propositions, that is, the senses of performative sentences like *I hereby promise to return your bagels,* in Katz (1977a).

above meaningfulness, the objects or sets of objects that the proposition is about must exist.

The justification of a notion of presupposition must establish adequate grounds for introducing a stronger condition on statementhood than Russell's. Russell's is the simpler theory, and hence, the onus of proof falls on the presuppositionalist. The failure of many philosophers and linguists to recognize this onus has led to the numerous unconvincing arguments for presupposition. Their dismal showing, in turn, has contributed to producing a false sense of confidence on the part of Russellians. I will try to present an argument for introducing presupposition that dispenses the onus of proof successfully.[5]

Russell's position assumes that the sheer meaningfulness of a sentence is necessary and sufficient for it to make a statement, be true or false; the sentence does not have to have a true presupposition. Now, a sentence like (2) is undeniably meaningful. After all, the sentence listed as (2) might have been $2 + 2 = 5$ so that (2) would have been true; any sentence that can be true (on a literal use) must be meaningful.

(2) *The sentence* (2) *is false.*

Consequently, on Russell's assumption, sentence (2) is either true or false. However, if the sentence (2) is true, then, since what sentence (2) asserts is that it is false, (2) is false; and if (2) is false, then, since what it asserts is the case, (2) must be true. But, since (2) is either true or false, it follows by elementary logic that (2) is both true and false. This is a contradiction and so it cannot be that (2) is either true or false. Insofar as Russell's assumption is what enables us to say that (2) is either true or false, this assumption is refuted. The deduction of the contradiction constitutes a reductio ad absurdum of Russell's assumption. Since the presuppositionalist theory provides the only alternative account of the conditions for statementhood, this reductio is an argument for this theory.[6]

[5] Presented originally in Katz (1972, p. 136).

[6] I should like to remark in passing that I find the discussion of my argument in S.-Y. Kuroda (1974) puzzling. Kuroda's first point is that "the Epimedian paradox is not essential for this conclusion [that metalinguistic sentences which contain predicates related to the concept of truth may not necessarily be assumed to have a truth-value]." I certainly grant that an argument from this paradox is not the only way to establish the conclusion; what I claimed is that such an argument is a way of establishing it. Kuroda's second point is even more curious. He says that the difficulty "caused by Epimedian sentences [is] not a matter of conflict between extensionalist logic and the semantics of natural language" because "It takes a form of antinomy that can arise within the extensionalist framework, given a language satisfying a certain effability condition. Its rele-

We said above that the justification for introducing presupposition determines the nature of the concept introduced. The justification here shows that what is needed in connection with (2) is a condition that the subject refers to a statement. That is, the predicate of (2) is *is false,* and our account says that truth and falsehood can only be predicated of statements. [The assertion of (2) will be true if the *statement* it makes is false and false if the *statement* is true.] Presuppositionalists thus avoid paradox because their account of the logical form of (2) says that reference to a statement is the presupposition of (2) and such reference must fail. Sentence (2) cannot refer to a statement because, in referring to itself, (2) refers to a statement only if it refers to one. Therefore, its deferring of reference returns to the deferring sentence, forming a referential loop and thereby guaranteeing that (2) will fail to refer to a statement.[7] This case is simply the case of the shortest book in which each page contains exactly one sentence saying the next contains a falsehood and the last saying the first contains one too. THIS justification commits one to Fregean presuppositions, namely, ones taking the form of conditions that terms refer to appropriate objects or sets of objects. The appropriate object will be a statement in the case of (2) and a unique King of France in the case of *The King of France is bald.*

---

vance . . . comes through the assumption that natural language possesses the effability condition in question." The issue as I made perfectly clear is whether a theory of the logical structure of natural language based on extensional logic can be adequate. I tried to argue that it cannot. Tarski's work on artificial languages showed that purely extensional languages which meet the condition in question are inconsistent, so I tried to turn this argument around, to show that natural languages are not extensional, and hence theories of their logical structure based on extensional logic are inadequate. Of course, both Tarski and I assume that natural languages meet a completeness condition (at least in the weak form that such languages contain a pair of sentences for any sentence in them, one member of which asserts that the sentence is true and the other which asserts that the sentence is not). So, of course, one might deny this, but the strength of the argument I proposed lies in there being no easily imaginable way to deny the effability of natural languages (in the weak form just specified). Of course, as Kuroda says, the relevance to the theoretical issue comes through the assumption about the effability of natural languages. Thus, if Kuroda wishes to deny the relevance, he ought to give some reason for thinking that the assumption is false. But this he does not do. Kuroda's third and final point is that my argument cannot be properly evaluated until a theory that associates presuppositions with metalinguistic sentences is developed. What is strange about this is just why my argument cannot be properly evaluated until then. We properly evaluated Chomsky's argument for transformational grammars well in advance of the development of any transformational grammars of natural languages. Kuroda again fails to supply a reason.

[7] Sentence (2) is ungrounded in the sense of Herzberger and Katz (1967), Herzberger (1970), and Kripke (1975).

Note that this commitment does not encompass "presuppositions" of the kind for which Geach (1954), and following him I (Katz, 1972), once argued. Sentences like (3) and (4) were said to presuppose states of affairs, to

(3) *I have stopped beating my wife.*

(4) *Have you stopped beating your wife?*

presuppose that the speaker in (3) and the addressee in (4) had been beating his wife. For, an affirmative or a negative response to (4) is "out of place" if the addressee had not been beating his wife. These "presuppositions," which are not about the successful reference of a term, are thereby not covered under the above justification. Moreover, they also seem not to be genuine presuppositions, but better thought of as predications upon which other predications are stacked. (See the fuller discussion in Katz, 1977, pp. 208–209.) The stacking is confused with the ordering of presupposition and assertion.

Related to the preceding justification are a number of considerations that further support the notion of presupposition. We mentioned one parenthetically above: Russell's account of the logical form of propositions forces us to adopt a highly unnatural theory of what simple copula sentences, among others, are about. Intuitively, one would say that the use of a sentence like (5) is about the Jimmy Carter who is now president

(5) *The president of the U.S.A. is bald.*

of the United States, and that the use of a sentence like (6) is not about anything.

(6) *The King of France is bald.*

On Russell's account, however, we have to say that (5) and (6) are both about everything in the world, and hence about the same thing. This is because Russell represents the logical form of such sentences using the universal quantifier to express the uniqueness of the definite article. In contrast, on our account, we can use the notion of presupposition to frame a general definition of aboutness that avoids these counterintuitive consequences. We can say that sentences are about the object or objects that satisfy their presupposition and about nothing if their presupposition is not satisfied.[8] This definition predicts that (5)

[8] We can characterize aboutness for sentences as well as for uses of sentences because presupposition can be defined in terms of the notion of type-reference. See Katz (1977b).

and (6) are about different things, President Carter in the case of (5) and nothing in the case of (6). Thus, it conforms to our intuitions concerning what these sentences are about.

3. ON DEFINING THE NOTION OF PRESUPPOSITION

Our solution to the projection problem for presupposition must first provide definitions that express this notion of presupposition in the normal form for definitions of semantic properties and relations in semantic theory. To do this, we start with some distinctions between kinds of definitions for semantic properties and relations.

All definitions of semantic properties and relations are framed in terms of the formal features of semantic representations. They explicate a property or relation on the basis of the constructs formalized at the semantic level. But the properties and relations themselves may be properties and relations of different things, such as linguistic expressions, their senses, or their relations to objects in the world. Definitions that explicate semantic properties and relations of linguistic expressions or senses, for example, definitions of semantic anomaly, ambiguity, analyticity, and so on, will be called MEANING DEFINITIONS, whereas those that explicate semantic properties and relations of objects and states of affairs, for example, definitions of "has a referent," "is true," and so on, will be called REFERENCE DEFINITIONS.

Cross classifying with the categories of meaning definition and reference definition are the categories of STRUCTURAL DEFINITION and INTERPRETIVE DEFINITION. A definition is a STRUCTURAL DEFINITION in case it explicates the structure of a semantic property or relation in a way that permits us to identify its instances on the basis of their exemplifying the structure. A definition is an INTERPRETIVE DEFINITION in case it logically interprets exemplifications of a semantic property or relation. The category of MEANING STRUCTURAL DEFINITIONS contains the most familiar definitions from semantic theory, for example, the definition of semantic anomaly as the absence of a reading, the definition of ambiguity in terms of the assignment of two or more readings, and the definition of synonymy in terms of the assignment of the same reading to different linguistic expressions. These definitions characterize a semantic property or relation in terms of a configuration of symbols in the readings of sentences or constituents. They say what formal structure the readings of a sentence or constituent must have for the sentence or constituent to have the semantic property or relation in question. Meaning structural definitions express generalizations, across the sentences of natural languages, about the common semantic structure underlying semantic properties and relations.

Reference structural definitions characterize a semantic property or relation in terms of the features of objects and states of affairs that determine the connection between a linguistic expression and some portion of the world. For example, this category of definitions contains the definition of *x* IS THE REFERENT (OR DESIGNATION) OF *w* in terms of the condition that, for every semantic marker *M* in the reading for *w* (in an optimal grammar), *x* falls under the concept represented by *M*. It is important to note here that the referential notions defined in this connection are under the same idealization as the semantical notions; that is, the notion of a referent of a word is the notion of its referent in the language, not the notion of what some use of the word refers to on that use.[9]

Interpretive definitions, on the other hand, explain the logical significance of the semantic properties and relations characterized in the structural definitions. The interpretive definition of a semantic property or relation expresses the logical feature of the sense of a linguistic construction attributable to its having that particular semantic property or relation. The interpretive definition of semantic anomaly is that such sentences express no proposition and so do not enter into logical (deductive) relations with other sentences. The interpretive definition of ambiguity is that sentences express more than one proposition and so enter polymorphously into logical relations. The interpretive definition of synonymy is that such sentences express the same proposition and so enter into exactly the same logical relations with other sentences (have the same role in arguments).

Crossclassifying with the categories of STRUCTURAL DEFINITION and INTERPRETIVE DEFINITION are the categories of EXPRESSION DEFINITION and SENSE DEFINITION. This dichotomy partitions structural and interpretive definitions into those that characterize semantic properties and relations of EXPRESSIONS (that is, sentences and their constituents) and those that characterize semantic properties and relations of SENSES (that is, concepts and propositions expressed by sentences and their constituents). The former category includes the structural and interpretive definitions of semantic anomaly, ambiguity, synonymy, and translation, whereas the latter includes the structural and interpretive definitions of analyticity, contradiction, and se-

[9] Katz (1972b) develops a new theory of reference based on a strict distinction between TYPE REFERENCE (reference in accord with the principles of the language) and TOKEN REFERENCE (reference in accord with context).

mantic entailment. A definition belongs in the category of expression definitions in case it defines a feature that cannot apply to propositions; for example, it makes no sense to say that a proposition is ambiguous or meaningless. A definition belongs in the category of sense definitions in case it defines a feature that can apply in different respects to the same (ambiguous) expression (Katz and Katz, 1977).

The account of presupposition in semantic theory must take the form of two definitions of the notion "presupposition," one a structural definition and one an interpretive definition. Both will be sense definitions because it makes sense to apply the property of having a presupposition to propositions and because this property applies in different respects to one and the same (ambiguous) sentence. For example, we can apply this notion to (7) in different respects.

(7) *The bat flew past my ear.*

We can say that (7) presupposes (on one sense) the existence of a flying mammal and that (7) presupposes (on another) the existence of a stout stick.

The problem of constructing the structural definition is to set up the projection apparatus so that the notions needed to state the structural definition of presupposition are available. To attack this problem, we construct a first approximation to a structural definition of presupposition, one that seems to embody the basic idea of Frege's notion, then construct formalizations of the notions employed in the first approximation, and finally rework the first approximation and the formalizations to reach a reasonably satisfactory structural definition.

Our first approximation to a structural definition is (8).

(8) i. A proposition *P* has a presupposition just in case there is at least one referring term in *P*.
ii. The presupposition of a proposition *P* is the requirement that each referring term in *P* has its appropriate designatum.

We shall make no attempt to actually explain what the term "appropriate designatum" means. The notion that we require for (8) is the notion of the designatum of a referring term which is picked out in a use of the term in a NULL CONTEXT, that is, one that contributes nothing to how the meaning of the term is understood.[10] This designatum can be taken as whatever in that context has all those features repre-

[10] The meaning of the term in such a context is the meaning of the term in the language.

sented in the meaning of the term in question. The term has a reading, the reading represents certain concepts, and the designatum is every object in a null context that falls under all of those concepts. The designata of tokens, what the use of expressions refer to on the occasion of their use, are not considered here because they are typically not determined solely by the grammatical structure of the sentence in which they occur but are influenced by, and sometimes fully determined by, contextual factors. The designata of tokens is a matter of performance, whereas the designata of expressions in the null context is a matter of competence (Katz 1977b).

The structural definition of presupposition tells us what condition has to be fulfilled to satisfy the presupposition of a proposition; the interpretive definition tells us what it means to satisfy the presupposition. Frege's conception of presupposition can be seen as the proposal that the interpretive definition be given in terms of statementhood. Frege's view is that the existence of "appropriate designata" for the referring terms in a sentence is a necessary and sufficient condition for it to state a truth or falsehood. If there are appropriate designata, there is something for the assertion of the sentence to be about, and the sentence is either true or false. If the designation requirement is not met and there is nothing that the assertion is about, the sentence can be neither true nor false. Given that a proposition's making a statement is its having a truth value and that the truth values are true and false, Frege's conception of presupposition suggests the interpretive definition (9).

(9) The presupposition of an assertive proposition *P* is the condition under which *P* makes a statement, that is, under which *P* is a truth or a falsehood.

4. THE SOLUTION

Langendoen and Savin (1971) proposed their "cumulative hypothesis" as a solution to the projection problem for presupposition. This hypothesis says that "the presuppositions of subordinate clauses stand as part of the presupposition of the complex sentences containing them [p. 58]."

This hypothesis was falsified on the basis of various counterexamples.[11] But I am not concerned with them at present. What is more im-

[11] Morgan (1969) points out that conditional sentences like "*If Jack has children, then all of Jack's children are bald*" do not presuppose that Jack has children, although their consequents do. In *Semantic Theory* I pointed out that opaque constructions block presuppositions.

portant here is that the entire discussion of the projection problem has been carried on at the purely descriptive level. Hypotheses take the form of simple empirical generalizations from examples, criticisms are further examples that do not fit the hypotheses, and reformulations (Karttunen, 1973)[12] are amended empirical generalizations. This has been responsible for the difficulties in finding revisions of such empirical generalizations that succeed in capturing the relations between presuppositions of clauses and presuppositions of the sentences containing them. The discussion has failed to go beyond the descriptive level. In particular, the trouble is that, by remaining at this level, one never looks for formal explanations of how the presuppositions of sentences derive compositionally from the meaning of their parts. Thus, theoretical constructs necessary to state the relations between presuppositions of clauses and the presuppositions of the sentences containing them are not constructed.

Our discussion of the projection problem departs radically from the descriptive approach and concentrates on the structure of a formal explanation of the compositional basis of presupposition. Contrary to the descriptive approach, we assume that the projection problem for presupposition is not separable from the general projection problem, and that the solution is a formal model of the compositional process in which readings are assigned to sentences that permit us to predict ALL of their semantic properties and relations.

Given the structural definition (8), the projection problem for presupposition boils down to formalizing the notion REFERRING TERM on the basis of readings. Our strategy will be the following. We first motivate taking the notion of a referring term to be that of a term that contributes a clause to the presupposition of the proposition. We then explain how to set up lexical readings in which referring terms are represented. For this we appeal to the notation of enclosure in heavy parentheses.[13] Then, we introduce projection apparatus that generates readings of sentences with heavy parentheses at just the right places to predict the presuppositions of sentences.

We interpret the notion of a referring term (or referential position) on the basis of presupposition rather than on the basis of the standard notion of a term (or position) for which (at which) coreferential terms may be substituted preserving truth. The theory we are developing construes presupposition as a condition guaranteeing a nonempty domain for a predication. A term is a referring term if the predicates asso-

[12] For all of the formalism this paper uses, its account of presupposition remains at the descriptive level, using metaphorical notions like "hole," "plug," and "filter" to refer to the phenomena that should be formally reconstructed (see Katz and Langedoen, 1976).

[13] The notation of heavy parentheses **(**and**)** was first introduced in Katz (1972).

ciated with the position the term occupies make assertions about its referent. Correspondingly, a position is referential if readings occurring in it determine the objects about which the predicates associated with the position make assertions. This notion of a referential position can be distinguished from the notion of a position that permits substitutivity of coextensive terms on the basis of examples like (10) and (11).

(10) *Honest politicians actually exist.*

(11) *Toadstools are real things.*

On the latter notion, the positions occupied by *honest politicians* and *toadstools* are referential positions, but they are not on the former notion. For suppose that *toadstools* is coextensive with *poisonous mushrooms.* Then, we can validly infer (12) from (11), and so ______ *is a*

(12) *Poisonous mushrooms are real things.*

real thing is referential in the substitutivity sense. But such contexts cannot be taken as referential in our sense of contributing to the presupposition of the sentence, for then a sentence like (11) would be marked as analytic rather than synthetic. If the term occupying such a position were to contribute a clause that makes statementhood depend on the term having an appropriate designatum, the presupposition of such sentences would include their truth conditions. For example, the presupposition of (10) would be that there is appropriate designata of *honest politicians,* but insofar as the truth conditions of (10) is that there are honest politicians,[14] these would be included in the presupposition, and therefore, we would be forced to make the false prediction that (10) is an analytic sentence (and could, accordingly, not be false).[15] Hence, the substitutivity notion of referentiality is not appropriate.

It is important to note in this connection, and this, I think, constitutes another strong argument for presupposition, that our theory will

[14] On a presuppositional theory of logical form, (10) is not synonymous with *Some politicians are honest.* The latter can be either false or not true. It is false when there are politicians but none is honest, and it is not true when there are no politicians.

But in both cases, (10) is false. Note also that we are not saying that sentences like (10) and (11) carry no presupposition. They could conceivably be analyzed as presupposing the existence of an appropriate universe, say of material objects in space–time, and asserting the presence of honest politicians and toadstools therein.

[15] In connection with sentences like *There are no poisonous mushrooms, Santa Claus does not exist,* and other negative existentials, we would falsely predict that the sentence is contradictory, since their alleged presupposition conflicts with the truth conditions (see Katz, 1972, pp. 178–181).

provide a very natural solution to the traditional puzzle about negative existential sentences, namely, how can a sentence of the form *X does not exist* ever be true if to assert that *X* does not exist requires us to refer to *X* and we can refer to something only if it exists? Previous solutions all seem inadequate because they do not explain what the problematic assumption is and why it should not be made (see Donnellan, 1974; Erwin, *et al.*, forthcoming). Our theory offers the following solution: As we have seen in Footnote 15, we must avoid saying that the position marked by *X* in sentences of the form *X does not exist* is referential, or else we must mischaracterize such sentences as contradictory. But if *X* does not have to refer to something in order for the negative existential to assert that *X* does not exist, then the first of the two assumptions is false and the puzzle disappears. This solution says that the assumption should not be made because it assigns the wrong logical form to negative existential sentences. (It is not wholly clear what logical form should be assigned to them, but we may conjecture that it presupposes a world of things and asserts that *X*s are not among them.)

One further matter before we turn to the formalization. The core of our conception of presupposition is the idea that the use of proposition to make a statement depends on the successful reference of its referring terms because the existence of the object(s) to which these terms refer is the condition on which the predicate(s) can be truly or falsely asserted. Failure to make a statement means that some predicate(s) in the proposition fails to be about something. Hence, our conception implies that each referring term in an assertive proposition contributes a necessary condition to the necessary and sufficient condition for its statementhood. Each referential term in the proposition is treated on a par.

This is the simplest and most coherent development of the Fregean notion of presupposition, which is why we have adopted (8). But it is clearly not the only one. It is possible to imagine alternatives to (8) that maintain the requirement that some referring terms must refer but drop the requirement that they all must. Such alternatives would be more complex because they would have to specify the further properties of referring terms that qualify them as contributing a condition to the presupposition of the proposition. It would also be necessary to explain why the absence of these further properties should block the contribution of a referring term's presupposition.

One such alternative is this: It might be held that successful reference of the subject is not a necessary condition for statementhood except when the subject is the only term in the sentence (or perhaps just when no direct object occurs) and that when there is a direct object, its successful reference is the condition for statementhood. On this view, (13) makes a (false)

(13) *Santa Claus visited some children last night.*

statement, even though its subject fails to refer.[16]

Given our original justification of presupposition, there is a quick reply to such alternatives, namely, that they land us right back in the paradox from which the theory of presupposition was to save us. We may illustrate this reply in connection with the alternative just mentioned. Suppose A and B take turns uttering a sentence, A first, then B. A's sentence is *Snow is white,* and B's sentence is *This statement of mine follows A's statement and is false.* Since the direct object of B's sentence, the expression *A's statement,* succeeds in referring (because A makes the statement that snow is white), on the proposal we are considering, B's utterance makes a statement. Thus, it is true or false. But, then, since it is also Epimenidean, it is both true and false.

It should be noted that this argument does not depend on any special feature of the example. The fact, for instance, that the example is a conjunction is clearly not essential. The argument is trivially restated in terms of an example like *This false statement of mine follows A's statement.* No matter how the alternative to (8) is formulated, that is, no matter what term is exempted from the requirement of successful reference, it will be possible to construct similar counterexamples. As long as it is granted that my Epimenidean argument shows that the existence of an appropriate designatum for some referring term in a proposition is a condition of its statementhood, it will be possible to show that the existence of appropriate designata for each of the other referring terms in the proposition is also a condition.

[16] I am indebted to Robert Fiengo and Janet D. Fodor for suggesting this kind of case. (See J. D. Fodor, "In Defense of the Truth Value Gap," in the present volume.)

To complete the argument against such proposals, we should also mention the following: They lack an explanation of how the failure of some terms to contribute to the presupposition can be consistent with the general motion of the thing(s) to which the referring terms refer being the thing(s) that the assertion is about. Further, it looks very much as if the plausibility of the claim that the use of a sentence like (13) makes a statement derives only from a confusion of falsehood with nontruth—which is a distinction that our hypothetical critic, in subscribing to a version of the Fregean theory of presupposition, is committed to drawing. What the critic wants to say is that it cannot be the case that Santa Claus visited the children, since there is no Santa Claus or we know that nobody visited them. It is possible, however, to express this sort of denial by saying that the assertion in question is not or could not be true. There is no reason to make the stronger claim that the assertion is false. We shall look more closely at this fallacy in the next section in connection with our examination of Harnish's and Wilson's arguments.

I shall assume on the basis of these considerations that there is no serious obstacle to our using the simplest structural definition for the notion PRESUPPOSITION OF AN ASSERTIVE PROPOSITION, and turn directly to the question of how to state the referential requirement in (8) as a condition on the formal structure of readings. The solution we obtain will be needed even if this assumption ultimately proves false, since any alternative to (8) will employ the notion of a referring term.

Technically, we ought to speak of a REFERRING OCCURRENCE OF A TERM rather than of a REFERRING TERM, insofar as the notion of a referring term is a relative one; that is, no term in and of itself is a referring term, but it is so when it occurs in a referential context. But the looser usage does no harm so long as it is understood that we are speaking relative to referential positions. On this understanding, the formalization of the referential requirement in (8) requires (α) apparatus for distinguishing referential and nonreferential positions, (β) a notation for representing a term occurring in a position, and (γ) an account of the referentiality of a term on the basis of (α) and (β).

The notation for representing the occurrence of a term in a position consists of the reading expressing the term written slightly below the semantic marker(s) representing the predicate concept(s) with which the position is associated. The notation thus consists of the reading occupying the place of the categorized variables in figure (14) or (15). We cannot define the

(14)
$$((M)_{[\quad]})$$
$$\mathbf{(}X\mathbf{)}$$
$$\langle\ \rangle$$

(15)
$$((M)_{[\quad]})$$
$$X$$
$$\langle\ \rangle$$

notion of a term occurring in a position directly in terms of its being the value of a categorized variable because some occurrences of categorized variables do not mark positions corresponding to argument places, but there is a simple principle for going from occurrences of categorized variables to argument places (see Katz, 1977a, p. 68).

The apparatus of HEAVY PARENTHESES distinguishes referential from nonreferential positions (Katz, 1972, p. 167f). Referential positions are represented by categorized variables enclosed within heavy parentheses and non-referential positions are represented by categorized variables not enclosed within heavy parentheses. Accordingly, the referentiality of a term is formally determined when the projection rule puts it inside heavy parentheses in substituting the term for an occurrence of a categorized variable. We could, therefore, take a step toward the formalization of (8) if we restate (8) using the notion of a reading enclosed within heavy parentheses to do the work of referring term.

In order to restate (8), however, we have to use the notion of a reading of a sense of a sentence in place of the informal notion of a proposition. This, then, nicely expresses a condition of adequacy on a solution to the projection problem for presupposition—namely, that it provide a satisfactory account of how the dictionary and projection rule generate readings for senses of sentences such that their subreadings enclosed in heavy parentheses determine all presuppositions of these senses. The solution therefore starts at the lexical level. What must be determined at this level is where heavy parentheses appear around occurrences of categorized variables and where categorized variables in lexical readings are free of them. Then the formulation of the solution moves to the level of complex constituents. What must be determined at this level is where applications of the projection rule remove or introduce heavy parentheses.

We already found one example of an argument place that must be represented as a nonreferential position, namely, that associated with the constructions *exists* and *there is*.[17] Another is the class of opaque verbs of propositional attitude, such as *believe, want, hope,* and *imagine*. Although (16) presupposes the existence of Santa Claus, (17) does not.

(16) *Santa Claus is sick with the flu.*

(17) *Billy believes Santa Claus is sick with flu.*

Thus, the lexical reading of such a verb must contain categorized variables that are not enclosed in heavy parentheses and that are categorized for the readings of constituents of the complement sentence such as the reading of the subject of the complement sentence in (17). When readings representing referential terms in the proposition expressed by the complement sentence are embedded in the reading for the opaque verb, they enter positions not enclosed in heavy parentheses and thereby become non-referential.

[17] The Kantian objection that *exists* is not a predicate (*The Critique of Pure Reason*, trans. N. K. Smith [London: Macmillan, 1958, pp. 504–505]) does not apply here. We are not saying that *exists* is a delimiting predicate of the kind that can figure in definitions.

Without attempting to offer a lexical reading for *believe*, we might indicate the form of the reading in a sentence like (17). In doing so, we distinguish two propositions that the agent is represented as thinking true. On the one hand, since (17) entails (18), there is the proposition that the referent of the reading of the subject of the complement sentence exists, and on the other, there is a proposition asserting that the referent has the property attributed to it in the proposition expressed by the complement sentence.

(18) *Billy believes that Santa Claus exists.*

Thus the form of the reading for *believe* in (17) is something like[18]

(19)

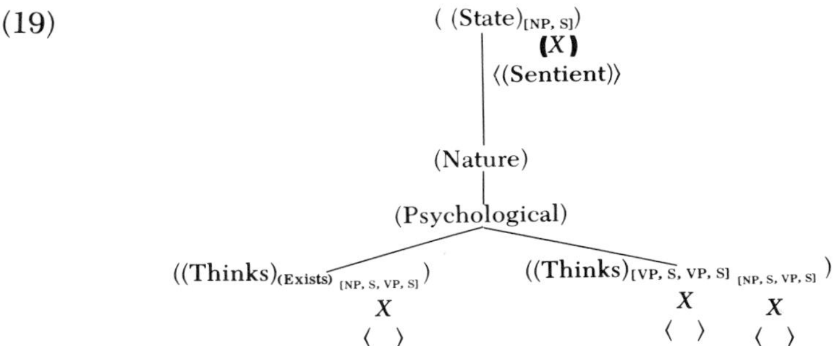

(19) represents the "opaque sense" of *believe*. It says that the only presupposition of (17) is that the reading of its subject has an appropriate designatum. The statementhood of an assertive use of this sentence depends solely on the existence of a believer. (19) says also that the truth conditions are the following: The believer is in a state, which implies that the believer is not an agent, since the definition of agent reading contains semantic markers like (Act) or (Activity) but not (State) (Katz, 1977a, pp. 77–87). Also, the state is psychological, contrasting *believe* with *frozen* (where the state is physical) and with *drunk* (where it is partly physical and partly psychological). Also, the psychological state is that of thinking that the person the belief is about exists. Here, the formulation of a lexical reading requires the formalization of the generalization that the believer thinks that there exists a referent of each of the REFERENTIAL terms in the proposition

[18] The tree notation for semantic markers is adopted because it is easier to read than the former parentheses notation. The interpretation is the same. The topmost semantic marker in the tree represents the basic predicate with its argument(s). The semantic markers labeling the nodes on the branching down to the roots represent the other predicate concepts out of which the meaning is composed. The branches represent them as predicate functions which complete the specification given in the basic predicate (see Katz, 1977a, Chap. 3).

functioning as the object of belief.[19] Finally, the psychological state is also one of thinking that the person the belief is about has the property he or she is attributed in the proposition functioning as the object of the belief.[20]

Verbs like *visit*, *chase*, and *kill* contrast with verbs of propositional attitude because all the argument places of the relation expressed by the former are referential positions. We have to write their lexical readings with categorized variables enclosed in heavy parentheses in order to reflect the semantic fact that each term of such relations contributes to the presupposition of sentences in which these verbs appear as main verbs.

There is no generalization to determine when an argument place in the sense of a lexical item is referential, though often there are generalizations like the one above about verbs of propositional attitude. This aspect of lexical readings has to be determined, more or less on a case-by-case basis, by comparing a heavy parentheses treatment with one that makes no use of them to discover which provides the best predictions about the semantic properties and relations of the complex constituents and sentences in which the lexical item appears. Our treatment of the question of whether *exists* and *there is* have nonreferential positions can be taken as paradigmatic. We decided that their positions are nonreferential on the grounds that this better predicts semantic properties and relations: The opposite decision would mistakenly predict that sentences like (10) and (11) are analytic.

We have said everything that needs to be said here about the projection problem for presupposition at the lexical level. The rest concerns the projection process from the lexical level to sentence readings. We need to explain how the apparatus of heavy parentheses interacts with other semantic apparatus as a result of projection rule applications that supply readings for a whole sentence on the basis of its lexical readings. We also need to explain how the derived readings that represent terms are built up out of lexical readings and how such derived readings are routed into their proper positions in the readings of sentences.

[19] The nonreferential terms in this proposition (that expressed by the complement sentence) do not give rise to a clause of the truth condition about what the believer thinks exists. Note that in the sentence *John believes that Sam believes that Santa Claus is sick with the flu* there is no clause of the truth condition that John thinks Santa Claus exists.

[20] We have not tried to explicate the concept of thinking in (19) or to specify completely the components of the propositions thought to be true (relative to the reading of the complement that represents them).

Nothing about term formation requires special comment in connection with the projection problem for presupposition. The readings representing terms are formed from lexical readings in the standard way. There is also nothing about term routing that requires special comment here. The readings representing terms are routed into positions in the readings of sentences on the basis of the grammatical function that determines the constituents to which the readings of terms are assigned and on the basis of the grammatical functions that categorize the variables in the lexical readings of other constituents. The projection rule thus relates terms to positions (representing argument places) by substituting readings representing terms for occurrences of categorized variables having the proper categorization. Thus, terms may be put into referential positions or nonreferential positions. Terms in referential positions may stay there or be moved out. A term that is moved out may be moved into a referential position or a nonreferential position, and so on. The process terminates in a finite number of steps with a term ending up in either a referential or nonreferential position, and each step is determined by the grammatical functions of constituents and the categorizations of variables.

At the beginning of this section, we criticized previous discussions of the projection problem for presupposition for remaining at a purely descriptive level. We argued that the practice discourages searching for formal explanations of how the presuppositions of complex sentence derive, compositionally, from the meanings of their constituents. We may now illustrate how even on the partial account of the general solution to the projection problem that has been presented so far we can formally explain why an initially plausible empirical hypothesis like Langendoen and Savin's cumulative hypothesis fails.

Attention to what happens in the process of making substitutions of readings for occurrences of categorized variables reveals why Langendoen and Savin's hypothesis fails in the case of sentences with opaque contexts, such as (17). Let us suppose that the lexical reading for its main verb *believe* has the form represented in (19). Let us suppose further that the syntactic structure of (17) is, roughly, that in (20), where (B), (19), (SC), and (SWF) are, respectively, the lexical readings for the substrings in (20). The two long dotted lines in (20) indicate that the reading of *Santa Claus* and the reading of *is sick with flu* will be combined with the reading of the verb *believe* in the semantic interpretation of (20). In combining these readings to form a derived reading for the verb phrase of (17), the reading of Santa Claus will be substituted for the variables in (19) that are categorized [NP, S, VP, S]. *Santa Claus* is the subject of the complement sentence and the gram-

(20)

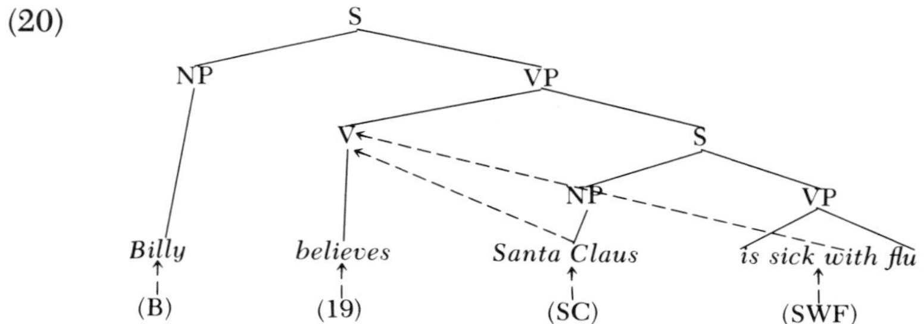

matical function [NP, S, VP, S] categorizes these variables so that their values will be the reading of the subject of the embedded sentence that is the complement of the main verb. Now, since the argument place for the predicate expressed by *is sick with flu* is referential, that is, since (16) has the presupposition that there is a Santa Claus, the combination of readings that forms a derived reading for the verb phrase of (17) lifts the reading of *Santa Claus* out of a position enclosed in heavy parentheses and substitutes it for occurrences of categorized variables in positions that are NOT enclosed in heavy parentheses. Since the final step in the semantic interpretation of (20) is simply to substitute the reading of the subject of (17) for the occurrence of the categorized variable in the topmost semantic marker in (19), no further operations are performed in connection with the other argument places of *believe.* Therefore, on the basis of (8), we predict that, although (17) presupposes the existence of some individual bearing the name *Billy,* (17) does NOT presuppose the existence of a Santa Claus (even though its complement sentence does).

The process of semantic interpretation just described is the way in which the presuppositions of sentences would be determined by the meanings of their constituents and their syntactic structure were there no interaction between occurrences of categorized variables and devices in lexical readings that remove or install heavy parentheses. But it is clearly possible for there to be operations that remove heavy parentheses, thereby transforming a referential position into a nonreferential position, and operations that install heavy parentheses, transforming a nonreferential position into a referential one.[21] Thus, we have to inquire now whether such interaction occurs in the semantic interpretation of sentences.

[21] Within the framework of semantic theory, each such transformation could be accomplished by an operator belonging to the same category of readings as the antonymy operator, an operator that makes some fixed change in the readings that fall in its scope (Katz, 1972, pp. 160–171).

It should be noted before undertaking this inquiry that we have now reduced the projection problem for presupposition to determining whether these possibilities of heavy parentheses installation and removal are empirically realized in natural languages (and if so, in what forms), since in the absence of any interaction between categorized variables and rules for introducing and deleting heavy parentheses, categorized variables remain throughout the projection process as they are lexically presented, either enclosed in heavy parentheses or unenclosed in them. We shall claim in what follows that both possibilities exist, and provide examples of each that will describe the kind of operators that remove and install parentheses.

The first possibility is the transformation of a categorized variable enclosed in heavy parentheses into one not so enclosed. Genericness is an example of a device that can dereferentialize a referential context. The verb *eats* is clearly like *chase, kill,* or *visit: eats* expresses a relation all of whose argument places are referential positions. An ordinary sentence like (21) presupposes the existence of a cow.

(21) *The cow is eating the grass.*

When the argument place of *eats* that takes agent readings falls in the scope of a generic element in the sentence, the argument place turns into a nonreferential position. This is the case with (22).

(22) *Cows eat grass (the cow eats grass).*

Sentence (22) has no presupposition about the existence of cows, since it would be true even if no cows exist. Similarly, the sentence (23) is known to be true even if black holes are not known to exist.

(23) *A black hole exerts tremendous gravity.*

Or, (24) is clearly false even though chances are that no one is perfectly virtuous.

(24) *The man of perfect virtue is deceitful when it is to his advantage.*

The truth of these sentences does not depend on the existence of referential relations because they are not about particular objects in the world.

Generic sentences are not the only presuppositionless sentences in natural languages. Hypotheticals like (25)–(27) also lack referential conditions on their statementhood.

(25) *If something is a cow, it eats grass.*

(26) *If something is a black hole, then it exerts tremendous gravity.*

(27) *If anyone is a man of perfect virtue, he is deceitful when it is to his advantage.*

These types of sentence fill a definite need in language. For both scientific and ordinary purposes, such types of sentence are needed to express assertions about possibilities that can be true or false independently of whether existential conjectures about them prove true. Scientific investigation of controversial entities like black holes, the unconscious, ether, and so on requires the formulation of true sentences about their properties in order to decide whether there is anything in the world that is such an entity.

I suspect that in other respects (see Katz, 1972, p. 178f) genericness and hypotheticality are different, although this is not part of my argument here. Generic sentences express a claim about the essential nature of some kind of entity (which may vary with whether the sentence is about a role such as president, an artifact such as a chair, or a natural kind such as cows). Hypotheticals express a claim about how things are, should a certain assumption be true. If this is correct, the hypothetical sentences (25)–(27) are not paraphrases of the generic sentences (22)–(24).

To represent the absence of referential condition on the statementhood of both generics and hypotheticals, we need an operator that serves as part of the lexical reading of syntactic genericness and of the hypothetical aspect of conditional constructions. Such an operator does not enter into the semantic interpretation of syntactic structures such as the abstract–concrete distinction or the tensed–untensed distinction, insofar as mathematical sentences like the sentence (1) with abstract noun phrases and having a timeless meaning nonetheless carry presuppositions.

(1) *The least convergent series is infinite.*

We represent the operator in the form (28):

(28) $$(M_1), \cdots, (\cdots (M_i)_{\substack{[\quad] \\ \mathbf{(}X\mathbf{)} \\ \langle\ \rangle}} \cdots), \cdots, (M_n)$$

$$\longrightarrow (M_1), \cdots (\cdots (M_i)_{\substack{[\quad] \\ X \\ \langle\ \rangle}} \cdots), \cdots, (M_n).$$

We assume it will be possible to define an appropriate notion of scope for its application. (28) operates on any reading of a constituent in its scope by simply erasing the heavy parentheses in the reading. Such an operator accounts for the argument places of *eats*, being referential positions without claiming that sentences like (22) have presuppositions. We need only assume that the scope of the operator includes the argument place in which the agent reading occurs.

The question of characterizing the proper notion of scope here is both complex and important. Normally, the scope of a syntactic symbol is the entire constituent it labels, but in this case scope has to be defined so as also to include anaphoric constituents. As an example, consider (29).

(29) *If Jack has children, then all of* $\left\{\begin{matrix} \textit{Jack's children} \\ \textit{them} \end{matrix}\right\}$ *are bald.*

This kind of sentence was presented by Morgan (1969) as a counterexample to the Langendoen–Savin solution to the projection problem for presupposition. Morgan argued that the sentence in the consequent presupposed that there are children one of whose parents is Jack, but that, contrary to the Langendoen–Savin solution, the entire conditional sentence does not presuppose their existence. The interesting question is which step in the compositional process by which the meaning of (29) is obtained blocks the presupposition of the subordinate clause from becoming a presupposition of the sentence.[22]

The explanation we propose is that it is blocked by an application of (28) to the heavy parentheses in the reading of the consequent sentence. First, consider the conditional formulations used in (25)–(27). Such forms express what would be the case were some possibility to be an actuality. This is accomplished by taking the sentence appearing in the antecedent of a conditional to state the hypothesis we are asked to assume in the assertion. Thus, (25) asks us to assume the existence of cows and (29) to assume the existence of Jack's children.

Just this hypothetical element is lost when the meaning of conditionals in natural language is represented in quantification theory using material implication. The proof of this is an old philosophical chestnut. Suppose someone were to claim that if God exists then so does the devil and you wish to deny the claim. Suppose, further, that their claim is construed on the basis of the notion of material implication, that is, (*God exists*) ⊃ (*the devil exists*). Your denial would take the form ~ ((*God exists*) ⊃ (*the devil exists*)), and since this implies

[22] A version of this explanation appears in Katz and Langendoen (1976, pp. 6–8, 15–16).

that God exists, in stating your denial you commit yourself to God's existence. This commitment results from the fact that use of the material conditional eliminates the hypothetical element in the claim and denial. The absurdity of the commitment shows that such an element had been present.

We might express the effect of this hypothetical element by saying that it acts as a block for truth conditions of the component clauses of conditionals in just the way that opacity acts as a block for presuppositions of component clauses of complex sentences like (17). Without trying to say how this hypothetical element blocks such truth conditions, we can observe that conditionals are the inverse of generics. Whereas in generics the presupposition is wiped out but the truth conditions remain, in the antecedent of a conditional the truth condition is wiped out but the presupposition remains [for example, that the noun *Jack* refers in a use of (29)].

Second, note that the subject of the consequent sentence in (29) bears some kind of anaphoric or inclusional semantic relation to a component of the truth conditions that have been wiped out. It is not quite right to say that the subject of the consequent sentence of (29) is syntactically anaphoric to the predicate nominal in the antecedent of this sentence, since aside from the syntactic questions that arise, sentences like (30) would seem to be exactly parallel to sentences like (29).

(30) *If Jack is the father of spinsters, then all of Jack's unmarried adult daughters are bald.*

This semantic relation, properly specified, will provide an extension of the scope of (28) that explains why sentences like (29) do not presuppose the existence of the designata or referring terms in their consequent sentences. We can make the existence of such semantic relation the condition under which (29) applies to the reading representing such terms and removes the heavy parentheses enclosing them.[23] The reading of *Jack's children* in the reading of the consequent (29) has its heavy parentheses removed, and we predict that (29) will be a counterexample to the Langendoen–Savin hypothesis that the presupposition of a complex sentence includes the presuppositions of its clauses.

[23] This might be done as a universal condition on semantic components, which says that if some rule wipes out a subreading r_i of a sentence R, and there is another subreading of R, r_j, which bears the appropriate inclusional semantic relation to r_i, then any erasure operation of the semantic component that can apply to r_j does.

The complexities to be encountered in attempting to complete the statement of (28) include at least the further consideration that this operator might well have to be stated as a context-sensitive rule. We want to supplement (9) with a definition that allows generic sentences to make statements (that is, to be either true or false) independently of having a satisfied presupposition. Suppose we were to reformulate (9) so that it says that the presupposition expresses the condition under which nongenerics make a statement, and that statementhood obtains in cases where the presupposition is satisfied or a proposition has no presupposition. What would we then say about the propositions, in their generic sense, expressed by sentences like (31)?

(31) *A married bachelor is a bachelor, A round square is round,* . . .

Structurally, they are both analytic and contradictory: If they have a truth value, they are both true and false. Since they are generic, our reformulation of (9) in its present form would accord them a truth value, and our characterization of statementhood would have the consequence that such sentences are true and false.

There are various ways to avoid this consequence. One is to rewrite the definitions so that genericness does not always imply statementhood. Another way, which ties in better with other constructions in semantic theory, is to make the operator (28) context-sensitive by restricting its application to heavy parentheses that enclose only readings representing consistent terms. That is, we prevent (28) from applying to readings appearing in term positions that contain two semantic markers from the same antonymous *n*-tuple (Katz, 1972, pp. 157–171). The fact that the heavy parentheses remain in the reading of sentences like (31) provides a solution to the difficulty, since, on the basis of them, the propositions of such sentences will be marked INDETERMINABLE, that is, semantically incapable of making a statement (Katz, 1972, pp. 144–148).

This context restriction has systematic relations that justify our choosing this way of avoiding the problem. If we were to spell out the lexical reading for *believe* given in (19), it would be necessary to write it with a schema that moves each reading R inside heavy parentheses within the reading of the complement sentence into a distinct component reading of the full sentence (where such a component reading represents the predication that the referent of the subject of *believe* thinks that there is something that is the appropriate designatum of R). In (32), the schema would introduce one such component reading, whereas in (33) it would introduce two such component readings.

(32) *John believes that Sue wants a unicorn.*

(33) *John believes that Sue phoned Ralph.*

(34) *John believes that a cow eats grass.*

Now in terms of the treatment of generics, (34) (taking the complement in its generic sense) would have no such component reading, which is clearly right. But on the basis of our context restriction on the rule (28), a belief sentence in which a sentence like (31) appears as the complement of the verb is represented as reporting someone's "impossible belief," namely, that a proposition that can be neither true nor false (for logical reasons) is true. In such cases, it seems right to take the belief sentence as entailing that the referent of its subject thinks that the impossible object exists, and this provides further justification for the context restriction previously discussed. With this restriction, the heavy parentheses are not removed from around readings representing contradictory concepts, so that the schema referred to above will provide a component reading in the reading of the full sentence that represents the belief of the referent of its subject that the (contradictory) concept has a non-null extension.[24]

We now turn to the possibility of introducing heavy parentheses that enclose a categorized variable that had no heavy parentheses in the lexical reading from which it originated. This case represents the last possibility to be considered in formally characterizing the projection problem for presupposition. Once we have determined whether there is a rule of heavy parentheses introduction parallel to the rule (28) for heavy parentheses elimination, we complete our characterization of the solution to the projection problem for presupposition. Details about what formal devices are used in what lexical readings remain to be worked out.

Although the reading of the subject of the complement sentence in (35) is a nonreferential term and (35) does not presuppose the existence of a king of France, the reading of the subject of the complement sentence in (36) is referential and (36) does presuppose the existence of a king of France.

(35) *Sue believes that the king of France is a philosopher.*

[24] I am indebted to D. T. Langendoen and Robert Fiengo for their help in working out the context restriction and applications discussed here. It is worth noting that this interpretation of belief sentences with contradictory concepts appearing as terms in the propositional object of belief is an example of the ordering of semantic rules, namely that these rules operate where applicable in a projection process that proceeds from bottom to top of phrase markers.

(36) *Sue believes of the king of France that the king of France is a philosopher.*

Sentence (36) is the kind of sentence that philosophers and logicians use to express what they allege to be a transparent sense of *believes*.[25]

We can account for such referentialization of the subject of the complement of *believes* and similar opaque verbs by making the rule (37) the reading of phrases like *of* NP where the NP is the subject of the complement sentence.[26]

(37)
$$(M_1), \cdots, (\cdots (M_i)_{\substack{[\quad] \\ \boldsymbol{(}X\boldsymbol{)} \\ \langle\ \rangle}} \cdots), \cdots, (M_n)$$
$$\longrightarrow (M_1), \cdots, (\cdots (M_i)_{\substack{[\quad] \\ X \\ \langle\ \rangle}} \cdots), \cdots, (M_n)$$

There seems to be good independent reason to treat (37) as the semantic representation of an important component of the meaning of the preposition in *of the so-and-so* phrases, since such phrases mean the same, or very close to the same, as phrases like *about the so-and-so, concerning the so-and-so,* and so on, which function to specify the object(s) of which some predication will be made.[27] Evidence for taking the scope of the lexical reading of such phrases to be the verb is that their free occurrence at different positions in a sentence like (38) makes it reasonable to treat them as adverbial phrases.

(38) *Mary believes the worst things of Sue.*

(39) *Of Sue, Mary believes the worst things.*

Moreover, since the noun phrase of such prepositional phrases is syntactically identified with the subject of the embedded sentence, as (40) shows,

(40) **Sue believes of them that he is a philosopher.*

the operation of heavy parentheses introduction can be restricted to the categorized variable whose values are readings of the subject of the embedded sentence.

[25] Or, *The king of France is such that Sue believes that the king of France is a philosopher.* See Quine, (1960, p. 147).

[26] Note that (37) enters into the semantic interpretation of constructions like NP *is such that* . . . in sentences like the example in Footnote 25.

[27] I owe this observation to D. T. Langendoen.

5. FACTIVE PRESUPPOSITION AND ITS CRITICS

Factive presuppositions are usually associated with sentences like (41).

(41) *Boris regrets* (*remembers, realizes, knows,* etc.) *that he made an appointment with the dentist.*

They arise from "factive verbs" and take the form of a requirement that the sentence appearing as the complement of a factive verb be true. Our interest in factive presupposition stems from whether it can be brought under the treatment of Fregean presupposition outlined in the previous section.

The formulation of factive presupposition proposed in *Semantic Theory* (pp. 135–136) was that a proposition P is presupposed by a sentence S just in case P follows from both S and its denial $\sim S$. This formulation was thought to be an acceptable test for presupposition in general, so that, insofar as both (41) and its denial imply that Boris made an appointment with the dentist, the formulation entails that (41) presupposes that Boris made an appointment with the dentist. But I now do not think that this formulation is an acceptable general test for presupposition (Katz, 1973), and consequently, the fact that both (41) and its denial imply that Boris made an appointment with the dentist is no longer grounds for me to claim that there are factive presuppositions. Thus, one argument for the existence of this kind of presupposition disappears. But my intuition is still that the truth of the complement sentence in a case like (41) is the condition under which the sentence makes a statement (asserts something true or false). It seems reasonable to say that factive presuppositions are the same sort of things as Fregean presuppositions: Just as there has to be a king of France for some assertion about the king of France to be true or false, so there has to be a state of affairs in which Boris made an appointment with the dentist for some assertion about it to be true or false.

However, Harnish (1972) and Wilson (1975) have raised doubts about the notion of factive presupposition by constructing two arguments against it. We could not simply accept their arguments and restrict the notion of presupposition to Fregean presupposition because, to the degree that it is reasonable to think that factive presupposition can be brought under Fregean presupposition, it is also reasonable to think that if factive presupposition has to be abandoned, then so does Fregean presupposition.

We should thus attempt to save factive presupposition. I will try to show that both arguments fail to eliminate factive presupposition, and I will try to show how factive presupposition can be treated together with the standard Fregean presupposition.

The first attack on factive presupposition is Harnish's argument that the notion leads to absurd consequences. He argues as follows. Assume that the relation between the sentences (42) and (43) is that the former is the logical presupposition of the latter.

(42) *Snails exceed the speed of light.*

(43) *Einstein knew that snails exceed the speed of light.*

Since it is false that snails exceed the speed of light, (43) must be neither true nor false. But, by the same token, (44), the denial of (43), is also neither true or false.

(44) *Einstein did not know that snails exceed the speed of light.*

We may thus infer that (45) is neither true nor false.

(45) *Einstein knew and Einstein did not know that snails exceed the speed of light.*

Sentence (45) is a contradiction and hence false, and therefore, we arrive at the absurdity that (45) is false and not false. We must therefore reject the notion of factive presupposition.

This argument seems convincing until we realize that its plausibility rests entirely on adopting an assumption that no consistent presuppositionalist can accept. Harnish is arguing against a view of presupposition that explicitly denies his assumption that (45) is a contradiction and hence false. The consistent presuppositionalist will say that (45) is not a statement at all because its presupposition (42) is false. There is no absurdity, then, because (45) is no more a contradiction than the assertion that the present king of France is both bald and not bald.[28]

The second argument (due originally to Harnish, but found in essentially the same form in Wilson) runs as follows. It is clearly the case that (46) implies (47).

(46) *Richard III did not commit murder.*

(47) *Historians do not (cannot) know that Richard III committed murder.*

[28] I am indebted to Yuji Nishiyama for pointing out this fallacy (see Nishiyama, 1975, pp. 55–93).

Now assume that Richard III did not commit murder. It follows that (47) is true. But, then, the falsity of the presupposition of (47) is compatible with the truth of the sentence (47), contrary to the presuppositionalist position.

This argument commits a fallacy by equivocating between external and internal negation.[29] The interpretation of the premise of the argument under which the premise is true is not the one under which it implies the conclusion, and the interpretation under which the premise implies the conclusion is not the one under which the premise is true. The premise of the argument, that is, the conditional *If (46), then (47)*, can be accepted as true only when the occurrence of negation in the consequent is external negation. This is to say, the sentence (48) cannot be true unless Richard III committed murder, but there is no reason to concede that (48) is false if Richard III did not commit murder.

(48) *Historians know (can know) that Richard III committed murder.*

[Presuppositionalists take the assertion of (47) to be that the relation 'believes on adequate evidential grounds' (or something like it) holds between historians and the state of affairs, so that (48) is false in case the state of affairs of Richard III having committed murder obtains and historians either do not believe that it does or fail to have adequate evidence for thinking it does.] But reading the negation as external negation makes the argument irrelevant to the controversy about factive presupposition, because presuppositionalists can accept the truth of (47) in the form (49).

(49) *It is not the case that historians know (can know) that Richard III committed murder* [that is, (48) is either false or has no truth value].

On the other hand, if the negation in (48) is internal negation, that is, (47) says that it is false that (48), then there is no reason for a presuppositionalist to grant the truth of the premise that is, the conditional *If* (46), *then* (47). The point is again the same. Therefore, either the premise is true but the troublesome conclusion does not follow, or the conclusion follows but from a premise begs the question by assuming the falsehood of the position that the argument is intended to refute.

To treat factive and nonfactive presupposition within a common

[29] External negation is paraphrasable as *It is not the case that* S which is true in case S is false or S has no truth value. The external negation of S says that S is in the complement of the true sentences. Internal negation is paraphrasable as *It is false that* S. A sentence of the form X *is not* (= internal negation) Y is thus true just in case X *is* Y is false.

framework, it is necessary to recognize that factive verbs do not form a natural semantic class but are defined in contrast to nonfactive verbs. Standard examples of nonfactive verbs include *suppose, assert, allege, claim, believe, conjecture, intimate,* and so on.[30] Sentences with these verbs as the main verb never have presuppositions, clauses of which are determined by aspects of the meaning of the complement sentence. Standard examples of factive verbs include *regret, know, remember, realize, be aware of, resent, surprise, deplore,* and so on. Factives are thus definable as verbs such that sentences with them as main verbs have presuppositions, SOME clauses of which are determined by aspects of the meaning of the complement sentence. But, the class of factives (and that of nonfactives) is not a class whose members belong to it because of their common semantic structure. We have already explained the structure underlying the nonfactivity of *believe;* we can provide an explanation of the different structure underlying the nonfactivity of *assert, claim,* and so on, in terms of the performative nature of these verbs (Katz, 1977a, pp. 218–219).

We now turn to factive verbs. Here the statementhood requirement is the existence of some particular state of affairs, roughly, that the proposition expressed by the complement sentence describe an actual state of affairs. The propositional content of the complement sentence functions as a referential term in essentially the manner of ordinary Fregean presuppositions. In a sentence like *Nixon regrets taping conversations,* there are two terms, one referring to the agent and one referring to the state of affairs. These terms pick out the things that the sentence is about, and the assertion made in the use of such a sentence is true just in case these things bear the relation to one another.

Given that the notation of heavy parentheses is not restricted to readings of concepts, it is natural to use the notation to represent the regret type of factive. The use of this notation is illustrated with the highly simplified lexical reading (50) for the verb *regret,* where

(50)

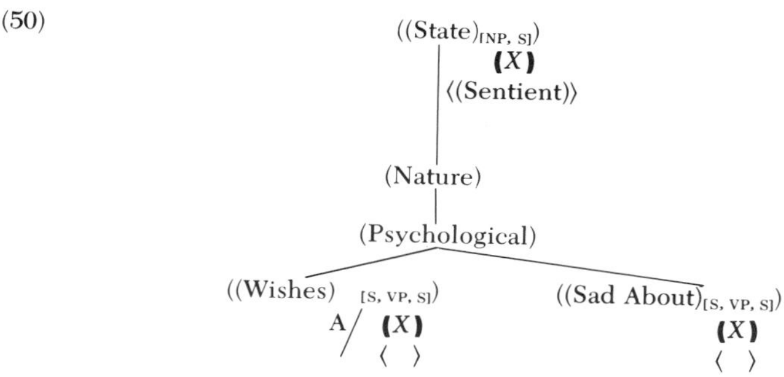

[30] The term FACTIVE comes from Kirparsky and Kirparsky (1970).

the symbol A/ is the antonymy operator. The semantic marker labeling the terminal node of the leftmost branch in (50) is a predicate function that says that the agent wishes that the event described in the complement did not occur.

A sentence like (51) does not (on the standard analysis) presuppose that the

(51) *John knows that the child laughed.*

complement sentence describes some state of affairs about which the sentence as a whole predicates something (in the sense in which a regret sentence predicates that the agent is sad about that state of affairs). This is supported by the observation of Kirparsky and Kirparsky (1970):

> There are some exceptions to this second half of our generalization. Verbs like *know, realize,* though semantically factive, are syntactically non-factive, so that we cannot say **I know the fact that John is here,* **I know John's being here,* whereas the propositional constructions are acceptable: *I know him to be here* [p. 146].

Rather, in the case of sentences like (51), there is a truth condition to the effect that the proposition expressed by the complement sentence is true. Accordingly, the only contribution that the meaning of the complement sentence makes to the presupposition of the whole sentence is a clause requiring that each referring term in the proposition expressed by the complement sentence designate. This can be represented by constructing the lexical reading of *know* so that heavy parentheses in the reading of the complement sentence are not removed in the projection process.[31] We thus restate the structural definition of presupposition in the form (52).

(52) The presupposition of a proposition *P* is the requirement that every reading enclosed in heavy parentheses appearing in the reading of *P* have its appropriate referent.

We note that factive sentences generally may have generic complement sentences, for example, (53), (54), and (55).

(53) *Biologists know that the owl is nocturnal.*

(54) *Bill is surprised that the owl is nocturnal.*

[31] As they would be in the case of sentences in which the main verb is *believe* instead of *know*.

(55) *May regrets that the owl is nocturnal.*

In the "know" type case, this is handled automatically, since the absence of referential terms in generic propositions means that they contribute nothing to the presupposition of the whole sentence. Hence, (53) presupposes only the existence of some non-null set of biologists. On the other hand, the "regret" type case is different, insofar as the logical reading for *regret* contains categorized variables enclosed with heavy parentheses for which readings from the complement sentence will be substituted. The simplest way of handling this situation is to promote (28) from its present status as a lexical reading for a syntactic feature to the status of a clause of the projection rule. To do this, we shall have to specify conditions for its application in the semantic interpretation of sentences, one of which will be genericness, where the rule will apply as it did when it was a lexical reading of this element. Another condition for the application of this rule will be the occurrence of pairs consisting of a categorized variable and a generic constituent satisfying its categorization. In such cases, (28) operates to wipe out heavy parentheses enclosing the categorized variable. This accounts for *regret* type cases such as (55), because the rule wipes out the heavy parentheses in the lexical reading of the main verb enclosing the variables categorized for readings of the embedded sentence.

REFERENCES

Donnellan, K. Speaking of nothing. *Philosophical Review*, 1974, *83*, 3–31.

Erwin, E., Kleiman, L., and Zembach, E. The historical theory of reference. (Forthcoming)

Frege, G. On sense and reference. In *Translations from the philosophical writings of Gottlob Frege*. P. Geach and M. Black (Eds.), Oxford: Basil Blackwell, 1952. Pp. 56–78.

Geach, P. Russell's theory of descriptions. In *Philosophy and analysis*. New York: Philosophical Library, 1954, Pp. 32–36.

Harnish, R. M. Studies in logic and language. Doctoral dissertation, Massachusetts Institute of Technology, Cambridge, Massachusetts, 1972.

Herzberger, H. Paradoxes of grounding in semantics. *The Journal of Philosophy*, 1970, *17*, 145–167.

Herzberger, H., and Katz, J. J. The concept of truth for natural languages. Unpublished manuscript, Cambridge, 1967.

Karttunen, L. Presuppositions of compound sentences. *Linguistic Inquiry*, 1973, *4*, 169–193.

Katz, J. J. *The underlying reality of language and its philosophical import*. New York: Harper and Row, 1971.

Katz, J. J. *Semantic theory*. New York: Harper and Row, 1972.

Katz, J. J. *Propositional structure and illocutionary force*. New York: Crowell, 1977. (a)

Katz, J. J. A proper theory of names. *Philosophical Studies*, 1977, *31*, 1–80. (b)

Katz, J. J. The theory of semantic representation. *Erkenntnis*, 1978, *13*, 63–110.

Katz, J. J. Chomsky on meaning. *Language*. (To appear.)

Katz, J. J. On defining the notion of "presupposition". *Linguistic Inquiry*, 1973, 4, 256–260.

Katz, F., and Katz., J. J. Is necessity the mother of intension? *The Philosophical Review*, 1977, *86*, 70–96.

Katz, J. J., and Langendoen, D. T. Pragmatics and presupposition. *Language*, 1976, *52*, 1–17.

Kirparsky, P., and Kirparsky, C. Fact. In *Progress in Linguistics*. The Hague: Mouton, 1970, Pp. 143–173.

Kripke, S. Outline of a theory of truth. *The Journal of Philosophy*, 1975, *72*, 1975, 690–716.

Kuroda, S.-Y. Geach and Katz on presupposition. *Foundations of Language*, 1974, *12*, 195.

Langendoen, D. T., and Savin, H. The projection problem for presupposition. In C. J. Fillmore and D. T. Langendoen (Eds.), *Studies in linguistic semantics*. New York: Holt, 1971, Pp. 55–62.

Morgan, J. L. On the treatment of presupposition in transformational grammar. In *Papers from the Fifth Regional Meeting*. Chicago: Chicago Linguistic Society, 1969, Pp. 167–177.

Nishiyama, Y. *The structure of propositions*. Tokyo: Keio University Press, 1975.

Quine, W. V. O. *Word and object*. Cambridge, Massachusetts: M.I.T. Press, 1960.

Russell, B. *Introduction to mathematical philosophy*. London: Allen and Unwin, 1919.

Strawson, P. F. On referring. *Mind*, 1950, *59*, 320–324. [Reprinted in J. F. Rosenberg and C. Travis (Eds.), *Readings in the philosophy of language*. Englewood Cliffs, New Jersey: Prentice-Hall, 1971, Pp. 175–194.]

Wilson, D. *Presuppositions and non-truth-conditional semantics*. Doctoral dissertation, Massachusetts Institute of Technology, Cambridge, Massachusetts, 1975.

ON PRESUPPOSITIONS IN COMPLEX SENTENCES[1]

Traugott Schiebe
University of Stockholm

1. INTRODUCTION

What is wrong with (1b) as opposed to (1a)?

(1) a. $_{S_1}$[*It is raining*] *and* $_{S_2}$[*it will not stop raining until tomorrow*].
b. *It will not stop raining until tomorrow and it is raining.*

A very simple description of the relevant difference between (1a) and (1b) might run as follows: Someone who utters a sentence like S_2 in (1a) normally presupposes that the listener knows that it is raining. When uttering S_2 in the context of (1a), the speaker is entitled to presuppose that it is raining because, by uttering S_1, he has just informed the listener of this fact. That is, in (1a) the speaker first tells the listener something that he then presupposes. In (1b), however, the speaker first presupposes something that he then tells the listener, which of course is an odd thing to do.

[1] This chapter presents and elaborates some main ideas in Schiebe (1975), to which I refer the reader for further discussion. For the sake of simplicity of presentation I am going to use English examples, although the views presented here are based on the analysis of German and Swedish examples, which I can judge with greater confidence than I can their English counterparts. I should be surprised, however, if the English examples turned out to behave in a radically different way.

Syntax and Semantics, Volume 11: Presupposition

ISBN 0-12-613511-8

Now compare (1) with (2):

(2) a. *Is it true that it is raining and that it will not stop raining until tomorrow?*
b. *Is it true that it will not stop raining until tomorrow and that it is raining?*

The parallel between (1) and (2) is obvious. Essentially the same thing seems to be going on in both cases. But if so, then certain embarrassing questions such as the following arise: Does it really make sense to say that a speaker who utters (2a) tells the listener something by uttering the first *that*-clause, something that is then presupposed in the second *that*-clause? What would that be? Obviously, the speaker cannot be said either to assert or to presuppose that it is raining, because that belongs to what he is asking about. So what then is first asserted and then presupposed in (2a)? There does not seem to be any immediately obvious answer, and the difficulty of answering such questions might even lead one to suspect that there is no real parallel between (1) and (2) after all or that the straightforward description of (1) just given is mistaken in some important respect. On the other hand, one could try to take intuitions about (1) and (2) seriously and to investigate the consequences of such a position. That is what I have tried to do in Schiebe (1975) (henceforth PZS). Although my results are in part very preliminary, they seem to me to be rather encouraging. I thus believe that there is a plausible way of looking at cases like (1) and (2) according to which it does make sense to say that something is first asserted and then presupposed in (2a) and which seems to allow one to describe the behavior of presuppositions in complex sentences in a fairly natural and adequate way. The following informal answer to the embarrassing questions just mentioned may perhaps give a preliminary idea of one aspect of the approach I advocate: Someone who utters (2a)—and presumably also someone who utters (1a)—tells a little story, as it were, asking whether the story is true—asserting that it is true, in the case of (1a). Thus, in (2a), the speaker does not assert or presuppose that it is true in reality that it is raining, but he does first assert and then presuppose that it is true in the "world" of his little story, that is, the imagined situation that he is describing in his story.

In Section 2, I shall outline my approach more strictly. Then, in Section 3 I shall present some central arguments for my position. In Section 4 further aspects of my approach and the main features of its formalization will be presented. In Section 5 I shall mention some points where my present views differ from or go beyond what I said in PZS.

Finally, in Section 6 I shall point out an important theoretical implication of my approach.

2. PRESENTATION OF THE APPROACH

2.1. Statement of the Main Theses

The central question in connection with presuppositions in complex sentences may be formulated as follows: How are the presuppositions of a complex sentence determined by relevant characteristics of the presuppositional constructions that it contains? Another way of stating the main problem can be found in Langendoen and Savin (1971) and Karttunen (1973), where it is said that the question is how the presuppositions of a complex sentence are determined by the presuppositions of the clauses it contains. In a certain sense that would also be a correct formulation, but those who have used it seem to have assumed that the presuppositions of a certain embedded sentence are the same as those of a corresponding independent sentence, and that is in general not the case, as we shall see.

My discussion will mainly be based on the following pragmatic concept of presupposition[2]: That a certain linguistic expression with a certain meaning presupposes A shall mean that a speaker who wants to use this expression with this meaning in a normal, correct, and sincere way must take A for granted. That he takes A for granted shall mean that he believes A to be true and feels entitled in relation to the listener to consider A something that is not at issue for the moment and need not be pointed out but may rather serve as a starting point in formulating the real issue. Normally, the speaker is considered to be right in taking something for granted if the listener knows it or at least does not find it very surprising. The set of assumptions that correspond to what the speaker is taking for granted at a certain moment will be referred to as the CONTEXT at that moment. Thus, mainly following Karttunen (1973), we can say that, in determining what the pragmatic presuppositions of a given expression with a given meaning are, we thereby define a class of contexts in which it could be sincerely uttered.

We shall concentrate on "classical" presuppositional constructions

[2] This does not imply that I deny the usefulness of certain other concepts of presupposition, such as logical or semantic concepts, but only that these other concepts represent points of view that are too restricted for the present purpose.

like aspectuals, factives, and definite descriptions. Our main interest will be in presuppositions that are somehow directly associated with the content that the speaker wants to convey at a certain moment rather than with the means he employs in that situation in trying to make clear to the listener what this content is. Thus, whereas we are interested in existential presuppositions, we shall, for instance, not be concerned here with the conditions under which persons, times, and places may be referred to by words like *I*, *now*, and *here*, respectively. Things like topic and comment will not be discussed either, although they no doubt are of great importance for the understanding of presuppositional phenomena. We shall try to minimize their influence on the present discussion by means of appropriate indications of stress in the examples used.[3]

An important aspect of pragmatic presuppositions is time: When is what is presupposed presupposed? As we saw in (1) and (2), it seems that the same thing can be first asserted and then presupposed during the utterance of one and the same complex sentence. Thus, we cannot simply regard the pragmatic presuppositions of a sentence as conditions on the context at the time of the utterance of the sentence as a whole. Rather, we shall have to differentiate between the various contexts corresponding to different times of utterance of different parts of the sentence and ask to which of these contexts a certain presupposition relates. In other words, we shall have to take into consideration that the context changes during the utterance of a sentence and that this change at least in part is due to the very utterance of the sentence.

An aspect of presuppositions perhaps still more important than the WHEN aspect is the WHAT aspect: What exactly is presupposed at a certain moment? As we saw already in connection with (2a), it seems necessary to recognize the possibility that what is presupposed is not necessarily assumed to be true in reality but may instead be assumed to be true in some other "world," for how else could one explain the fact that the speaker seems to be taking the truth of *It is raining* for granted in some sense, when he utters the second embedded clause in (2a), although he obviously does not take it for granted that it is really raining? That some notion such as that of "worlds" different from reality is needed to explain presuppositional phenomena in complex sentences has already been argued by Morgan (1969), and I believe that what I mean by "world" is in certain respects similar to what he had in

[3] I believe that there are several factors that may affect, or may seem to affect, the presuppositional character of presuppositional constructions and that must be kept track of if confusion is to be avoided. For some discussion see PZS and Schiebe (to appear).

mind. I have already indicated how I want to use "world," by talking about the "world of a story" in connection with (2a). Indeed, I think that "world," as I use it, has roughly the same range of meanings as have words like "world" and "situation" in everyday speech when we use them to talk about fiction, art, and imagined situations.

Strictly speaking, I shall use two different concepts of "world,"[4] neither of which is exactly the same as that of "possible world" in the sense of modal logic. One of them more specifically covers what I referred to as "the world of a story" in connection with (2a). In order to distinguish it from the other concept and from the possible worlds of modal logic I shall refer to it as a "model of a possible world" or, simply, "model world." In general, a certain model world may be said to define a certain set of possible worlds, namely, those which are compatible with what is stipulated to be true in the model world. While the identity of a possible world may be thought of as being determined by a complete description of what exists and is true in it, in a model world most things are left unspecified and are regarded as irrelevant to the definition of the corresponding set of possible worlds. Perhaps one could say that the identity of a certain model world is primarily determined "historically," that is, by the occasion of its creation. At any rate, we shall assume that the identity of the linguistically relevant model worlds that we are interested in here is determined token-reflexively, that is, that the identity of a certain such world is determined by the speech event in connection with which the world is introduced, created by imagination. In principle, each abstract sentence structure can be said to be associated with its own model world, namely, the imagined situation that is described when the speaker utters the corresponding surface structure expression.

The other concept of world, the one I shall be referring to when I use "world" without further qualifications, is more comprehensive and covers cases like "the world of a person." That something is "true in Peter's world," for instance, shall mean that Peter believes it to be true. I also want to be able to say that an individual or a fact is taken primarily to exist in Peter's world or to "originate" from Peter's world. By this I mean that the individual or fact in question is considered as something that may have come into being in Peter's head, so to speak, by virtue of what he believes to be the case. If something exists in Peter's world without originating from it, it must originate from somewhere else, usually from reality. It is then a real individual or fact, which Peter is acquainted with. Thus, a world in this sense is con-

[4] In PZS, I did not distinguish between these two concepts consequently enough.

ceived as some kind of REGION or SPHERE that can be the provenance of entities like individuals and facts. The real world and, when taken in isolation, model worlds are likewise assumed to be worlds in this sense.

As for the relation between the model world aspect and the "sphere world" aspect of presuppositions, I assume that an individual or a fact that is presupposed to originate from a certain model world as seen in isolation at the same time is taken to represent a certain other entity which is presupposed to originate from a certain world that is not a model world, if the function of the model world in the whole utterance is considered.

These remarks about "world" are admittedly rather vague, but I hope they will suffice for the moment.

We are now in a position to state the following main theses:

(3) a. A presuppositional construction PC in a sentence S presupposes that the truth of a certain proposition (or perhaps rather the existence of an entity such as an individual or a fact) relative to a certain world (or certain worlds) belongs to what is assumed in the context at the time of the utterance of PC. If one disregards the question of how the context is influenced by the utterance of S, one may simply say that the presuppositions of S are the presuppositions of the different individual presuppositional constructions of S.

b. If the influence of the utterance of S on the context is taken into account, the question of the presuppositions of complex sentences must be formulated in the following way: What conditions must be met by the initial context of S if, in an otherwise unchanged situation, the influence of the utterance of S on the context is to have the effect that, for every moment *t* in the course of the utterance of S, the presuppositions relating to *t* will be fulfilled?[5]

[5] An approach that is in certain respects similar to (3b) is to be found in an important paper by Karttunen (1974). However, one important difference between Karttunen (1974) and the approach I advocate is clear already from (3), namely, that I relate presuppositions to the times of utterance of the presuppositional constructions and not to LOCAL CONTEXTS defined by constituent sentences, as Karttunen does. Further differences will emerge in the rest of the present chapter. Cf. also the criticism of Karttunen (1974) in the Appendix of PZS.

Accordingly, the following central questions will have to be asked:

(4) a. How is the presupposition of a certain presuppositional construction determined by its position in the whole sentence uttered?
b. What mechanisms determine how the context changes during the utterance of the sentence due to the utterance of the sentence?

2.2. Preliminary Discussions

Before going on to discuss the general view just presented I would like to make (3) and (4) more concrete by demonstrating how I want to answer the questions in (4) with respect to some examples.[6]

2.2.1. Presupposition Determination within a Sentence. Condition A and Condition B

Consider (5).

(5) $\left\{\begin{array}{l}\textit{Mary believes}\\ \textit{Does Mary believe}\end{array}\right\}$ $_{S_1}$[*that Peter is in London now*] *and* $_{S_2}$[*that he will never leave England again*].

Let us start with Question (4a) and concentrate on the presuppositional construction with *leave . . . again* in S_2. The meaning of S_2 is such that the proposition, the truth of which relative to some world(s) constitutes what is presupposed at the time of the utterance of the presuppositional construction, can be said to be *Peter is in England.* As for the worlds with respect to which this is assumed to be true, there is a fourfold ambiguity here, depending on whether the stay, the duration of which is talked about in S_2, is taken to be a real stay, a stay that exists according to Mary's beliefs, a stay that according to Mary exists if Peter is in London, or a stay that does in fact exist if Peter is in London. Thus, we must distinguish between four different presuppositional readings, the main difference between them having to do with whether the fact described by *Peter is in England* is taken to originate from the world described in (6a), (6b), (6c), or (6d).

(6) a. the real world
b. Mary's world in the real world
c. the world-of-the-truth-of-S_1 in Mary's world in the real world
d. the world-of-the-truth-of-S_1 in the real world

[6] The following analyses differ somewhat from those I gave of similar examples in PZS.

Let us call the corresponding readings A, B, C, and D, respectively. In order to make it easier to see the differences between them I would like to point out that (7) has two different presuppositional readings, which are similar to the readings A and B of (5) in that the presupposed fact is taken to originate from (6a) and (6b), respectively:

(7) *Does Mary believe that Peter will never léave England again and that he is in London now?*

In a situation in which neither reading A nor reading B is possible because it is not assumed either that Peter is in England or that Mary believes that he is, the most natural reading of (5) is D, since it is generally known that London is in England. To get reading C one could imagine a situation in which speaker and listener are convinced that London is not in England and that Mary erroneously believes that London is in England. In all four readings of (5), and thus not only in C, the presupposed fact is assumed to exist in the "lowest" world involved, that is, in (6c). In A, B, and D, where this is not the world of origin, the fact in question is thus presupposed to exist both in the world it originates from and in the lowest world (6c). Moreover, in the case of A the presupposed fact is assumed to exist in world (6b), because it cannot, so to speak, get down into (6c) from (6a) without passing (6b). That means that in reading A it is presupposed that Mary knows that Peter is in England. In summary, the four readings presuppose the existence of the respective fact in sequences of hierarchically related worlds in the following manner:

A: (6a), (6b), (6c)
B: (6b), (6c)
C: (6c)
D: (6d), (6c)

What presuppositional readings are possible here of course depends on what constructions contain the presuppositional expression. That is, it has to do with the fact that the expression with *leave* in S_2 in (5) is contained in the complement of *believe* and in the conjunction with S_1. In Section 4, I shall present a formalism that enables one to determine the presuppositional possibilities, given the constructions that contain the presuppositional expression in question.

In addition to the kind of presupposition just discussed—which we will henceforth call Type A—there is another presuppositional condition associated with the construction with *leave* in S_2 in (5), a condition of a type that we will refer to as Type B.[7] Whichever of the read-

[7] In PZS I did not distinguish between Conditions A and B consequently enough.

ings A, B, C, and D the presuppositional construction is used in, there is also the presupposition that the model world primarily being described at the moment of utterance, that is, the model world of S_2, functions in the structure of (5) in such a way that the fact presupposed in the reading in question may be expected to appear in it. We shall have more to say about this aspect of presuppositions.

2.2.2. Contextual Change by an Utterance of a Sentence. More on Condition B

We now turn to Question (4b), concentrating as before on the presuppositional construction with *leave* in S_2 in (5). We are thus going to consider how the context changes during the utterance of (5) and what, accordingly, the initial context must be like if the change is to have the effect that the presupposition associated with the construction in S_2 is fulfilled when the construction is uttered. The main aspects of what happens may be roughly described as follows. When a speaker who utters (5) has reached the beginning of the complement of *believe*, it is clear from what he has said so far that the complement is going to express something the truth of which in relation to what Mary believes to be true is at issue. This means that, when describing the model world of the complement, the speaker may take for granted whatever it is taken for granted that Mary believes to be true. Moreover, having characterized the model world by uttering S_1 and going on to utter S_2, the speaker may take for granted whatever it is taken for granted that Mary believes to follow from S_1. Thus, when the speaker is about to utter the presuppositional construction in S_2, it is clear from what he has said so far that, in formulating what he is about to say, he is entitled to take for granted everything the truth of which in world (6c) is taken for granted at that moment. If, therefore, the context at that moment contains, say, the assumption that there is the fact corresponding to reading A and that this fact exists in (6c)—and in the intermediate (6b)—in addition to existing in its world of origin, then the presuppositional construction in S_2 can be correctly used in the sense of reading A. As opposed to a sentence like (8),

(8) *Mary believes that Peter, who has been in England for some time, is in London now and* $_{S_2}$[*will never léave England again*].

where the speaker tells the listener something that may be relevant to the presupposition in S_2 by inserting an appositive relative clause, nothing of the kind happens in (5), so here the relevant assumptions must be present already in the initial context—if we disregard the possibility that the context changes due to factors other than the utterance of (5).

Now it is not necessary that the initial context primarily contains exactly what is presupposed in the respective reading A, B, C, or D since there are certain general principles of deduction and expectation that the speaker can use. Especially important is the principle of expectation that says, roughly, that if an entity such as an individual or a fact originating from a certain world is known as such to the listener, the speaker is entitled to presuppose its existence not only in its world of origin but also in a sequence of hierarchically related lower worlds,[8] if he believes it to exist in these worlds and if there is no expectation to the contrary. This means that if the context contains one of the assumptions in (9),

(9) a. *Peter is in England.*
b. *Mary believes that Peter is in England.*
c. *Mary believes that if Peter is in London now then he is in England.*
d. *If Peter is in London now, he is in England.*

this is usually enough to entitle the speaker to use the presuppositional construction in S_2 in (5) in the sense of A, B, C, or D, respectively.

This principle of expectation is also relevant to the presuppositional conditions of Type B, which I am now going to characterize in somewhat greater detail. Corresponding to the model world MW of the sentence structure S immediately containing a certain presuppositional construction PC, there is a world W such that taking something for granted with respect to MW is equivalent to taking it for granted with respect to W. The identity of W depends on the function of MW in the whole utterance, that is, on what constructions contain S. W is the lowest world to which the presuppositional condition of Type A associated with PC relates. Now Condition B says that at the moment at which PC is uttered it must be clear from the speach situation that the function of MW is such that W is a world with respect to which the existence of the entity presupposed according to Condition A may be taken for granted. Due to the principle of expectation, this means that enough must be known about the function of MW and thus about W to allow the conclusion that W is identical to, or in the relevant sense lower than, the world of origin of the entity presupposed according to Condition A, so that this entity may be expected to occur in W. Condi-

[8] For a definition of such sequences of worlds see Section 4.2.

tion B is always satisfied in S_2 in (5) if the presupposed fact with its world of origin is known to the listener, since the FULL specification of W—that is, (6c)—and, a fortiori, its relevant relation to the world of origin can always be deduced from the preceding parts of the utterance in the way indicated earlier, irrespective of the assumptions in the initial context. An example of a violation of Condition B would be (10a), as opposed to (10b),

(10) a. $_{S_1}$[*Would Peter léave England again*] $_{S_2}$[*if he were in Lőndon now*]?
b. *If Peter were in Lőndon now, would he then léave England again?*

if the speaker wanted (10a) to be understood as being about the duration of a counterfactual stay in England (taking for granted that Peter was, say, in Hamburg) and if he uttered it in a situation where there had not been any talk about such a counterfactual stay and the conditional clause had to be regarded as representing "new information" with a certain extra stress on *London.* In such a situation it would not be clear that, when uttering S_1, the speaker was, so to speak, dwelling in a world that was identical to, or lower than, the world-of-the-truth-of-S_2 in the real world. On the other hand, it would of course be clear in such a situation that he was dwelling in a world identical to, or lower than, the REAL world. Accordingly, there seems to be a clear tendency to interpret (10a) as being about a real stay in England when uttered in a situation of this kind. This is in contrast to both an utterance of (10b) in such a situation and an utterance of (10a) in a situation where the initial context contains the assumption that what is going to be said may be expected to be about the counterfactual situation that Peter is in London and thus in England and where, accordingly, it is natural to utter S_2 without any stress. In both cases the utterance may very well be interpreted as being about a counterfactual stay in England.

Besides the principle of expectation just discussed there is a principle of deduction of which the speaker may make use. This principle enables him to take something for granted if it follows in a natural way from what is being assumed otherwise. Thus, instead of containing one of the assumptions in (9), the context of (5) may contain an assumption of the following kind:

(11) a. *Peter is in the East of England.*
b. *Mary believes that Peter is in the East of England.*

c. *Mary believes that if Peter is in London now then he is in the East of England.*
d. *If Peter is in London now he is in the East of England.*

If, for instance, the speaker wants to use (5) in accordance with A in a situation where the context contains (11a), then, according to the principle of expectation, the speaker may take the existence of the fact corresponding to (11a) for granted with respect to the sequence of worlds (6a)–(6b)–(6c) and, due to the principle of deduction, he may then also take the existence of the fact that Peter is in England for granted with respect to this sequence of worlds, which is what he needs in order to be able to use the presuppositional construction correctly. One might ask why the speaker could not instead be assumed to use the principle of deduction in such a way that he simply took (9a) for granted in addition to (11a), from which it follows, then go on to use the principle of expectation in the same way as he would have done if the context had contained only (9a). While I am not sure that this would be impossible in the case of (5), there often seems to be a strong tendency to use these principles in a way corresponding to the first alternative mentioned, if there are no special, interfering assumptions in the context. Consider (12), for example:

(12) $_{S_1}$[*Peter is in London now.*] $_{S_2}$[*Mary believes that he will never léave England again.*]

If S_2 in (12) is intended to be about a real stay in England known to Mary, as would normally be the case, the utterance of S_1 is enough to create the necessary background, given the principles of expectation and deduction. However, the principles do not seem to cooperate in such a way that first it is deduced from S_1 and the relevant geographical facts that Peter is in England and then this fact is taken also to exist in Mary's world, that is, to be known to her. Rather, what normally seems to happen is that the principle of expectation is applied first: The fact described by S_1 and the relevant geographical facts are assumed to be known to Mary, and from this it is then also deduced that the fact that Peter is in England is known to her. Thus, (12) has more in common with (13a) than with (13b),

(13) a. *Peter is in London now. Mary knows that he is in London now and believes that he will never leave England again.*
b. *Peter is in London now. Mary knows that he is in England and believes that he will never leave England again.*

which may be seen from the fact that it is usually rather odd to continue (12) with an utterance like (14a) or (14b).

(14) a. *But I am sure that she does not even know that he is in London.*
b. *But I am sure that she does not even know that London is in England.*

Such an utterance could, however, be a continuation of (13b). Consider also (15),

(15) *Is it true that* $_{S_1}$[*Peter is in London now*] *and that Mary believes that* $_{S_2}$[*he will never léave England again*]?

where, roughly speaking, the same thing that happens in (12) with respect to the real world happens with respect to the model world of the complement of *true*. This means that a speaker who wants to use (15) in such a way that the presuppositional construction in S_2 is associated with the presupposition that if Peter is in London it is the case both that he is in England and that Mary knows this, must in addition assume that if Peter is in London Mary knows that he is in London and knows the relevant geographical facts. Whatever the explanation of these phenomena, it seems interesting to me that there are restrictions on the applicability of the principles of deduction and expectation that may force a speaker who wants to take advantage of the principles to make stronger assumptions than would seem minimally necessary and thus to take a stand on questions that could otherwise have been left open. Notice that if the speaker refrains from relying on the principles and instead specifies the background explicitly—compare, for example, (13b)—he may use the same sentence with the same meaning and the same presuppositions proper without making those extra assumptions.

3. FURTHER DISCUSSIONS

3.1. The Time Sensitivity of Presuppositional Constructions

An essential feature of the general view I advocate is the claim that a presupposition constitutes a condition on the context AT THE MOMENT OF THE UTTERANCE OF THE PRESUPPOSITIONAL EXPRESSION. This claim concerns both aspects of a presupposition, that is, both the condition that the existence of a certain entity originating from a certain world is taken for granted with respect to a sequence of worlds—what we have called Condition A—and the condition that the existence of this entity is taken for granted with respect to the model world primarily being described—Condition B.

3.1.1. Time Sensitivity with Respect to Condition A

As for Condition A, we saw already in connection with (8) that the speaker can create the background needed for the correct use of a certain presuppositional construction by inserting an appositive relative clause that gives the relevant information. Of course, he must do this in such a way that the appositive clause comes to be uttered before the presuppositional construction. This, however, appears to be the only restriction in this respect, that is, it seems that the clause may, as a principle, be uttered at any point up to the utterance of the presuppositional construction. If the appositive clause appears later than the presuppositional construction, the result is felt to be odd or the clause is given a special interpretation such as that it merely repeats "old information" or that it corrects an earlier mistake in the sense of "I ought perhaps to have told you that . . ." or something similar. Compare, for example, (16a) and (16b):

(16) a. $_{S_2}$[*Mary is sure that Charles,*] $_{S_1}$[*whom she believes to be negotiating with Peter,*] $_{S_2}$[*will soon stóp negotiating with him*].

b. $_{S_2}$[*Mary is sure that Charles will soon stóp negotiating with Peter*] $_{S_1}$[*whom she believes Charles to be negotiating with*].

Example (16a), where the appositive clause precedes the presuppositional construction, is correct, but (16b), where it does not, is odd or presupposes some very special interpretation of the kind mentioned. Evidence of this sort thus supports the intuitively plausible claim that the presupposition relates to the moment of utterance. Now perhaps someone might want to argue that the difference between (16a) and (16b) should rather be explained as a reflection of a difference in underlying structure having to do with how the relative clause, S_1, and the rest of the sentence, S_2, are related by some abstract asymmetric relation. One could then also say that the difference between (17a) and (17b) reflects the same difference in the abstract relation between S_1 and S_2:

(17) a. $_{S_1}$[*Mary believes Charles to be negotiating with Peter*] *and* $_{S_2}$[*she is sure that he will soon stóp negotiating with him*].

b. $_{S_2}$[*Mary is sure that Charles will soon stóp negotiating with Peter*] *and* $_{S_1}$[*she believes him to be negotiating with him*].

However, even granted that such an approach were possible, it is worth noticing that one would have to correlate this abstract relation between S_1 and S_2 not with the surface order of the surface manifestations of S_1 and S_2 but with the surface order between the manifestation of S_1 on the one hand and THE PRESUPPOSITIONAL CONSTRUCTION in S_2 on the other hand. As a matter of fact, such an approach can be shown to be inadequate in principle. Suppose we have a sentence S_1 with an inserted sentence S_2:

(18) $_{S_1}/X/_{S_2}/Y/_{S_1}/Z/$

(arrows: from X to Y, and from Y to Z)

Suppose further that the relation between background-creating and presuppositional expressions is as indicated by the arrows, that is, that uttering portion *X* of S_1 creates the background needed for the correct use of a presuppositional construction in *Y*, that is, in S_2, and that uttering S_2 in turn creates the background for a presuppositional expression in portion Z of S_1. In such a case there is no relation R between S_1 and S_2 that could be used in explaining the correct distribution of background-creating and presuppositional expressions. R would have to be asymmetric, since otherwise it could not explain anything about the asymmetric behavior of sentence pairs like (17a) and (17b). But, in contradiction, in a case like (18) one would have to assume both S_1RS_2 because of the first arrow and S_2RS_1 because of the second arrow. In PZS I used a sentence like (19) as an example of (18):

(19) $_{S_1}$[*Charles was convinced that Peter was married and that Mary,*] $_{S_2}$[*who he believed had been given a dréss by Peter's wife*] $_{S_1}$[*had got a present from Peter, too.*]

Here the utterance of the first part of S_1 could be said to create the background for the presuppositional construction *Peter's wife*, whereas the utterance of S_2 creates the background for the presuppositional construction with *too* in the second part of S_1.[9] Notice that both (20a) and (20b),

(20) a. $_{S_1}$[*Charles,*] $_{S_2}$[*who believed that Mary had been given a dress by Peter's wife,*] $_{S_1}$[*was con-*

[9] For a more detailed analysis of this example and the following ones see PZS, pp. 32–34.

vinced that Peter was married and that Mary had got a present from him, too.]

b. $_{S_2}$[*Charles,*] $_{S_1}$[*who was convinced that Peter was married and that Mary had got a present from him, too,*] $_{S_2}$[*believed that she had been given a dréss by Peter's wife.*]

where S_1 and S_2 are essentially as in (19), differ from (19) in their presuppositional properties and that these differences seem to depend on how the order of background-creating and presuppositional expressions differs from that in (19). This seems to be rather strong evidence for the assumption that chronological order is an essential factor here.

3.1.2. Time Sensitivity with Respect to Condition B

Condition B requires that it is clear from the speech situation that the model world primarily being described has such a function in the entirety of the uttered sentence that the entity the existence of which is presupposed according to Condition A may be expected to appear in it. Since this expectation is relative to the presupposed entity with its world of origin, Condition B is in principle dependent on Condition A in the sense that the former cannot be fulfilled unless the latter is. Therefore, if Condition A need not be fulfilled until the presuppositional construction is uttered, as seems to be the case, neither can Condition B be required to be fulfilled until then. That, on the other hand, Condition B must be fulfilled by the time t of the utterance of the presuppositional construction is clear from the asymmetric behavior of sentence pairs like (10a) and (10b), which show that the relevant property of the model world in question must be deducible at t from what has been said so far or from special assumptions in the context about what is going to be said.

The differences between (5) and (7) and between (2a) and (2b) may also be assumed to demonstrate the nature of Condition B in this respect. Let us consider (2) once more:

(2) a. *Is it true that* $_{S_1}$[*it is raining*] *and that* $_{S_2}$[*it will not stop raining until tomorrow*]?

b. *Is it true that* $_{S_2}$[*it will not stop raining until tomorrow*] *and that* $_{S_1}$[*it is raining*]?

If we merely consider one aspect of what happens in (2a), looking at the model world MW of the complement of *true* in isolation, we could say that, having characterized MW by uttering S_1, the speaker may take the truth of S_1 in MW for granted when he reaches the presuppositional construction with *stop* in S_2. Taking into account the final effect of using this presuppositional construction in the entirety of the structure of (2a), we may say that taking the existence of a certain fact originating from a certain world W other than MW for granted in formulating S_2 normally implies taking it for granted with respect to the world-of-the-truth-of-S_1 in the real world and that the presupposition ultimately associated with the presuppositional construction in question consists in the requirement that, first, the existence of the fact described by *It is raining* and originating from the world-of-the-truth-of-S_1 in the real world is taken for granted with respect to this same world (Condition A) and, second, an expression associated with Condition A may be expected to occur in S_2 (Condition B). Notice that Condition A is equivalent to the requirement that it is taken for granted that it is raining if it is raining. The truth of such a tautology may of course always be taken for granted, so the context cannot be assumed to change in this respect. However, it changes in a way that is relevant to Condition B, since only after the utterance of S_1 is it clear that, in formulating S_2, the speaker is dwelling in a world where the fact whose existence is required in Condition A may be expected to appear. If one tried to use (2b) with the same presuppositional reading as (2a), Condition A would of course also be fulfilled, but Condition B would be violated. The reason for this is that it is not clear from what has been said when S_2 in (2b) is uttered that the model world being described has the property required by Condition B, the relevant information being given only afterwards in S_1, and that, in contrast to cases like (10), the context cannot normally contain any special assumption about what is going to be said from which the property in question could be deduced, probably because (2b) usually cannot have a topic-comment structure that would fit in with such a situation and would allow S_1 to represent "old information." Accordingly, S_2 in (2b) tends to be interpreted as being about a real rain. But under such an interpretation the continuation with S_1 is felt to be redundant. Thus (2b) is odd either way.

3.2. Presuppositional Difference of Independent and Embedded Sentences

If presuppositions are seen as conditions associated with the utterance of individual presuppositional expressions, the presuppositions of a sentence containing several presuppositional expressions may simply be said to be the presuppositions of the presuppositional expressions contained in it. Since the presuppositional expressions of a certain sentence are the presuppositional expressions of its clauses, one could also say that, in this rather trivial sense, the presuppositions of a complex sentence are determined by the presuppositions of the clauses it contains. However, as was already pointed out, this does not imply that the presuppositions of a certain clause are in general the same as those of a corresponding independent sentence. The main reason for this is that the clause may be contained in constructions that make it necessary to use the presuppositional expressions in the clause with other presuppositional readings than they would normally have had if the clause had appeared as an independent sentence. It is thus an important feature of the approach I advocate that the main alternative is not between an embedded clause having the same presuppositions as it would normally have had as an independent sentence and its merely having a proper subset of these presuppositions or no presuppositions at all. Rather, as we saw, its presuppositions may differ from those of a corresponding independent sentence in a way having to do with the worlds to which they relate. Consider (21):

(21) *Peter believes that it will not stop raining until tomorrow.*

Condition A of the presupposition associated with the construction with *stop* in (21) requires that it is taken for granted either that there is a real rain that also exists in Peter's world or that there is a rain originating in Peter's world. This means that it is presupposed either that it is raining and that this fact is known to Peter or that Peter believes that it is raining, irrespective of whether it is assumed actually to be raining or not and, if it is assumed to be raining, it being left open whether or not Peter knows that it is raining.[10] Accordingly, a natural way of creating the background for the two readings of the construction with *stop* in (21) is to give the information in (22a) or (22b).

(22) a. *It is raining* [*and Peter knows that*].
b. *Peter believes that it is raining.*

The brackets in (22a) indicate what may be left out owing to the principle of expectation. If the presuppositional construction is used in (23) instead of (21),

(23) *It will not stop raining until tommorow.*

[10] It should perhaps be pointed out here that knowing something is not simply the same as believing something that is true. Someone who, on the basis of false assumptions, has come to believe something that happens to be true cannot be said to be acquainted with the corresponding real fact, although, of course, there is a corresponding fact in his world.

of course, it cannot be associated with the same presuppositional readings—provided (23) is asserted to be true with respect to the same world as is (21), for example, the real world, as in the normal case. It is worth noting in this connection that in many cases the differences between the presuppositional readings in respect of the worlds that the presupposition relates to are directly correlated with differences as to the identity of an element belonging to the content proper of the clause in question. Consider (24), for example:

(24) *Does Mary believe that you are going to kill it?*

Here the thing referred to by *it* either may be presupposed to exist in reality and to be known to Mary or may be presupposed to be something that Mary believes exists. Sentence (24) may, for example, be used in a dialogue where (25a) or (25b) has just been uttered, (25a) corresponding to the first reading of (24) and (25b) corresponding to the second reading:

(25) a. *There is a mad dog that Mary believes to be in our garden.*
b. *Mary believes that there is a mad dog in our garden.*

Obviously, *it* in (24) cannot be taken to have the same referential value when it is associated with the first kind of existential presupposition as when it is associated with the second kind. On the other hand, in (26), as opposed to (24),

(26) *Are you going to kill it?*

it cannot normally be used as referring to something that is assumed to exist only in Mary's imagination. In such cases, then, not only are the presuppositional readings of the embedded clause different from those of a corresponding independent sentence, but the differences between the presuppositional readings of the clause are coupled with differences in content proper that could not normally have occurred in an independent sentence.

4. TOWARD FORMALIZATION OF THE ROLE OF CONSTRUCTIONS ON THE ABSTRACT STRUCTURE LEVEL

4.1. Dyers

What presuppositional readings a certain presuppositional expression may be used in depends on how the sentence structure S immediately containing it—and thus the model world primarily being described when it is used—is assumed to function in the context of the whole utterance. This in turn depends on what constructions S is contained in in the abstract structure of the whole sentence uttered. Considering the role of different kinds of constructions in this respect we may start from the classification in Karttunen (1973), where Karttunen distinguishes between "plugs," constructions which block off the presuppositions in their domain, "holes," which leave them unaffected; and "filters," which under certain conditions cancel some of them.

I shall not have much to say here about plugs and holes. As for plugs, I believe that it is correct to say that presuppositional constructions contained in the complement of a verb of saying may lose their presuppositional character, but it should be pointed out that they need not. When they retain their presuppositional character, the effect of the verb of saying seems to be that of a "double-dyer." The "plugging" effect of verbs of saying may perhaps best be seen as being due to their constituting a context that favors a special way of using presuppositional constructions that also occurs otherwise and that has been referred to as "semi-quotation" (cf. Fillmore, 1969, p. 122).

As for the class of holes, I believe that such a class must be postulated but that one should not include as many constructions in it as Karttunen did. For instance, alongside such constructions as aspectuals and one- and two-way implicatives, he considered all factives to belong to this class. However, while factives like *be significant* may be considered as holes, factives like *regret* are not holes but a special kind of "dyers."

The constructions that Karttunen considered filters were *if . . . then, and,* and *either . . . or.* These and several other similar constructions, on the one hand, and constructions with verbs like *believe, wish, dream,* and many others, on the other hand, seem to me to form one class, because they share the important feature that presuppositional expressions contained in them have presuppositions that differ from those they would have had if they had not been contained in them. Thus, to use Karttunen's metaphors, these constructions neither "block" presuppositions like plugs, nor let them through unaltered like holes, but rather modify them with respect to their truth levels. I have, accordingly, called them DYERS.[11] The DYEING may sometimes have the effect that the presupposition ultimately associated with a certain presuppositional expression will be equivalent to a very trivial condition [cf. (2a) and its discussion in 3.1.2]. This may then give the impression that the presupposition has been entirely "filtered out."

[11] Karttunen (1974) mentions an observation by S. Peters which has made him aware of the possibility that presuppositions are modified and not just filtered out or blocked.

I cannot discuss the different types of dyers here, but would like at least to mention two kinds of constructions which seem to me of particular theoretical interest. Consider (27).

(27) a. *Is there anybody among the passengers who is ill and whose disease is dangerous?*
b. *Is there anybody among the passengers whose disease is dangerous and who is ill?*

There are similar questions to be asked here as in the case of (2), and I believe that an attempt to answer those questions leads to the postulation of what I have called "model individuals." I thus believe that it is a model individual of whom it is first asserted and then presupposed in (27a) that he is ill. As in the case of a model world, the identity of a certain model individual is determined token-reflexively, and the model individual corresponds to a set of (possible or real) individuals satisfying its characterization in a similar way as a certain model world corresponds to a set of possible worlds. More exactly, it must be assumed that a model individual is always introduced together with a model world in which it is taken to exist and in which its characterization is true. Such a pair of a model world and a model individual then corresponds to a set of pairs consisting of a possible world and an individual of whom the relevant characterization is true in that world.

The other kind of construction I would like to mention is illustrated in (28).

(28) a. *There is a rat in our cellar. Last night Mary dreamed that I killed the poor animal.*
b. *Mary imagines that there is a rat in our cellar. Last night she dreamed that I killed the poor animal.*
c. *Last night Mary dreamed that there was a rat in our cellar. She dreamed that I killed the poor animal.*

As opposed to a dyer like *believe*, the dyer *dream* seems to define not just one but two steps in the hierarchy of worlds, since there is the possibility that the rat referred to by *the poor animal* in (28) not only is assumed to be a real rat as in (28a) or a rat originating in a dream world of Mary's in the real world as in (28c), but also may be taken to originate in Mary's world in the real world as in (28b). Verbs like *want* and *hope* behave similarly. I have called such dyers DOUBLE-DYERS. Presumably, one will also have to assume the existence of what might be called MULTIPLE DYERS because of cases like (29):

(29) a. 1. *Peter has got a car.*
2. *If Peter lives in Europe, he has got a car.*
3. *If Peter lives in England, he has got a car.*
4. *If Peter lives in London, he has got a car.*
b. *But isn't it rather unlikely that* $_{S_1}$[*he lives in London*] *and uses the car?*

The dyeing construction relevant to the existential presupposition associated with *the car* in (29b), the conjunction with S_1, provides not only the possibility that the car is taken to be real, as in (29a1) + (29b), or to originate in the world-of-truth-of-S_1 in the real world, as in (29a4) + (29b). Rather, as indicated by (29a2) + (29b) and (29a3) + (29b), there seems to be a whole set of possibilities having in common that for some S the car is assumed to originate in the world-of-the-truth-of-S in the real world, S being taken to follow from S_1.

4.2. Formalization

I am the first to admit that the formalism presented in PZS has a very preliminary character. Nevertheless, I believe it is valuable, since it enables one to determine what predictions are made by my analysis in several important respects. I am now going to present in an informal way a simplified (and in one respect modified—cf. footnote 12) version of the formalism that gives some idea of how it works in principle.

Suppose we want to find out with what presuppositional readings (Condition A) a certain presuppositional construction PC in the independent sentence S^0 containing no constructions that function as plugs can be associated. For this we must know in what dyeing constructions the sentence structure S^n immediately containing PC is contained in the abstract structure of S^0. We therefore scan all the constructions in the abstract structure of S^0 that contain S^n, starting with the outmost one and moving inwards. We disregard the holes, but for every dyer we meet we write down a symbol representing relevant information about the dyer. By arranging these symbols from left to right and putting a special symbol in front of them that stands for the world that S^0 is uttered in, usually the real world, we get a string of symbols that represents the lowest world that the possible presuppositional readings of PC relate to, this world being common to all of them. By operating on this string in a special way we then arrive at the other characteristics of the different readings. Suppose the string symbolizing the lowest world is (30).

(30) $W^0W^1W^2W^3W^4W^5$

Now, proceeding from right to left, we delete an arbitrary number of these symbols except W^0, for example, as in (31):

(31)
$$W^0\underset{3}{\not{W}^1}\underset{2}{\not{W}^2}W^3\underset{1}{\not{W}^4}W^5$$

Before we start and after each deletion we write down what is left of the original string, arranging the strings we get in that way from right to left. The result is a representation of a sequence of four worlds:

(32) $W^0W^3W^5$, $W^0W^1W^3W^5$, $W^0W^1W^2W^3W^5$, $W^0W^1W^2W^3W^4W^5$

Example (32) corresponds to one of the possible presuppositional readings of PC, the entity concerned being assumed to exist in all four worlds, originating from the first world, $W^0W^3W^5$, and getting down into the lowest world $W^0W^1W^2W^3W^4W^5$ through the intermediate worlds. The set of all sequences derivable from (30) in the same way as (32) corresponds to the set of the possible presuppositional readings of PC.

The derivation of sequences of worlds like (32) is of course subject to many additional restrictions and specifications, some of which are discussed in PZS. For instance, in order to be able to capture the behavior of double-dyers one has to allow not only deletions of symbols as in (31) but also substitutions of symbols.

The set of possible sequences of worlds such as (32) that is defined by the formalism not only is needed in determining the possible presuppositions of Type A but also occurs in the formulation of the principle of expectation and in the specification of conditions of Type B.

I conclude this section by showing how the formalism can be applied to some concrete examples in determining the presuppositional conditions of Type A. For simplicity's sake, we assume that the surface structure of the sentences involved yields the structural information needed. In each case I first give the sentence in question, emphasizing with boldface the central part of the presuppositional construction examined and indicating by labeled brackets the relevant dyers and the symbols used to represent them. Then I indicate what kind of entity's existence we are concerned with, and last I give the sequences of worlds in which this entity is presupposed to exist in the different readings, together with an adequate background-creating utterance, where what is in brackets may be left out owing to the principle of expectation.

(33) a. *It is not the case that Peter will never* ***léave England*** *again and that he is in London now.*

b. A fact describable as *Peter is in England.*

c. W^0
Peter is in England.

(34) a. *It is not the case* $_{W^{S_1}}$[*that* $_{S_1}$ (*Peter is in London now*) *and that he will never* ***léave England*** *again.*][12]
b. A fact describable as *Peter is in England*
c. $W^0W^{S_1}$
If Peter is in London now, he is in England.
d. W^0, $W^0W^{S_1}$
Peter is in England [*and if he is in London now, that does not, of course, affect the fact that he is in England.*]

(35) a. $_{W^{P,x}}$[*Mary*$_x$ *is sure that* $_{W^{P,y}}$ [*Peter*$_y$ *believes that I am going to kill* ***the poor animal***$_z$.]]
b. A referent of z
c. $W^0W^{P,x}W^{P,y}$
Mary believes that Peter believes that there is a mad dog in our garden.
d. $W^0W^{P,x}$, $W^0W^{P,x}W^{P,y}$
Mary believes that there is a mad dog in our garden [*and that Peter knows of this dog.*]
e. W^0, $W^0W^{P,x}$, $W^0W^{P,x}W^{P,y}$
There is a mad dog in our garden [*and Mary knows of this dog and believes that Peter knows of it.*]

[12] In PZS, I should here have used a symbol like $W^{S,x}$ instead of W^{S_1}, the token-reflexively determined index x referring to the model world involved. I now believe that a better formulation of the presuppositional conditions of Type A can be achieved if one disregards the model world aspect in this connection. Thus, wherever I used a token-reflexively indexed symbol like $W^{S,x}$, I now prefer a symbol of the type W^S, where S represents the content of the relevant part of the dyeing construction in question.

The question then arises, what is the relevant part? While it seems rather clear, for instance, that in the logically asymmetric construction *If A then B* (or *B if A*) A dyes a presuppositional expression in B, but not vice versa, things are less clear in the case of logically symmetric constructions like conjunctions. In (33) and (34) it is simply assumed that the presuppositional expression considered is dyed by the conjunction of the conjuncts that are to the left of it in surface structure, that is, S_1 in (34) and none in (33). However, I am not sure that there is a corresponding asymmetry in abstract structure. In fact, I am rather inclined to assume that, for each conjunct C, a presuppositional construction in C is dyed by the conjunction of all conjuncts other than C and to rely on Condition B to explain the asymmetric behavior, cf. the discussion of (2) in 3.1.2. In the case of (33) this would mean that, potentially, there are the same readings as in (34), Condition B allowing only W^0, $W^0W^{S_1}$ to be realized.

f. $W^0W^{P,y}$, $W^0W^{P,x}W^{P,y}$
Peter believes that there is a mad dog in our garden [and Mary knows that he believes that.]

(36) [=(5)]
a. $_{W^{P,x}}$[*Does Mary$_x$ believe* $_{W^{S_1}}$[***that*** $_{S_1}$(*Peter is in London now*) *and that* ***he will never léave England*** *again*]]?
b. A fact describable as *Peter is in England*
c. $W^0W^{P,x}W^{S_1}$
Mary believes that if Peter is in London now then he is in England.
d. $W^0W^{P,x}$, $W^0W^{P,x}W^{S_1}$
Mary believes that $_z$(*Peter is in England*) [*and that, if Peter is in London now, that does not affect this fact$_z$.*]
e. W^0, $W^0W^{P,x}$, $W^0W^{P,x}W^{S_1}$
$_z$(*Peter is in England*) [*and Mary knows that and believes that, if Peter is in London now, that does not affect this fact$_z$.*]
f. $W^0W^{S_1}$, $W^0W^{P,x}W^{S_1}$
If Peter is in London now, then he is in England [and Mary knows that if he is in London now he is in England].

5. TOWARD AN EXPLANATION OF CONDITIONS A AND B

As I have pointed out already, there are a few points where the present account differs from that in PZS. Thus I now distinguish more clearly between the model world aspect and the "sphere world" aspect of presuppositions and have accordingly arrived at what I believe to be a more consequent and adequate formulation of the behavior of certain dyers (cf. footnote 12). I also believe that I now have a more consequent view of the difference between the presuppositional conditions of Type A and those of Type B than I had in PZS. In this section I would like to point out a possibility, not considered in PZS, of giving a kind of explanation of certain aspects of the question of why there are presuppositional readings of the kind we have been discussing. It seems to me that one might distinguish between certain central aspects of a presupposition and certain secondary aspects that may be derived from the central aspects on the basis of some general assumptions. One could assume that the primary aspect of a presupposition is the condition that the existence of a certain entity originating from a certain world is taken for granted, the entity either belonging to or being closely connected with the content of the sentence immediately containing the presuppositional expression in question. Another central aspect of the presupposition would then be the condition that the speaker takes it for granted that the entity occurs in the model world MW primarily being described. Given the way MW is intended to function in the entirety of the utterance, to take the existence of something for granted with respect to MW seems to be equivalent to taking its existence for granted with respect to a certain other world W. Accordingly, the speaker seems to be entitled to take the existence of the entity for granted with respect to MW if enough is known about the function of MW to allow the conclusion that the corresponding world W is such that the speaker is entitled to take the existence of the entity for granted with respect to W. (This is, of course, what we have called Condition B.) Now the question arises of how to explain the relation between MW and W. It seems to me that one could perhaps arrive at a better understanding of this by means of the following considerations. In connection with a model world or a model individual, that is, as I see it, things that may be symbolized by variables, there usually seems to be the presupposition that the members of the corresponding set are picked out from some other set. In other, more traditional words, a variable is usually associated with a range of possible values. Now, to take something for granted with respect to an entity that could be symbolized by a variable seems to be equivalent to taking it for granted with respect to all members of what would be the range of the variable. If the speaker conceives of the range as being specified in a certain way, he will be committed to the truth of the assumption in question with respect to all members of the set thus specified. Consider, for example, (37):

(37) *Is there anybody$_x$ among the passengers whose$_x$ disease is dangerous?*

Here the speaker will normally be committed to the assumption that all members of the set of passengers he is letting x range over are ill. If one assumes that the meaning of (38a) and (39a) is at least roughly equivalent to that of (38b) and (39b), respectively (where variables w range over possible worlds and specifications of ranges are in parantheses), one may conceive of such cases in a similar way:

(38) a. *If Peter is in London now* $_{S_1}$[*he will never leave England again*].

b. $\wedge w$ (in w Peter is in London now): in w he will never leave England again.

(39) a. *Mary believes that* $_{S_1}$[*Peter will never leave England again*].

b. $\wedge w$ (what Mary believes is true in w): in w Peter will never leave England again.

What is important about (38b) and (39b) is not the exact formulation but rather that they show that it is not implausible to assume that S_1 in (38a) and (39a) functions in such a way in the utterance that the speaker will normally be committed to conceiving of the range of the model world of S_1 as being specified in the way indicated and thus to assuming that *Peter is in England* is true in all the possible worlds of the range thus specified. This is more or less equivalent to his assuming the truth of *Peter is in England if he is in London now* in the case of (38a) and the truth of *Mary believes that Peter is in England* in the case of (39a). The first of these assumptions will in turn be affected by the same phenomenon, if (38a) occurs embedded as in (40):

(40) *Does Mary believe that if Peter is in London now he will never léave England again?*

The result is the commitment of the speaker to the truth of something like *Mary believes that if Peter is in London now he is in England.* Thus, if we assume that dyers differ from holes in that they affect the ranges of model worlds in the way indicated whereas holes restrict the range of a model world to containing the immediately "higher" model world as its only member, we may begin to understand why the relation between MW and W is such that W can be determined on the basis of the dyers that the sentence S describing MW is contained in and why all presuppositional conditions of Type A that may be associated with a presuppositional construction in S relate to W, W being the lowest of the worlds in which the presupposed entity is assumed to exist. Why this entity gets down into W from its world of origin in the way previously demonstrated is still another question, certain aspects of which I have discussed in PZS.

6. THEORETICAL IMPLICATIONS

I think it is clear from what has been said that if the views presented here are mainly correct this will have certain consequences for our conception of the logical structure of natural languages. In these concluding remarks I would like to stress another theoretical implication of this approach. To the extent that the approach is adequate it shows that it is important to bear in mind that distributional regularities involving different parts A and B of one and the same sentence may not —or may not only—be due to syntactic or semantic rules defining allowable structural configurations in which A and B are to occupy certain positions. Rather, they may be due to the fact that A, being uttered first, usually affects the speech situation in a way relevant to the question of whether B may be correctly used in it, the rules that govern the correct use of B in the relevant respect only relating to certain features of the situation at the moment of the utterance of B and being in principle indifferent to how this situation has arisen and how B is structurally related to A. According to the views presented here we may have such a case if B is a presuppositional expression. I have argued that the presuppositional conditions associated with a presuppositional construction PC as used in a certain utterance relate to the moment *t* at which PC is uttered. The features of the context at *t* that are assumed to be relevant to the conditions are of such a kind that they may in principle have been introduced in many different ways, for example, by the utterance of earlier sections of the same sentence or the same discourse, but obviously also by nonlinguistic events such as gestures, pictures or events being watched by speaker and listener. It thus seems that restricting oneself to the question of how the context may change due to the utterance of a sentence *in an otherwise unchanged situation* ((3b)), as we have done in this chapter, is in a sense a quite arbitrary and artificial decision, in view of the nature of the phenomena discussed.

REFERENCES

Fillmore, C. J. Types of lexical information. In F. Kiefer (Ed.), *Studies in syntax and semantics*, Dordrecht, Holland: D. Reidel, 1969.

Langendoen, D. T., and Savin, H. B. The projection problem for presuppositions. In C. J. Fillmore and D. T. Langendoen (Eds.), *Studies in linguistic semantics*, New York: Holt, 1971.

Morgan, J. L. On the treatment of presupposition in transformational grammar. In R. Binnick *et al.* (Eds.), *Papers from the Fifth Regional Meeting*. Chicago: Chicago Linguistic Society, 1969.

Karttunen, L. Presuppositions of compound sentences. *Linguistic Inquiry*, 1973, *4*, 169–193.

Karttunen, L. Presuppositions and linguistic context. *Theoretical Linguistics*, 1974, *1*, 181–194.

Schiebe, T. *Über Präsuppositionen zusammengesetzter Sätze im Deutschen*. Stockholm: Almquist och Wiksell, 1975.

Schiebe, T. Review of D. Wilson "Presuppositions and Non-Truth-Conditional Semantics," *Studies in Language*. (To appear.)

A NEW SEMANTIC COMPUTATION WHILE PARSING: PRESUPPOSITION AND ENTAILMENT[1]

RALPH M. WEISCHEDEL
University of Delaware, Newark

1. INTRODUCTION

Though there is not yet complete agreement on what the definition of presupposition should be, a pattern has emerged among the concrete examples cited to justify various definitions of presupposition. For those examples in the literature which have not been successfully refuted, presuppositions seem to be associated with particular lexical items and certain grammatical constructions. (Karttunen and Peters, 1975, make this observation as well.) This suggests that a parser and lexicon might predict the presuppositions of a sentence, using a purely structural computation. I have constructed such a parser and lexicon which, when given an input sentence, compute the presuppositions of the sentence. A solution to the projection problem for compound sentences is also included.

Many examples of entailment also seem to be associated with particular lexical items; for instance, Givón (1973) and Karttunen (1970) offer many instances. These, too, can be generated while parsing a sentence. Furthermore, the solution to the projection problem for pre-

[1] The work was carried out while the author was in the Department of Computer and Information Science, University of Pennsylvania, Philadelphia. It was partially supported by NSF Grant SOC 72-0546A01.

Syntax and Semantics, Volume 11: Presupposition

ISBN 0-12-613511-8

suppositions has been extended to compute the entailments of compound sentences.

This chapter describes the parser and lexicon at an intermediate level of detail. A higher level description may be found in Joshi and Weischedel (1977); an in-depth description appears in Weischedel (1975), including background material on the formalism of the grammar and a complete analysis of the lexical information.

For the purposes of this chapter, assume that a completely satisfactory definition of presupposition and entailment will soon be found, incorporating the rich and diverse examples of Fillmore (1971), Givón (1973), Keenan (1971), Kiparsky and Kiparsky (1971), Karttunen (1970), and Karttunen and Peters (1975). I shall use the terms PRESUPPOSITION and ENTAILMENT to refer to those examples which appear to be associated with particular lexical items and syntactic constructions. I use the term CONTEXT to mean previous text, cultural rules, universal laws, etc. All phenomena attributable to the effect of context and all computations modeling such phenomena are termed PRAGMATIC.

Assume that the goal of a natural language parser is to translate from sentences to semantic representations for those sentences. My parser translates to the type of semantic representations posed by Keenan (1972), which are also amenable to semantic analyses using factorization of verbs. However, my computation presumes only that the semantic representations are a subset of a context-free language. Thus, the only assumption is that they may be represented by a tree or bracketed string.

Let S and S' be sentences with semantic representations L and L'. We say that sentence S' may be SUBFORMULA-DERIVED from sentence S if there is a tree transformation f and a subtree t of L such that

$$L' = f(t).$$

The chief result of this research is to demonstrate that presuppositions and entailments may be subformula-derived and to demonstrate how to write a parser and lexicon for this purpose.

My grammar is written in the formalism of the augmented transition network (ATN) of Woods (1970, 1973), and is patterned after the linguistic string parser of Sager (1967, 1973). (The linguistic string parser is based on the theory of grammar by Harris, 1970.)

The fact that presupposition and entailment may be computed while parsing is quite important from the viewpoint of a computational linguist. The process of drawing inferences is computationally quite complex, though crucial to model many semantic and pragmatic phenomena. Furthermore, how to guide the inference process to make the important inferences rather than all inferences is an unsolved problem. (Charniak, 1976, discusses these problems.) Since computing the semantic representation of a sentence is central to processing the sentence, the fact that we can also compute presuppositions and entailments as part of the parsing process is important. Furthermore, presupposition and entailment are central to the meaning of a sentence, in the sense that they arise from the meaning of particular words and syntactic constructions.

One chief advantage of a computational approach in linguistic research is that it offers interacting computational processes as a model of the use and interpretation of language. Interacting computational processes potentially provide a model of the interaction of syntax, semantics, and pragmatics, which is evident in anaphora, ambiguity, paraphrase, contradiction, presupposition, and discourse.

Let us consider this with respect to presupposition. Much of the literature raises difficulties for a purely semantic view of presupposition, as well as difficulties for a purely pragmatic view of presupposition. Kempson (1975, Chapter Four) discusses many difficulties. However, interacting computational processes could offer a solution to these difficulties.

For instance, a pragmatic view of presupposition might claim that presuppositions must be in the common ground of speaker and audience in order that the sentence be uttered felicitously. However, sentences such as (1) may be uttered to inform the audience of the truth of the presupposition expressed by the complement.

(1) *I regret that smoking is not permitted in this auditorium.*

The process described in this chapter computes presupposition by purely structural means, thus reflecting the intuition that presupposition is semantic in nature. A second process could verify whether the presuppositions computed are true in the context of the utterance, thus reflecting the pragmatic aspects of presupposition. If they are not, a third process would be invoked to hypothesize the speaker's intent, whether perhaps to inform that smoking is not permitted, to make a joke, or to be sarcastic. Psycholinguistic evidence for such processes appears in Clark and Haviland (1977).

On the other hand, a purely semantic view of presupposition has difficulty explaining the projection algorithm. For instance, *and* is not symmetrical with respect to affecting presuppositions of embedded sentences. However, a process model can reflect this well, since the common ground may be augmented by the proposition to the left of *and* before verifying presuppositions of the right side.

We make no pretence that the ideas of the two previous paragraphs are a scientific model; however, the sections that follow present a concrete process which could become a portion of such a model. In fact, that process has been applied by Weischedel, Voge, and James (1977) toward sophisticated computer-assisted language instruction. The interacting processes in that system are used to pinpoint a student's mistakes in use of language as the student gives (sentential) answers to questions about a given short text. If a presupposition of a student's answer does not correspond to the text, the system points out the lexical item that was used inappropriately. Furthermore, using the presuppositions of a question, the system identifies a student's failure to comprehend the question if an inference process cannot infer from the student's answer the proposition corresponding to the presupposition. We feel there is great potential in exploiting interacting computational processes as a model of linguistic phenomena.

The remainder of this chapter is organized as follows. Sections 2, 3, and 4 detail the computation of presupposition, of entailment, and of those entities in compound sentences, respectively. Section 5 suggests a criterion for including semantic information in a lexicon, and Section 6 concludes. The syntactic constructions in the implemented system are given in Appendix A; some sample output appears in Appendix B.

2. COMPUTING PRESUPPOSITIONS

While parsing a sentence, my system computes the presuppositions and entailments of that sentence, using an ATN and a lexicon for detailed information about each word. (We will not attempt to provide a description of the ATN formalism. Woods, 1970, 1973, gives this.)

The ATN enables one to write natural language parsers which are close to the surface structure of sentences, yet which can do the equivalent of inverse transformations while parsing a sentence. Therefore, my parser can compute semantic representations (as defined by Keenan, 1972) without operating on surface structure trees. Furthermore, while it computes the semantic representation of the sentence, it also computes the semantic representations for presuppositions and entailments.

The ATN is a generalization of finite state machines, so rich that they are equivalent to unrestricted production rules, and therefore equivalent to a Turing machine. Since an ATN is a generalization of a finite state machine, I will frequently refer to finding a particular parse as traversing a particular path in the graph of the ATN. The designer of a parser may associate a specific computation with any such path or parse (which is a way that the equivalent of inverse transformations may be achieved).

For two reasons, sets are an adequate data structure for storing presuppositions during the computation: No presuppositions interact with each other in elementary (unembedded) sentences. For embedded sentences, a simple tree transformation depending upon the embedding predicate gives the set of presuppositions at the current sentential level from the sets of presuppositions of embedded sentences.

Presuppositions are added to the set in one of three ways. First, those arising from syntactic constructs are added as soon as the construct has been parsed. Second, when a word having a presupposition is encountered, a tree transformation is retrieved from the lexical entry and added to the set of such tree transformations. At the completion of parsing at the current level, the tree transformations are performed, yielding presuppositions from lexical entries. Third, after parsing the sentence at the current level including all of its embedded sentences, the appropriate tree transformation is applied to the sets computed for embedded sentences, thereby computing the effect of the embedding on presuppositions. The first two ways are discussed in Sections 2.1 and 2.2, the third in Section 4.

2.1 Presuppositions from Syntactic Constructs

There are two keys to understanding how to compute presuppositions that arise from syntactic constructs. One is that since they arise from syntactic constructs, their occurrence is syntactically marked. Suppose we construct the ATN graph such that there is a path which corresponds exactly to that syntactic construct; that is, the path is taken if and only if those syntactic clues for that construct are present. Then, we can associate with the arcs of that path a function to select the proper well-formed subformula and apply the proper tree transformation to it.

The second key is that when there is ambiguity, when two different syntactic constructs yield the same surface sentence but differ in presuppositions, the responsibility of any parser and of our system is not to resolve all ambiguity, but to be able to generate both readings so that semantic and pragmatic components can choose between them.

Two examples are cleft sentences and definite noun phrases. The cleft sentences, with a noun phrase extracted, are represented by the following path, where REL represents relative clause and the double circle indicates final state.

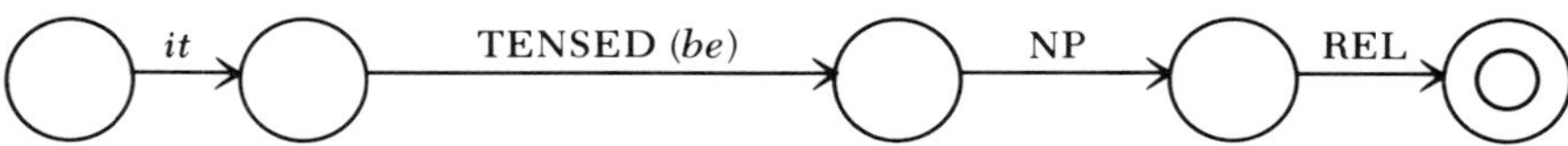

A cleft sentence presupposes that there is some individual (person or thing) having the property mentioned in the relative clause REL. To obtain the semantic representation of the relative clause, the binding of the variable representing the noun phrase must be changed to that of a constant representing "some individual." Associating this new binding with the representation of the relative clause gives the semantic representation of the presupposition. Since the REL arc computes the representation of the relative clause, the binding can be changed as an action of that arc, and the new presupposition added to the set of presuppositions.

A second example is noun phrases whose determiner is *the*. (Possessives and noun phrases with relative clauses are other definite noun phrases having presuppositions; the system handles these in an analogous way.) A noun phrase such as *the extremely big, red dog* presupposes that ***there is** an extremely big, red dog* in the shared information of the dialogue participants. In a function argument notation we might represent this as (L).

(L): (binding (*UNTENSED (IN-THE-SHARED-INFO variable)))

IN-THE-SHARED-INFO is a predicate meaning "in the shared information of the dialogue participants"; the *UNTENSED indicates that the tense is not known. If "binding" gives the binding of "variable," then we need to fill in "binding" with the semantic representation of the noun phrase itself except that an existential quantifier replaces the determiner (quantifier) *the*.

Thus, after parsing noun phrases with determiners, the corresponding path must check to see if the determiner of the head noun is *the*. If it is, a presupposition is generated by replacing that determiner by the existential quantifier, and by embedding that semantic representation in the place of "binding" in (L) and by replacing "variable" in (L) by the variable assigned to the noun phrase as a whole. This presupposition is added to the set of presuppositions and returned among the values of the noun phrase graph.

2.2. Presuppositions from Lexical Entries

The organization of lexical entries is patterned after the linguistic string parser (Sager, 1967, 1973, and Grishman, 1973), which has a lexicon of 9000 words and has been very successful. The linguistic string parser relies on restrictions placed on co-occurring constituents; these can be encoded in an ATN via the conditions on arcs.

In the linguistic string parser each word is classified into one or more hierarchically arranged subcategories. The characterization is so precise that one may compute both the constituents with which a subcategory can co-occur and the syntactic paraphrases that are possible. Another feature of the subcategories is that words having affixes are associated with their stem words.

In the lexical entry for a word, we must encode the tree transformation for a particular presupposition. The left hand side of a tree transformation gives the pattern to be matched and names for the subtrees which are to be manipulated. We have found that the pattern is encoded by the lexical subcategories of the linguistic string parser and the constituents with which they can co-occur. Therefore, by associating the right-hand side of the transformation with the word plus lexical subcategory, pattern matching occurs naturally as the ATN parses the sentence. Since my ATN parser assigns pieces of semantic representation to registers according to logical role in the sentence rather than syntactic role, the naming of subtrees involved in the transformation occurs automatically in parsing according to a convention for naming the logical roles.

Thus, we need only store the right-hand side of the transformation under the word plus syntactic category. The function BUILD of the ATN is a natural choice to encode the right-hand side, for it offers a general way to combine subtrees to form a new tree. However, the restriction that BUILD use only the contents of registers to fill "vacant slots" is too rigid. For instance, (2a) presupposes (2b).

(2) a. *John stopped running at noon.*
b. *At a time immediately before noon, John had been running.*

Corresponding to *a time immediately before noon,* a new variable must be generated for the logical notation. This cannot be part of the representation of (2a), and is therefore not available as a register in the augmented transition network. Thus, the computation is not merely a composition of the contents of registers. The function we need is similar to BUILD, but the list elements for filling "vacant slots" in the tree may be any computable function of the registers.

We may call this new function NEWBUILD. It has one argument, a list (*L*1, *L*2, *L*3, . . . , *Ln*), where *L*1 is the tree structure and each L*i*, $i > 1$, is evaluated to fill the slots.

This allows more complex computations than tree transformations. However, in all cases the arguments specifying what subtrees to insert are simply register names or else the LISP function that generates a unique variable for the logical notation. Therefore, the computation is like that of a tree transformation.

As an example, the verb *resent* presupposes that its logical subject is human, and that the embedded sentence is true. For instance, (3) presupposes (4) and (5).

(3) *John resented that he was forced to move.*

(4) *John is human.*

(5) *John was forced to move.*

In the lexical entry for *resent* (taking a *that SENTENCE* complement) we would have a list consisting of elements (6) and (7).

(6) ((*UNTENSED (HUMAN +)) LSUBJ);

(7) (+ COMP).

For Sentence (3), register LSUBJ, the logical subject, would be *John*. Thus, NEWBUILD applied to (6) yields (*UNTENSED (HUMAN John)), which may be paraphrased *John be* (unknown tense) *human*. For Sentence (3), COMP, containing the embedded complement sentence, is *John was forced to move*, which is also the result of applying NEWBUILD to (7).

Sentence (2) provides an example that the computation of presupposition is not merely manipulation and composition of the contents of ATN registers. Sections 2.2.1–2.2.4 present other complex aspects of the computation. For the remainder of Section 2, I adopt a convention that a sentence labeled (a) presupposes a sentence labeled (b).

2.2.1. Internal and External Negation

There are at least two types of negation in language. With internal negation, only the assertion of the affirmative form of the sentence is negated. For instance, the sentence *Mary did not leave when John came*, would normally be interpreted as *At the time John came*, *Mary did not leave*. *John came* is presupposed, demonstrating that presuppositions are not affected by internal negation.

External negation denies at least one of the presuppositions of the affirmative form of the sentence. For instance, the previous sentence in the context of (8) does not presuppose that John came.

(8) HERMAN: *Did Mary leave when John came?*
FRANK: *Mary did not leave when John came, because John never came.*

Context determines which interpretation is intended.

My system is written to compute (if need be) both interpretations for negation. Selection of an intended reading would occur in a pragmatic component, designed for all context-dependent computations. My system has not implemented a pragmatic component.

2.2.2. Assigning Tense

Assigning the proper tense to a presupposition can be crucial semantically, as example (9) demonstrates.

(9) a. *John stopped beating Mary at 10:00.*

b. *Immediately before 10:00, John had been beating Mary.*

The tense of a presupposition seems to be completely determined by the tense of the surface sentence and the lexical item which has the presupposition. Thus, for each presupposition, one can associate a function whose argument is the tense of the surface sentence. Each such function has a name; we have chosen the class of names *TENSE*i**, where *i* is a positive integer.

Let *L* be the lexical entry to generate a particular presupposition, represented as a tree. In *L*, place the name of the appropriate tense function *TENSE*i** where the tense should appear in the complete presupposition. By definition NEWBUILD will not move the atom *TENSE*i**. If we define a function APPLYTENSE to search for any *TENSE*i**, apply that function name to a tense, and insert the result in the tree where *TENSE*i** is, then

APPLYTENSE (NEWBUILD(*L*), tense)

gives the properly tensed presupposition. ("Tense" is assumed to be the tense at this sentential level.) This solves the problem of assigning tense to presuppositions.

2.2.3. Effect of Syntactic Environment

The syntactic environment of a word can affect whether it has a presupposition, thus, differentiating shades of meaning. For instance, (10a) presupposes (10b), but (11) has no such presupposition.

(10) a. *John knows that Henry is coming.*
b. *Henry is coming.*

(11) *John knows whether Henry is coming.*

The lexical subcategories (of the linguistic string parser [Anderson, 1970]), that are assigned to a word provide a way to compute the syntactic environments in which a word may occur. We have found that where the syntactic environment differentiates between a sense of a word having a presupposition and one which does not, there are two different syntactic subcategories of the word. (Or, where this is not the case, we may further subdivide the subcategory to make it so.) Corresponding to two different syntactic subcategories of the word, there are two different paths in the ATN graph. After completing the parse at the current sentential level, the path taken determines which of the two syntactic subcategories of the word was used. Thus, ASSOCIATING PRESUPPOSITIONAL ENTRIES IN THE LEXICON WITH THE WORD AND ITS SYNTACTIC SUBCATEGORY IS A SOLUTION TO THE EFFECT OF SYNTACTIC ENVIRONMENT ON COMPUTATION OF PRESUPPOSITIONS.

For example, *know* has at least two syntactic subcategories: one corresponding to "that SENTENCE" as complement, and one corresponding to "whether SENTENCE or not" as complement. With the first syntactic subcategory we would associate a lexical entry for presuppositions; with the second, the lexical entry would be empty.

This is analogous to having two senses of *know*: $know_1$ and $know_2$. Figure 1a shows an operation that gives the presupposition of $know_1$.

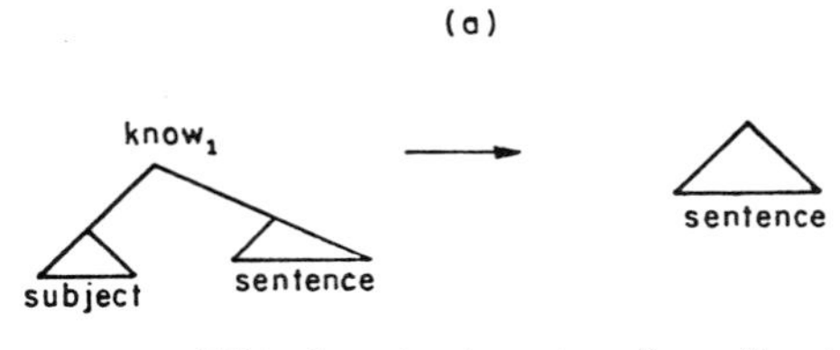

(b)

NP V that S

FIGURE 1

Traversing the path in Figure 1b enables the ATN to recognize that $know_1$ is intended in the sentence. NEWBUILD and APPLYTENSE, as described earlier, perform the equivalent of the operation in Figure 1a at the end of the path in Figure 1b.

2.2.4. Stem Words and Affixes

In the lexicon, one would like to have as little redundant information as possible for words that are derivatives of some stem. As mentioned earlier the lexical subcategories relate words with affixes to their stem words. Since we associate the presuppositional information in the lexicon with the word plus its subcategory, we have been able to relate the similar presuppositions of words such as *disappoint, disappointed,* and *disappointment.* In many instances, one need only have a pointer to the stem word in the lexicon, rather than having the lexical information replicated.

3. COMPUTING ENTAILMENTS

The computation of entailments is more complex than it is for presuppositions because the computation depends on the presence or absence of negation. For instance, sentence (12a) entails (12b), but (13) has no entailment. Throughout the remainder of this section, an (a) sentence entails a (b) sentence.

(12) a. *John was not able to leave.*
b. *John did not leave.*

(13) *John was able to leave.*

Karttunen (1970) studies the effect of negation on the entailments of numerous lexical items.

A chain of entailments must be computed, because entailments at a given sentential level in the semantic representation may be affected by embedding predicates and syntactic structures arbitrarily many levels above the current one. For instance, (15a) entails (15b) and (15c), since (15b) entails (15c). However, from (14a), one cannot conclude anything about whether Mary won.

(14) a. *It is false that John prevented Mary from winning.*
b. *John did not prevent Mary from winning.*

(15) a. *It is true that John prevented Mary from winning.*

b. *John prevented Mary from winning.*
c. *Mary did not win.*

The embedded sentences of (14a) or (15a) could have been preposed, therefore the computation must wait until the entire sentence is traversed. A tree is built during the parse; every node in the tree corresponds to a propositional or sentential level. Upon reaching the period (or question mark) marking the end of the sentence, the information in the tree is used to compute the chain of entailments.

At each node of the tree, three units of information are needed: an atom indicating whether there is negation present in the surface sentence at this sentential level, the surface tense (if any) at this level, and a list of the lexical entries for potential entailed propositions arising from words at this level. After parsing the complete sentence, a function CHAIN of three arguments is applied to each node of the tree. The arguments are the tree just described, an atom indicating whether negation is passed from the higher sentential level, and the tense from a higher level. The function computes entailments by checking the negation requirements of the possible entailments at this level against the negation actually present. If the negation conditions of none of the possible entailments at this level are satisfied, the remainder of the subtree is ignored. This corresponds to the fact that (14a) entails nothing about whether Mary won or not. I shall refer to this tree as a TREE OF POTENTIAL ENTAILMENTS.

The tree is formed in the following way. One of the entities returned from any embedded sentence is the tree constructed from that sentence. Each tree is stored in a list according to logical role rather than syntactic order. As each word that could have entailments is encountered at this sentential level, its lexical information is added to a set of such information at this level. At the end of this level, each member of this set is modified by applying NEWBUILD to its argument in the member. Also, an atom telling whether or not negation is present at this level and the surface tense at this level is added, forming a new node of the tree.

The lexical information for entailments is associated with the word plus subcategory, just as it was for presupposition. The information is a set of elements, one element per possible entailment.

For each set element, four items are necessary. The first is an atom indicating whether negation must be present or absent. The second is the argument to NEWBUILD, which will yield the logical form of the potential entailment. The third item is an atom indicating whether the entailed proposition would be positive or negative. This is necessary to verify that the negation conditions are satisfied for potential entailments of embedded sentences. The fourth unit is necessary for predicates which have two embedded sentences. It is an atom indicating whether the left or right subtree is associated with the entailment (for purposes of continuing the chain of entailments).

In addition to the effect of negation, there are two other phenomena that prevent potential entailments from being added to the set of entailments of a sentence.

3.1 Blocking Entailments

Examples (16) and (17) demonstrate the behavior of *prevent* with respect to negation.

(16) a. *John prevented Mary from leaving.*
b. *Mary did not leave.*

(17) *John did not prevent Mary from leaving.*

(18) *Did John prevent Mary from leaving?*

(19) *I ask you whether John prevented Mary from leaving.*

If the proposition of (16a) is asked as a yes–no question or embedded in a "whether" clause, as in (18) and (19), there is no entailment corresponding to *prevent*. This is due to the dependence of entailment on negation.

Modeling this computationally is straightforward. In a yes–no question, the tree of potential entailments at the top sentential level is simply the null tree. Similarly, the sentential level of a "whether" clause has the null tree as well. However, entailments of embedded sentences must still be computed, as Section 3.2 demonstrates.

3.2. Promoting Entailments to Presuppositions

Any entailment of a presupposition is also a presupposition. Since (20) presupposes (16a), (16b) is also presupposed by (20).

(20) *Did John know that he prevented Mary from leaving?*

The entailment of *prevent* has been promoted to a presupposition, because of the meaning of *know*.

A way to reflect this is to add an entailment entry in the lexicon under *know* and its appropriate subcategory. However, the negation condition would be *T*, for universally true. At the end of the current sentential level, the system checks the set of possible entailments for any condition marked *T*. If it finds one, the subtree of potential entailments is used to calculate the entailments immediately and add them to the set of presuppositions. The subtree is then set to null.

That is a way to compute entailments promoted to presuppositions because of the effect of lexical items. A similar computation occurs for the effect of syntactic constructs having presuppositions; rather than marking the lexical entry, the path of that syntactic construct is appropriately marked.

4. COMPOUND SENTENCES

The search for a recursive rule that would give the presuppositions and entailments of a compound sentence from those of its embedded sentences has been called the PROJECTION PROBLEM. A solution has evolved over several years. It is summarized in Joshi and Weischedel (1977); a more thorough account appears in Weischedel (1975).

The solution involves placing the predicates that take embedded sentences in four classes: holes, speech acts, predicates of propositional attitude, and connectives. Associated with each class is a simple structural computation which gives the presuppositions and entailments of the compound from those of its embedded sentences. The lexicon records to which of the four classes each such predicate belongs.

The parser is designed such that a "pushdown" occurs whenever an embedded proposition is expected, whether or not it has the syntactic form of a sentence. The set of presuppositions and the tree of potential entailments of the embedded proposition are returned as values. At the end of the sentence at the current level, the recursive rule or projection rule is applied. First, I describe the rule for presuppositions, then the one for entailments.

4.1. Presuppositions

The broadest of the four classes of predicates has been called HOLES, because presuppositions of embedded sentences become presuppositions of the compound. *Regret*, *fail*, and *begin* are just a few prediates in this class. Numerous examples of this class and the other classes may be found in Karttunen (1973). For this class, presuppositions of embedded sentences are merely added to the set of the current level.

The two classes of speech acts and of predicates of propositional attitude exhibit similar behavior. Speech acts are verbs of saying. Predicates of propositional attitude include verbs such as *think* and *hope.* Presuppositions of sentences embedded under these predicates become presuppositions of the compound, but under the speaker's claims (for speech acts) or the actor's "beliefs" (for predicates of propositional attitude). For instance, (21a) presupposes (21b), not (21c).

(21) a. *John said that Mary regretted that she left.*
b. *John claimed Mary left.*
c. *Mary left.*

To reflect this, every presupposition of a sentence embedded under a speech act becomes embedded under a predicate *CLAIM*, which is a semantic primitive; the logical subject of the speech act is an additional argument to *CLAIM*. For predicates of propositional attitude, the same computation occurs, except using a primitive *BELIEVE*.

An exception to this case arises with presuppositions that definite noun phrases have referents. When the noun phrase makes transparent reference (that is, all participants in the communication agree that there is a referent), those presuppositions are not embedded under the speaker's claims. Opaque reference is the case of the referent existing only in the world of the speaker or actor; in this case, presuppositions of definite noun phrases must be embedded under the speaker's claims or actor's beliefs.

We can easily separate those presuppositions that pertain to existence of referents of noun phrases, because they arise from syntactically distinguished strings. The projection algorithm must generate two interpretations. The one corresponding to opaque reference embeds all presuppositions of embedded sentences in the world of the speaker's claims (for speech acts) or the world of the actor's beliefs (for predicates of propositional attitude). The interpretation corresponding to transparent reference embeds only the subset of presuppositions not pertaining to noun phrases under the speaker's claims or actor's beliefs; each member of the subset pertaining to noun phrases becomes a presupposition of the compound without such embedding.

A fourth class is connectives, such as *and*, *or*, and *if . . . then . . . .* As in the previous paragraphs, presuppositions of embedded sentences become presuppositions of the compound, but embedded under a world created by the connective. For instance, presuppositions of *if A then B* (interpreted as material implication) are the presuppositions of *A* plus all propositions *if A then C*, where *C* is a presupposition of *B*. (Examples involving other connectives appear in Joshi and Weischedel, 1977, and Karttunen, 1973).

4.2. Entailments

A significant new contribution of the research was demonstrating that the analysis for presuppositions carries over to entailments, subject to the constraint that the negation conditions are satisfied. Therefore, the projection algorithm acts on the tree of potential entailments, rather than a set as in the case of presuppositions.

For the class of predicates which are holes, the tree of potential entailments for the embedded sentence is unchanged, and becomes a subtree at the current level as described earlier.

For speech acts and predicates of propositional attitude, entailments of embedded sentences must be embedded under the speaker's claims (for speech acts) or the actor's beliefs (for predicates of propositional attitude). However, the speech act or predicate of propositional attitude itself has negation conditions on the embedded entailment becoming an entailment of the compound sentence. For instance, (22a) entails (22b). When part of a compound as in (23a), (23b) is entailed. However, (24) has no such entailment.

(22) a. *John forced Mary to leave.*
b. *Mary left.*

(23) a. *Jack said that John forced Mary to leave.*
b. *Jack claimed Mary left.*

(24) *Jack did not say that John forced Mary to leave.*

To account for this, the projection algorithm modifies the tree of potential entailments from embedded sentences; each potential entailment in the tree must be embedded under a predicate *CLAIM* (for speech acts) with an additional argument specifying the speaker. For predicates of propositional attitude, potential entailments are embedded under a predicate *BELIEVE*, with an additional argument specifying the speaker.

To account for the negation conditions of the speech act or predicate of propositional attitude, we can encode these negation conditions in the lexicon for each such predicate with the same four units of information described in Section 3. In this case, the proposition entailed by a speech act or predicate of propositional attitude is the trivial, universally true proposition *T*.

The fourth class of embedding predicates is the connectives. *A and B* entails *A*, *B* and the entailments of each. However, if *A and B* is negated as in *I doubt that A and B*, none of the entailments of *A* or of *B* become entailments of the whole. For material implication, if *B* entails *C*, then the entailments of *if A then B*, are of the form *if A then C*.

By now, the projection rule for connectives should be clear, for the phenomena to account for are analogous to those for speech acts. For *if A then B*, we embed each entailment in the list or tree structure in (25).

(25) (IF *a c*)

Of course, *a* is a register containing the semantic representation of *A*, and *c* contains a potentially entailed proposition of *B*.

There are negation conditions for *and* and *or* just as there were for speech acts and predicates of propositional attitude. The type of lexical entry described for speech acts will work for the connectives as well.

5. A SUGGESTION ABOUT THE LEXICON

I have demonstrated here and in Joshi and Weischedel (1977) that the presuppositions and entailments for a given interpretation or reading of a sentence may be computed independent of nonstructural context. As the parser generates the various readings of a sentence, my system computes the presuppositions and entailments for each reading. Of course, since context alters which reading is intended by a speaker or author, the presuppositions and entailments alter depending on context. In my computation, the lexicon contains the information used to compute those presuppositions and entailments associated with particular words.

THIS LEADS ME TO SUGGEST THAT THE TEST OF WHAT SHOULD BE INCLUDED IN A PARSER AND ITS ASSOCIATED LEXICON IS WHETHER THE LANGUAGE PHENOMENON IS INDEPENDENT OF NONSTRUCTURAL CONTEXT. If it is independent of nonstructural context, then it may be included.

Similar principles have been implicit in the design of the lexicon of the linguistic string parser, described in Section 2. It is based on a theory of grammar by Harris (1970). The empirical basis of his model is not acceptability itself, but rather whether hypothesized syntactic transformations preserve the acceptability or unacceptability of sentences. That empirical test largely factors out the effect of nonstructural context. (This theory of grammar has been studied formally in Joshi, Kosaraju, and Yamada, 1972, and its relation to transformational grammar has been considered in Joshi, 1973.)

To summarize, I suggest that the test of what should be included in a parser and its associated lexicon is whether the phenomenon is independent of nonstrutural context. Presupposition and entailment have this property.

6. CONCLUSION

This chapter has demonstrated how a parser, written as an augmented transition network, and its associated lexicon may compute the presuppositions and entailments of a sentence. The system achieves this by computing them for each reading or interpretation of a sentence as the parser generates the various readings. The computation is structural in nature, using tree transformations. Presupposition and entailment are examples of semantic information that may appropriately be included in a parser. A solution for the projection problem for presuppositions has been included in the system. Furthermore, that solution has been extended to include entailments.

This chapter has described a concrete computational model of computing presuppositions and entailments of sentences, and has sketched in Section 1 how interacting computational processes might predict the diverse phenomena of presupposition, which embrace semantics and pragmatics. I feel that interacting computational processes potentially offer powerful means for modeling linguistic phenomena, such as anaphora, paraphrase, contradiction, presupposition, entailment, and discourse. This is important since many linguistic phenomena embrace aspects of each of syntax, semantics, and pragmatics.

APPENDIX A

Compared to grammars appearing in linguistic literature, this one is of modest size. However, since it is patterned after a subset of the lexicon of the linguistic string parser of Sager, it is very general in nature. Furthermore, compared to many grammars that have been implemented on a computer, it is somewhat extensive.

Since one way to evaluate a natural language system is by the extent and complexity of syntactic constructions in the system, this appendix specifies a context-free language which includes all sentences the system is prepared to handle. The context-free language is specified by a recursive transition network (Woods, 1970).

A recursive transition network (RTN) is a generalization of a finite-state machine. An RTN is a graph with labeled states, labeled directed arcs, a distinguished start state, and a subset of final states. Arc labels may be either terminal symbols or state names. An input string of terminal symbols is accepted by an RTN if there is a path from the start state to the final state which consumes the string. A transition from one state to another in such a path may be made in one of two ways: (*a*) an arc labeled by a terminal symbol is taken if that terminal is currently pointed to in the input string; (*b*) an arc labeled by a state name is taken if there is a substring beginning at the current symbol in the input such that the substring is accepted by a path from the state named on the arc to a final state.

I have used the following nonterminals to represent syntatic categories (which would appear in the lexicon for a word). This is a shorthand for a subgraph of two states; the first state being labeled by that syntactic category, and the second state being a final state. The arcs between the two states would each be labeled by a word in the lexicon having that syntactic category.

V	verb
VN	nominalized verb
VEN	past participle of verb
VING	present participle of verb
PRO	pronoun
DET	determiner
TITLE	title
A	adjective
D	adverb
N	noun
P	preposition

The six graphs are DS for declaratives, NP for noun phrases, LS for subject shapes, OBJ for object shapes, POBJ for passive forms of object shapes, and $T(x)$ for tensed verbs x.

All items in lower case are constants. All upper case items are state names, corresponding to nonterminal symbols. Some special symbols follow:

λ	null symbol, that is, a jump
/s	ending for plural nouns or present tense, third person, singular
*poss	possessive ending

I have not included in this appendix graphs for relative clauses or questions (although these are included in the system); the reader can easily ascertain the relative clause and question constructions allowable from the DS, LS, OBJ, and POBJ graphs, by extraction of a noun phrase.

The nonterminal S–NP refers to any noun phrase not modified by *only* or by relative clauses. The $T(x)$ graph assumes that when it is called, it has been given (via SENDR) a particular syntactic subcategory or stem word to match, specified as x.

DS (Declarative Sentences)

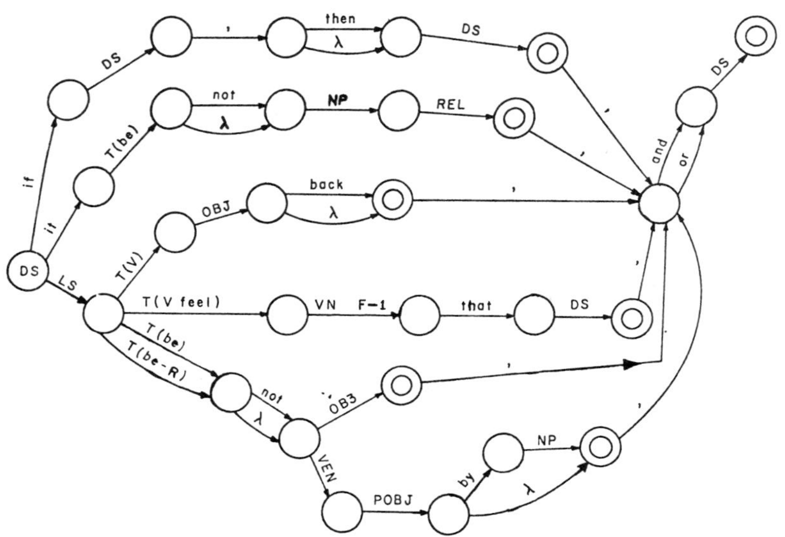

NP (Noun Phrases)

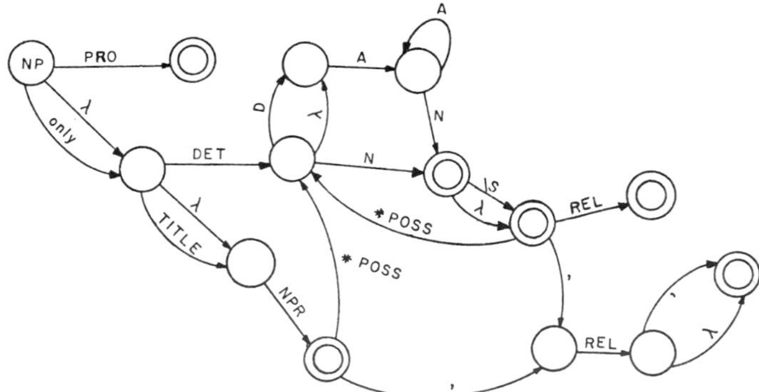

LS (Subject Shapes)

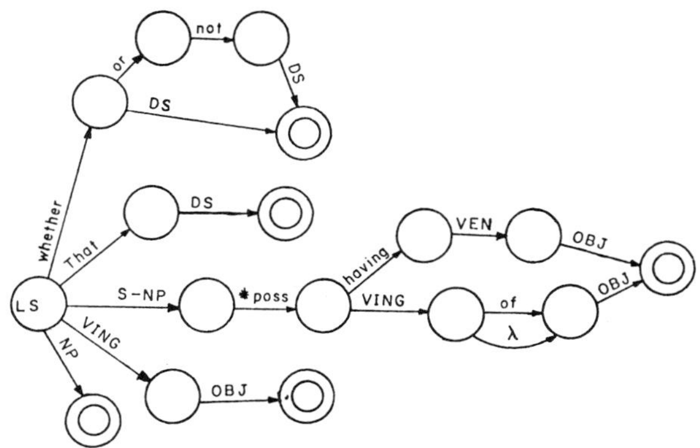

OBJ and OB3 (Object Shapes)

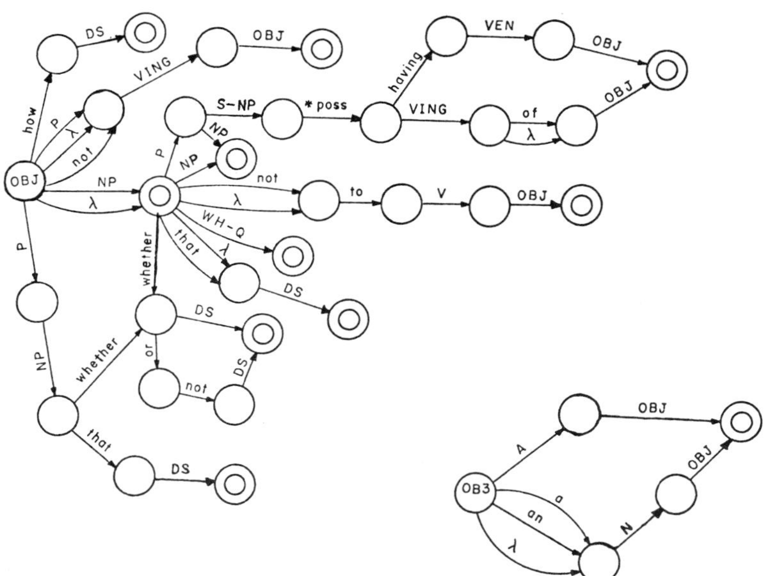

POBJ (Object Shapes for Passive Sentences)

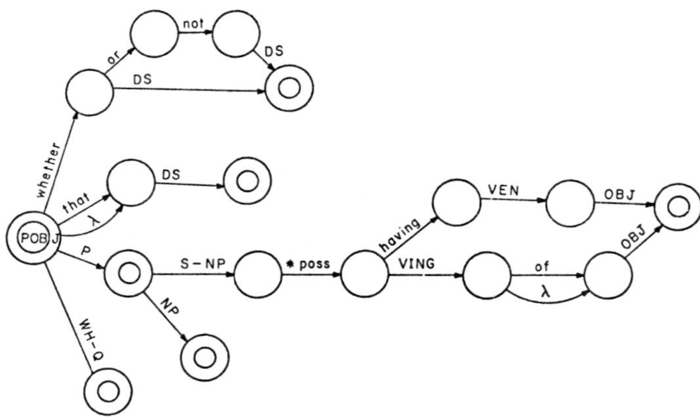

T(x) (Tensed Elements)

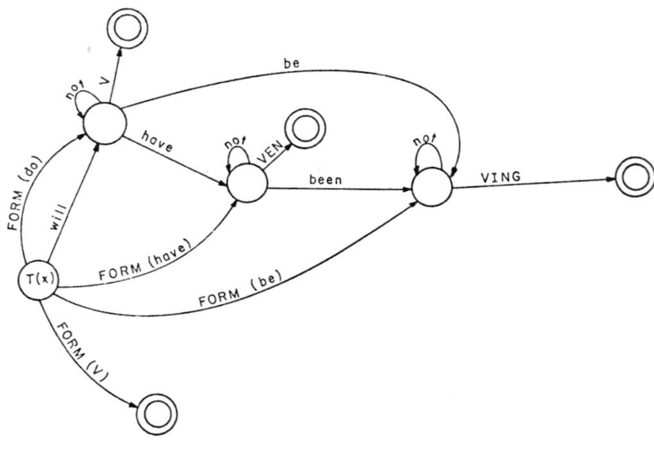

APPENDIX B: SAMPLE OUTPUT

Several example sentences are presented here with their computed presuppositions and entailments. The semantic representations used follow those suggested by Keenan (1972). It is a predicate and argument notation, encoded as list structures. The predicate is the first argument of a list and its arguments are the remaining list elements. The bindings (corresponding to noun phrases) for variables are encoded in lists one at a time. If *b* is a binding and *r* is a sentence in this notation, the sentence with the additional binding is (*b r*).

In the output, periods and commas are preceded by a slash because of LISP conventions. The input sentence appears first followed by a semantic representation of it.

The two sets of presuppositions computed are labeled NON-NP PRESUPPOSITIONS, those not associated with noun phrases, and NP-RELATED PRESUPPOSITIONS, those corresponding to the referents of noun phrases. Entailments are printed last. For presuppositions and entailments, the semantic representation of the proposition is printed first, followed by a simple translation to English. The symbol -UNTENSED- indicates that the tense of the proposition is not known.

Example 1 illustrates the presupposition of a *wh* question. Almost all of the examples include presuppositions of definite noun phrases. Examples 2 and 3 reflect the effect of syntactic environment on whether the predicate *be a problem* has a presupposition. Examples 4 and 5 show entailments corresponding to *force* and *prevent*. Example 6 is a yes–no question; the entailment of *continue* is therefore blocked, but the presupposition of *continue* remains. Examples 7 and 8 illustrate the projection algorithm.

Example 1

WHO TRANSLATED THE ASSIGNMENT?

SEMANTIC REPRESENTATION

((THE ASSIGNMENT /, X0077) ((E ONE /, X0076) (ASK I YOU (*WH*-SOME X0076 (IN-THE-PAST (TRANSLATE X0076 X0077))))))

NON-NP PRESUPPOSITIONS

NP-RELATED PRESUPPOSITIONS

((E ASSIGNMENT /, X0077) (*UNTENSED (IN-THE-SHARED-INFO X0077)))
SOME ASSIGNMENT EXIST -UNTENSED- IN THE SHARED INFORMATION.

((THE ASSIGNMENT /, X0077) ((E ONE /, X0076) (IN-THE-PAST (TRANSLATE X0076 X0077))))

SOME ONE TRANSLATED THE ASSIGNMENT.

ENTAILMENTS

Example 2

THAT THE DISCUSSIONS ARE IRRELEVANT IS A PROBLEM /.

SEMANTIC REPRESENTATION

((((COLLECTIVE DISCUSSION /, XØØ13) (NUMBER XØØ13 TWO-OR-MORE)) /, XØØ14) (ASSERT I (IN-THE-PRESENT (PROBLEM (FACT (IN-THE-PRESENT (NOT (RELEVANT XØØ14))))))))

Non-NP Presuppositions

((((COLLECTIVE DISCUSSION /, XØØ13) (NUMBER XØØ13 TWO-OR-MORE)) /, XØØ14) (IN-THE-PRESENT (NOT (RELEVANT XØØ14))))

THE DISCUSSIONS ARE IRRELEVANT.

NP-Related Presuppositions

((((E DISCUSSION /, XØØ13) (NUMBER XØØ13 TWO-OR-MORE)) /, XØØ14) (*UNTENSED (IN-THE-SHARED-INFO XØØ14)))

SOME DISCUSSIONS EXIST -UNTENSED- IN THE SHARED INFORMATION.

Entailments

Example 3

WHETHER THE DISCUSSIONS ARE IRRELEVANT IS A PROBLEM /.

Semantic Representation

((((COLLECTIVE DISCUSSION /, XØØ17) (NUMBER XØØ17) TWO-OR-MORE)) /, XØØ18) (ASSERT I (IN-THE-PRESENT (PROBLEM (WHE (IN-THE-PRESENT (NOT (RELEVANT XØØ18))))))))

NON-NP Presuppositions

NP-Related Presuppositions

((((E DISCUSSION /, XØØ17) (NUMBER XØØ17 TWO-OR-MORE)) /, XØØ18) (*UNTENSED (IN-THE-SHARED-INFO XØØ18)))

SOME DISCUSSIONS EXIST -UNTENSED- IN THE SHARED INFORMATION.

ENTAILMENTS

Example 4

MARY WAS FORCED TO LEAVE /.

Semantic Representation

((MARY /, XØØ52) (ASSERT I (IN-THE-PAST (CAUSE NIL (COME-ABOUT (EVENT (LEAVE XØØ52)))))))

Non-NP Presuppositions

NP-Related Presuppositions

((MARY /, XØØ52) (*UNTENSED (IN-THE-SHARED-INFO XØØ52)))
MARY EXIST -UNTENSED- IN THE SHARED INFORMATION.

Entailments

((MARY /, X0052) (IN-THE-PAST (LEAVE X0052)))
MARY LEFT.

Example 5

THE CROWDED LECTURES PREVENTED THE STUDENTS FROM LEARNING /.

SEMANTIC REPRESENTATION

((((COLLECTIVE STUDENT /, X0059) (NUMBER X0059 TWO-OR-MORE)) /, X0060) ((((((COLLECTIVE LECTURE /, X0056) (CROWDED X0056)) /, X0057) (NUMBER X0057 TWO-OR-MORE)) /, X0058) (ASSERT I (IN-THE-PAST (CAUSE X0058 (NOT (COME-ABOUT (EVENT (LEARN X0060 NIL)))))))))

NON-NP PRESUPPOSITIONS

NP-RELATED PRESUPPOSITIONS

((((((E LECTURE /, X0056) (CROWDED X0056)) /, X0057) (NUMBER X0057 TWO-OR-MORE)) /, X0058) (*UNTENSED (IN-THE-SHARED-INFO X058)))

SOME CROWDED LECTURES EXIST -UNTENSED- IN THE SHARED INFORMATION.

((((E STUDENT /, X0059) (NUMBER X0059 TWO-OR-MORE)) /, X0060) (*UNTENSED (IN-THE-SHARED-INFO X0060)))

SOME STUDENTS EXIST -UNTENSED- IN THE SHARED INFORMATION.

ENTAILMENTS

((((COLLECTIVE STUDENT /, X0059) (NUMBER X0059 TWO-OR-MORE)) /, X0060) (NOT (IN-THE-PAST (LEARN X0060 NIL))))

IT IS NOT THE CASE THAT THE STUDENTS LEARNED.

Example 6

DID MARY CONTINUE STRIKING JOHN?

SEMANTIC REPRESENTATION

((JOHN /, X0109) ((MARY /, X0108) (ASK I YOU (WHE (IN-THE-PAST (CONTINUE (EVENT (STRIKE X0108 X0109)) NIL))))))

NON-NP PRESUPPOSITIONS

((JOHN /, X0109) ((MARY /, X0108) ((((E TIME /, X0110) (IMMEDIATELY-BEFORE X0110 NIL)) /, X0111) (AT-TIME (IN-THE-PAST (HAVE-EN (BE-ING (STRIKE X0108 X0109)))) X0111))))

MARY HAD BEEN STRIKING JOHN.

NP-RELATED PRESUPPOSITIONS

((MARY /, X0108) (*UNTENSED (IN-THE-SHARED-INFO X0108)))

MARY EXIST -UNTENSED- IN THE SHARED INFORMATION.

((JOHN /, X0109) (*UNTENSED (IN-THE-SHARED-INFO X0109)))

JOHN EXIST -UNTENSED- IN THE SHARED INFORMATION.

ENTAILMENTS

Example 7

THE PROFESSOR DOUBTED THAT JOHN MANAGED TO TRANSLATE AN ASSIGNMENT /.

SEMANTIC REPRESENTATION

((E ASSIGNMENT /, X0042) ((JOHN /, X0041) ((THE PROFESSOR /, X0039) (ASSERT I (IN-THE-PAST (BELIEVE X0039 (NOT (IN-THE-PAST (COME-ABOUT (EVENT (TRANSLATE X0041 X0042)))))))))))

NON-NP PRESUPPOSITIONS

((THE PROFESSOR /, X0039) (*UNTENSED (HUMAN X0039)))

THE PROFESSOR BE -UNTENSED- HUMAN.

((E ASSIGNMENT /, X0042) ((JOHN /, X0041) ((THE PROFESSOR /, X0039) (IN-THE-PAST (BELIEVE X0039) (IN THE PAST (ATTEMPT (EVENT (TRANSLATE X0041 X0042)))))))))

THE PROFESSOR BELIEVED THAT JOHN ATTEMPTED TO TRANSLATE SOME ASSIGNMENT.

NP-RELATED PRESUPPOSITIONS

((E PROFESSOR /, X0039) (*UNTENSED (IN-THE-SHARED-INFO X0039)))

SOME PROFESSOR EXIST -UNTENSED- IN THE SHARED INFORMATION.

((JOHN /, X0041) (*UNTENSED (IN-THE-SHARED-INFO X0041)))

JOHN EXIST -UNTENSED- IN THE SHARED INFORMATION.

ENTAILMENTS

((E ASSIGNMENT /, X0042) ((JOHN /, X0041) ((THE PROFESSOR /, X0039) (IN-THE-PAST (BELIEVE X0039) (NOT (IN-THE-PAST (TRANSLATE X0041 X0042))))))))

THE PROFESSOR BELIEVED THAT IT IS NOT THE CASE THAT JOHN TRANSLATED SOME ASSIGNMENT.

Example 8

JOHN WON /, AND MARY FELT DISAPPOINTMENT THAT HE WON /.

SEMANTIC REPRESENTATION

((MARY /, X0050) ((JOHN /, X0048) (ASSERT I (AND (IN-THE-PAST (WIN X0048)) (IN-THE-PAST (DISAPPOINT (FACT (IN-THE-PAST (WIN X0048))) X0050))))))

NON-NP PRESUPPOSITIONS

((JOHN /, X0048) (IF-THEN (IN-THE-PAST (WIN X0048)) (IN-THE-PAST (WIN X0048))))

IF JOHN WON THEN JOHN WON.

((MARY /, X0050) ((JOHN /, X0048) (IF-THEN (IN-THE-PAST (WIN X0048)) (*UNTENSED (HUMAN X0050)))))

IF JOHN WON THEN MARY BE -UNTENSED- HUMAN.

NP-RELATED PRESUPPOSITIONS

((JOHN /, X0048) (*UNTENSED (IN-THE-SHARED-INFO X0048)))

JOHN EXIST -UNTENSED- IN THE SHARED INFORMATION.

((JOHN /, X0048) (IF-THEN (IN-THE-PAST (WIN X0048)) ((MARY /, X0050) (*UNTENSED (IN-THE-SHARED-INFO X0050)))))

IF JOHN WON THEN MARY EXIST -UNTENSED- IN THE SHARED INFORMATION.

ENTAILMENTS

((JOHN /, X0048) (IN-THE-PAST (WIN X0048)))

JOHN WON.

((MARY /, X0050) ((JOHN /, X0048) (IN-THE-PAST (DISAPPOINT (FACT (IN-THE-PAST (WIN X0048))) X0050))))

THE FACT THAT JOHN WON DISAPPOINTED MARY.

REFERENCES

Anderson, B., Transformationally based english strings and their word subclasses. *String Program Reports No. 7.* New York: Linguistics String Project, New York University, 1970.

Charniak, E., Inference and knowledge I. In E. Charniak and Y. Wilks, (Eds.), *Computational semantics.* Amsterdam: North-Holland, 1976.

Clark, H. H., and Haviland, S. E., Comprehension and the given-new contract. In R. Freedle, (Ed.), *Discourse production and comprehension.* Hillside, New Jersey: Lawrence Erlbaum Associates, 1977.

Fillmore, C. J., Verbs of judging: An exercise in semantic description. In C. J. Fillmore and D. T. Langendoen (Eds.), *Studies in linguistic semantics.* New York: Holt, 1971.

Fitzpatrick, E. and Sager, N., The lexical subclasses of the linguistic string parser. *American Journal of Computational Linguistics,* 1974, *1*, microfiche 2.

Givón, T., The time-axis phenomenon. *Language,* 1973, *49*, 890–925.

Grishman, R., Implementation of the string parser of English. In R. Rustin (Ed.), *Natural language processing.* New York: Algorithmics Press, 1973.

Harris, Z. S., Two systems of grammar: Report and paraphrase. In Z. S. Harris (Ed.), *Structural and transformational linguistics.* Dordrecht, Holland: D. Reidel, 1970.

Joshi, A. K., A class of transformational grammars. In M. Gross, M. Halle, and M. Schutzenberger (Eds.), *Formal analysis of natural language.* Amsterdam: North-Holland, 1973.

Joshi, A. K., and Weischedel, R. M., Computation of a subclass of inferences: Presuppo-

sition and entailment. *American Journal of Computational Linguistics,* 1977, 4, microfiche 63.
Joshi, A. K., Kosaraju, S., and Yamada, H. M., String adjunct grammars I and II, *Information and Control, 21,* 1972, 93–116; 235–260.
Karttunen, L., On the semantics of complement sentences. *Papers from the Sixth Regional Meeting of the Chicago Linguistic Society.* Chicago: University of Chicago, 1970.
Karttunen, L., Presuppositions of compound sentences. *Linguistic Inquiry,* 1973, *IV,* 169–193.
Karttunen, L. and Peters, S., Conventional implicature in Montague grammar. Paper presented at the First Annual Meeting of Berkeley Linguistic Society, Berkeley, California, February 15, 1975.
Keenan, E. L., Two kinds of presupposition in natural language. In C. J. Fillmore and D. T. Langendoen (Eds.), *Studies in linguistic semantics.* New York: Holt, 1971.
Keenan, E. L., On semantically based grammar. *Linguistic Inquiry,* 1972, *4,* 413–461.
Kempson, R. M., *Presupposition and the delimitation of semantics.* Cambridge: Cambridge University Press, 1975.
Kiparsky, P. and Kiparsky, C., Fact. In D. Steinberg and L. Jakobovits (Eds.), *Semantics.* New York: Cambridge University Press, 1971.
Sagar, N., Syntactic analysis of natural language. In F. Alt. and M. Rubinoff, (Eds.), *Advances in Computers, 8.* New York: Academic Press, 1967.
Sager, N. The string parser for scientific literature. In R. Rustin (Ed.), *Natural language processing.* New York: Algorithmics Press, 1973.
Weischedel, R. M., Computation of a unique subclass of inferences: Presupposition and entailment. Unpublished doctoral dissertation, University of Pennsylvania, 1975.
Weischedel, R. M., Voge, W., and James, M. An artificial intelligence approach to language instruction. *Artificial Intelligence,* in press.
Woods, W. A., Transition network grammars for natural language analysis. *Communications of the ACM,* 1970, *13,* 591–606.
Woods, W. A., An experimental parsing system for transition network grammars. In R. Rustin (Ed.), *Natural language processing.* New York: Algorithmics Press, 1973.

KATZ AND LANGENDOEN ON PRESUPPOSITION

S.-Y. KURODA
University of California at San Diego

(1) *Jack has children and all of Jack's children are bald.*

Concerning this sentence Karttunen (1973) says, "As far as I can see, it does not presuppose that Jack has children. If it should turn out that the first conjunct is false, then the whole conjunction surely ought to be false, not indeterminate or truthvalueless [p. 178]." And concerning this statement by Karttunen, Katz and Langendoen (1976) write, "This is all that Karttunen says by way of justifying his claim that sentences like [1], in which the first clause asserts what the second clause presupposes, do not contain a presupposition associated with the second clause [p. 16]." They then admonish Karttunen: "Thus the claim that *and* and *or* results in filtering rests ultimately only on the intuitions of the investigator [p. 16]."

Linguistic theory ultimately rests on the intuitions of the speaker–investigator, but if linguistic investigation ultimately rests ONLY on the intuitions of the investigator, that is when empiricism arises again, as Katz and Bever (1976) have warned, and romanticism will also return.

* * *

(2) a. *Jack has children, and all of Jack's children have children.*
b. *Jack and all of Jack's children have children.*

But rationalists may not always agree with rationalists in performance.

Syntax and Semantics, Volume 11: Presupposition

ISBN 0-12-613511-8

> Suppose that Jack does not have children. On Karttunen's analysis, (2a) is false and (2b) is truthvalueless (fails to make a statement). On our analysis, both (2a) and (2b) are truthvalueless. Thus (2a) and (2b), on Karttunen's analysis, cannot have the same logical form; this will force him to give up the generalization that conjoined sentences and their counterparts with conjoined NP's always have the same logical form. . . . On our analysis, on the other hand, the generalization is secure. Hence our analysis . . . is preferable to Karttunen's [Katz and Langendoen, 1976, p. 16].

This is all Katz and Langendoen say by way of justifying their claim that *and* is "not associated with presupposition filtering." That is, a definite description like *Jack's children* carries the existential presupposition, and the presupposition is not filtered out by the conjunction *and*, as Karttunen claims it may be.

But if a secure generalization over the two sentence patterns in question is all that counts, we might as well take both as **FALSE**, as the "Russellian" theory of definite descriptions would have it. Indeed, according to a nonpresuppositionalist theory, each of these sentences entails the existence of Jack's children, and hence, if Jack does not have children, logic simply dictates it to be false. The question as to whether *and* is associated with presupposition filtering—or some such extralogical mechanism in the semantic component—does not even arise in a nonpresuppositionalist semantic theory. Is not this analysis, then, preferable to Katz and Langendoen's (and a fortiori to Karttunen's)?

* * *

(3) a. *If Jack has children, then all of Jack's children are bald.*
b. *If Jack has sisters, then all of Jack's children are bald.*

Suppose that Jack does not have children. "If Jack has sisters, then aren't all of Jack's children bald?"—"?! . . . If Jack has sisters, then all of Jack's children are bald?! That doesn't make sense."

Suppose that Jack does not have children. "But **if** Jack has children, then aren't all of Jack's children bald?"—"Surely, bald as Jack has been since he was fifteen, if Jack has children, then all of Jack's children must be bald."

Thus, Katz and Langendoen, with Karttunen, observe that *Jack's children* carries an existential presupposition with *if Jack has sisters,* but not with *if Jack has children,* and conclude that the subject position in the consequent of conditionals behaves like a "hole" on some occasions and like a "plug" on others.

Katz and Langendoen, however, admonish Karttunen for jumping to the conclusion that he has found a new type of semantic entity with the properties of both holes and plugs. They abhor such an idea, which is reminiscent of the logic of quantum physics. They would rather simply plug holes by the heavy-parentheses wipe-out rule (HPWR), which is claimed to be independently motivated and provides a mechanism for presupposition filtering.

"The details of how [they] represent this plugging do not concern us here [Katz and Langendoen, 1976, p. 7]." What concerns us here is their claim that unless otherwise specified by HPWR a definite description carries with it an existential presupposition in the subject position in the consequent of conditionals.

When the presuppositionalist says truthvalueless, the nonpresuppositionalist is supposed to say false. When the presuppositionalist says something presupposes something else, the nonpresuppositionalist is supposed to say something entails something else.

Putting Katz and Langendoen's claim in his framework, the nonpresuppositionalist would have to say that (3b) entails *Jack has children* and he would have to formulate a counterpart of HPWR and introduce entailment filtering—an extralogical mechanism, the question of whose existence has previously been said not even to arise—in order for (3a) not to entail *Jack has children.*

It would now seem that the choice between the presuppositionalist and the nonpresuppositionalist semantic theory ultimately rests on the intuitions of the investigator. Where the presuppositionalist intuits presupposition and absence of truth value, the nonpresuppositionalist intuits entailment and falsehood.

* * *

(4) a. *If Jack has sisters, Jack's sisters have insisted his wife have children.*
b. *If Jack's sisters have insisted his wife have children, Jack's wife has let herself have children.*
c. *If Jack's wife has let herself have children, Jack's wife has become neurotic.*
d. *If Jack's wife has become neurotic, all of Jack's children are bald.*

Therefore, if Jack has sisters, then all of Jack's children are bald. But we have yet to find out whether Jack indeed has children. This sentence hence does not entail *Jack has children.* More generally, a conditional sentence, we conclude, does not entail entailments of its consequent, and we need not introduce an extralogical mechanism of entailment filtering for the sake of conditional sentence, either.

Insofar as the above argument has persuasive power for the presuppositionalist, he cannot insist that our concluding sentence, that is, (3b), is truthvalueless due to presupposition failure. But, as we have noted earlier, Katz and Langendoen observe that *Jack's children* carries an existential presupposition in (3b). Is it their intuition, not presupposition, that has failed here?

* * *

(5) a. *I pledge allegiance to the flag of the United States of America.*
b. *We have a genius in the White House now.*
c. *If Jack has grandchildren, then all of Jack's children are bald.*

"A beginning was made in studying the role of the competence–performance distinction in semantics during the early 1960's . . . . Chomsky's distinction of 'wellformedness' versus 'acceptability' is paralleled by the distinction of 'meaningfulness', which is a property of sentence types, vs. 'significance', which is a property of tokens, or utterance." Thus, the pledge of allegiance to the flag of the United States of America "is meaningful in English—but a token of [5a] incomprehensibly spoken by nursery school children would not be significant [Katz and Langendoen, 1976, p. 11]."

Likewise, (5b) could have significance (utterance meaning) not solely predictable from its grammatical meaning, as the case may be.

"According to [Karttunen's] account," Katz and Langendoen further warn, "sentences like . . . [5c] also do not presuppose that Jack has children . . . ." But "by the formal semantic theory sketched in §2, . . . the presupposition remains that Jack's children exist. If users of sentences like . . . [5c] conclude that that presupposition does not obtain, the carrying out of their deduction must be viewed as being performed outside the grammar itself, . . . [Katz and Langendoen, 1976, p. 15]."

Thus, quite rightly, the intuitions of the speaker–investigator as well as nursery school children, could either reflect competence more or less adequately, as when the pledge is uttered with the right understanding of its grammatical meaning and with the right intention, OR diverge from it significantly, as the contexts of utterance might dictate.

Katz and Langendoen claim that (3b) grammatically presupposes the existence of Jack's children. But they must recognize, we insist, that the TOKEN of (3b) is truthfully uttered as the conclusion of the argument given in (4) without that presupposition. The logic of the competence–performance distinction, then, must tell us that in the context of the above argument the presupposition of (3b) is suppressed outside the grammar, and that in contrast the speaker–investigator's intuition responds correctly to the grammatical meaning of (3b) and records a faithful intuitive representation of its presupposition when (3b) is given him in isolation as an example in linguistic discussion.

Such logic, at best, sounds a bit peculiar. A contingent sentence like (3b) can be said to be true or false, or truthvalueless, only in actual or imaginary use with a specific context with respect to which the sentence is to be given a valuation. Put another way, the predicates *true*, *false*, and *truthvalueless* are to be predicated of sentence TOKENS, not sentence TYPES, at least as far as contingent sentences are concerned.[1] To say this does not imply that these predicates do not belong to semantic theory, a competence theory concerned with sentence TYPES. In fact, we are facing the claim in semantic theory that (3b) semantically presupposes the existence of Jack's children, which means that for each TOKEN of (3b) it is either true or false if and only if *Jack has children* is true in the TOKEN context. But one is advised, it would seem, that in order to test this claim against our intuition we should not conjure a TOKEN with a sufficiently specified context where the valuation of (3b) is determined clearly, but rather we should on the contrary contemplate (3b) in isolation, trying not to simulate any situation of possible use which would allow the valuation of (3b) to be specified concretely.

* * *

(6) a. *Jack is a bachelor.*
b. *Jack is unmarried.*

A direct, intuitive grasp of entailment is possible for our faculty of understanding. For example, we have intuitive, direct understanding of the fact that (6a) entails (6b). This by itself does not guarantee, however, that the intuitive feel of entailment is always necessarily a form of intuitive manifestation in our consciousness of the semantic concept entailment, a concept belonging to semantic theory. Nor, for that matter, does the intuition of entailment by itself justify entailment as a semantic concept. What we identify as our intuitive feel for entailment might only be rooted at the level of performance, like our sense of acceptability presumably produced by various competence and performance factors.

[1] I put the word type in small capitals when it is used in the sense coupled with TOKEN, lest it should be confused with the sense referring to different categories of sentences such as declarative or interrogative. Correlatively, I also put the word TOKEN in small capitals for the sake of symmetry.

But the concept of entailment belongs to logic. To the extent that we can assume linguistic competence contains the faculty of reasoning, we are justified to assume that semantic theory contains logic in some form and that entailment also belongs to semantic theory as a semantic concept. Thus, entailment is both a semantic concept and an intuitive notion. In accordance with the fundamental theoretical assumption of the competence–performance distinction, the entailment relation holding between two specific sentences may not be directly accessible to our intuitive understanding. Nor may a specific instance of intuition of entailment necessarily be a form of intuitive manifestation of the semantic concept of entailment.

The earlier argument (4) convinces us that (3b) does not entail *Jack has children.* But this fact may not be grasped directly by our intuitive understanding. On the contrary, given (3b) in isolation, our immediate intuition might perceive, as Katz and Langendoen's apparently does, that it entails *Jack has children.*

Such apparent conflict between immediate intuition and theoretical reason of course does not disturb us. What such apparent conflict suggests is the distinction between the concept of entailment belonging to semantic theory and the notion of entailment, better labeled "apparent" entailment, belonging to performance theory, parallel to the distinction between grammaticality and acceptability. Example (3b) might "apparently" entail Jack has children, which it in fact does not entail.

So far as the concept of entailment is concerned it is a vain hope, apparently, that without context Katz's PRAG (Katz and Langendoen, 1976, p. 8) can be left alone, dormant. Lack of context may also interfere with the workings of intuition in the unfathomable depths of consciousness. Only with the help of appropriately selected contexts can theoretical reason help us see the meaning of a sentence when intuition fails us.

* * *

Recall that Katz and Langendoen, as well as Karttunen, claim that (3b) PRESUPPOSES *Jack has children.* Equivalently, they claim that the former is truthvalueless unless the latter is true. But our earlier example of an argument (4) and the preceding discussion must, I believe, convince any rationalist presuppositionalist that Katz and Langendoen's intuition has failed them on this account.

To be fair to the faculty of intuition, however, we should perhaps not say it has failed them. For intuition is doomed not to fail! Katz and Langendoen must have sensed by intuition what they identify as absence of truth value when they put (3b) before their consciousness, imagining that they did not know that Jack has children. For when we read that "as Morgan (1969) and Karttunen (1973) both observe, sentences like [3b] presuppose that the person referred to by the subject in the antecedent has children [Katz and Langendoen, 1976, p. 9],"[2] it would be fair to assume that Katz and Langendoen have made this statement on the basis of their confidence in their intuition, since what they are concerned with here is OBSERVATION. We do not have to cast any doubt on the sincerity of their reported observation. The intuition of absence of truth value must be real. But two cases arise.

First, absence of truth value may in fact be a semantic concept, a concept to be accounted for in semantic theory and ultimately understood by theoretical reason. If so, what Katz and Langendoen have sensed as absence of truth value must be a form of intuitive manifestation of this concept. Even so, though, a particular TOKEN of this category of intuition may not be a faithful reflex of a TOKEN of the underlying concept, and properly speaking, we may only talk about the intuition of "apparent" absence of truth value.

Or, secondly, absence of truth value may not be a concept belonging to linguistic competence. In that case what Katz and Langendoen have sensed as absence of truth value is, though real, not a form of intuitive manifestation of a semantic concept and can merely be justified on the level of performance, like acceptability. Absence of truth value could be a highly illusory amalgam of heterogeneous intuitive factors activated by the interactions of various concepts and notions, among them perhaps the concept of falsehood.

Whichever the case, what has failed Katz and Langendoen is reason, not intuition.

If the claim that absence of truth value is a semantic concept should ultimately rest only on the intuitions of the investigator, it cannot convincingly silence the dissidents who cast doubt on the epistemologi-

[2] Katz and Langendoen refer to Morgan in this context, but as far as I can see Morgan (1969) does not contain statements from which one can infer that he has made the same observation.

As far as Karttunen (1973) is concerned, his formula (13b), which specifies that a presupposition of the consequent clause of a conditional sentence is a presupposition of the entire conditional sentence unless it is entailed by the antecedent clause, indeed predicts that the existence of Jack's children is presupposed by our (3b). However, in a later section Karttunen reformulates his (13b), taking the effect of the context into consideration; compare his (17b′). If we apply the new formula to (3b) in the context given in the argument (4a)–(4d), it would rightly predict that (3b) does not (pragmatically) presuppose the existence of Jack's children, since the existence of Jack's children would be judged as entailed by the existence of Jack's sisters in the given context. Thus, my concern in the present chapter has no bearing on the validity of the judgments and the claims made by Karttunen (1973) that relate to pragmatic presupposition.

cal origin of the intuitive perception of so called absence of truth value and who wonder if it might only be a matter of intuition and not grounded on the level of competence, like the sense of acceptability. In any case, the case for semantic presupposition, needless to say, would not get much help from discussions based on examples where intuition, apparently, but not reason, recognizes absence of truth value.

* * *

(7) *The king of France is healthy.*

Sentence (7), said of the present actual world, is, we are told, truth-valueless. Upon hearing such a sentence we will have our sensitivity for absence of truth value activated. But the skeptic might attempt to imagine contexts where the use of such allegedly truthvalueless sentences do not plausibly excite our sense of absence of truth value.

Imagine, first, a scene of a cat chasing Fido. Assume that our John, observing the scene, states: "A rabbit is chasing Fido." We know that John is wrong, since his statement implies the existence of a rabbit but there is no rabbit in the scene. Imagine, now, that Bill is chasing Fido, and assume that our John pronounces: "The king of France is chasing Fido." Do we not know that John is mistaken, since his statement implies the existence of the king of France, but there is, we know, no king of France? These two cases are comparable. But, of course, we might simply conclude that John is out of his mind, using such a simple sentence out of place. Those who have thought that John is wrong must have carried out the deduction out of the grammar.

* * *

(8) a. *Is the king of France healthy?*
b. *The king of France is not healthy.*

In order to get out of everlasting disputes on intuition and on its evidential value, it would be incumbent on the proponent of the presuppositional theory to justify the notion of absence of truth value not solely relying on immediate intuition. Expounding on an idea by Geach, Katz has made such an attempt. He couples an affirmative sentence like (7) with the corresponding negative (8b), and considers them in light of the fact that they are THE proper possible answers to the corresponding interrogative sentence (8a). If there is no king of France, one cannot answer this question either by *yes* or *no;* the question should not arise and its possible answers are neither true nor false.

I have argued elsewhere that Katz's argumentation is spurious (Kuroda, 1974). Basically, Katz is mistaken in two respects: failing to see a correct generalization in one direction, and making a rash and wrong generalization in the other.

For one thing, the fact that the question posed by (8a) cannot be answered with either of the possible answers, *yes* (7) or *no* (8b), has nothing to do with the semantic presupposition or the statementhood condition. It is simply subsumed as a special case under a more general fact, that is that a disjunctive interrogative must, properly speaking, be answered by the declarative counterpart of one of its disjuncts, if one only assumes, as in fact Katz himself did elsewhere (Katz and Postal, 1964), that a yes–no interrogative is underlyingly the disjunction of a pair of corresponding positive and negative interrogatives. For example, *Is John a linguist or a philosopher?* may, properly speaking, be answered either by *John is a linguist* or by *John is a philosopher.*[3] If neither is true, the question should not have been raised, and if raised, it cannot be answered properly. However, from this observation one would not conclude that, if John is neither a linguist nor a philosopher, both *John is a linguist* and *John is a philosopher* are truthvalueless.

* * *

(9) a. *Make the king of France healthy.*
b. *Oh, were the king of France healthy.*

For another thing, Katz would have it not only that "the case where a question does not arise must coincide with the case where its corresponding assertion is neither true nor false" but also that "one can make a more general point," namely, "the propositions expressed by a declarative, its corresponding interrogative, corresponding imperative, corresponding hortatory, and so on, are respectively a statement, question, request, wish, and so on, by virtue of the same condition [Katz, 1972, p. 134]." Apparently Katz sees "asymmetry in the treatment of different sentence types [ibid]" and abhors it, if one considers the proposition expressed by a declarative as a statement, when its corresponding interrogative, corresponding imperative, or corresponding hortatory, etc., is out of place.

But such formalist argumentation to attain simple simplicity can only cover up important distinctive characteristics of different cases and ultimately fail to lead to adequate understanding of the real issues. I claim such is the case with Katz's argument for symmetry.

The interrogative, the imperative, the hortatory sentence, etc., are each associated with a particular type of speech act. The characteristic property of such a speech act determines the condition by virtue of

[3] Here I put aside the question of whether *or* can be read "inclusively," which does not affect the essence of the following argument.

which the interrogative, the imperative, the hortatory sentence are respectively a question, request, wish, etc.

Take, first, the imperative sentence (9a). The speaker issues an order, makes a request, gives an advice, offers an invitation, etc., by uttering this imperative sentence.[4] For the addressee to obey the order, respond to the request, follow the advice, accept the invitation, etc., the addressee must be in a position to be able to bring about a situation in which the addressee could state: "I have made the king of France healthy." Thus, for (9a) to constitute an appropriate speech act, it must presently be the case not only that there exists a king of France, but also that the king of France is not healthy. Or, consider the hortatory sentence (9b). For this to express a wish, it must likewise be the case that the king of France is presently not healthy.

If the speaker is sincere in issuing an order, etc., by uttering (9a), or expressing a wish by uttering (9b), the speaker must hold the belief that the king of France is not healthy. But assume that the king of France is healthy, or that there is no king of France. Then, though the speaker is sincere, the intended order, etc., does not constitute an actual order, etc., since it cannot be properly responded to, and the intended wish does not count as a wish, since nothing desired is left to be fulfilled.

The interrogative (8a), as noted earlier, requests from the addressee the information as to which of the two, (7) or (8b), is true. For this request to be properly responded to, it must be the case that the king of France is healthy or the king of France is not healthy. If the speaker is sincere in asking a question by uttering (8a), the speaker must hold the belief that either (7) or (8b) is true. But assume neither (7) nor (8b) is true. Then, though the speaker is sincere, the utterance does not make a question, since it cannot be answered.

Thus, the characteristic properties of the speech acts associated with the interrogative, the imperative, and the hortatory sentence determine the conditions under which they each properly make a TOKEN of the associated speech act. Put in another perspective, those are the conditions for the speaker to be SINCERE in properly using those sentences. They are not empirical conditions for conversational efficacy, for example, but conditions, dictated by practical reason, of what each speech act should be.

Now, consider the declarative sentence (7), and assume that the speaker is sincere in uttering this sentence. Then the speaker must hold the belief that the king of France is healthy! If the king of France

[4] For the speech act characterization of the imperative see Patrick Murray's forthcoming work.

is not healthy, or if there is in fact no king of France, the utterance does not make a TRUE statement, since there is mismatch between the reality and the intended statement.

These sincerity conditions differ among sentence types. The existence of a king of France is indeed entailed by each of them, but generally is not equivalent to them. It does not by itself make the utterance of each sentence a proper TOKEN of the associated speech act.

Note furthermore that if the proper use of the interrogative sentence is to ask a question, that of the imperative to issue an order, and so on, that of the hortatory to make a wish, then the proper use of the declarative sentence is to make a TRUE statement. The sincerity conditions of speech acts cannot determine the condition under which an utterance makes a false statement, and hence cannot determine the condition under which an utterance makes a true OR false statement. Practical reason does not know how one sincerely lies or deceives.

* * *

(10) *Is John a linguist or a philosopher?*

Thus, Katz's attempt to justify the concept of absence of truth value and that of semantic presupposition with the help of theoretical reason fails, I judge, and we have seen that practical reason cannot justify them, either. However, practical reason provides us with a rational foundation for the concept of PRAGMATIC presupposition in the case of INTERROGATIVE sentences.

Consider (10) again. A speech act made by uttering this sentence demands a choice between *John is a linguist* and *John is a philosopher* as a true statement. For this choice to be possible, it must be the case that either one or the other of these is true, and, hence, for the speaker to be sincere in asking the question, he must hold the belief that *John is a linguist or a philosopher* is true. Furthermore, the speaker must believe that the addressee is capable of answering the question, hence, that the addressee knows that either John is a linguist or John is a philosopher. It follows then that the speaker believes that the addressee knows, a fortiori, that *John is a linguist or a philosopher* is true.

To summarize, in a context in which (10) is properly uttered, the speaker believes that both the speaker and the addressee know *John is a linguist or a philosopher* is true. But, then, by the very definition of pragmatic presupposition, this disjunctive declarative sentence is a pragmatic presupposition of (10), the corresponding disjunctive interrogative.

The argument can be generalized to conclude that a disjunctive interrogative pragmatically presupposes the corresponding disjunctive declarative.

It follows from this that the unique existence of a king of France is in fact a pragmatic presupposition of (8a). For, to recall again, (8a) is assumed to be underlyingly identified with the disjunctive interrogative *Is the king of France healthy or is the king of France not healthy?* Then, the disjunction *The king of France is healthy or the king of France is not healthy* is a pragmatic presupposition of (8a), but this is logically equivalent to the unique existence of a king of France!

The reason why the sincerity condition of a speech act enables us to draw a conclusion of pragmatic presupposition in the case of interrogative sentences is that the speech act associated with interrogative sentences requires the addressee to respond with another speech act. This is a characteristic property of question as a speech act. The other speech acts do not relate to speech acts of the addressee, and their sincerity conditions do not relate to the addressee's belief system.

* * *

(11) a. *No one is healthy in France.*
b. *The president of the Senate is out of his mind.*

The interrogative sentence (8a) pragmatically presupposes the unique existence of the king of France, we have confirmed. In contrast, the claim that the unique existence of a king of France is a pragmatic or semantic presupposition of the declarative sentence (7) is not, I maintain, established on a rational basis. The claim still rests empirically on the intuitions of the investigator.

The declarative sentence is associated with the speech act of making a statement. This is a generic characterization of the declarative sentence in speech act theory, and may be considered as a property belonging to each sentence TYPE. However, the speech act characteristics of each TOKEN of the sentence TYPE, may, needless to say, deviate from this characterization, or may need modification of it.

The declarative (7), for example, may be used as an answer to the question posed by uttering the interrogative (8a). In such use, (7) not only performs the function of making a statement but also that of ANSWERING A YES–NO QUESTION PROPERLY. Answering the question posed by the interrogative (8a) means, among other things, that speaker A (the one who answers) knows what the utterance of (8a) indicates that speaker Q (the one who questions) believes, and A has accepted Q's belief without contradicting it. In particular, when A is about to answer properly by uttering (7), A knows that Q believes that either the king of France is healthy or the king of France is not healthy, that is, equivalently, that there exists one and only one king of France. Furthermore, A knows that A holds the same belief. Thus, (7), used as a proper answer, quite naturally pragmatically presupposes what is pragmatically presupposed by the interrogative sentence to which (7) is a proper answer.

Compare the speech act of answering properly with that of evading an answer. Assume, upon Q's (8a), A responds by uttering (11a). This is not a proper answer to (8a). Q must realize that, and can only evaluate (11a) as a statement. Q should now doubt whether what has been pragmatically presupposed by Q uttering (8a) is in fact adequate in the context. A may not believe that either (7) or (8b) is true. Example (11a) entails that the king of France is not healthy, if there is one and only one king of France, but it does not entail that there is in fact a king of France.

Or, assume A answers by uttering (11b). In that context, (11b) does not function as a proper answer, only as a statement. Hence it entails, but does not, in this context, pragmatically presuppose, the unique existence of a president of the Senate. Q may not conclude from this evasive answer of A's that A believes that Q has known that there is a person characterizable as the president of the Senate.

* * *

An affirmative sentence S is generally paired with a negative sentence $\bar{S}$ so that S and $\bar{S}$ constitute the set of properly possible answers to the corresponding yes–no interrogative S?. Let us call $\bar{S}$ the denial negation of S, and the pair S, $\bar{S}$ a denial pair. For example, (8b) is the denial negation of (7); (7) and (8b) are a denial pair, that is, each is the denial of the other. We can generalize the preceding discussion and conclude that a declarative sentence, either affirmative S or negative $\bar{S}$, pragmatically presupposes S *or* $\bar{S}$ in the speech act of answering a yes–no question properly. S *or* $\bar{S}$ is a condition under which S and $\bar{S}$ are contradictories of each other, that is, under this condition S is false if and only if $\bar{S}$ is true.[5] (This conclusion holds whether one assumes presuppositional semantics or nonpresuppositional semantics.) Giving a proper answer to S? by S is effectively stating S and rejecting $\bar{S}$ as its contradictory. The role of S and $\bar{S}$ may of course be interchanged. Let us agree to call this condition, or any proposition logically equivalent to it, the semantic$_2$ presupposition of S and $\bar{S}$, without committing ourselves to presuppositionalist semantics. As a proposi-

[5] This characterization does not apply to conditional sentences, however. For more discussion about the concept of denial negation, semantic$_2$ presupposition and other matters related to presuppositional phenomena, see Kuroda (1977), of which this article is both a summary and a continuation.

tion the semantic$_2$ presupposition would generally be identical to what the presuppositionalist would take as the semantic presupposition. But their definitional meanings differ.

Thus, rephrasing what we have established earlier, we may state that (7) or (8b), in a speech act of answering a yes–no question properly, pragmatically presupposes its semantic$_2$ presupposition, the unique existence of a king of France. In contrast, we may not state that (7) or (8b) in a speech act of pure statement pragmatically presupposes its semantic$_2$ presupposition.

Now, when a declarative sentence is used in discourse, even though no question is posed explicitly, there might be contexts in which the sentence is felt to be answering an implicitly put yes–no question. To the extent that one can justify this characterization of the particular use of a declarative sentence in discourse, one may maintain that that sentence pragmatically presupposes its semantic$_2$ presupposition in context, and making a statement by this utterance is accompanied by a supplementary effect of rejecting its "denial," that is, its partner in the denial pair, as its contradictory. Let us call the speech act of using a declarative sentence with this effect assertion$_2$. Then, to the extent that the declarative sentence makes an assertion$_2$ it may be said to pragmatically presuppose its semantic$_2$ presupposition.

* * *

We have first justified the concept of pragmatic presupposition for the disjunctive interrogative and, as a special case, for the yes–no interrogative, which has led us to justification of pragmatic presupposition for the declarative sentence in the speech act of properly answering a yes–no question. Finally, for the declarative sentence in general, pragmatic presupposition is justified to the extent that the notion of assertion$_2$ can be justified. In this procedure of justification the concept of yes–no interrogative and the assumption that the yes–no interrogative is only a special case of the disjunctive interrogative have played a crucial role. But putting *wh*-questions aside, why then must all questions be put in disjunctive form? Why can a statement not be questioned without being disjoined?

One might say that to question a statement is to demand a choice between it and its negation, and this is exactly what our assumption about the yes–no interrogative claims. Not exactly. Our assumption claims that a yes–no interrogative is underlyingly a disjunct with the interrogative of its denial negation. For example, (8a) is underlyingly identical with *Is the king of France healthy or is the king of France not healthy?* The denial negation is a particular, syntactically determined form of negation. Logically, it is not trivial, to say the least, whether it can be called THE negation. The everlasting dispute between the "Russellian" and the presuppositionalist would be good testimony. Besides, it cannot be denied that theoretical reason can conceive of a wider scope of negation than denial negation and construct and understand a formal language that incorporates such negation. So why can one not question a statement without disjoining it with a particular synactic form of negation, or for that matter without disjoining it with anything?

* * *

Can we in fact not question without disjunction? Apparently not, syntactically. But can we not doubt without questioning?

The statement *The king of France is healthy* may be put in doubt in a number of ways. The king of France, of course, may not be healthy, even though he looks so. The man said to be the king of France, even though he behaves like a king and the people surrounding him treat him as one, may not in fact be the king of France. Or, what is France? Perhaps there should not be such an entity as a nation–state France.

Or, take a quotidian example. *The cat is chasing Fido.* Is the cat really chasing Fido? The two animals may be just running in the same direction separated by some distance. Is it really a cat that is running after Fido? Or is it perhaps a false vision? And is that Fido? Might it not be altogether an illusion that I see a cat running after a dog? Am I not dreaming?

Reason can descend into depths of doubt that the syntax of negation may not open readily to the faculty of immediate understanding. But with the help of reason rising again out of skepticism, we might understand the notion of truth in a new perspective. Immediate reality is examined and evaluated more adequately with an ever expanding horizon of possibilities and conceivables, that is, negations of reality, as reason exposes hidden "presuppositions."

But we also need prudential reason to set a utilitarian frame for ordinary language to function smoothly. Syntax provides the form of negation with respect to which the declarative sentence is understood as making an "assertion." In this ordinary context, to "assert" is to recognize reality understood in opposition to the specific possible or conceivable defined by the denial negation, that is, to "assert" is, to wit, simultaneously to "assert" and to "deny" the denial.

* * *

To conclude, the concept of entailment is, I claim, grounded on theoretical reason, the concept of pragmatic presupposition of the interrogative on practical reason, and the function of semantic_2 presupposition as pragmatic presupposition of the declarative on prudential reason. The concept of denial negation and correlatively that of semantic$_2$ presupposition are to be accounted for by grammatical theory.

In contrast, the notion of semantic presupposition, and correlatively absence of truth value, as conceived by the presuppositionalist semantics, are not theoretically grounded on reason, and their justification can perhaps rest only on the intuitions of the investigator. The recognition of these notions might simply reflect the perception of a category of intuition that is a product of various competence and performance factors.

Katz and Langendoen are concerned with the significance of the distinction between competence theory and performance theory. I share this concern with them. It should be clear that entailment, the pragmatic presupposition of the interrogative that is justified in the previous discussion, denial negation and semantic$_2$ presupposition belong to grammatical theory, a competence theory. The notion of pragmatic presupposition IN GENERAL is not discussed here and needs more deliberation. It would, however, not be justified without reference to a theory of language use, a performance theory complementing grammatical theory. Finally, the intuitions of the investigator about the notions of semantic presupposition (in the sense of the presuppositionalist semantics) and absence of truth value are perhaps accounted for by a performance theory.

REFERENCES

Karttunen, L. Presuppositions of compound sentences. *Linguistic Inquiry*, 1973, *4*, 169–193.

Katz, J. J. *Semantic theory*, New York: Harper and Row, 1972.

Katz, J. J., and Bever, T. G. The fall and rise of empiricism. In T. G. Bever, J. J. Katz, and D. T. Langendoen (Eds.), *An integrated theory of linguistic ability*, New York: Crowell, 1976.

Katz, J. J. and Langendoen, D. T. Pragmatics and presupposition. *Language*, 1976, *52*, 1–17.

Kuroda, S.-Y. Geach and Katz on presupposition, *Foundations of Language*, 1974, *12*, 177–199.

Kuroda, S.-Y. Description of presuppositional phenomena—from a nonpresuppositionalist point of view. *Linguisticae Investigationes*, 1977, 1, 63–161.

Morgan, J. L. On the treatment of presuppositions in transformational grammar," Papers from the Fifth Regional Meeting of the Chicago Linguistic Society. Chicago: University of Chicago, 1969. Pp. 169–177.

IN DEFENSE OF THE TRUTH VALUE GAP[1]

JANET DEAN FODOR
University of Connecticut
Storrs, Connecticut

1. INTRODUCTION

Truth value gaps appear to have had their heyday. In the last few years, less effort has been devoted to the business of explaining where and why they occur than to the attempt to explain them away.[2] Certainly, intuitive discriminations between false sentences and neither-true-nor-false sentences do tend to waver. Further, the logic for natural languages would be considerably simplified if we could classify all of these sentences as false, and attribute contrary intuitions to pragmatic factors.

The plausibility of this move toward a Russellian theory supplemented by principles of conversation has gained by the expansion of the data base from the standard examples of reference failure discussed by Frege, Russell and Strawson, to include also sentences containing words like *already, yet, but,* and *even*. For those who have any inclination to accept the existence of truth value gaps, failure of reference has always provided the most convincing examples. But the de-

[1] This chapter was first drafted in 1974, when I was teaching at the Linguistics Institute at the University of Massachusetts at Amherst, and participating in the Mathematical and Social Sciences Board Workshop on Syntax and Semantics, funded by the National Science Foundation. The material in this chapter has since been presented at University College London, City University of New York, and Mount Holyoke College. My thanks to all those who were kind enough to hear me out, and to offer contributions or criticisms.

[2] As, for example in Kempson (1975) and Wilson (1975).

Syntax and Semantics, Volume 11: Presupposition

ISBN 0-12-613511-8

scriptive study of sentences suffering from reference failure has been so extraordinarily simplistic that it is not surprising that the influence of these cases is on the wane.

What I hope to demonstrate is that not all instances of reference failure are alike. It must be conceded that some do NOT exhibit truth value gaps, but this can serve to strengthen, by contrast, the claim that others do. Furthermore, the search for principles subtle enough to distinguish between the two types of example leads to a new theory of the source of truth value gaps. This theory is much more general than those that have gone before, sufficiently general that it promises to be applicable to many of the *already–yet–even* types of example, too, and thus to tip the balance back again towards an account of presupposition which relates it to truth and falsity rather than to the use of language in conversational exchanges.

2. THE KING OF FRANCE AS A FICTION

I maintain that the intuition that Sentences (1)–(4) are not true and are not false is a veridical one.

(1) *The present king of France is* {*bald.* / *hairy.* / *fat.* / *thin.* / *an atheist.* / *a male chauvinist pig.*}

(2) *The present king of France* {*has a cat.* / *is married to a Dutchwoman.*}

(3) *The present king of France* {*likes Camembert.* / *grows roses.*}

(4) *The present king of France* {*loves his daughter.* / *is standing next to the queen of France.*}

Talk of SENTENCES with and without truth values is a convenient shorthand which I shall make use of. More correctly, it should be said that the sentences above cannot, under current circumstances, be used to make a statement which is either true or false. This formulation, which is common in Strawson's writings, is itself imprecise, for it hides a distinction between two slightly different views. One is that such sentences cannot be used to make any statement at all; the other is that, though they may be used to make statements, these statements are neither true nor false. The latter position is somewhat obscure, and I will return to it later. For present purposes the important point is that, however we choose to characterize a truth value gap, the gaps exhibited by (1)–(4) must not be attributed wholly to the absence of a referent for the definite description *the present king of France*. For this phrase appears also in Sentences (5)–(6), which intuition declares to be false.

(5) *The present king of France* { *is standing next to me.* / *is standing next to the queen of England.* / *has his hand on your shoulder.* }

(6) *The present king of France* { *is married to a friend of mine.* / *ate some Camembert that you bought.* }

Let us concentrate on Sentences (7) and (8), and consider whether there is any rationale for our inclination to call the latter false but not the former.[3]

(7) *The king of France is bald.*

(8) *The king of France is standing next to me.*

An obvious point is that the phrase *the king of France* is the ONLY referring expression[4] in (7), while in (8) there is also the word *me*, which in normal use will succeed in referring. This suggests a diagnosis as follows: Sentence (7) does not connect with the real world at all, because it says nothing about anybody or anything that is present in the real world; but sentence (8) does, for it says something about me, and the reason we judge it to be false is that what it says about me is false.

There are two ways of pursuing this account of the contrast between (7) and (8), and I shall start with one which, though superficially appealing, turns out to lead nowhere. The idea here is that the existence or nonexistence of a king of France is IRRELEVANT to the valuation of (8). We need not know whether there is a king of France in order to determine that (8) is false; all we need establish is that there is no king of France standing next to me; that is, either that there is no one stand-

[3] Like Strawson, I shall drop the word *present* in the description of the king of France, but it is to be understood.

[4] Strawson (1964) says: "Let us call an expression *as and when used in a statement with the role of identifying reference*—whether or not it suffers in that use from radical reference failure—*a referring expression*." I shall follow this usage.

ing next to me or that the person or persons standing next to me are not king of France. Depending on the degree of our ignorance about the political situation in France, we could happily use one or another of Sentences (9)–(11).

(9) *Whether or not there's a king of France, the king of France is not standing next to me.*

(10) *If there's a king of France, he's not standing next to me.*

(11) *Even if there's a king of France, he's not standing next to me.*

This seems promising, for the corresponding sentences about baldness are quite bizarre. What justification could there possibly be for the assertions (12)–(14)?

(12) !!*Whether or not there's a king of France, the king of France is not bald.*

(13) !!*If there's a king of France, he's not bald.*

(14) !!*Even if there's a king of France, he's not bald.*

Notice that for the predicate *is standing next to me*, Sentence (8) is just like Sentence (15), for which there is no reference failure. Statements (16)–(18) are quite coherent and reasonable if one is unsure about the existence of a queen of England but is sure that the only person in the vicinity is, for instance, Robert Redford.

(15) *The queen of England is standing next to me.*

(16) *Whether or not there's a queen of England, the queen of England is not standing next to me.*

(17) *If there's a queen of England, she's not standing next to me.*

(18) *Even if there's a queen of England, she's not standing next to me.*

To put it informally, and in overtly verificationist terms, this theory says that (7) has no truth value because to evaluate it we would need to look at the king of France and we cannot; and that (8) does have a truth value because to evaluate it we need only look at me and at those people who are near me. But this is unsatisfactory for it simply shifts the puzzle one step further back. If we can make a list of the people standing next to me and determine that no king of France is on it, why could we not also make a list of the people who are bald and establish that no king of France is on IT? More formally, why is the argument (19) valid and the argument (20) not?

(19) *No one who is standing next to me is the king of France; therefore it is false that the king of France is standing next to me.*

(20) *No one who is bald is the king of France; therefore it is false that the king of France is bald.*

Of course, it is likely to be much harder in practice to make an exhaustive list of all the bald people in the world than of the people standing next to me; that is, harder to establish the truth of the premise in (20) than in (19). But that is a practical matter only, and should have no bearing on the validity of the inference if we allow ourselves to imagine, at least, that the premise has been established as true.

In fact, the explanation of the invalidity of (20) is quite obvious. On the reading on which it is true, the premise of (20) quantifies over EXISTING bald people. It therefore entails only that, IF the king of France exists, it is false that he is bald. Since he does not, we can draw no conclusion about the state of his head from this premise.[5] Thus, an additional existence premise would be needed for argument (20) to be valid. And then by parity, it would seem that argument (19) should likewise be valid only in conjunction with an existence premise. In the absence of any explanation of why (19) and (20) should differ in this respect, we must conclude that the apparent validity of (19) is an illusion.

The temptation to accept the invalid argument (19) can perhaps be explained. Perhaps we construe it as enthymemic for the more elaborate argument (21).

(21) *No one who is standing next to me is the king of France; therefore if there is a king of France he is not standing next to me; and if there is no king of France then the king of France is not standing next to me.*

The last clause here is the important one, and it leads to a rather different account of the contrast between our original Sentences (7) and (8).

[5] If the premise of (20) is read as quantifying over all bald individuals, existing and nonexisting alike, then the argument (20) will be valid. But it will not be sound, for the premise will not be true. This is evident from the fact we began with, namely, that it is neither true nor false that the king of France is bald.

Our working assumption so far has been that the existence or nonexistence of the king of France is irrelevant to the truth value of (8). But (21) makes it clear that this is a mistake. The nonexistence of the king of France is SUFFICIENT to render (8) false. In other words, the key to the problem lies not in the preceding *even if–whether or not* statements, but in the much stronger *because* statement (22).

(22) *Because there is no king of France, the king of France could not be standing next to me.*

As before, the corresponding sentence about baldness is bizarre.

(23) !!*Because there is no king of France, the king of France could not be bald.*

What is needed now is an explanation of why (22) is acceptable and (23) is not; that is, of why the nonexistence of the king of France is sufficient to establish that he is not standing next to me but not sufficient to establish that he is not bald. For this purpose I shall assume an ontology of possible worlds, which is familiar from recent work in modal logic, and which I think reflects the way in which many (if not all) people conceptualize propositions about nonexistent individuals and states of affairs. The "psychologically real" ontology is the one relevant to explaining the semantics of a natural language, even if upon examination it proves indefensible as a theory of what "really exists" in our universe. But in any case, as far as I can determine the references in what follows to nonreal worlds and individuals are innocent and could be translated by anyone who is squeamish about them into less loaded (though also less vivid) terms.

The assumption, then, is that there is a universe of worlds, one of which is the real world. To say that the king of France does not exist is to say that there is no king of France in the real world. But since the existence of a king of France is possible, then there IS a king of France in at least one possible but nonreal world. If we permit worlds to be incompletely specified, we can say that there is just one nonreal world which contains a king of France and it is unspecified for almost everything except his existence—for example, unspecified for his age, marital status, tastes and actions, and also of course for his baldness or lack of it, as well as for the properties and even the number of other individuals who inhabit the same world. Alternatively, we can say that there are infinitely many nonreal worlds containing a (the) king of France, each of which is fully specified but specified differently with respect to the king's age, marital status, baldness, and so on. (See van Fraassen, 1966.)

A similar reconstruction has been given for talk about fictional individuals (see Lewis, 1978). Winnie the Pooh does not inhabit the real world, but there is an incompletely specified nonreal world (or a set of fully specified nonreal worlds) created by A. A. Milne in which Winnie the Pooh does exist. It is a fact about this world that Winnie the Pooh is fat and makes up poems and likes honey; it is not specified in this world exactly how tall Winnie the Pooh is, or whether he prefers Mondays to Tuesdays. My assimilation of the king of France to Winnie the Pooh is quite deliberate. My proposal is that we respond to sentences containing the phrase *the king of France* in the same way as to sentences about any fictional individual. The only difference is that the king of France is a very thin fiction, specified for no properties at all except for being king of France.

An utterance of sentence (7) could be intended or construed in two different ways. As an attempt to state something about the real world it fails, for it does not say anything about anything that is in the real world.[6] As an attempt to say something about a nonreal world it succeeds. But WHAT it says about that world cannot be assigned a truth value for the quite straightforward reason that the world is not fully specified and it is neither true nor false within it that the king of France is bald. (Equivalently, not every member of the infinite set of fully specified worlds containing the king of France is such that it is true that he is bald and not every member is such that it is false that he is bald.) All of this is exactly analogous to the situation for sentences like (24)–(26) about Winnie the Pooh.

(24) *Winnie the Pooh likes Mondays.*

(25) *Winnie the Pooh likes honey.*

(26) *Winnie the Pooh hates honey.*

None of these sentences can be used successfully to make a statement about the real world, hence none of them can be evaluated with respect to the real world. All of them can be used to make a statement about Winnie the Pooh and hence about the world of Milne's creation. Sentence (26) is false of that world, (25) is true of it, and (24) is neither true nor false of it.

Note that this account explains the tension between the alternative characterizations mentioned earlier of the nature of the failure of a sentence like (7). On one construal, relative to the real world, there is a failure to make any statement at all; on the other, relative to the

[6] If stating is defined in terms of intentions, we may say that any sincere utterance of a declarative sentence constitutes the making of a statement. But I am using *statement* to mean an abstract object which is associated with some such utterances but not others.

nonreal world which contains the fictional individual, the statement that is made fails to engage any fact in that world that would render it either true or false. Since the traditional examples of reference failure fail on BOTH counts, they tend to obscure this distinction. But that there ARE these two construals is quite clear in the case of familiar fictions. If a child asks, "Is it true that the tooth fairy takes your tooth away if you put it under your pillow?" we do not know how to answer until we have determined whether the question is about the real world or about the world inhabited by the tooth fairy.

A statement cannot be true or false *simpliciter* but must be true or false OF some world or other. The failure to specify WHICH world is under consideration can lead to pointless disputes, such as whether sentences like (27) and (28) are true or without truth value.

(27) *The king of France is male.*

(28) *The round square is round.*

Sentence (27) does not apply to the real world and *a fortiori* has no truth value with respect to the real world; but it says something true, analytically true, about a nonreal world that contains the king of France. Sentence (28) does not apply to the real world, nor to any other possible world, since there is none that contains a round square. (But it would presumably apply to, and be both analytically true and analytically false of, an impossible world—if it should by any chance turn out that impossible worlds can be coherently incorporated into the model.)

Sentence (8), with its two referring expressions, must now be fitted into this picture, and it offers us three different kinds of construal. Uttered with the intention of making a statement just about the real world it fails, for the attempt is to describe a relationship holding between two individuals in that world, but only one of them is present in it. As an attempted statement wholly about a nonreal world its status is more controversial, for it depends on whether we are prepared to allow that a nonreal world containing the king of France could also contain me.[7] But in any case, the most natural construal for a hearer who knows that I (the speaker) exist and knows that the king of France does not, is as a statement about both worlds at once. What is asserted is that the relation of standing next to holds between me, an inhabitant of the real world, and the king of France, an inhabitant only of some nonreal world.

Now there ARE some relations (which I shall discuss in Section 4)

[7] See the discussion in Section 5.

which can hold among individuals in different worlds, but the relation of standing next to is not one of them. It is what I shall call a SAME-WORLD RELATION; that is, whatever else is involved in its holding between two individuals, they must at the very least be in the same world. This is why the nonexistence of the king of France is sufficient grounds for judging (8) false. Of course, it is not sufficient grounds for judging (29) false.

(29) *The king of France is standing next to the queen of France.*

For the queen of France does not exist in the real world, and could exist in the king's world, so (29) cannot be accused of asserting that a same-world relation holds between individuals in different worlds. However, the general principle does extend to every case, whether or not the real world is involved, for which we know that the individuals in question do not coexist in the same world. For example, if we can assume that there was no tooth fairy in the world of Sherlock Holmes, any more than there is in the real world, then we know that (30) is false.

(30) *Sherlock Holmes tickled the tooth fairy.*

It is worth noting that this talk of same-world relations is not motivated solely by instances of reference failure, for a very similar principle governs sentences about real individuals who existed at different times. Thus (31) is false for exactly the same kind of reason (8) is, even though William the Conqueror and Elizabeth I were both real enough in their day.

(31) *William the Conqueror took tea with Elizabeth I.*

These examples introduce extra complications, however, for the class of same-time relations is not coextensive with the class of same-world relations. Sentences (32) and (33) might be true, though (34) and (35) cannot be.

(32) *Elizabeth I sat in a chair that William the Conqueror had sat in.*

(33) *Elizabeth I beheaded a descendant of William the Conqueror.*

(34) *Sherlock Holmes sat in a chair that the tooth fairy had sat in.*

(35) *Sherlock Holmes beheaded a descendant of the tooth fairy.*

The conclusion that emerges from these observations is that sentences which contain referring expressions that do not refer to real world individuals, though they cannot be evaluated with respect to the real world alone, can be evaluated, at least in principle, with respect to those possible worlds in which their referring expressions do refer. Whether or not they can be evaluated in practice depends on how fully specified those worlds are. For thin fictions like the king of France there are only two kinds of facts that can be used in assigning a truth value to sentences. One kind is facts which follow from his description, for example, that he is a king or that he is male. The other kind is facts which follow from the world in which he exists, for example, that he cannot stand in any same-world relation to an individual in some other world such as the real world.

These observations can now be converted into predictions about the distribution of truth value gaps. Sentences like (1) and (7), which have a one-place predicate and an unsuccessful referring expression, will lack a truth value unless the predicate expresses a property for which the nonreal referent happens to be specified in the nonreal world in which it exists. A sentence with a two-or-more-place predicate will have the value False if the predicate expresses a same-world relation but its referring expressions do not all have referents in the same worlds; in particular, if one or more of them does refer in the real world and one or more of them does not. It should follow that, as long as we continue to restrict ourselves to same-world predicates, any sentence which contains at least one expression with a referent in the real world will have a truth value, whether or not it also purports to refer to nonexistent entities.[8] Failure of reference does not automatically de-

[8] Katz (this volume) has argued that this theory reinstates the paradoxes of self-reference which are resolved by his own theory that ANY reference failure deprives a sentence of a truth value.

Katz and I are agreed that the sentence *This sentence is false* cannot be used to make a statement about the real world, and this is just as well for if we suppose that it can be used to make a statement, we would have to admit that that statement was true if false and false if true.

Katz illustrates the difference between the two theories with a sentence which expresses a same-world relation, one of whose noun phrases does refer. A says "Snow is white," and then B says, for example, "This false statement of mine follows A's statement." By hypothesis, the phrase *A's statement* refers in the real world, so on pain of paradox we must assume that the phrase *this false statement of mine* does not. For Katz, this failure of reference entails that B's utterance does not express a statement. There is no paradox, because what B says is neither true nor false. But my theory maintains that the phrase *this false statement of mine* can be construed as referring in a nonreal world, and it permits B's utterance to express a statement about this nonreal world. My theory is obviously defective if it acknowledges any circumstances in which B's utterance expresses a statement that has paradoxical consequences. In fact, as I will illustrate, B's utterance either does not express a statement at all, or else expresses a nonparadoxical statement.

prive a sentence of a truth value; it has the effect of doing so in some cases only because nonreal individuals, unlike real ones, are typically unspecified for many of their properties.

3. STRAWSON AND ABOUTNESS

In one of his later discussions of presupposition, Strawson (1964) gives some attention to sentences with two-place predicates, and offers an account of them which is similar in some respects to the one I have given. But Strawson strains harder, too hard I believe, to preserve as many truth value gaps as possible. He does not concede that successful reference is only incidentally related to a sentence's having a truth value. Instead, he retains the spirit of his earlier view that ANY failure of reference results in a truth value gap, and he simply exempts one special class of referring expressions from this general rule.

Strawson notes that sentence (36) is intuitively judged false. (We are to assume that there really is an Exhibition in town.)

(36) *The Exhibition was visited yesterday by the king of France.*

The reason Strawson gives is very much like the one given in Section 2 (although he makes no explicit mention of same-world relations): A nonexistent king cannot visit an Exhibition that exists in the real world. Thus Strawson agrees that, despite the reference failure, Sen-

---

Let us consider first whether B's utterance can express a statement about a single world, real or nonreal. For this to be possible, both the subject phrase and the object phrase of B's sentence must refer in that world. But the standard *reductio ad absurdum* argument entails that the subject phrase does not refer in any world in which what B says is true. Therefore both phrases refer only in a world in which B makes a false statement and A makes a statement, but B's false statement does NOT follow A's statement. What B says can express a statement only about a world with these properties, and the statement it expresses is not paradoxical but simply false. (Note that, as on Katz's theory, if in the real world B's utterance does follow a statement by A, then it does not express a statement about the real world.)

Now we must consider whether B's utterance can express a statement about a pair of distinct worlds. This will be possible just in case the subject phrase refers in one world and the object phrase refers in the other. Hence what B says expresses a statement just in case the subject phrase refers, in one world, to a statement by B about both worlds, and the object phrase refers, in the other world, to a statement by A. But once again there is no paradox. Since following is a same-world relation, the statement that is made about these two worlds is simply false.

Other examples can be handled in a similar fashion. The analysis is inevitably more tedious than on Katz's theory, but the solution to the apparent paradoxes is fundamentally the same, for both theories allow that there are sentences that cannot be interpreted as expressing statements about certain worlds.

tence (36) can be assigned a truth value. But he maintains that the explanation for this is that the unsuccessful referring expression is "absorbed into the predicate-term" in (36), so that the sentence is not ABOUT the king of France at all but is construed as a simple subject–predicate sentence about the Exhibition. The general principle that the referents of referring expressions must really exist in order for the sentence to have a truth value is then restricted to just those referents that the sentence is about.

Strawson offers a "recipe" for determining aboutness. We are to form a description of the utterance of the form (37).

$$\text{(37)}\qquad \textit{He}\ \text{(i.e.,}\ \textit{the speaker}\text{)}\ \textit{was} \begin{Bmatrix} \textit{saying} \\ \textit{describing} \\ \textit{etc.} \end{Bmatrix} \begin{Bmatrix} \textit{who} \\ \textit{what} \\ \textit{how} \\ \textit{which} \\ \textit{etc.} \end{Bmatrix} \underline{\qquad\quad}.$$

In the case of (36), the appropriate description would be something like (38).

(38) *He was stating who the Exhibition was visited by yesterday.*

Those noun phrases which appear in the utterance description are the ones whose referents the sentence is about, and they must refer in the real world or else deprive the sentence of a truth value. Any noun phrase which is eliminated in the utterance description counts as having been absorbed into the predicate in the original sentence. If it lacks a real-world referent, the only consequence will be that the predicate expresses a property (e.g., having been visited by the king of France) which no real-world entity could possess, and so the sentence must be false.

Strawson refers to what a sentence is about as its topic, and his distinction between the two parts of the sentence is reminiscent of the distinctions between topic and comment, theme and rheme, focus and presupposition, and so on, that have been drawn in the linguistics literature. Without going into an extensive survey of these distinctions and their relation to each other, it is worth noting how closely Strawson's analysis fits with the focus and presupposition analysis of Chomsky (1970) and Jackendoff (1972). Chomsky illustrates the presupposition (henceforth the F-presupposition, to distinguish it from logical presuppositions whose failures lead to truth value gaps) of a sentence by appeal to its appropriateness as an answer to certain questions, and so does Strawson. Thus Chomsky (1970) observes: "It would, for example, be impossible to answer [*Were the Yankees beaten by the* ***Red Sox?***] by saying: *No, the Red Sox beat the* ***Tigers.*** Or, to be more precise, this would be an answer only . . . by failure to accept the presupposition [p. 75]." And Strawson discusses Sentence (7), *The king of France is bald,* as an answer to the questions *What is the king of France like?* and *What bald notables are there?* In answer to the first question, (7) is about the king of France and has no truth value; in answer to the second (admittedly less natural) question, (7) is about bald notables and so it does have a truth value. Strawson also talks of the topic as an antecedently introduced class, for example, the class of bald notables for the sentence ***The king of France*** *is bald,* which does have a truth value. And Jackendoff identifies the F-presupposition of a sentence as the proposition that a certain set is a coherent set in the present discourse, is well defined in the present discourse, is amenable to discussion, or is under discussion. The set in question is the set of values which can truly be substituted for the focus of the sentence. For the sentence *John* ***likes*** *Bill,* this is the set of all attitudinal relations which hold between John and Bill. For the sentence *The king of France* ***is bald,*** it is presumably the set of all properties of the king of France; and for the sentence ***The king of France*** *is bald,* it would be the set of all (or perhaps all notable) people who are bald.

Given these parallels, we can reformulate Strawson's proposal about the distribution of truth value gaps as follows. All and only those sentences whose F-presuppositions contain one or more referring terms which fail to refer in the real world lack a truth value; that is, all and only those referring expressions within the F-presupposition of a sentence carry a logical presupposition of existence. To put it yet another way: Only those referring expressions that are within the focus of the sentence are excused from having to refer in the real world. This formulation brings with it some descriptive advantages, since as Chomsky makes clear, the focus and F-presupposition of a sentence are affected by stress and intonation and not solely by surface structure and context as Strawson implies. Thus (37), with emphasis on the subject phrase, is interpreted, like (36), as about the Exhibition rather than about the king of France.

(37) ***The king of France*** *visited the Exhibition today.*

My objection to Strawson's theory is not that the proposed influence of F-presupposition on logical presupposition is incorrect, but that it is insufficient to account for all sentences which have truth values despite containing unsuccessful referring expressions. A sentence can be uttered with a neutral intonation pattern so that it has no marked focus. In that case it is interpreted as about the referents of ALL of its referring expressions. Thus (38), uttered quite neutrally and not in the context of a prior question or an antecedently introduced class of individuals, seems to be about the Exhibition and the king of France equally.

(38) *The king of France visited the Exhibition yesterday.*

The appropriate utterance description for (38) would therefore be (39) or (40), in which both noun phrases survive.

(39) *He was telling us whether or not the king of France visited the Exhibition yesterday.*

(40) *He was saying what relation holds between the king of France and the Exhibition.*

Hence by Strawson's theory, (38) should lack a truth value. And yet there is a very strong temptation to call it false.

Also, having extended our sights from one-place to two-place predicates, we should not stop there. A sentence like (41), with three referring expressions, one of them within its focus, still has two in its F-presupposition.

(41) *The king of France gave me* ***this gold plated cake knife.***

Strawson's prediction would be that (41) lacks a truthvalue, since it suffers from reference failure within the F-presupposition. But in fact the sentence strikes one as false, as predicted by the more radical theory presented in Section 2, according to which only TOTAL reference failure (within the F-presupposition?) will result in a truth value gap.

Strawson's discussion of aboutness and exemptions from the need to refer can thus be accepted as a contribution to the prediction and explanation of truth value gaps. Discourse phenomena like focus and F-presupposition do appear to be implicated to some extent. But this observation supplements rather than supplants the observations of Section 2, and those observations seem to demand an explanation based not on discourse phenomena but on the relation between sentences and worlds.

4. CROSS-WORLD RELATIONS

There are sentences containing two-place predicates which, however they are pronounced, whatever their focus is taken to be, do not have a truth value. Consider (42), for example.

(42) *Morris Halle resembles the king of France.*

Whether or not it is also about the king of France, this sentence is about Morris Halle, who does exist, and yet it is neither true nor false.

Resembling is a CROSS-WORLD RELATION; that is, a relation which CAN hold between individuals in different worlds.[9] For instance, Sentence (43), with a more fully specified fictional individual than the king of France, could perhaps be held to be true.

(43) *Morris Halle resembles Santa Claus.*

The mere fact that a sentence attributes a resemblance relation between two individuals in different worlds is thus not sufficient to render it false—though it might happen to be false for other reasons, as with (44).

(44) *Sherlock Holmes resembles the tooth fairy.*

Sentences with the two place predicate *resemble,* and other cross-world predicates such as *is taller than* and *knows as much mathematics as,* thus exhibit a different pattern of truth value gaps than the sentences with same-world relational predicates discussed in Section 2. They can be EITHER true OR false when one referring expression refers in the real world and the other does not, but they can also be neither. However, a single generalization covers both kinds of predicate: Only sentences which could be true can be neither true nor false. It is because the king of France could be bald that we cannot say whether he is bald or not. And it is because the king of France could resemble Morris Halle that we cannot say whether he does or not.

It is interesting to speculate on what makes a predicate same-world or cross-world. Not surprisingly, predicates which implicate spatio-temporal relations are same-world predicates. Examples are *is standing next to, kicked, had tea with,* and *sat on the same chair as.* The

[9] Van Fraassen (1964) argues for the falsity of sentences which assert that the identity relation holds between an individual who exists and one who does not. He says: "For example, that Santa Claus does not exist is sufficient reason to conclude that the president of the United States is not Santa Claus; that the Scarlet Pimpernel is a fictional character, sufficient reason to conclude that the man in the iron mask was not the Scarlet Pimpernel."

For our purposes, resemblance and the cross-world comparative relations are more interesting than the identity relation, since they can give rise to the unusual phenomenon of (affirmative) sentences about individuals in different worlds which are judged to be TRUE. However, van Fraassen does also note that sentences with the predicates *worshipped* or *conceived of* can be true across worlds. These fall into the class of OPAQUE predicates, which I shall discuss shortly.

cross-world predicates appear to be (or at least to include) those expressing relations which follow from singulary properties of each of their arguments. For example, if we are given that Santa Claus is jolly, and also that Morris Halle is jolly, we can infer that (at least in this respect) Morris Halle resembles Santa Claus. And since being jolly is a singulary property which can be possessed by both parties, each in his own world, the premises for this inference can both be true. The relation of resemblance demands no interaction between the resembling individuals, and this is why it does not require them to exist in the same world.

There is another class of predicates which, if they express relations at all, express cross-world relations. These are the opaque predicates like *pray to, think of,* and *admire.* Sentence (45) is true, even though I am in the real world and the king of France is not.

(45) *I am writing about the king of France.*

Such sentences are often described as containing opaque, or nonreferential, noun phrases in object position. It is said that (45) refers to me but not to the king of France, and that this is why it can have a truth value even though there is no king of France. On the other hand, (46) is said to refer (or to purport to refer) to the king of France but not to refer to me, and this is why it has no truth value, even though I do exist.

(46) *The king of France is writing about me.*

This analysis is compatible with the general theory I have outlined. Like Strawson's exemption of focused noun phrases, it would simply remove certain expressions (the objects of opaque predicates) from the domain of the theory. However, given an ontology which admits nonreal individuals, we can at least explore the possibility that a sentence like (45) refers both to me and to the king of France, and is true of us even though we exist in different worlds. To preserve the general theory developed in Section 2 it must then be shown that the fact that the subject of *admire* typically must refer in the real world, while the object of *admire* need not, is simply a consequence of the more fundamental requirement that the person who does the admiring must be specified for certain properties while the person who is admired need not be. It is this ASYMMETRY of the opaque predicates with respect to truth value gaps which most needs explanation.

We have seen that the cross-world relations like resemblance and being taller than engage with facts about each individual alone. If Xenon is 5 feet tall and Yolande is 6 feet tall, then Yolande is taller than Xenon. And we can create or destroy such relations between Xenon and Yolande by acting on either one alone. Given that Xenon is 5 feet tall, we can make it true or false that Yolande is taller than Xenon, just by making Yolande more or less than 5 feet tall, (either by stipulation, if Yolande is nonreal or, for example, by the use of growth hormones if Yolande is real). And quite symmetrically, given that Yolande is 6 feet tall, then acting upon Xenon alone can be sufficient to determine the truth value of the claim that Yolande is taller than Xenon. Conversely, suppose that Yolande is a fictional individual of our own creation whose height we have not yet specified. Then we are free to stipulate that Yolande is taller than Xenon. No fact about Xenon's world, even about Xenon's height, could possibly conflict with the stipulation of this relation. And clearly the same is true if we exchange Yolande for Xenon here, and vice versa.

The asymmetry of an opaque relation like thinking of stands out by contrast. There is nothing we can do to Xenon alone to make it true that Yolande is thinking of Xenon.[10] But we CAN work on Yolande. For example, if someone were to talk to Yolande about Xenon and could somehow manage to ensure that Yolande was understanding and concentrating on what was being said, then Yolande would be thinking about Xenon. Again, suppose we are in the business of stipulating relations between a nonreal Xenon and Yolande. Then we could freely stipulate of Yolande's world that Yolande was thinking about Xenon, without danger of conflict with any fact solely about Xenon. But we might not be free to stipulate of XENON'S world that Yolande was thinking about Xenon, for it might already have been determined about Yolande's world that Yolande is asleep and not thinking at all. Thus the assertion that Yolande is thinking about Xenon appears to engage with other facts about Yolande but not with other facts about Xenon.

In case it seems that these observations have taken us beyond the realm of rational discourse, it is worth pointing out that similar asymmetries are to be found in relations between quite ordinary, real individuals. I can see you (really see, as opposed to hallucinating) only if you exist. Seeing behaves with respect to nonexistence and truth value gaps exactly like other same-world relations such as touching, kicking, and taking tea with. And yet there is some sense in which my

[10] There are some apparent counterexamples to this claim. Thus, given that Yolande is thinking about everyone who is eating cheese, then by getting Xenon to eat cheese it would appear that we could make it true that Yolande is thinking about Xenon. There is pretty clearly something wrong here, but I am not sure at present how to describe what is wrong.

seeing you impinges on me but not on you. If there were an analysis of a person's brain (or big toe) that permitted the reconstruction of all of his physical and mental interactions with the world, we would expect that analysis to reveal who and what he had seen, but not by whom or what he had been seen. Your being seen by me is not an event that AFFECTS you[11] (even though it may lead to events which do, such as my kicking you). Thus the asymmetry of the thinking of relation is at least partly independent of its opacity, of its being a cross-world relation. Table (47) shows how these properties interact. (The apparent lack of examples for the lower left section suggests that relations which affect both parties require them to coexist in the same world.)

(47)

	Affects both parties	Affects only one party	Affects neither party
Same-world	e.g., kicking	e.g., seeing	e.g., being 3 miles away from
Cross-world	?	e.g., thinking of	e.g., being taller than

This notion of AFFECTING clearly deserves further attention, but the asymmetry of affectedness exhibited by the opaque relations does not obviously invalidate their analysis AS relations. Hence we can incorporate them into the general theory. Sentences attributing opaque relations to individuals will have a truth value just in case the individuals are specified for the relation in question. The only idiosyncrasy of such sentences is that specification for the relation must proceed from the world of the subject, and is inherited indirectly by the world of the object. Because I exist I am (vagueness apart) a fully specified individual, and therefore it must be either true or false that I am thinking of the king of France. Because the king of France does not exist, he need not be a fully specified individual and in fact is notably underspecified. Therefore it need not be, and in fact is not, either true or false that the king of France is thinking of me.

[11] There may be a connection worth exploring between this fact and the failure of substitutivity of coextensive descriptions for the object position of *see*. On one reading of *I see my best friend* it does not entail *I see my greatest rival* even in conjunction with the additional premise that my best friend is in fact my greatest rival. However, this failure of substitutivity is at least partly independent of existence entailments, as argued in Fodor (1970). Seeing can be opaque with respect to the description of its object and nevertheless be a same-world relation; that is, require existence of the object in the same world as its subject. Perhaps, then, the absence of "affectedness" rather than of existence conditions is the source of description opacity.

5. WORLD SHIFTING AND OTHER PRAGMATIC EFFECTS

I have argued that whether a sentence is true, false, or neither of some world is a matter of fact (and fiction). The role of pragmatics is only to determine which world(s) we will in practice choose to evaluate the sentence with respect to.

One very general pragmatic principle is that we tend to relate sentences to the real world if it is possible to do so. In normal circumstances, if I were to utter (48), it would be judged true; and it would be so judged because it would be judged relative to the real world rather than to some nonreal world in which I might yet be single.

(48) *I am married.*

In other words, the *I* of (48), since it does refer in the real world, is understood as so referring. The origin of this principle is no doubt very similar to that of the principle that, in the absence of contrary indications, we tend to interpret noun phrases as referring in the present rather than in the past or future. Thus Sentence (49), in isolation, will tend to be judged true; that is, will tend to be understood as referring to the present president than to some still alive but past (or future) president.

(49) *The president of the United States has unusually large teeth.*

There is another general pragmatic principle which may conflict with the real world principle. This is that we tend to evaluate a sentence with respect to a world in which it has a truth value; that is, we tend (perhaps out of charity towards the speaker) to construe a sentence as intended to be about a world which it could be about, rather than as about one which it could not be about. This accounts for our uncertainty, in the absence of contextual cues (as when a linguist requests intuitions from an informant), about how to respond to a sentence like (50).

(50) *Santa Claus is jolly.*

Should we evaluate it with respect to the real world or to the world in which it has a truth value? Very often the two desiderata converge. The real-world evaluation of (48) guarantees that it will have a truth value, while a nonreal-world evaluation does not. But in cases like (50) the principles pull in opposite directions.

In the discussion of two-place predicates in Section 2, it was observed that the most natural interpretation of a sentence like (51) is about two worlds simultaneously.

(51) *The king of France is standing next to me.*

The real world principle tells us to construe *me* as referring to the real me (that is, the me in the real world), while the principle of maximizing truth values tells us to construe *the king of France* as referring within some nonreal world in which there exists a king of France. When one of the noun phrases in such a sentence is indefinite, however, yet another principle takes over. Sentence (52) is naturally judged to be false, and sentence (53) to have no truth value, even though the predicate *is married to* expresses a relation which presumably affects (in the sense of Section 4) both of its arguments.

(52) *A Dutchwoman is married to the king of France.*

(53) *The king of France is married to a Dutchwoman.*

This contrast between (52) and (53) might be attributed to nothing more than variations in focus and aboutness as described by Strawson. But the effect seems to be much stronger than that. For example, the falsity of (52) appears to be resistant to the shift to a truth value gap that is predicted to result from focusing on the subject noun phrase. More importantly, the reasons behind our judgements on these sentences show that the indefinite phrase *a Dutchwoman* shifts its reference (or more precisely, its domain of quantification) from one sentence to the other. We call (52) false because a Dutchwoman, a REAL one, could not be married to an unreal king of France. We say (53) has no truth value because the king of France is unspecified for the property of being married to a Dutchwoman—a NONREAL one existing in the nonreal world he inhabits himself. Either sentence might be interpreted in either way, but a pragmatic principle governs the PREFERRED interpretation. This principle is context-sensitive and operates, apparently, from left to right. An indefinite noun phrase is taken to refer to an individual (to quantify over individuals) in the same world as the noun phrase on its left, if there is one, and otherwise to an individual in the real world. The preference for real-world interpretations is present, but it can be overruled by contextual dependencies.

Two further points should be made. First, the world-shifting principle for indefinites applies only to those phrases that are not INTERNALLY specified for their world of reference. Sentence (54) is false, because though the king of France's world may contain Dutchwomen, it cannot contain Dutchwomen I used to be in school with.

(54) *The king of France is married to a Dutchwoman I used to be in school with.*

In fact, the relation of being in the same world as is passed along like the black spot. Sentence (55) is also false, for since I exist in the real world, so must my mother and anyone my mother was in school with. Hence, any such person is in a different world from the king of France.

(55) *The king of France is married to a Dutchwoman my mother used to be in school with.*

Secondly, definite noun phrases also sometimes shift world like indefinites. Sentence (56) may be judged to lack a truth value.

(56) *The king of France lives in Paris.*

A king in a nonreal world obviously cannot live in a city that exists only in the real world; the relation of living in is a same-world relation. If, nevertheless, we do not judge (56) false, this is because we allow that Paris might exist in the king's nonreal world too. It is an interesting fact, and one which lends credence to the assimilation of all nonexistent individuals to fictions, that the real-world entities which we are prepared to acknowledge as existing in nonreal worlds seem to be just those publicly familiar entities which we are not surprised to find referred to in fictions. As long as they are not specifically excluded (the period is right, and so on), we assume the existence of trees, houses, Dutchwomen, Paris, London, the queen of England, Richard Nixon, the White House, and so on, in the world that a storyteller creates, even if he does not explicitly mention them. HOW public a figure one has to be in order for one's existence to be taken for granted in a nonreal world has no precise answer. I would be very surprised to encounter either myself or my mother in a novel, and this is why I am inclined to judge (55) false. But the queen of England (or at least, A queen of England) is sufficiently public property that one might allow the same world relation expressed in (57) to be possibly true.

(57) *The king of France is married to a Dutchwoman that the queen of England's mother used to be in school with.*

In summary, for definite terms referring to widely known people, places and things, the real world principle may be in competition with a world-shifting principle like that which governs indefinite noun phrases.[12] Which principle someone will follow in a particular instance is likely to be influenced by certain inherently imprecise matters of factual knowledge and precedents set by standard fictions as to how freely the imagination is to be exercised.

Finally, I must mention yet another principle which contributes to the selection of a world or worlds against which to evaluate a given sentence. In Fodor (1970) I argued against the commonly held view that definite noun phrases carry no existential commitments when they appear in the complements of opaque verbs opaquely construed. Demonstrative noun phrases as in (58) had already been recognized as exceptions, but some nondemonstratives as in (59) are too.

(58) *John wants to meet that man over there.*

(59) *John wants to meet the man who is hanging from the chandelier.*

Given that the final noun phrase in (59) fails to refer in the real world, then the mere fact that John BELIEVES there is a man hanging from the chandelier (and wants to meet this man he believes to exist) is NOT sufficient to warrant the use of Sentence (59). Rather, in uttering (59), the speaker would appear to be endorsing John's mistaken belief. There are, however, some noun phrases which do not commit the speaker in such contexts. These include phrases referring to standard fictional characters, as in (60); superlative phrases, as in (61); and what I have called role descriptions, as in (62) and (63), since they pick out constant roles whose incumbents vary over time.

[12] It is possible, especially if the world shifting principle is sensitive to stress and intonation as well as to left-to-right sequence, that this principle provides the true explanation for Strawson's observations. Perhaps we are inclined to say that *The Exhibition was visited by the king of France* is false, NOT because *the king of France* is "absorbed into the predicate," but because the early appearance in the sentence of *the Exhibition* forces its interpretation as referring to the Exhibition in the real world rather than to its counterpart in the king's nonreal world.

The absorption-into-the-predicate story does seem to provide the simplest account of the preferred interpretations of negation in such sentences. *The Exhibition was not visited by the king of France* is naturally construed as saying that the Exhibition does not have the property of having been visited by the king of France; *The king of France did not visit the Exhibition* is naturally construed as saying that the king of France does not have the property of having visited the Exhibition. But this simply points up the need for a world shifting principle. For, given that visiting is a same-world relation, BOTH negative sentences should equally be judged to be true. So if in fact we regard the king as unspecified for the property of having visited the Exhibition, then it must be that the Exhibition we take to be relevant is one to which a nonreal king COULD have access.

(60) *John wants to meet the man in the moon.*

(61) *John wants to meet the cleverest girl in the room.*

(62) *John wants to meet the captain of the cricket team.*

(63) *John wants to meet the king of France.*

It seems that any one of these sentences could be truly uttered, even if their final noun phrases fail to refer.

It is of particular interest that the superlatives and role descriptions behave here like the descriptions of established fictional or mythical characters, for we find just the same grouping in transparent contexts of the kind we have been concerned with in this chapter. Assuming reference failure in all cases, the sentences of (64) can be so construed that they will be judged false, while for the sentences of (65) this is very much less natural.

(64) { *The man in the moon* / *The cleverest girl in the room* / *The captain of the cricket team* / *The king of France* } *visited the Exhibition yesterday.*

(65) { *That man over there* / *The man who is hanging from the chandelier* } *visited the Exhibition yesterday.*

None of these individuals exists in the real world. The question, then, is why we can construe only the noun phrases in (64) as referring to nonreal people. The difference cannot be due to a difference in the incidence of false beliefs about the real existence of these various individuals, for it is perceptible even to informants who are fully convinced that none of them exist. Could it be that it is more plausible that there MIGHT have been a king of France or a captain of the cricket team even though there is none, than that there might have been a man hanging from the chandelier even though there is none? I think this comes closer to providing an explanation, but that we can come closer still by noting, once again, the parallels with standard fictions. A storyteller who has let us know that France exists in the story world can go on to mention the king of France without having to explicitly assert that there is a king. A storyteller who has already introduced the cricket team can later refer to its captain without explicitly stating that the team has a captain. But a storyteller who describes the chandelier and then simply refers to the man hanging from it, without first having said that there IS a man hanging from it, has either made a mistake or has indulged in a selfconscious literary artifice. A role description identifies a sort of stock character who hovers in the wings ready to appear whenever called upon.

It has already been shown that the degree to which we take for granted the existence of certain people and things in an incompletely specified nonreal world can influence the application of the world-shifting principle. Now it looks as if it also influences the interplay between the real-world principle and the principle of maximizing truth values. If the real-world principle fails, for lack of a real-world referent, how readily do we conjure up a nonreal referent which will permit us to assign a truth value? For role descriptions like *the king of France* we do so easily enough; for other kinds of noun phrase, failure of the real-world principle leaves us with nothing to fall back on.

With this last observation I have conceded that not all cases of reference failure lend themselves to an analysis as instances of successful reference to nonreal individuals, even though the well-worn examples with which we confront informants generally do. The point of exploring the latter kind of example at such length has been to establish (a) that we can expect wide variation in informants' judgements unless we take care to pin down what SORT of judgment is being offered (in accord with which of the various competing principles? relative to which world or worlds?); and (b) that we need not throw up our hands in despair at this profusion of kinds of judgment, since once the world or worlds against which the sentence is being judged have been established, one very general principle predicts what the judgment will be. A truth value will be assigned JUST IN CASE THERE IS SOME FACTUAL BASIS FOR ASSIGNING ONE, RELATIVE TO THE WORLD OR WORLDS IN QUESTION, that is, just in case the individual(s) referred to (exist and) are specified in those worlds for the properties or relations attributed to them. This principle explains so many very different kinds of example that it is hard to doubt that it is true. And if it is true, it follows that, judged relative to the REAL world only, many sentences do exhibit truth value gaps.

6. CONCLUSION

There are two words *false:* the word *false* as an item in the vocabulary of common or garden English, and the word *false* as a technical term in the metalanguage (based on everyday English but not identical with it) that we use for talking about English and other languages.

In the metalanguage we can, if we see fit, define the word *false* to be equivalent to *not true*. Or we can define it in such a way that the predicate *neither true nor false* is coherent. For example, we could define truth as correspondence to the facts, falsity as conflict with the facts, and then lack of a truth value would consist in failure to engage any facts. Which of these moves we make is of no great importance, for we could easily introduce other terms to achieve the same effect. Thus if *true* and *false* are defined as contradictory predicates rather than merely contrary ones, we could still divide the false sentences into those which are false because they conflict with the facts and those which are false because they fail to engage the facts.

The case against truth value gaps in natural language must be more than just a terminological quibble. It can proceed on one of two levels. It might be said that English speakers do in fact use the words *true* and *false* as contradictories and acknowledge no third alternative. This seems to be just factually wrong, and has been admitted as such even by proponents of a two-valued logic. So the argument must be that English speakers do not use the words *true* and *false* consistently, and that they could not do so because there is no valid basis for the distinction within nontrue sentences which English speakers take themselves to be making by their restriction of the word *false* to only some nontrue sentences.

I have tried to show that the disagreements and doubts about the application of the word *false* which have brought this distinction under attack are susceptible to explanation. In finding an explanation for them I have looked at a far wider range of examples than usual, which is good, and have made use of a much more liberal ontological framework than is usual, which may be bad. My hope is that the things I have said, even if they cannot properly be said as I have said them, can properly be said somehow.

REFERENCES

Chomsky, N. "Deep structure, surface structure, and semantic interpretation." In R. Jakobson and S. Kawamoto (Eds.), *Studies in general and Oriental linguistics. Presented to Shiro Hattori on the occasion of his sixtieth birthday. Tokyo* TEC Co., 1970. [Also in Chomsky, N. *Studies on semantics in generative grammar,* The Hague, Mouton, 1972; and in D. Steinberg and L. Jakobovitz (Eds.), *Semantics: An interdisciplinary reader in philosophy, linguistics, and psychology.* Cambridge: Cambridge University Press, 1971.]

Fodor, J. D. *The linguistic description of opaque contexts,* Ph.D. dissertation, Massachusetts Institute of Technology, 1970. Distributed by Indiana University Linguistics Club. (to be published by Garland Publishing Inc., New York)

Jackendoff, R. S. *Semantic interpretation in generative grammar.* Cambridge, Massachusetts: MIT Press, 1972.

Katz, J. J. *A solution to the projection problem for presupposition.* (this volume)

Kempson, R. M. *Presupposition and the delimitation of semantics.* Cambridge: Cambridge University Press, 1975.

Lewis, D. Truth in fiction, *American Philosophical Quarterly,* 1978, *15,* 1.

Strawson, P. F. Identifying reference and truth-values." *Theoria,* 1964, *30,* 96–118.

van Fraassen, B. C. Singular terms, truth-value gaps, and free logic. *Journal of Philosophy,* 1966, *63,* 481–495.

Wilson, D. *Presupposition and non-truth-conditional semantics,* London: Academic Press, 1975.

PRESUPPOSITIONAL GRAMMAR[1]

CHOON-KYU OH AND KURT GODDEN
University of Kansas at Lawrence

1. INTRODUCTION

Various works such as Karttunen and Peters (1975) and Gazdar (1976) deal with the presupposition projection problem, and each of these works proposes a solution of some form. Karttunen and Peters, for instance, propose to enrich Montague's PTQ (Proper Treatment of Quantification) system by equipping it with a device that computes what they call conventional implicature. In their system, the translation procedure assigns to each generated phrase a complex of three types of expressions of intensional logic language: extension expression, implicature expression, and heritage expression. The intensional logic language is an interpreted formal language which Montague (1974) uses as an intermediary step for natural language semantics. It seems quite obvious that any adequate grammar would have to assign to each generated phrase including lexical items its "implicature" meaning as well as extension, but one cannot help wondering whether assigning the "heritage" information to all expressions would be the better way of dealing with the projection problem. Even if their theory brings out solutions for "a number of long-standing problems about presupposition," one suspects that there would be more natural explanations as far as the projection problem is concerned.

Gazdar (1976) provides interesting definitions and rules which rank

[1] This work was supported by the University of Kansas General Research Grant.

Syntax and Semantics, Volume 11: Presupposition

ISBN 0-12-613511-8

order the entailments, implicatures, and presuppositions of a sentence. When a sentence is uttered that might give rise to a contradiction of semantic information, his rules provide for the cancellation of that information that takes part in the contradiction and lies on the lower end of the rank order. Thus, in the sentence *John's teacher was either a bachelor or a spinster*, the opposing presuppositions of the subject's maleness and femaleness, since they are on the same level, are both canceled and the desired result follows that the sentence as a whole carries no presupposition of the sex of John's teacher. While Gazdar supplies formally satisfactory rules which account for a large number of problematic cases for the "projection problem," his rules provide no natural explanation for why they function as they do.

We intend to suggest an alternative theory of grammar that not only is able to account for many of the troublesome cases of presupposition projection, but also provides a natural explanation for the account.

2. PRESUPPOSITIONAL GRAMMAR[2]

We will start out by characterizing the presuppositional grammar we are proposing.

Presuppositional grammar = $\langle S, C, A, R \rangle$, where

$S = \{s_1, s_2, \ldots\}$ such that each s_i is a sentence of a natural language;

$C = \{c_1, c_2, \ldots\}$ such that each c_i is a context, which in turn is a set of propositions;

$A = \{a_1, a_2, \ldots\}$ such that each a_i is a proposition set that 'translates' some $s_j \in S$;

$R = A \times C \longrightarrow S$

In this grammar presuppositions for a sentence s_i may be defined in two ways: as members of $c_j \in C$ such that $r(a_k, c_j) = s_i$ for some $r \in R$ or as those propositions in c_j that are crucially utilized by r in mapping a_k into s_i, the propositions that must be in the context for the sentence in question to be selected. We will base our analysis on the second definition. Tautologies are presuppositions of all sentences according to the standard definition of presupposition since all sentences and

[2] A presuppositional grammar is not a complete theory of grammar, but rather a subpart of one. We assume rules to derive well formed sentences to make up the members of S.

their negations entail tautologies. It should be obvious that in the definition that we have chosen this need not be the case.

To show how this grammar works, we will illustrate first by a case of lexical choice and then another example of how some syntactic constructs are selected.

(1) *John has stopped smoking.*

(2) *John does not smoke.*

(3) *John has started smoking.*

(4) *John continues smoking.*

Sentences (1) and (2) share the propositional content, namely, that John does not smoke, but differ in the context of use in that only the context for the first contains the proposition that John smoked sometime before. Similarly sentences (3) and (4) assert the identical proposition that John now smokes but their contexts include the mutually contradictory values of the proposition that John smoked before. Our illustration might be further clarified, if we name the propositions and types of contexts involved in the previous discussion as follows:

[*John now does not smoke*] = a_1 $(\in A)$[3]
[*John now smokes*] = a_2 $(\in A)$
[*John smoked before*] = c_1 $(\in C)$
[*John did not smoke before*] = c_2 $(\in C)$

Now, if r is the English grammar, r can be characterized as the following:

$$r(a_1, c_1) = s_1$$
$$r(a_1, c_2) = s_2$$
$$r(a_2, c_2) = s_3$$
$$r(a_2, c_1) = s_4$$

For an example of how our grammar selects syntactic constructs, let us consider the cleft construction. Suppose a speaker wants to assert the proposition that John's fiancée called from Seoul today, his choice of sentences between

(5) *It was John's fiancée who called from Seoul today.*

(6) *John's fiancée called from Seoul today.*

will depend on whether the context includes the proposition that

[3] [ ] is a function from sentences into propositions. See Gazdar (1976).

somebody called from Seoul today. If it does, (5) will be selected. Otherwise (6) will be used.

3. FILTERS IN PRESUPPOSITIONAL GRAMMAR

Most proposed projection rules in recent literature are based on the notion of presupposition cancellation. For a typical example, Karttunen (1973) treats sentential connectives such as *if A then B, A and B*, and *A or B* as "predicates which, under certain conditions, cancel some of the presuppositions of the complement," and calls them FILTERS. The heritage expressions in Karttunen and Peters (1975) are to control exactly such presupposition cancellations. Gazdar's "satisfactory incrementation" of implicatures and presuppositions is similarly motivated. Let us consider Karttunen's original examples:

(7) a. *If baldness is hereditary, then all of Jack's children are bald.*
 b. *If Jack has children, then all of Jack's children are bald.*

(8) a. *Baldness is hereditary and all of Jack's children are bald.*
 b. *Jack has children and all of Jack's children are bald.*

(9) a. *Either baldness is not hereditary or all of Jack's children are bald.*
 b. *Either Jack has no children or all of Jack's children are bald.*

All the (a) sentences presuppose that Jack has children. For the (b) sentences, while the consequent sentences do presuppose the same sentence, the whole sentences do not. This is why presuppositions are described as having been canceled. The presupposition distribution in the preceding sentences follows from the following perfectly natural principles:

GENERAL OPERATING PRINCIPLE (GOP) I: *No proposition may be asserted, questioned, or conditionalized with the intention of conversationally implicating any proposition already in the context.*

GOP II: *No proposition already in the context may be contradicted.*

The reason for adopting the stricter version of GOP I by blocking the intended conversational implication of some contextual propositions instead of blocking just their entailment—as in GOP I′—is to be able to treat the following examples discussed extensively in recent literature (see Karttunen, 1973, Katz and Langendoen, 1976):

GOP I′: *No proposition may be asserted, questioned, or conditionalized with the intention of* **entailing** *any proposition already in the context.*

(10) *If Geraldine is a Mormon she has given up wearing her holy underwear.*

(11) *If Nixon appoints J. Edgar Hoover to the cabinet, he will regret having appointed a homosexual.*

(12) *If the secretary has destroyed the tape, Nixon is guilty too.*

These sentences may or may not have the relevant presuppositions depending on the contexts in which they are uttered. According to GOP I′ (10) as a whole sentence is expected always to have the presupposition that Geraldine used to wear her holy underwear. The antecedent of (10) above does not entail the presupposition, therefore one cannot say that the sentence was used with the intention of making that entailment, and consequently GOP I′ will not block (10) from being associated with any context. But the fact is that whenever (10) does not have the presupposition, it is invariably the case that the antecedent sentence of (10) *together with some proposition(s) in the context* entails the presupposition. This fact is reflected in the stricter form of GOP I.

We would like to claim that these principles are universal restrictions on the forms of R to be used for natural languages. These principles say only that if a proposition is already registered in a discourse context it should be totally unnecessary to assert, improper to question or hypothesize, and wrong to contradict that proposition. GOP I blocks the (b) sentences in (7)–(9) from being mapped with any context which contains the proposition that Jack has children. Sentence (7b), for instance, cannot be uttered in a context which includes the proposition for in that context one's hypothesizing something that is already known would be grossly unjustifiable. GOP II can handle the nasty problems for most of the presupposition projection treatments discussed in Wilson (1975). Consider, for example, (13) and (14):

(13) *John's teacher will be either a bachelor or a spinster.*

(14) *If John's teacher was a bachelor he was lucky, but if his teacher was a spinster he was unlucky.*

These sentences could not be uttered in the context that includes either the proposition that John's teacher was a male or that John's teacher was a female since in either context one of the conjuncts in (13) and (14) will contradict the presupposed proposition.

Notice that one should be allowed to speculate on the consequences of the falsehood of some proposition that is in the context. This is what counterfactuals are used for. Karttunen and Peters (first paper in this volume) summarize the difference between the two kinds of *if A then B:*

If A then B conventionally implicates
a. Indicative mood—*it is epistemically possible that A*
b. Subjunctive mood—*it is epistemically possible that −A*

As Karttunen and Peters spell out, "In a situation where it is agreed upon or evident that the antecedent clause is false, only the subjunctive conditional can be used." Karttunen and Peters further add, "In a situation where it is evident or agreed upon that the antecedent clause is true only the indicative conditional is acceptable." This should not be taken as contradicting our analysis of conditionals. While it is true that the subjunctive conditional cannot be used in the situation Karttunen and Peters describe, one should note that in such a situation use of a conditional, even an indicative one, is the exception rather than the rule. Otherwise the bizarre nature of a sentence such as (15) would remain unexplained.

(15) *?*If John's natural father has ever made love to a woman, he is not a Catholic priest.*

4. PLUGS IN PRESUPPOSITIONAL GRAMMAR

Plugs are defined as predicates which block off all the presuppositions of the complement sentence. These include performative verbs and propositional attitude verbs. Thus the following (a) sentences do not necessarily presuppose their corresponding (b) sentences:

(16) a. *Harry has promised Bill to introduce him to the present king of France.*
b. *The king of France exists.*

(17) a. *Sheila accuses Harry of beating his wife.*
b. *Harry has a wife.*

(18) a. *Cecilia asked Fred to kiss her again.*
b. *Fred has kissed Cecilia before.*

(19) a. *Bill believes that Fred kissed Cecilia again.*
b. *Fred kissed Cecilia before.*

Notice that this does not mean that the speaker of the (a) sentences may not presume the truth of the (b) sentences in any context. In fact, we would like to claim that there is a systematic ambiguity here, an ambiguity just as systematic as that for the negation and implication as illustrated in (20) and (21):

(20) a. *John has not stopped smoking. (I just caught him smoking in the barn.)*
b. *John has not* **stopped** *smoking.* (He never smoked before.)

(21) a. *If John has stopped smoking, the color of his lungs must be changing. (They must be getting pink again.)*
b. *If John has* **stopped** *smoking, the color of his lungs must be changing.* (If John has *stopped* smoking, he smoked before. And if he smoked before, the color of his lungs must be changing.)

We might explain the different readings in (20) and (21) in terms of sentential versus propositional operations. A sentence in this theory is the representation of a proposition in a certain context. From the purely truth-conditional semantic point of view, one could identify a sentence s_i with the conjunction of a_j with the propositions in c_k if there exists r_l such that $r_l(a_j, c_k) = s_i$.

Defining sentences this way allows us to talk about sentential operations as well as propositional operations as illustrated in the following analysis of (20):

(20′) 1. Propositional negation:
a_j = (−(*John does not smoke*))
c_k = (*John smoked before*), . . .
2. Sentential negation:
$s_i = (-s_j)$ where
s_j = '*John has stopped smoking*' (=*John smoked before and John does not smoke now.*)

Once it is agreed upon that a logical operator may operate on the members of *A* or the members of *S* as earlier defined, the treatment of plug verbs becomes rather straightforward. We admit that the utterers of the (a) sentences of (16)–(19) need not believe the corresponding (b) sentences. In fact, contrary to what has often been claimed, the speakers need not believe even that the subjects have such beliefs. Thus it is not necessary for the speaker of (16a) to presume that (16b) or that Harry believes that (16b). But it is not possible for the speaker not to have either presumption. In other words, (16a) does not presuppose that the king of France exists or that Harry believes that the king of France exists, but rather THAT EITHER THE KING OF FRANCE EXISTS OR HARRY BELIEVES THAT THE KING OF FRANCE EXISTS.

It is interesting to note what happens when sentences (16a)–(19a) are negated. The negation of (16a) presupposes that either the king of France exists or someone (not necessarily Harry any more) believes so. As far as the semantic presuppositions are concerned, both the sentences (16a)–(19a) and their negations presuppose more general presuppositions, namely the presuppositions of the negated sentences. How is this fact explained in the presuppositional grammar? Simply by allowing *r* to relate (16), for instance, to two distinct contexts, one which contains the proposition that the king of France exists and the other the proposition that the king of France exists is believed by someone.

5. THEORETICAL IMPLICATIONS

The reader will have noticed that GOPs I and II have their foundations in the widely accepted conversational rules presented in Grice (1972). To violate our principles is to violate a Gricean maxim. For example, if *p* is accepted by all conversants and is therefore in the context, to contradict *p* is to violate the QUALITY MAXIM. Likewise, if *p* is in the context and *q* is used only to conversationally implicate *p*, then questioning or hypothesizing *q* perhaps violates some extended version of the RELATION MAXIM and asserting *q* violates the MAXIM OF QUANTITY. This interaction with Gricean rules is then the natural explanation for the account that GOPs I and II provide for presuppositional phenomena.

One interesting aspect of our presuppositional grammar is the way it relates presuppositions to sentences. We may embed this theory within a larger framework of generative transformational grammar. The relation *R* can associate contexts, hence presuppositions, and propositional contents with natural language expressions. The transformations in such a model can be sensitive not only to forms, but also to presuppositions in the context. In fact, we claim that presuppositions are applicability conditions for transformational rules. Thus, it was seen that the use of a cleft sentence was dependent upon the presence of some presupposition in the context. All transformations are obligatory in this theory. Optional transformations of other theories are obligatory in the present theory but dependent on the presence or absence of certain propositions in the context.

Notice also that with this new model, there is no question of presupposition projection. We need not say that presuppositions of embedded expressions are canceled or filtered out by higher expressions. Canceled presuppositions are symptomatic of either the cases where the embedded expressions are never assigned these presuppositions or those cases where the expressions are related to a group of contexts at least one of which does not include the presuppositions in question. Our approach is a simple and natural restriction on R to disallow certain constructions from being related to certain presuppositions, instead of allowing the relations and then canceling or filtering them out later. With this view it is seen that linguistic expressions are not invariably associated with certain presuppositions. It makes no sense to say that factive verbs presuppose the truth of their complements. Sometimes they do; and sometimes they do not, for example, when they are in the scope of plug type verbs.

The present theory provides an interesting explanation for some ingenious observations made in Wilson (1975) and summarized as follows:

Only tautologies can be both logically presupposed and entailed by a given sentence.

Only tautologies can logically presuppose and be entailed by a given sentence.

These observations are employed as one of the major criteria throughout Wilson's book in determining whether a certain meaning component of a sentence is a presupposition or entailment. Notice that GOP I implies that an assertion set a_i is not empty and is disjoint with its presupposition set c_i and thus supplies a natural explanation for Wilson's observations.

The theory presented here may also clarify some common mistakes made during second language acquisition. It is widely noticed that language learners tend to overgeneralize words or expressions to contexts in which they should not apply. As familiarity with language increases, the overgeneralizations decrease until, if learned thoroughly, they apply only to the correct situations. Within our grammar, the logical form of an expression is learned first and the learners will try to guess at the set of contexts of which the initially learned context is a member. In many cases, these guesses prove wrong. When this is discovered, the learner modifies his internal relation *r* to disallow that incorrect association, and in this way step-by-step he arrives at the correct form of *r* for the target language.

REFERENCES

Gazdar, G. *Implicature, presupposition, and logical Form.* Ph.D. dissertation. University of Reading. Distributed by the Indiana Linguistics Club.

Grice, H. P. Logic and conversation. In P. Cole and J. L. Morgan (Eds.), *Syntax and Semantics III: Speech Acts* New York: Academic Press, 1972. Pp. 41–58.

Karttunen, L. Presuppositions of compound sentences, *Linguistic Inquiry, 1973, 4,* 169 –193.

Karttunen, L. and Peters, S. Conventional implicature in Montague Grammar. In *BLS I Proceedings of the First Annual Meeting of the Berkeley Linguistics Society.* Berkeley, California. Pp. 266–278.

Katz, J. J. and Langendoen, D. T. Pragmatics and presupposition. *Language,* 1976, 52, 1–17.

Montague, R. The proper treatment of quantification in ordinary English. In R. H. Thomason (Ed.), *Formal philosophy: Selected papers of Richard Montague.* New Haven: Conn. Yale University Press, 1974.

Oh, C.-K. Presupposition and meaning change by transformational rules. In R. W. Shuy and C.-J. N. Bailey (Eds.), *Towards tomorrow's linguistics.* Washington, D.C.: Georgetown University Press, 1974.

Wilson, D. *Presuppositions and Non-Truth-Conditional Semantics.* London: Academic Press, 1975.

WHERE PRESUPPOSITIONS COME FROM

DEREK BICKERTON
University of Hawaii at Honolulu

Hitherto, accounts of the presupposition phenomenon have treated it as a pragmatic or a logical one. In the present chapter, I shall suggest that it arises because of certain syntactic facts.

Logical definitions typically have been framed in terms of a three-valued logic (as in, for example, Keenan, 1971) and suggest that a sentence *S* presupposes a proposition *P* if both *S* and $-S$ logically imply *P*. If *P* is false, then *S* is generally held to lack a truthvalue. However, Wilson (1975) points out that sentences such as

(1) *John didn't stop working.*

which are generally held to presuppose

(2) *John was working.*

may be true even if their presuppositions are false, since

(3) *John didn't stop working, he never even started.*

is both true and semantically well formed even if (2) is false. Pragmatic accounts, on the other hand, have sought to define presuppositions in terms of felicity conditions (Karttunen, 1974), context (Thomason, 1974) or COMMON GROUND (Karttunen and Peters, 1975). These and similar proposals have been criticized by Gazdar (1976) on a variety of grounds, of which perhaps the most compelling is that a sentence such as

Syntax and Semantics, Volume 11: Presupposition

ISBN 0-12-613511-8

(4) *Was it you who ate the cookies?*

presupposes

(5) *Someone ate the cookies.*

whether or not there exists any context or COMMON GROUND—(4) is perfectly possible as the first utterance of a conversation—and whether or not it is felicitously uttered. While this very cursory treatment does not begin to do justice to the richness and diversity of Wilson's and Gazdar's arguments, I shall henceforth assume that existing logical and pragmatic accounts of presupposition are inadequate.

Two more recent works have tried to handle presupposition rather differently. Karttunen and Peters (1975) suggest that presuppositions might be treated as conventional implicatures, though they are rather hesitant about this: "We certainly do not claim that everything that has been called a case of pragmatic presupposition is a case of conventional implicature. More likely, the former term . . . covers a heterogeneous class of phenomena [p. 267]." However, Gazdar (1976) has shown that while implicatures (such as *if* clauses, which conventionally implicate that their converse is possible) can cancel presuppositions, the reverse does not hold. Thus, if we treat presuppositions as implicatures, we are left with no principled grounds for deciding when one implicature ought to cancel another, and when one should fail to do so. Furthermore, while conversational implicatures are derivable from Gricean maxims (Grice, 1968), conventional implicatures are primitive concepts as opaque as GRAVITY or INSTINCT; what they implicate seems to be, in some sense, governed by lexical entries and structural descriptions of sentences.

However, Gazdar's own position seems essentially little different from that of Karttunen and Peters which he criticizes. Gazdar defines the potential presuppositions of sentences (that is, what will become the presuppositions of those sentences unless canceled by entailment, implicature or context) "in terms of their components and constructions AS IF POTENTIAL PRESUPPOSITIONS WERE SOMETHING GIVEN TO US BY THE LEXICON AND THE SYNTAX, but I do this without prejudice to the possibility of some future general explanation as to why these lexical and syntactic sources of presupposition are such [Gazdar, 1976, 188, emphasis added]."

In what follows, I shall try to show that presuppositions are indeed given by the nature of syntax, and in showing how this comes about I hope to provide the kind of general explanation Gazdar envisaged. This will involve a reversal of the recent trend toward expressing sentences of natural languages in logical terms; that is, translation of logical and quasi-logical categories into syntactic terms.

Let us begin by considering analytic sentences:

(6) *Bachelors are unmarried adult males.*

(7) **The winner of the race won the race.*

(8) **That red box is a red box.*

Katz (1964) observed that "sentences that are fully analytic are not found in natural language, except in areas where a highly technical nomenclature is in use [p. 527]." Of the three preceding sentences, (6) might be used to explain to an adult learner of English what the word *bachelor* means. It is, however, virtually impossible to conceive of any set of circumstances (setting aside pure facetiousness) in which (7) and (8) would be regarded as well-formed sentences of English. The same is true to an even greater extent of (9)–(11).

(9) **John is a bachelor and he is an unmarried adult male.*

(10) **Mary stopped her car and brought her automobile to a halt.*

(11) **That box was here yesterday and it was here yesterday.*

Sentences such as these strictly speaking are not analytic but they are bad for the same reason that analytic sentences are bad: They repeat information which has already been given. The rule that is at work here can be still better illustrated by observing the behavior of confirmatory tag sentences:

(12) *John says that Mary is pregnant, which she is.*

(13) **John regrets that Mary is pregnant, which she is.*

(14) *John regrets that Mary is pregnant, which she is through no fault of her own.*

Here, (12) is good because the tag adds a piece of information which was not recoverable from the original sentence, which merely reports John's assertion that a certain situation exists. In (13), however, no new information is added. The fact that Mary is pregnant is somehow implicit in the use of the verb *regret*. However, (14) becomes good again because here the tag includes additional information about

Mary's condition. We can assume, from Examples (5)–(14), that there is a general principle of language which may be stated as follows:

(15) *The second member of a pair of conjoined sentences must add substantive information if the resulting sentence is to be well formed.*

Although (15) has been stated so as to apply only to pairs of conjoined sentences, it is not suggested that it is the act of conjunction per se that makes resultant sentences ill formed. Similar results would be obtained if the members of the pair simply followed one another as independent units.

In what follows, sentences such as (7)–(11) and (13), which violate Principle (15), will be asterisked. However, since I do not wish to get into irrelevant arguments about the precise status of the data, I shall be quite satisfied even if some speakers find some asterisked sentences permissible, provided always that, given any two sentences in which the same pair of conjuncts are placed in different orders, the reader accepts that the asterisked order is at least clearly worse than the nonasterisked order.

Let us now consider the behavior of certain pairs of sentences which exhibit logical or quasi-logical relationships. I shall distinguish the following three types of conjoint-pair:

1. Conjoint-pairs in which S_1 strongly entails S_2
2. Conjoint-pairs in which S_1 presupposes S_2
3. Conjoint-pairs in which S_1 weakly entails S_2

A word should be said here about the definition of the above relationships. The distinction between STRONG ENTAILMENT and WEAK ENTAILMENT was suggested by Wilson (1975, p. 4), who observed that entailment could be defined strongly ("a sentence *S* entails another sentence *P* iff *if S* is true *P* must also be true, and if *P* is false *S* must also be false") or weakly ("if *S* is true *P* must also be true, but . . . no claim is made about the consequences for *S* if *P* is false"). I propose to use the terms rather differently, since I am interested in the extent to which the truth or falsity of a matrix sentence *S* affects the truth or falsity of an embedded sentence *P*. For the purposes of this discussion it will be immaterial what effect the truth value of *P* has on that of *S*. I shall therefore more fully define the relationships of strong and weak entailment and presupposition, using the terms ENTAIL and IMPLICATE in the following senses: *X* entails *Y* iff *Y* must be true if *X* is true, and *X* implicates *Y* iff, when *X* is false, *Y* will be assumed to be true unless it is separately negated.

1. Strong entailment: *S* entails *P*, -*S* entails -P.
2. Presupposition: *S* entails *P*, -*S* implicates *P*.
3. Weak entailment: *S* entails *P*, -*S* is compatible with either *P* or -*P*.

The relationship of presupposition is well known from the literature (although it is not always defined as here) but the other two relationships may require illustration. As an example of strong entailment,

(16) *John managed to get to the party.*

entails

(17) *John got to the party.*

and

(18) *John didn't manage to get to the party.*

entails

(19) *John didn't get to the party.*

As an example of weak entailment,

(20) *John left the party early.*

entails

(21) *John left the party.*

but

(22) *John didn't leave the party early.*

entails neither

(23) *John didn't leave the party.*

nor (21), provided that we assume noncontrastive intonation patterns (we shall later have to confront the problems posed for logical analysis by the fact that a single orthographic sentence may represent two or more utterances which have quite different implications).

The rules for the conjunction of pairs of sentences in relationships may be stated and illustrated as follows:

1. Conjoint pairs showing strong entailment: Given a pair of sentences, *S*1 and *S*2, where *S*1 strongly entails *S*2, *and*-conjunction of *S*1 and *S*2 will result in ill formed sentences irrespective of the order of conjuncts.
   Consider examples (24)–(31).

(24) **John got to the party and he managed to get to the party.*

(25) **John managed to get to the party and he got to the party.*

(26) **Mary did not win and she failed to win.*

(27) **Mary failed to win and she did not win.*

(28) **Bill succeeded in borrowing $5 and he borrowed $5.*

(29) **Bill borrowed $5 and he succeeded in borrowing $5.*

(30) **Bill did not succeed in borrowing $5 and he did not borrow $5.*

(31) **Bill did not borrow $5 and he did not succeed in borrowing $5.*

The bilateral relationship illustrated holds for all cases of strong entailment that I have examined. However, it might seem that Principle (15) is in danger from the claim (due to Karttunen and Peters, 1975, following numerous earlier writers) that items such as *manage* and *fail* do carry conventional implicatures (for example, in the case of *fail*, that the subject tried to, or was expected to win) and should therefore add substantively to the meaning of sentences such as (24) or (26). However, Coleman (1975) gives good grounds for thinking that such claims are at best shaky, and it is not hard to devise even more telling counterexamples than those in her paper. Consider (32) for example.

(32) *Mary failed to win, which was hardly surprising, since no one including herself had really expected her to, and she didn't even try.*

Any serious claims about the conventional implicature of *fail* would have to assert that (33) is contradictory, which it clearly is not.

2. Conjoint pairs showing presupposition: Given a pair of sentences, $S1$ and $S2$, where $S1$ presupposes $S2$, *and*-conjunction will result in ill formed sentences if $S1$ is the first conjunct, but not if $S2$ is the first conjunct.

Consider examples (33)–(48).

(33) *Someone ate the cookies and it was you who ate them.*

(34) **It was you who ate the cookies and someone ate them.*

(35) *John wanted something and what he wanted was a cigarette.*

(36) **What John wanted was a cigarette and he wanted something.*

(37) *A man came in and the man who came in was Bill's brother.*

(38) **The man who came in was Bill's brother and a man came in.*

(39) *Bill was a fool and Mary knew he was a fool.*

(40) **Mary knew Bill was a fool and he was a fool.*

(41) *John couldn't swim and Mary regretted that he couldn't swim.*

(42) **Mary regretted that John couldn't swim and he couldn't swim.*

(43) *John was working and he didn't stop working.*

(44) **John didn't stop working and he was working.*

(45) *There is now a king of France, and the present king of France is bald.*

(46) **The present king of France is bald, and there is now a king of France.*

(47) *Mary smokes and the fact that she smokes upsets Bill.*

(48) **The fact that Mary smokes upsets Bill and she smokes.*

The asymmetric relationship illustrated holds for all the cases I have examined of sentences treated in the literature as presuppositional. It can further be shown that the syntactic distinction made between strong entailment conjunction and presupposition conjunction will hold even when the same pair of conjuncts includes elements with both presuppositional and strong entailment relationships. Consider, for instance,

(49) *Caesar managed to conquer the Gauls.*

which entails

(50) *Caesar conquered the Gauls.*

while

(51) *Caesar didn't manage to conquer the Gauls.*

entails

(52) *Caesar didn't conquer the Gauls.*

However, (49) only presupposes

(53) *The Gauls were conquered.*

because (51) does not entail either (54) or

(54) *The Gauls were not conquered.*

When the appropriate conjunctions are carried out, we get exactly the results which 1. and 2. predict; that is,

(55) **Caesar conquered the Gauls and he managed to conquer them.*

(56) **Caesar managed to conquer the Gauls and he conquered them.*

(57) *The Gauls were conquered and Caesar managed to conquer them.*

(58) **Caesar managed to conquer the Gauls, and they were conquered.*

However, when we come to examine weak entailment conjunctions, we find what at first appears to be a much less distinct pattern. Some sentences that show weak entailment relationships can have their conjuncts in any order. Thus, for instance,

(59) *John was trying to catch the fish.*

entails

(60) *John had not caught the fish yet.*

–although

(61) *John was not trying to catch the fish.*

does not entail or implicate either (60) or

(62) *John had already caught the fish.*

But both conjoining orders for (59) and (60) yield well formed sentences:

(63) *John was trying to catch the fish and he hadn't caught it yet.*

(64) *John hadn't caught the fish yet and he was trying to catch it.*

However, it is also true that (20) entailed (21), while the negation of (20) did not entail either (21) or (22). Yet when these are conjoined, we get a result quite different from the one we obtained by conjoining (59) and (60):

(65) *John left the party and he left it early.*

(66) **John left the party early and he left it.*

On the face of things, there are some weak entailment pairs which behave exactly like presuppositional pairs. This is an undesirable finding, since it does not appear that (20) presupposes (21). However, if we examine the problem more closely, we will see that there are at least two ways in which we can distinguish "true" presuppositional pairs from those weak entailment pairs that seem to mimic them.

The first way involves pointing out the ambiguity of sentences such as (20). Sentence (20) is ambiguous between two intonational patterns,

(20) a. *John left the party early.*
b. *John left the party* ***early***.

Now (20b) DOES presuppose (21), for (21b), *John didn't leave the party* ***early***, is an exact paraphrase of (21c), *It wasn't early when John left the party*, and both (21b) and (21c) implicate (21), *John left the party*. In other words, weak-entailment sentences such as (20) always have a presuppositional reading in addition to their weak-entailment reading, and (for reasons still far from clear) *and*-conjunction brings out, indeed forces, the presuppositional reading. Compare the following examples:

(67) *The cake was eaten and Mary ate it.*

(68) **Mary ate the cake and it was eaten.*

(69) *Bill writes in his room and he writes poetry in his room.*

(70) **Bill writes poetry in his room and he writes in his room.*

Note that, according to Chomsky–Halle stress rules, we would expect primary stress to fall on *ate* in (67) and *room* in (69). In fact, these sentences are acceptable only if primary stress falls on *Mary* in (67) and on *poetry* in (69); that is, (67) and (69) are equivalent, respectively, to

(71) *The cake was eaten and it was Mary who ate it.*

(72) *Bill writes in his room and it is poetry that he writes in his room.*

Where members of a weak-entailment pair differ from one another only by the presence or absence of a single constituent—as in (65), (67) and (69)—there seems to be no way in which the weak-entailment reading can be salvaged from the presuppositional reading. However, where they differ by more than a single constituent, as in (63), no problem from presuppositional readings arises.

The second way of distinguishing weak entailment pairs from "true" presuppositional pairs is less dependent upon ambiguities. It involves the use of *but*-conjunction instead of *and*-conjunction. Much about *but*-conjunction remains obscure, and it has hardly been touched on in the literature. However, R. Lakoff (1971) points out that, for *but*-conjunction to be grammatical, the second conjunct must in some way deny the expectations of the first. From this, it would follow that *but* is inappropriate if the second conjunct, instead of denying, in fact fulfills the expectations of the first. Take, for example,

(73) *John walked and walked.*

(74) **John walked but walked.*

(75) *Mary aimed the pistol and fired.*

(76) **Mary aimed the pistol but fired.*

(77) *The Lone Ranger mounted his horse and rode off into the sunset.*

(78) **The Lone Ranger mounted his horse but rode off into the sunset.*

It should follow that, in the case of presuppositions, *but*-conjunction (where *S*1 precedes and presupposes *S*2) should yield results no different from those of *and*-conjunction; that is, ill formed sentences. And indeed,

(79) **It was you who ate the cookies but someone ate them.*

is fully as bad as (35).

It might be thought that weak-entailment sentences would behave in the same way. Indeed, it is true that, in both types of sentence, if *S* is true, then *P* must also be true, and from this one might deduce that *P* cannot be repeated in a *but*-conjunct. However, this omits a vital difference between presuppositional and weak entailment sentences. Granted that *P* for (35)—*Someone ate the cookies*—must be true if (35) is true, and that *P* for (20)—*John left the party*—must be true if (20) is true, there is still this difference between (35) and (20): (35) PRESUPPOSES *P*, whereas (20) merely ASSERTS P—if (35) were denied, it would still implicate *P*, whereas if (20) were denied, it would no longer implicate *P*.

Thus

(80) *John left the party early, but he left it.*

is quite acceptable as a counter to the expectation that, if John had left the party at all, he would have left it late. Similarly acceptable—though they require slight shifts of wording or emphasis if they are not to sound awkward—are the *but*-equivalents of (68) and (70):

(81) *Mary ate the cake, but it* ***was*** *eaten.*

(82) *Bill writes poetry in his room, but he* ***does*** *write there.*

Weak entailment sentences that do not have presuppositional readings will accept *but*-conjunction without even these minor adjustments:

(83) *John was trying to catch the fish but he hadn't caught it yet.*

(84) *Mary has left but she was here.*

(85) *John had sold Mary the house but it used to be his.*

On the other hand, presuppositional sentences such as the odd numbered ones between (33) and (48) will not accept *but*-conjunction under any circumstances:

(86) **It was you who stole the cookies but* {***someone*** *stole* ***them*** / *someone* ***did steal*** *them* / *someone stole* ***them***}.

(87) **Mary knew Bill was a fool but* $\left\{\begin{array}{l} \textbf{\textit{he}}\ \textit{was a fool} \\ \textit{he}\ \textbf{\textit{was}}\ \textit{a fool} \\ \textit{he was a}\ \textbf{\textit{fool}} \end{array}\right\}$.

(88) **John didn't stop working but* $\left\{\begin{array}{l} \textbf{\textit{he}}\ \textit{was working} \\ \textit{he}\ \textbf{\textit{was}}\ \textit{working} \\ \textit{he was}\ \textbf{\textit{working}} \end{array}\right\}$.

The behavior of weak entailment sentences may be summarized as follows:

3. Conjoint pairs showing weak entailment: Given a pair of sentences, $S1$ and $S2$, where $S1$ weakly entails $S2$, *but*-conjunction will yield well formed sentences irrespective of the order of conjuncts, while *and*-conjunction will also yield only well formed sentences except for those cases which carry a presuppositional reading, which will behave like the presuppositional sentences described under 2.

Our findings in general may be summarized as follows:

(89) If $S1$ strongly entails $S2$, $S1$ may neither precede nor follow $S2$; if $S1$ presupposes $S2$, $S1$ may follow but not precede $S2$; if $S1$ weakly entails $S2$, $S1$ may either precede or follow $S2$.

We have therefore demonstrated that there is a syntactic hierarchy, statable in terms of surface ordering relations, among strong entailment, presupposition and weak entailment, showing them to be ranked in that order; that is, with presupposition intermediate between the two kinds of entailment. We noted earlier that logical and pragmatic definitions alike had failed to explain why presuppositions presuppose. We are now in a position to suggest that presuppositions derive from the facts of surface ordering previously shown, and that these in turn derive from principle (15). Unlike entailments of both kinds, presuppositions critically involve pairs of items—the presupposition itself and the sentence in which it is subsequently embedded —which can only be ordered unidirectionally. From this fact, it should be possible to see why presuppositions behave as they do. The utterance of any sentence in which a presupposition is embedded—felicitously or otherwise, in context or out of it—must carry the implication that either its presupposition has already occurred, and is therefore acceptable to both speaker and hearer (otherwise it would immediately have been challenged), or that, if it had already occurred, it would have been accepted. The only other possibility, that it might not yet have occurred in the discourse (and therefore would still be open to denial, assuming it occurred), is not open, because in all cases, the following of an embedded presupposition by the simple presupposition itself yields only unacceptable sentences—a fact which, though to the best of my knowledge not overtly observed before, must form part of our innate language faculty, since sentences such as have been examined here seem to be equally unacceptable in all languages, and not through any idiosyncracy of English grammar. Knowing this, any hearer will therefore accept the invited inference—that the presupposition is true—unless he has explicit knowledge which indicates that it is false. Thus, the manner in which presuppositions work (and are differentiated from cases of entailment) derives from syntactic, rather than logical, facts.

It would, of course, be possible to make the reverse claim: that the syntactic facts previously discussed arise simply from the nature of presuppositions. However, this would deprive us of any plausible explanation of why presuppositions work as they do. Any such proposal would have, quite literally, nothing to propose. Indeed, it might be easier to stand logic on its head and argue that the logical properties of strong and weak entailment derive from their syntactic relationships, rather than vice versa. But any such enterprise would be overly ambitious in the present chapter, which is merely an attempt to account in a new way for a very old phenomenon.

REFERENCES

Coleman, L. The case of the vanishing presupposition. In *BLS I Proceedings of the First Annual Meeting of the Berkeley Linguistics Society.* Berkeley, California, 1975. Pp. 78–89.

Fillmore, C. J., and Langendoen, D. T. (Eds.) *Studies in linguistic semantics,* New York: Holt, 1971.

Gazdar, G., 1976. Formal pragmatics for natural language: Implicature, presupposition and logical Form. Unpublished doctoral dissertation, University of Reading.

Grice, H. P., Logic and conversation. In P. Cole and J. L. Morgan (Eds.), *Syntax and Semantics III: Speech acts.* New York: Academic Press, 1972. Pp. 41–58.

Karttunen, L. Presupposition and linguistic context. *Theoretical Linguistics,* 1974, *1,* 181–194.

Karttunen, L. and Peters, S. Conversational implicature in Montague grammar. In *BLS I Proceedings of the First Annual Meeting of the Berkeley Linguistics Society.* Berkeley, California, 1975. Pp. 266–278.

Katz, J. J., Analyticity and contradiction in natural language. In J. A. Fodor and J. J. Katz (Eds.), *The structure of language.* Englewood Cliffs, New Jersey: Prentice-Hall, 1964. Pp. 519–543.

Keenan, E. L. Two kinds of presupposition in natural language. In C. J. Fillmore and D. T. Langendoen (Eds.), *Studies in Linguistic Semantics*, New York: Holt, 1971, Pp. 45–54.

Lakoff, R. If's, and's and but's about conjunction. In C. J. Fillmore and D. T. Langendoen (Eds.), *Studies in Linguistic Semantics*. New York: Holt, 1971. Pp. 115–150.

Stalnaker, R., 1974. Pragmatic presuppositions. Paper presented at the Texas Conference on Performatives, Presuppositions and Conversational Implicatures.

Wilson, D. *Presuppositions and Non-Truth-Conditional Semantics*, London: Academic Press, 1975.

PRAGMATIC PRESUPPOSITION: SHARED BELIEFS IN A THEORY OF IRREFUTABLE MEANING[1]

JOHAN VAN DER AUWERA
University of Antwerp

1. PAPERISM, PAUPERISM

A paper allows its author to restrict the topic so heavily that it can easily be given an air of reasonableness and consistency. There is the easy excuse of "leaving it to future research" and the fear of "going beyond the limits of the paper." It frightens me to see linguistics engender so many articles, working papers, squibs, proceedings, readers and so few books in which one or more linguists try to give a solid, integrated theory. Papers are valuable, but a monopoly of papers is unhealthy.

The subject matter of this paper, too, is really too broad to be dealt with in sufficient detail. I am forced to sketchiness. However, I am not flying balloons in a vacuum. The whole paper is a reference to a book on natural language meaning (Van der Auwera, 1977a). This chapter[2] partially owes its existence to the fact that this book is written in Dutch. I apologize, then, for too many high and mighty references to what this paper does not deal with, but what is dealt with in another work, written in non-English.[3] My concern is pragmatic presupposi-

[1] Thanks are due to the Commonwealth Fund of New York for sustaining our work.
[2] The same is true for Van der Auwera (1977b, 1977c).
[3] Compare Ballmer's complaint in Ballmer (1976, p. 45, Note 1).

Syntax and Semantics, Volume 11: Presupposition

ISBN 0-12-613511-8

tion. Everything else is dealt with to the degree that it helps to make my account of pragmatic presupposition more persuasive.

2. LINGUISTIC SEMANTICS VERSUS LINGUISTIC PRAGMATICS

It happens to be an insidious characteristic of most analyses of meaning that they are restricted to the use of language in reporting a state of affairs. Whether any other uses are regarded as beneath the investigator's notice, shelved as a problem for future research, or interpreted as variations or complications of the assertoric use, assertions have caught and held the attention. This remark is Urmson's (1969:196–199) and it is about philosophy up to and including British philosophy between the world wars, that is, logical atomism and logical positivism. Despite the liberating work of Wittgenstein (1968), Austin (1975), Searle (1969) and others, this remark is still valid with respect to the most important contemporary approaches, whether linguistic or language philosophical, logical or not logical.

A confinement to the study of assertion makes it difficult to see the differences between a speech act and a proposition. One can say that (1), (2), and (3) are speech acts and that they all contain the proposition (4).

(1) *John loves Mary.*

(2) *Does John love Mary?*

(3) *John, love Mary.*

(4) */John loves Mary/*

The assertion (1) and the proposition (4) look so very much alike that if one only studied (1), and not (2) and (3), one would not immediately see a reason for adopting something like (4).

Yet, a theory of natural language meaning needs the concept of proposition. Example (1) is an assertion, (2) a question, and (3) an order, but in all three, one, say, propounds the same state of affairs, one in which John loves Mary. The speaker calls attention, both his own and the hearer's, to the same state of affairs. One can assert, question, and order one and the same thing. Let us call the study of the meaning of the proposition LINGUISTIC SEMANTICS and the study of the meaning of speech acts LINGUISTIC PRAGMATICS.

The proposition has a number of properties. Since the speech acts contain propositions, there is a sense in which these properties can be shared by the speech act. Yet, a careless attribution of propositional features to speech acts leads to disaster or confusion.[4]

A proposition has a center or focus of attention, called SEMANTIC FOCUS. Now, the speech act has its own center or foreground, PRAGMATIC FOCUS. I believe that these tools greatly clarify the understanding of what goes on where one speaks about SUBJECT, TOPIC, THEME or FOCUS.

Another important characteristic is that a proposition has SEMANTIC IMPLICATIONS and SEMANTIC PRESUPPOSITIONS. A proposition p semantically implies a proposition q iff q has to be true for p to be true. A proposition p semantically presupposes a proposition q iff p semantically implies q and q can, but does not have to be true when p is false. It follows that every semantic presupposition is also a semantic implication. Here are some examples. Example (5) semantically implies (6); (7) semantically implies and presupposes (8).

(5) */John managed to escape/*

(6) */John escaped/*

(7) */John regretted that Mary had left/*

(8) */John believed that Mary had left/*

(9) */*John did not manage to escape but he escaped/*

(10) */John did not regret that Mary had left but he believed it/*

(11) */John did not regret that Mary had left because he did not believe it/*

(12) */John did not regret that Mary had left because he enjoyed it/*

There are circumstances in which (9) is still acceptable, but they are exceptional and of a different nature than the ones that admit (10). Whether one wants to use the terms IMPLICATION and PRESUPPOSITION or not, two concepts are needed.

I have not given a clear description of what a proposition is or of what a speech act is. I have spoken about the meaning of these things. This is not immediately clear because propositions are often regarded as meanings themselves. And if a speech act is really an act, how could we treat it in the same way as a proposition? I have not clarified the

[4] See Van der Auwera (1977a) and Note 7.

concept of semantic implication and the unorthodox definition of semantic presupposition. We have not even mentioned some other interesting propositional properties. I have not focused on the dangers of attributing propositional features to speech acts. I have relied on an intuitive understanding of the word *true*.[5] The purpose of this section is achieved, though, if (*i*) one is aware of the propositional similarity between assertions, questions and orders such as (1), (2) and (3), and (*ii*) one takes the distinction between speech act and proposition very seriously. The distinction is serious enough to motivate a distinction between linguistic semantics and pragmatics.

3. THE IRREFUTABLE MEANING OF AN ASSERTION

Notice that both semantics and pragmatics deal with meaning. Let us do some pragmatics. The question that will occupy us in this section is whether or not there is something that could be called the IRREFUTABLE meaning of an assertion, some kernel meaning that is necessary and sufficient for an expression to qualify as an assertion.

Suppose that A says that B loves carrots. Does this mean that B really loves carrots? Clearly not. A's information on B's feelings about carrots might be completely mistaken. Maybe A's assertion only means that A believes that B loves carrots. But, here again, suppose that A is lying or joking or simply giving an example of a grammatical sentence of English. A's assertion does not irrefutably mean that A believes that B loves carrots. At the most, it might irrefutably mean that A speaks as if he believes that B loves carrots.

The phrase *speaks as if such and such* is used here without its usual connotation that such and such is probably not the case. *Speaking as if one believes* is furthermore to be taken in a sense of complete conformity to the rules. The slightest breach and one is no longer speaking as if one believes that such and such. Yet, mistakes do not always produce gibberish. Suppose that A speaks about B's taste in vegetables and that he mistakenly says that B loves *barrots*. A might not even know that he used the sound *barrots* and he certainly intended to use the word *carrots*. A's speaking as if he believes that B loves barrots is ruled out as a meaning because *barrot* is not English. A's speaking as if he believes that B loves carrots is ruled out, too. The only way to speak as if one believes that B loves carrots is to say that B loves carrots and not, for example, to say that B loves *barrots*. Maybe, then, the

[5] Van der Auwera (1977c) is a critique of the use of the concept of "truth" that is being adopted in formal logic.

assertion at least irrefutably means that the speaker wants to speak as if he believes that B loves carrots.

Suppose now that A thinks that the English word for the orange vegetables which most speakers of English presumably call *carrot*, is *parrot*. A says that B loves parrots. What A wants, is to speak as if he believes that B loves carrots, even if he does not know that he should use the word *carrot*. A does not want to speak as if he believes that B loves parrots, parrots not being what A thinks they are. Nevertheless, A certainly speaks as if he wants to speak as if he believes that B loves parrots.

Is this then the irrefutable meaning of an assertion? For the purpose of this chapter the answer is positive. There are more refutations but we can prevent them by introducing four hearer-bound assumptions relative to which this meaning is irrefutable.

1. The hearer is competent.
2. The hearer is paying close attention to what the speaker says.
3. The hearer understands that the utterance is an assertion.
4. The hearer makes sense of every word that is used.

With respect to this ideal hearer, every assertion conveys the irrefutable meaning that the speaker speaks as if he wants to speak as if he believes that such and such. One might object that speakers never have these complicated desires and never act in these irrefutable ways and that hearers never assign such complicated meanings. First, there is a difference between a state or an action and being conscious of it. For the most part, people want to stay alive. But they are not conscious of this every minute. So, our irrefutable meaning approach is really immune against the objection that people never or seldom consciously behave in the way we have just been describing. Even so, in the second place, we fundamentally believe that people do sometimes consciously behave in these IRREFUTABLE MEANING ways. Incorporating this makes for a theory that holds good for all discourse. Finally, often speakers' acts and wants are not complicated but only their interpretation is. Suppose that A says that C loves pheasant. To say this and to know that *pheasant* refers to pheasant and to say this and to believe that *pheasant* refers to turkey are equally easy.

Lack of space prevents a detailed analysis of the reasons for denying irrefutability to any one meaning. I refrain from analyzing the assumptions people have to make for justifying the less outlandish and more refutable meaning. I cannot here investigate whether irrefutable meaning really concerns beliefs and wants and not, for example, knowledge and intentions. This chapter does not contain a comparison between this approach and speech act theory, Grice's account of meaning and possible worlds semantics. For these and other problems, see Van der Auwera (1977a,b).

Notice how the analysis stresses the importance of the speaker's volition. Still, I am far from riling Ryle (1965) and claiming that every speech act involves a separate act of volition. The analysis covers unwanted assertions, such as a spontaneous exclamation like *It hurts!* since the irrefutable meaning does not have a necessary wanting but a necessary acting as if one wants.

4. PRAGMATIC PRESUPPOSITION

In the first section, I proposed to take seriously the distinction between proposition and speech act. It is often remarked that, for any utterance to be understandable, speakers and hearers must rely on shared beliefs.[6] Let us take this remark seriously, too, and analyze in an IRREFUTABLE MEANING style. Are there any aspects of the meaning of a speech act that are irrefutably meant to constitute shared beliefs? What does the concept of shared beliefs look like in a theory of irrefutable meaning? PRAGMATIC PRESUPPOSITION will be the name of the speaker's act of relying on these shared beliefs. What, then, is a pragmatic presupposition?

That speaker and hearer would have some shared beliefs would be of no use if the speaker did not know that they are shared. So, these "shared" beliefs are really some beliefs of the speaker. What good are they? The answer refers to the well-known PRINCIPLE OF INERTIA. They make speaking easier. New information is communicated bit by bit. Each bit is kept small enough to be easily processible. Now, every bit serves as old information or shared beliefs for what follows. A new bit mostly contains an element that has been introduced before. The speaker does not have to take the pain of explaining it all again. He can simply mention it and rely on the shared beliefs hoping that the hearer knows exactly what the speaker is talking about. This reliance on shared beliefs also facilitates understanding. If some bit of information did not contain any old information, the hearer would not have anything to which to attach the new and the utterance would not be interpretable.

To ease his communicative task the speaker does not have to believe that he himself already believes that such and such. It is enough to believe that the hearer believes it. Suppose that the shared beliefs

[6] Or shared knowledge, but since we consider knowledge to be a peculiar sort of belief, the particular features of which are not of interest here, we prefer to speak about shared beliefs.

concern the existence of an old lady. The hearer has been trying to convince the speaker of her existence. Still, the speaker does not believe this but he can certainly refer to her and hereby rely on the "shared" beliefs. Now, what is it that the hearer already believes? Suppose that the speaker has been speaking about this lady for a while, trying to convince the hearer of her existence. The hearer does not believe him. But the speaker can certainly refer to her and rely on the "shared" belief about this lady that the hearer at least believes that the speaker believes that the old lady exists. As we shall see, this description is incomplete and therefore incorrect as a description of pragmatic presupposition. But at least we have laid bare the basic structure. Pragmatic presupposition concerns a belief of the speaker concerning a belief of the hearer concerning a belief of the speaker. We shall soon take down each component to its irrefutable foundations.

belief of the speaker
about
belief of the hearer
about
belief of the speaker
about
something

We may pause here to observe that our argument about the basic structure of pragmatic presupposition is really broken-backed. Why do we say that pragmatic presupposition concerns a belief of the speaker about a belief of the hearer about a belief of the speaker rather than this three-tiered belief about a belief of the hearer or even this four-tiered belief about a belief of the speaker, and so on? The analysis of the basic structure of pragmatic presupposition would be indefinitely regressive. At this point, no satisfactory answer can be given. The answer will be obvious, though, when I finish the irrefutability analysis. It will also be obvious why I cannot as yet give this answer.

Pragmatic presupposition deals with a speaker's belief. Now, the speaker cannot provide the hearer with a direct insight into the speaker's beliefs. The speaker has to express them. He has to speak as if he believes such and such. But he can make a mistake in his speech act while he still wants to speak as if he believes such and such. The speaker, however, might not really want this. He only speaks as if he wants to speak as if he believes it. So far, then, the pragmatic presupposition has been exposed as an act of the speaker as if he wants to speak as if he believes that the hearer believes that the speaker believes such and such. In other words, we claim that there is rule governed behavior by means of which one can express that one believes that the hearer already believes something one believes.

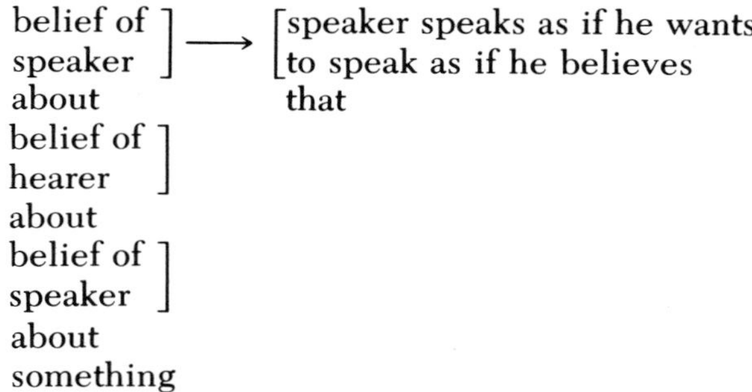

A similar analysis has to be carried out for the other components of the basic structure: a belief of the hearer and another belief of the speaker. Let us tackle the second one first.

We have seen that if the shared belief concerns, say, an old lady, the hearer does not have to believe in her existence. It is enough that the hearer believes that the speaker believes that she exists. But even this is too much. Suppose that the hearer's belief that the speaker believes in the old lady's existence is based on something the speaker has said. Now, the speaker could have been lying. And when the lady is mentioned again in the speech act under consideration, the speaker is lying again. So the hearer should only believe that the speaker speaks as if he believes such and such. And, once we have completed the descent into irrefutability, we see that the hearer's belief should really only concern a speaker's speech act as if he wants to speak as if he believes such and such. With this second step, the pragmatic presupposition appears as a speech act of the speaker as if he wants to speak as if he believes that the hearer believes that the speaker speaks as if he wants to speak as if he believes such and such. That is, there are ways of expressing that one believes that the hearer already believes that one is in the act of expressing that one believes such and such.

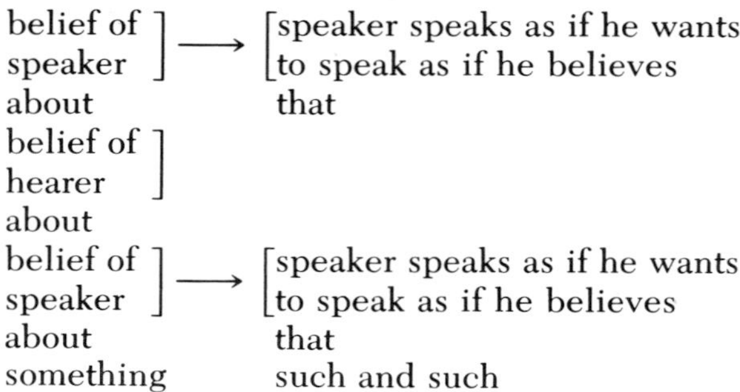

The middle component, the belief of the hearer, still stands unanalyzed. It is possible that the hearer does not hold this belief. The hearer could only act as if he holds it. In that case, the speaker can still rely on the shared belief, be it that it is not a real belief on the part of the hearer. But, then again, it does not have to be real in the case of the speaker, either. Now, while the speaker speaks, the only thing the hearer is doing, is listening. But maybe he is not listening at all, although he can surely want to be listening. Finally, he might not even want that but if he still acts as if he wants to listen as if he believes that such and such, nothing prevents the speaker from pragmatically presupposing.

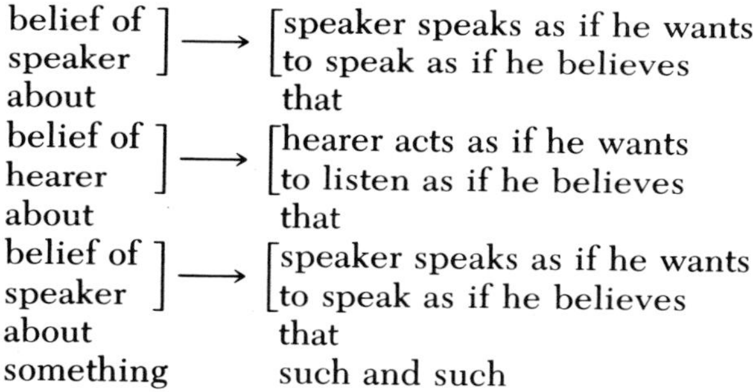

The expansion of the middle component completes the definition of pragmatic presupposition. When one pragmatically presupposes that *p*, one speaks as if one wants to speak as if one believes that the hearer acts as if he wants to listen as if he believes that one speaks as if one wants to speak as if one believes that *p*. Or, to be less exact but more immediately clear, the pragmatic presupposition deals with information about which the speaker expresses a belief that the hearer appears to already believe that the speaker is in the act of expressing the belief that such and such. This last act of expressing a belief is the same as the one in which the speaker expresses a belief about the hearer's belief.

We can now see why the definition of pragmatic presupposition does not involve an infinite regress. A pragmatic presupposition is really an act of the speaker concerning an act of the hearer concerning an act of the speaker. The two speaker's acts are the same, namely, a part of the one, complete speech act. The beliefs, on the other hand, that are connected with these acts, are different. When we were discussing the basic belief structure of pragmatic presupposition, we were not paying any attention yet to the acts that show these beliefs to be present. On their own, beliefs can concern other beliefs, which can concern other beliefs, and so on. However, since the second speaker's act does not concern any further act but only refers back to the first one, to which it is really identical, the second speaker's belief does not concern any further belief either.[7]

What are the signals for pragmatic presupposition? Or, how indeed, does one act as if one . . .? One example is that of the definite description. Another is the use of verbs like *regret*. Let us illustrate the *regret* case.

(13) *John regretted that Mary had left.*

We have already claimed that the proposition of (13), (7), semantically presupposes that John believed that Mary had left. From this one can derive that every assertion containing (7) also semantically presupposes that John believed that Mary had left. This derivation is subject to referential restrictions. But we do not have to go into this matter, here.[8] What interests us now is the complement *Mary had left*.

At a time when the distinction between what got called SEMANTIC PRESUPPOSITION and PRAGMATIC PRESUPPOSITION was not yet seen or was not very clear, researchers–for example, Kiparsky and Kiparsky (1970), Karttunen (1971), Hooper and Thompson (1973), and Hooper (1974)–felt that (13) presupposes that Mary had left or that at least the speaker believes that Mary had left. This is simply wrong. Despite these papers and some others–for example, Wilson (1975), Kempson (1975) and Gazdar (1975)–in which it is argued that (13) indeed does not presuppose but still implies that Mary had left, but in accord with at least Moravcsik (1973), Delacruz (1972), Klein (1975) and Van der Auwera (1975), I claim that one can certainly say that somebody regrets something which is false or which one believes is false.

(14) *You know that John believes that two and two is five. You see, he also regrets that two and two is five. He intensely dislikes the number five, especially when it is the result of a calculation.*

[7] Because of the identity of the two speakers' acts, an infinite loop is built in:

speaker speaks . . . hearer acts . . . speaker speaks . . . (hearer acts . . .
speaker speaks . . . (hearer acts . . . speaker speaks . . . (. . .)))

This is what we have called NON-MINIMAL irrefutable meaning. See Van der Auwera (1977b).

[8] The *John* and the *Mary* of the assertion and its potential semantic presupposition have to refer to the same people, the departure has to be the same event, and so on. In propositions reference plays no part.

Some workers, for example, Stalnaker (1973), Oh (1974), Karttunen (1974), Peters (1975), and Van der Auwera (1975) have tried to say that what is pragmatically presupposed has to be part of the SHARED KNOWLEDGE, COMMON GROUND, COMMON SET OF ASSUMPTIONS or CONTEXT. Part of this claim, expressed in different terminology, is that the speaker believes that the hearer believes the information that is pragmatically presupposed. With such a definition, however, *Mary had left* cannot be pragmatically presupposed.

(15) *How can I persuade you to believe that Mary had left? Well, John, too, believed and even regretted that Mary had left. Do you think John would regret something which he knows to be false?*

(16) *We regret to inform you that Mary is ill.*

And indeed, in our earlier work (Van der Auwera, 1975), *regret* was without a pragmatic presupposition. Karttunen (1974) claims that in actual discourse the hearer often does not already believe what he is supposed to believe according to the pragmatic presupposition and Stalnaker (1973) qualifies his definition by claiming that presupposition is really a matter of the speaker's acting as if he believes that the hearer already believes such and such.

Gazdar (1975) does not approve of the strategies of Karttunen (1974) and Stalnaker (1973), among other things, (i) because these would involve treating most ordinary discourse as something special, and (ii) because they would prevent any possibility of counterexamples. With respect to the first objection, we claim that these strategies do not have to be interpreted as treating most of ordinary discourse as something special but can and should be interpreted as attempts to find an account of presupposition that holds good for all discourse. The second objection is not valid because there are many counterexamples. Here is just one. It is not necessary for using (13) that the speaker act as if he believes that the hearer believes that Mary had left.

(17) *I know that you do not believe that Mary had left.*
You know that I believe it. John believes it, too.
You see, John regrets that Mary had left. . . .

Example (17) shows that it is enough that the speaker acts as if he believes that the hearer believes that the speaker believes that Mary had left. But this, too, is much too strong. There are again a huge number of counterexamples. One needs to bring up all possible counterexamples. One refines the analysis up to the point at which it no longer admits any counterexamples. One deepens it down to irrefutability. And this is exactly what we have done in the first part of the section. Thus an analysis of at least some research on presupposition points to the type of account that we arrived at from an independent consideration of what shared beliefs would look like in a theory of irrefutable meaning.

Despite the feasibility of a theory that has both a semantic and a pragmatic presupposition (see our conjectures in this chapter and in Van der Auwera, 1977a), presupposition is no longer as well thought of as a few years ago. Some of the following factors might have been involved. The term became very popular. But along with popularity came confusion about what presupposition really was and was not. Recently, the most interesting earlier accounts were found to be wrong. Their broad acceptance of a few years ago sharply contrasts with the clarity with which it was seen that they are faulty. Rather than to refine the notion of presupposition, critics started to shelve the whole idea and to reach out for another concept that was becoming increasingly popular, namely, Grice's (1975) IMPLICATURE, whether CONVENTIONAL (Karttunen and Peters, 1975, 1976) or CONVERSATIONAL (Boër and Lycan, 1976; Kempson, 1975; Wilson, 1975) and which had already been mentioned in connection with presupposition (Grice, 1972; Horn, 1972; Thomason, 1973; Kasher, 1974; Peters, 1975). If all this were just a terminological question, it would not be worth spilling ink over. Maybe some phenomena that were thought to be presuppositional, are truly a matter of implicature. And, as we shall see in Section 5 , even in the cases which I now believe to be pragmatically presuppositional, the notion of implicature has some bearing. But at least in the case of definite descriptions, factives such as *regret*, and *wh*-questions, as far as pragmatic presupposition goes, and constructions such as *regret*, as far as semantic presupposition goes, we believe there is enough continuity between what people thought was going on in the presuppositions of a few years ago and what I now believe presupposition is all about.

5. PRAGMATIC IMPLICATION

Grice (1975) and Griceans make a distinction, valuable though vague, between what is said and meant and what is suggested, implicated and meant. A similar but hopefully less vague distinction is the one between what is irrefutably meant and what is not. Irrefutable meaning exists because of some assumptions about the hearer (attention, competence, for instance). Refutable meaning owes its existence to some assumptions about the speaker (competence, veracity, for instance). One could say that refutable meaning is PRAGMATICALLY IMPLIED. In Van der Auwera (1977a) I have classified different types of refutable meaning as different types of PRAGMATIC IMPLICATION. The superassumption is the inertia principle. This is the pragmatic, or perhaps we should say pragmatist, principle that speakers and hearers generally expend the least effort possible. The cognitive work is generally kept as low as possible. I have tried to treat various problems such as referential opacity and Grice's conversational implicatures as pragmatic implications.

Pragmatic presupposition is irrefutable meaning. Let me briefly deal with one type of pragmatic implication that is derivable from pragmatic presupposition. Let us look at the *regret* pragmatic presupposition of (13) again. The speaker pragmatically presupposes that Mary had left. In other words, the speaker speaks as if he wants to speak as if he believes that the hearer acts as if he wants to listen as if he believes that the speaker speaks as if he wants to speak as if he believes that Mary had left. The hearer faces the task of understanding. The pragmatic presupposition is very difficult to process. Fortunately, if the hearer holds the right assumptions, he can simplify greatly. If the hearer believes that the speaker is really competent, then the hearer can drop, so to speak, the first occurrence of *speaks as if he.*[9]

> *speaker ~~speaks as if he~~ wants to speak as if he believes that the hearer acts as if he wants to listen as if he believes that the speaker speaks as if he wants to speak as if he believes that Mary had left*

This gives the pragmatic implication that the speaker simply wants to speak as if. . . . If the hearer also believes that (13) completely conforms to the rules of English, he can drop the first *wants to.*

> *speaker ~~speaks as if he wants to~~ speak as if he believes that the hearer acts as if he wants to listen as if he believes that the speaker speaks as if he wants to speak as if he believes that Mary had left*

If the hearer further believes that the speaker is sincere, he can drop the second occurrence of *speaks as if he.*[9] And so on. The point is, of course, that the hearer virtually always simplifies. He does hold the right assumptions, and most of the assumptions come so naturally that one is not even conscious of them.

[9] More assumptions are needed to make this step, but this is at least the most important one.

The number of possible pragmatic implications of this type is large but finite. Among them one will find paraphrases of some older definitions of pragmatic presupposition. Let us pick out some interesting pragmatic implications. Consider this:

> *speaker ~~speaks as if he~~ wants ~~to speak as if he believes that~~ the hearer ~~acts as if he wants~~ to listen as if he believes ~~that the speaker speaks as if he wants to speak as if he believes~~ that Mary had left*

This leaves open the possibility that the hearer does not yet believe that Mary had left. It is up to the hearer to decide whether he wants to comply with the speaker's desire that he believe it. Consider also these pragmatic implications:

> *speaker ~~speaks as if he wants to speak as if he believes that the hearer acts as if he wants to listen as if he believes that the speaker speaks as if he wants to speak as if he~~ believes that Mary had left*

> *~~speaker speaks as if he wants to speak as if he believes that the hearer acts as if he wants to listen as if he believes that the speaker speaks as if he wants to speak as if he believes that~~ Mary had left*

Notice that they no longer concern a shared belief. Consider a final illustration:

> *~~speaker speaks as if he wants to speak as if he believes that~~ the hearer ~~acts as if he wants to listen as if he~~ believes ~~that the speaker speaks as if he wants to speak as if he believes that~~ Mary had left*

Pragmatic implications can be present together. Suppose that it is pragmatically implied that the speaker believes that Mary had left and that the hearer believes that Mary had left. Suppose that (13) also semantically presupposes that Mary had left. Now speaker, hearer and regretter believe that Mary had left. Presumably this situation is very common. It is yet another application of the principle of inertia. Without information that suggests something else, the hearer will assume that the three of them believe that Mary had left. As a matter of fact, there is another type of pragmatic implication that takes care of the fact that Mary, too, in the vast majority of cases, believes that she left.

A final note: One might resent this very strong pragmatic ambiguity or vagueness. Let us bear in mind two things. First, many pragmatic implications describe the speaker's and the hearer's beliefs about Mary's departure. This is not the speaker's primary concern. He is really speaking about John's regrets. Second, utterances, of course, do not occur in isolation, but in a strongly disambiguating or clarifying context.

REFERENCES

Austin, J. L. *How to do things with words.* The William James Lectures delivered at Harvard University in 1955. 2nd ed. J. O. Urmson and Marina Sbisà, (Eds.). Cambridge, Massachusetts: Harvard University Press.

Ballmer, T. T. Logical language reconstruction and reference. In *Papers from the 12th Regional Meeting of the Chicago Linguistics Society,* Chicago: University of Chicago Press, 1976. Pp. 33–48.

Boër, S. E. & Lycan, W. G. The myth of semantic presupposition. *Ohio State University Working Papers in Linguistics,* 1976, *21,* 1–90.

Delacruz, B. Factives and proposition level constructions in Montague Grammar. In R. Rodman (Ed.), *UCLA Occasional Papers in Linguistics,* 1972, *2,* 101–126.

Gazdar, G. Implicature and presupposition. Paper presented to the Spring meeting of the L.A.G.B. Nottingham, 1975. Mimeo.

Grice, H. P. Lectures on language and reality. Unpublished paper, 1972.

Grice, H. P. Logic and conversation. In P. Cole and J. L. Morgan (Eds.), *Syntax and Semantics,* Vol 3. New York, Academic Press, 1975. Pp. 41–58.

Hooper, J. B. On assertive predicates. *UCLA Papers in Syntax,* 1974, *5,* 49–79.

Hooper, J. B. and Thompson, S. A. On the applicability of root transformations. *Linguistic Inquiry,* 1973, *4,* 465–497.

Horn, L. R. *On the semantic properties of logical operators in English.* Unpublished doctoral dissertation, University of California, Los Angeles.

Karttunen, L. Some observations on factivity. *Perspectives in Linguistics,* 1971, *4,* 55–69.

Karttunen, L. Presupposition and linguistic context. *Theoretical Linguistics,* 1974, *1,* 181–194.

Karttunen, L., and Peters, S. Conventional implicature in Montague grammar. In *Proceedings of the First Annual Meeting of the Berkeley Linguistic Society.* Berkeley: University of California Press, 1975. Pp 266–278.

Karttunen, L., and Peters, S. What indirect questions conventionally implicate. *Papers from the 12th Regional Meeting of the Chicago Linguistics Society.* Chicago: University of Chicago Press, 1976. Pp. 351–368.

Kasher, A. Mood implicatures: A logical way of doing generative pragmatics. *Theoretical Linguistics,* 1974, *1,* 6–38.

Kempson, R. M. *Presupposition and the delimitation of semantics.* Cambridge: Cambridge University Press, 1975.

Kiparsky, P., and Kiparsky, C. Fact. In: M. Bierwisch and K. E. Heidolph (Eds.), *Progress in linguistics.* The Hague: Mouton, 1970. Pp. 143–173.

Klein, E. Two sorts of factive predicate. *Pragmatics Microfiche,* 1975, *1,* B5–C14.

Moravscik, J. M. E. Comments on Partee's paper. In J. Hintikka *et al.* (Eds.), *Approaches to natural languages.* Dordrecht: Reidel, 1973. Pp. 349–369.

Oh, C.-K. More on degree of factivity. Papers from the 10th Regional Meeting of the Chicago Linguistics Society. Chicago: University of Chicago Press, 1974. Pp. 516–527.

Peters, S. Presuppositions and conversation. *Texas Linguistic Forum* 2, 1975, 122–134.

Ryle, G. *The concept of mind.* New York: Barnes & Noble, 1965.

Searle, J. R. *Speech acts. An essay in the philosophy of language.* Cambridge: Cambridge University Press, 1969.

Stalnaker, R. C. Pragmatic presuppositions. Paper presented at the Texas Conference on Performatives, Presuppositions and Conversational Implicatures, 1973.

Thomason, R. H. Semantics, Pragmatics, Conversation and Presupposition. Paper presented at the Texas Conference on Performatives, Presuppositions and Conversational Implicatures, 1973.

Urmson, J. O. *Philosophical Analysis. Its development between the two world wars.* London: Oxford University Press.

Van der Auwera, J. Semantic and pragmatic presupposition. *Antwerp Papers in Linguistics,* 1975, 2, 1–118.

Van der Auwera, J. *Inleiding tot de linguistische pragmatiek.* Leuven: Acco, 1977. (a).

Van der Auwera, J. Irrefutable meaning. Simplified version appears in *Proceedings of the Stanford Student Conference in Philosophy.* Complex version to appear in *Journal of Pragmatics,* 1977, (b).

Van der Auwera, J. Logic "hooked" on natural language. Paper presented at the California Linguistics Association Conference, 1977. (c).

Wilson, D. *Presuppositions and non-truth-conditional semantics.* London & New York: Academic Press.

Wittgenstein, L. *Philosophische untersuchungen—Philosophical investigations.* Oxford: Blackwell, 1968.

HOW LINGUISTICS MATTERS TO PHILOSOPHY: PRESUPPOSITION, TRUTH, AND MEANING[1]

JAY DAVID ATLAS
Pomona College, Claremont, California, and Wolfson College, Oxford

1. INTRODUCTION

Fifteen years ago J. A. Fodor and J. J. Katz suggested that philosophy of linguistics was philosophy of language enough. With the rapid development of transformational generative grammar, it seemed that the problems in philosophical logic, theory of meaning, and philosophy of language that preoccupied our predecessors in the late nineteenth and early twentieth centuries would find rigorous articulation and adequate solution within linguistic theory. Fodor and Katz shortly retreated from this provocative position, and, as Richard Rorty has observed, its promise has so far gone unfulfilled. In theory of reference,

[1] I am indebted to the Educational Foundation of America for its sponsorship of part of this research through a student–faculty research award in 1975–1976 to Mark Phillips and myself; to the Departments of Linguistics and Philosophy in the University of Kansas and to the organizers of the April 1977 Conference on Presupposition; to the Research Committee of Pomona College, Claremont; to the President and Fellows of Wolfson College, Oxford; and to Paul Benacerraf, Rene Coppieters, Michael Dummett, John Egan, Robert Evren, William Leach, Stephen Levinson, Michael R. Martin, Peter Nicholas, Kurt St. Angelo, Jerry Sadock, Dana Scott, and Rick Tibbetts.

I am particularly indebted to Mark Phillips; to Geoffrey Koziol; and to Allan Hunter of St. John's College, Oxford.

I am grateful to Peter Strawson for his intellectual example, his encouragement, and his kindnesses; this essay is for him.

Syntax and Semantics, Volume 11: Presupposition

ISBN 0-12-613511-8

stimulated by the causal theory outlined by Keith Donnellan, Saul Kripke, and Hilary Putnam, in theories of meaning, truth, and logical form for natural languages, guided by the work of Donald Davidson, and in theories of conversational and conventional implicature, initiated by H. Paul Grice, current research only rarely makes essential use of empirical linguistic theory either to suggest or to test proposals.

It is difficult to make precisely the right connection between philosophical proposals and linguistic hypotheses, and it is to be expected that the relationship is subtle, but one place to look is the phenomena of presupposition. Linguists have used the notion in multitudinous ways; philosophers of language and logicians have attempted to clarify and formalize the notion; and metaphysicians, for example, Collingwood, have appealed to the notion in limning conceptual frameworks. Rarely has one notion, or better a family of notions, been so ubiquitous in logic, semantics, and metaphysics, or entered so essentially into the central problems of logical form, truth, and meaning.

Presupposition has been a topic of discussion the historical foci of which have been G. Frege "On Sense and Reference" (1892), B. Russell "On Denoting" (1905), P. F. Strawson "On Referring" (1950), and M. Dummett "Truth" (1958). These discussions have had two subjects: (*a*) the concepts of truth, falsity, and the logical form of English sentences; (*b*) a theory of meaning underlying the concept of logical form and extending beyond it. It is the way the notion of presupposition brings together logical form, truth, and meaning that gives it its special interest.

In this essay I shall review the essentials of my earlier theory of the semantics of presuppositional sentences, comment on the way philosophical doctrines and linguistic distinctions interact, suggest difficulties for current Gricean accounts, and sketch a more coherent total theory that properly combines semantic and pragmatic components. Along the way I shall mention not only how my theory resolves the Russell–Strawson controversy but also how it contributes to the Davidson–Dummett debate over what it is to understand a language.

Those who know my views will find the first four sections familiar. The last four sections consider some new criticism of an earlier Gricean account of presupposition that I shared with a number of friends and colleagues. One metaphilosophical aim of this essay is to convince Richard Rorty that linguistics does contribute to the solution of philosophical problems and to show him precisely how it does so. In the process I provide a novel critique of Fregean semantics and support Dummett's defense of verificationist semantics.

2. GENERALITY VERSUS AMBIGUITY

In *Word and Object* (1960) Quine argued for the distinction between terms that are ambiguous and those that are merely general terms of wide extension. The distinction between generality and ambiguity has been employed in philosophical claims about terms like *exists.* Tables, chairs, and other such furniture of the universe exist. Sets and prime numbers exist. Are these different kinds of existence? Is *exist* ambiguous? Quine does not think so. *Exist* is merely a general term; it is semantically NONSPECFIC (in one sense of that term in linguistic theory) with respect to concreteness/abstractness. Another, less convincing example of Quine's is *hard.* Since chairs are hard and questions are hard, is *hard* ambiguous or is it a general term of heterogeneous extension and semantically NONSPECIFIC with respect to concreteness/abstractness? On grounds I shall not discuss here Quine suggests that *hard* is univocal. Whether or not Quine is right about *hard,* his distinction is intelligible and his question coherent.

There are familiar examples in linguistics of the same phenomenon. Is *fish* ambiguous, or is it NONSPECIFIC with respect to warmbloodedness/coldbloodedness so as to apply unambiguously, for example, to whales? Another case is the third person pronouns *he, she,* and *it,* which in English are nonspecific with respect to the age of the referent but specific with respect to gender.

3. PRESUPPOSITION AND AMBIGUITY

Bertrand Russell (1905, 1919) claims that ⌜*The A is not B*⌝ is ambiguous, having either WIDE or NARROW scope occurrences of the singular term ⌜*The A*⌝ (or equivalently, being either a predicate or a sentence negation). P. F. Strawson (1950) seems to take ⌜*The A is not B*⌝ to have univocally the WIDE SCOPE reading. The linguistic and philosophical literature assumes either a structural SCOPE AMBIGUITY or a lexical ambiguity in *not,* represented by choice (predicate) and exclusion (sentence) negation. A standard formalization of SEMANTIC PRESUPPOSITION relies on just this ambiguity: A presupposes B if and only if $A \vdash B$ and $-A \vdash B$, where $-A$, the choice negation of A, is true (false) if and only if A is false (true) under every admissible valuation of a nonbivalent language containing both choice and exclusion negation.

Atlas (1975b) and Atlas (1977a) discuss critically Zwicky–Sadock (1975) and show in detail that the claim that English sentences ⌜*The A is not B*⌝ are ambiguous is false; they are semantically NONSPECIFIC with respect to the choice/exclusion logical negations. There is no scope ambiguity of *not* in English, nor is *not* lexically ambiguous. (The linguistic claim has also been put forward independently by Ruth Kempson [1975]. For discussion of the linguistic claim and its significance for the theory of meaning, see Atlas [1975a].) As Atlas (1977a) reemphasizes, the absence of ambiguity implies the nonexistence of semantic presupposition and indefensibility of truth-value gaps. Russell's and Strawson's accounts, for years the subject of inconclusive debate, are demonstrably incorrect in essential respects. Defensible aspects of both accounts are radically reformulated and coherently united in my theory.

4. MEANING AND LOGICAL FORM

Students of Strawson's (1950) critique of Russell and of Quine's (1953) attack on "meaning = naming" in "On What There Is" recognize the connection often made between disputes about logical form and disputes about meaning. Russell makes the connection explicit in the second lecture "Logic as the Essence of Philosophy" of his Lowell Lectures *Our Knowledge of the External World* (1914). As a consequence of his comments on logical form, Russell adopts the view that a theory of meaning for a natural language, which has as its point an explanation of what it is to understand utterances in the language, necessarily contains as its core component a theory of truth for the language, and that to understand a statement is to know the conditions necessary and sufficient for its truth and falsity. Donald Davidson has recently made similar claims.

5. LINGUISTICS AND PHILOSOPHY

Just as the Russellian and the Strawsonian positions on truth-value and logical form are undermined by a linguistic analysis of the meaning of negative presuppositional sentences, so also is the Russellian and Davidsonian position on the form of a philosophical theory of meaning and its account of what it is to understand a sentence undermined by arguments suggested by the same analysis. (This claim is discussed in Atlas, 1978.) These analyses and arguments fulfill Katz and Fodor's 1962 promise that linguistics will do something to solve philosophical problems. Interestingly enough, it does so without philosophy of language being reduced to philosophy of linguistics. But even more surprisingly not only is the SEMANTICAL REALISM of Frege, the early Wittgenstein, the Russell of the 1910s, or Donald Davidson undermined, the SEMANTICAL ANTI-REALISM (or VERIFICATIONISM) of Friedrich Waismann, the later Wittgenstein, the Quine of "Epistemology Naturalized" (1969), Michael Dummett, and the Hilary Putnam of "Reference and Understanding" (1978) is supported by the same considerations. Here, by contrast, a theory of meaning for a natural language contains as its core component a theory of justification, and to understand a statement is to know the conditions that justify (warrant) asserting it.

Previously I have argued for the following propositions:

1. English sentences of the form ⌜*The A is not B*⌝ are not ambiguous. (It is also true that the interaction of negation with adverbs, "factive" verbs, and perhaps quantifiers fails to produce ambiguity.)
2. English sentences of the form ⌜*The A is not B*⌝ have no logical forms in the familiar languages of first or second order extensional or intensional logics.
3. The 1970 Davidson–Harman hypothesis—that underlying structures, as "full semantic representations," are logical forms—is false.
4. The semantical representation of the sentence ⌜*The A is not B*⌝ cannot be a "logical form" (Davidson, Harman), a "bracketed logical form" (H. P. Grice), a "meaning" (Montague, Stalnaker), or a "character" (Kaplan) of the sentence.
5. Semantical presupposition, as it is normally defined, is not a relation that actually obtains between English sentences, for example, between ⌜*The A is B*⌝ and ⌜*There is an A*⌝.
6. Philosophical arguments in twentieth century logical semantics for the existence of truth-value gaps in sentences of the form ⌜*The A is B*⌝ are exactly as cogent as physical arguments in nineteenth century electromagnetic theory for the existence of the luminiferous ether.
7. English sentences of the form ⌜*The A is not B*⌝ are semantically "non-specific" (Zwicky and Sadock), "general" (Quine), "indeterminate," or "vague" (G. Lakoff). The same holds for negative sentences with adverbs, "factive" verbs, and perhaps quantifiers.
8. ANTI-REALISM is the only theory of meaning and understanding that is consistent with the linguistic claim that negative presuppositional sentences are semantically NONSPECIFIC and that can explain linguistic intuitions about negative presuppositional sentences with singular terms, "factive" verbs, adverbials, or quantifiers.

9. As MODERN LOGIC was used by Russell in criticism of nineteenth century epistemological and metaphysical IDEALISM, so THEORETICAL LINGUISTICS can be used in criticism of twentieth century SEMANTICAL REALISM.

In what follows I shall discuss a pragmatic account of presuppositional inference, derived from the views of H. P. Grice, developed by a number of theorists in the early 1970s, and described, in one version, in Atlas (1975a,b). The account was originally intended as a logically conservative alternative to the semanticization of absolutely everything that the methodology of GENERATIVE SEMANTICS seemed to portend and also, in my version, as a theory that would prove compatible with, and even help to explain, the semantic observations listed previously.

The claims for the explanatory power of Gricean principles of conversational inference rest upon a highly convincing if vague account of the RELATIONSHIP between the CONVENTIONAL MEANING of the IMPLICANS, its conversational role, and the resulting IMPLICATA. But for words and sentences the theory posits CONVENTIONAL MEANINGS that are controversial, while seeming to assume that the adequacy of such posits of conventional word/sentence-meaning can never be tested directly, but—and this is a truism in the theory—only by their contribution to the speaker's utterance-meaning of words and sentences uttered in contexts of actual use. The theory's great success is its convincing explanation of how and what speakers are understood to mean when patently they do NOT mean what their words conventionally do. It would be perfectly cogent for the theory to claim, for some class of words or sentences, that NO speaker EVER means what his words conventionally or literally mean. For example, positing the truth-functional material conditional as the conventional meaning of the English *if . . . then* would yield a case very close to this theoretical extreme. Also, the obverse case, the theory treats as "degenerate" any case where the speaker means precisely what his words conventionally mean.

The theory is arguably adequate as a theory of conversational inference, in particular, as a theory of what a listener could infer from a speaker's sentence and its context if the listener assumed that the speaker's words such as *not, or, and,* and *if . . . then* and sentences were synonymous with $-$, $\vee$, &, and $\supset$ and with logical forms. Indeed, the account is enlightening. But how much CAN this kind of theory tell us about the ACTUAL conventional meanings of English expressions?

Suppose one could successfully sail, for example from Dover to Alexandria, by using a theory of ocean navigation in which it was assumed that the earth is uniformly flat. One might admire the theory because much might be learned from such a theory about the nature of rational principles governing the activity of navigating. In particular, one might learn much by studying the inferences employed in getting from paths in a two dimensional Euclidean plane to paths on a three dimensional almost-Euclidean sphere. It would be perfectly cogent for the theory to claim, for some class of theoretically possible voyages, that NO sailor EVER makes them, for example, a voyage beyond the edge of the world. Moreover, the theory treats a "degenerate" any case where the actual path of the voyage and the theoretical path of the voyage are (to a very close approximation) the same, for example, Dover to Calais. These are not very interesting voyages, since the theory's principles of inference do no interesting work—as it were, *A*, therefore *A*.

Despite telling us much that is interesting and even true about how to get from *a* to a distant *b*, how much CAN this kind of theory tell us about the way the world ACTUALLY is in the vicinity of *a*? Basically, for any *a* that is a possible port of call, the theory says it's very flat around *a*. Unfortunately, though our theory gets us from Anchorage to Seattle, we KNOW it is not very flat around Anchorage, and we did not do any sailing to find that out.

Now suppose, by using a theory of conversational inference in which it was assumed that some English words, among them adverbs, subordinating and coordinating conjunctions, were respectively synonymous with the various logical connectives, one could successfully explain what a listener could take a speaker to mean. How much CAN this kind of theory tell us about the ACTUAL, conventional or literal meanings of English words like *not*, *only if*, and *every*? Though our theory of conversational inference gets us from a negative presuppositional sentence to a choice negation understanding of an utterance of the sentence in the appropriate context, as we shall see, we KNOW that the *not* in the negative sentence is neither ambiguous between an exclusion and a choice negation nor identical with either, and we did not do any implicating to find that out.

In short, the structure of Grice's theory is problematic in two respects: On the one hand, the theory allows the possibility that speakers never mean what they literally say, and on the other hand, when they do, the theory provides no explanation of it. Grice's theory claims, falsely, that the literal meaning of the English word *not* is that of an ordinary logical connective. The version of the theory in Atlas

(1975a,b) makes a subtler claim, but it is open to subtler objections, as Atlas (1977a) and the following discussion show. To that pragmatic account of presupposition I now turn.

6. GRICE'S PRAGMATICS AND PRESUPPOSITION

My skepticism about the explanatory value of the concept of semantical presupposition not only is founded on showing that some linguistic data have been misdescribed, that the relation of semantical entailment suffices to account for the data, and that the lack of truth-value of sentences with false "presuppositions" is both unmotivated and theoretically incoherent; it relies also on an empirical linguistic claim that the semantical assumptions made about the properties of negation in English are demonstrably false.

Therefore it was my belief, and that of others, that a pragmatic account was essential to a correct theory. Stimulated by H. Paul Grice and encouraged by Stephen Levinson I began to formalize the characteristic Gricean argument schema for conversational implicature (see Brown and Levinson, 1978, pp. 92–96) and to apply it to the explanation of presupposition. I argued that rather than *The king of France is bald* semantically presupposing *There is a king of France*, *The king of France is bald* entails *There is a king of France* and that its denial *The king of France is not bald* IMPLICATES (in a speech context *K*) *There is a king of France* (that is, the speaker uttering *The king of France is not bald* in *K* conversationally implicates that there is a king of France).

Grice's description of the inference is roughly as follows. For a speaker S and an addressee A, A knows that in uttering *P*, S means to communicate *Q* because in the conversation S has said *P*; there is no reason to suppose that he is not observing the maxims (saying what he knows, being relevant, being informative, being clear) or at least the COOPERATIVE PRINCIPLE (make your conversational contribution such as is required, at that state at which it occurs, by the accepted purpose or direction of the talk-exchange in which you are engaged); S could not be observing the maxims unless he thought that *Q*; S knows (and knows that A knows that S knows) that A can see that the supposition that S thinks that *Q* IS required; S has done nothing to stop A thinking that *Q*; therefore S intends A to think, or is at least willing to allow A to think, that *Q*; and so—S has implicated that *Q*. (See Grice, 1975, p. 70.)

Atlas (1975a,b) suggested that the denial *The king of France is not bald* could have the sentential negation READING or LOGICAL FORM and claimed:

> To syntax, phonetics, and semantics are added principles of pragmatics, whose task is to explain the relation between ways of understanding sentences and the contexts in which they are uttered. These principles take as input the context and the logical form produced by the semantics. They yield as output a new logical form that renders the contextually determined meaning of the utterance.
>
> The speaker says *The king of France is not bald*, which he and I both realize can be understood in (at least) two ways. One is its READING, that it is false (not true) that the king of France is bald. But to tell me that this is false (not true) is to make [an uninformative claim]. (Ie. the simple denial that the supposed king is extant, unique, and bald.) [Since the utterance is about the king and about baldness,] unless the speaker is not cooperating in this conversation (not saying what he knows, being relevant, being informative, or being clear), he must mean something more than [the reading of the sentence.] [Atlas, 1975b, pp. G1–G2].

There is no reason to suppose that he is not observing the maxims. He could not be doing so unless he thought that the king of France were nonbald, the most informative (and relevant) literal claim he can make in uttering the sentence in any context *K*. He knows, and knows that I know he knows, that I can see that the supposition that he thinks that the (unique, extant) king of France is nonbald is required in the context about which we are reasoning. He has done nothing to stop me from understanding him this way. Therefore he intends me to think, by virtue of his uttering *The king of France is not bald*, that the unique, extant king of France is nonbald. That is, he implicates the predicate negation understanding of the sentence.

Such an account imputes to the speaker–hearer a knowledge of the READING of a sentence, a conversational competence to assess the cooperative fit between a given context and the READING, and an inferential capacity to discover or construct an alternative proposition from the READING and the context.

The account was offered in contrast to views that claimed that *The king of France is bald* semantically presupposed *There is a king of France* because both the sentence and its denial necessitated the truth of that sentence. The logical form of its denial was typically taken to be a predicate negation, and it was usually claimed (following Strawson or Russell, respectively) that the negative sentence was univocal, having only the predicate negation reading, or was ambiguous, having both predicate and sentential negation readings. The former view differed from mine in the assignment of the predicate negation logical form as the reading of the negative sentence. The latter view differed in its ambiguity claim. I had argued against the sentence's ambiguity and for the sentence's GENERALITY. I therefore did NOT take my hypothesized READING to give the intuitive, LITERAL meaning of the sentence. A fortiori I rejected the former view's claim that the meaning of the negative sentence was the predicate negation READING.

7. OTHER GRICEAN VIEWS

Some philosophers have had extreme difficulty understanding the claims just made, which to be comprehensible require only a knowledge of linguistic theory and a recognition that READING is a theoretical term. There were other theorists who were sympathetic to my attack on semantical presupposition but cautious about the controversial grounds for it. One attack (Boër and Lycan) chose to argue that IF the negative sentence were the sentential negation, it did not necessitate, and so the affirmative did not semantically presuppose, that there is a king of France; and that IF the negative sentence were the predicate negation, which does necessitate that there is a king of France, the negative sentence is not THE DENIAL of the affirmative. In either case, therefore, there is no semantical presupposition.

Their positive account was likewise a Gricean account, in which the addressee asks himself how the speaker knows, since he is enjoined by Grice's maxims to say what he knows or justifiably believes, that the king of France is not bald, and in answer infers that the speaker's evidence is that the (extant, unique) king of France is nonbald, the predicate negation reading. This reading entails the existence of a king, the EXISTENTIAL PRESUPPOSITION (Boër and Lycan, 1976, pp. 48–49).

If the description of the speaker's knowledge is given by the sentence *The king of France is not bald*, and a possible READING of that sentence is the sentential negation, then Boër and Lycan argued, as had Atlas, Levinson, and Allwood, that from the sentential negation different inferences as to the speaker's evidence are possible. Hence they were happy to acknowledge my observation that even the English sentence allegedly reporting this reading, *It's not true that the king of France is bald,* has "presuppositions." On the other hand, if the predicate negation is a READING of *The king of France is not bald,* once the sentence is so understood, the Gricean mechanism adds nothing to the understanding of the utterance.

8. RESERVATIONS ABOUT THE STANDARD GRICE VIEW

However congenial this strategy in 1975 I ultimately regarded it as unsatisfying. I objected to the implicit ambiguity claim for *The king of France is not bald,* or in Boër and Lycan to their explicit agnosticism, which was a decision not to ask which was or were the sentence's logical form or forms. Philosophers and linguists are still vexed by the relationship between logic and grammar. Despite enlightening work by Davidson, Harman, and Grandy as to what a theory of logical form is, and by Katz, McCawley, Lakoff, and others as to what semantic representations are, it is still controversial how to decide whether a theory of logical form will suffice as a theory of semantic representation. In what follows, I wish to suggest novel kinds of arguments in support of distinguishing semantic representation of sentences from classical logical forms and to raise questions about my earlier RADICAL PRAGMATICS view. I shall suggest that a methodoligcally satisfying RADICAL PRAGMATICS demands an equally RADICAL SEMANTICS. (Compare the notion of "partially specified semantics" in Lakoff, 1977.)

Taking the negative sentence in isolation, competent speakers know that it has (at least) two uses or understandings. Independently of context, the understandings are phenomenologically of equal status, neither judged less a function of the meaning of the sentence than the other. But the account in the theory is "unequal," in that it is split between the semantics and the pragmatics, and the understandings are of different theoretical status.

The classical pragmatic view, without the semantical generality of negation, permits the negative sentence interpreted as a sentence negation to implicate the EXISTENTIAL PRESUPPOSITION. The negative sentence interpreted as a predicate negation straightforwardly entails it. And of course there are contexts in which no implicature of the sentential negation is intended. Letting L^- stand for the sentential negation, L^+ for the predicate negation, the function PRAG for the Gricean inference, and K for kinds of context, we may abbreviate the claims by the formulas:

$$\mathrm{PRAG}(K^*, L^-) = L^+,$$
$$\mathrm{PRAG}(K^{**}, L^-) = L^-.$$

In the second case, the pragmatics adds nothing to the semantical interpretation; in the first case it obviously does. The standard view permits this kind of asymmetry in the theory. The first case is paradigmatic; the second case is degenerate. Why should there be this difference?

No explanation is given for the degenerate case, where we may view the implicature produced in the paradigm case as canceled by the contextual difference between K^* and K^{**}. One remark, appropriate in this theory but unilluminating, is that in K^{**} but not K^* the speaker means what his sentence (literally) means; another, equally circular, is that the speaker does not presuppose that there is a French king.

But if this choice of L^- is not made, there is a cost to the indecision as to which logical form, L^+ or L^-, to give to the negative sentence. This indecision opens the possibility that the statement:

$$\text{PRAG}(K'', L^+) = L^-$$

could be true for some K'', and that the theory could just as well be expressed by:

$$\text{PRAG}(K', L^+) = L^+$$
$$\text{PRAG}(K'', L^+) = L^-.$$

But given the assumptions of PRAG, that is, Gricean principles of inference, this is not an obvious possibility.

On Grice's account the semantic representation L^- would express the conventional meaning of the sentence; and the semantic representation would be a representation of the sentence's truth-conditions. On the Atlas (1975a,b) accounts the semantic representation was L^-, but the semantic representation did NOT express the conventional meaning of the sentence, NOR did it represent the SENTENCE'S truth conditions. The SENTENCE did not have truth-conditions; only propositions expressed by it in contexts had truth-conditions. The semantic representation, identified with the logical form L^-, was NOT taken to be a representation of the MEANING of the sentence; it was employed in a theory not of what the sentence means, but of what it is to UNDERSTAND utterances of the sentence. Gricean principles of inference constituted part of the theory of understanding, and inferential competence was taken to be part of one's capacity to understand an utterance of the sentence. One did not have knowledge of the truth-conditions of the utterance solely by virtue of knowing the meaning of the sentence uttered. Knowledge of those truth-conditions was arrived at by inference from knowledge of meaning, of persons, and of the world. Thus UNDERSTANDING an utterance typically requires a theory of reference and truth.

The shift in employment of logical forms, from their role in a theory of the meaning of sentences to a role in a theory of the understanding of utterances, was a deliberate conceptual revision of the notion of semantic representation. ["Theories of logical form are theories of propositions expressed by sentences of the language, though they sometimes masquerade as theories of meaning for sentences of the language" (Atlas, 1975b, p. G3).] In Atlas (1977a) this dual role of semantic representation in accounts of sentence-meaning and of utterance-understanding was again made explicit, the identification of semantic representations with logical forms was rejected, and the theoretical term SEMANTIC REPRESENTATION was returned to its original sense in the linguistic theory of meaning. It is important to point out that our distinction between the uses of MEANING and UNDERSTANDING follows Russell's and is very similar to, but not identical with, distinctions drawn by Dummett and Putnam, who use the same terms. But Putnam (1978) seems to REVERSE the Russellian use of them. This terminological inconsistency is unfortunate but momentarily inescapable.

I have surely said enough to indicate that the choice of L^- as the SEMANTIC REPRESENTATION in my 1975 Gricean theory did not tell me what represented the conventional meaning of the negative presuppositional sentence. Indeed, in my theory it was not intended to. And if my arguments are cogent, the choice of L^- in Grice's form of the theory could not actually tell me, despite the pretense of doing so. There is therefore only the appearance of inconsistency between the claim of these pragmatic theories that L^- is the semantic representation of ⌜*The A is not B*⌝ and my claim that because of the semantical nonspecificity of ⌜*The A is not B*⌝ L^- cannot represent its conventional meaning. The apparent inconsistency results from a mistaken conception of the role of L^- in the pragmatic theories. These theories do NOT provide an alternative semantical theory of negative, presuppositional sentences. I shall now proceed to show that with a more intuitive concept of a semantic representation, one that represents literal–conventional meaning, a more coherent Gricean theory is possible.

9. GRICE'S PRAGMATICS AND SEMANTICAL GENERALITY

I have already discussed the "asymmetry" in the standard pragmatic theory's account of the L^- and L^+ understandings of utterances of the sentence ⌜*The A is not B*⌝. A Gricean view combined with the representation of the semantical generality of negation, which was among the positions I advanced as viable options in the early 1970's, remedies this theoretical "asymmetry" in the standard Gricean view. Let $L^{=}$ stand for the nonspecific semantic representation of ⌜*The A is not B*⌝. Then the pragmatic theory does theoretical work in BOTH cases:

$$\mathrm{PRAG}(K^*, L^=) = L^+$$
$$\mathrm{PRAG}(K^{**}, L^=) = L^-.$$

Understandings that phenomenologically are of equal status are theoretically of equal status—produced in the same way by the same mechanism. The problem of explaining the degenerate case, that is, the case where $\mathrm{PRAG}(K^{**}, L^-) = L^-$, simply vanishes.[2]

Furthermore, understanding the speaker's utterance is NOT simply knowing a logical form that the context SELECTS from "the meanings" of an ambiguous sentence. Such a view would have been congenial during the palmy days of GENERATIVE SEMANTICS in the early 1970s when formal semantics was loved by linguists more fondly and less well than the subject deserved, and everything seemed cut and tailored to a logical form. On my view understanding the speaker's UTTERANCE is knowing a proposition that the context CONSTRUCTS from "the meaning" of a univocal, semantically nonspecific sentence. Not only is the nonspecific meaning of the sentence made specific in the understanding of the utterance, but the propositional content of the utterance that is constructed by inference is one that contributes to an explanation for the uttering of the sentence in the context. A mathematical model for what one knows when one knows the meaning of a sentence is not a set, for example, of possible worlds or of pairs of worlds with sets of worlds (truth-conditions), but a procedure, for example, a computer program modeling logical, practical, or inductive reasoning (verification-conditions). (For further discussion see Atlas, 1975a, 1977a, 1978.)

10. CONCLUSION

It seems to me that the standard pragmatic account of presupposition raises serious philosophical and linguistic questions, such as

[2] It may be helpful to linguists to consider a parallel with phonology. The sentence ⌜*The A is not B*⌝ in one context may be understood as L^- and in another as L^+. These understandings are related to the conventional meaning $L^=$ of the sentence as ALLOPHONES are to the PHONEME to which they belong.

what is the relationship between semantic and pragmatic properties of sentences within a unified theory of meaning? In a theory of presuppositional sentences, Grice's pragmatics without semantical nonspecificity is blind, and semantical nonspecificity without Grice's pragmatics is empty. It is this synthesis of the semantic and pragmatic that creates difficulties for the theorist of Logical Form, the Generative Semanticist, the Semantical Realist, the core of whose conception of meaning is truth-conditions, or the standard Gricean Pragmatist. And it is a mutually enriching synthesis of philosophy and linguistics that points to a more adequate theory.

In seeing concretely for the first time how linguistics contributes to the solution of philosophical problems, we discover that Fregean semantics is inadequate to our explanatory tasks. The age of classical semantics is over, and we are finally expelled from the Cantorian paradise.

> *"Glaub nicht immer, dass du deine Worte von Tatsachen abliest; diese nach Regeln in Worte abbildest!"*
>
> Don't always think that you read off what you say from the facts; that you portray these in words according to rules.
>
> —LUDWIG WITTGENSTEIN, *Philosophical Investigations* 292

REFERENCES

Allwood, J. Negation and the strength of presupposition. *Logical Grammar Reports No. 2*. Department of Linguistics, University of Göteborg, Sweden, December 1972.

Allwood, J. Truth, appropriateness and focus. In O. Dahl (Ed.), *Topic, comment, contextual boundedness, and focus*. Hamburg: H. Buske, 1974.

Atlas, J. D. Frege's polymorphous concept of presupposition and its role in a theory of meaning. *Semantikos*, 1975, *1*, 29–44.(a)

Atlas, J. D. Presupposition: A semantico-pragmatic account. *Pragmatics Microfiche*, 1975, *1.4*, D13–G9.(b)

Atlas, J. D. Negation, ambiguity, and presupposition. *Linguistics and Philosophy*, 1977, *1*, 321–336.(a)

Atlas, J. D. Presupposition revisited. *Pragmatics Microfiche*, 1977, 2.5 D5–D11.(b)

Atlas, J. D. On presupposing. *Mind*, 1978, *87*, 396–411.

Atlas, J. D. and Levinson, S. C. The importance of practical reasoning in language usage: An explanation of conversational implicature. Unpublished ms. Mathematical Social Sciences Board Research Workshop on the Formal Pragmatics of Natural Language, University of Michigan, July 1973.

Atlas, J. D. and Phillips, M. A. Art, imagination, and metaphor: Some consequences for the theory of meaning. Pomona College Research Reports, Pomona College, Claremont, California. December 1977.

Boër, S. E. and Lycan, W. G. The myth of semantic presupposition. In A. M. Zwicky (Ed.), *Papers in nonphonology*, Working papers in Linguistics No. 21. Department of Linguistics, The Ohio State University, Columbus, Ohio. May 1976. Pp. 2–90.

Brown, P., and Levinson, S. Universals in language usage: Politeness phenomena. In E. Goody (Ed.), *Questions and politeness: Strategies in social interaction.* Cambridge: Cambridge University Press, 1978. Pp. 56–310.

Davidson, D. Truth and meaning. *Synthese,* 1967, *17,* 304–323.

Davidson, D. On saying that. *Synthese,* 1968–1969, *19,* 130–146.

Davidson, D. Radical interpretation. *Dialectica,* 1973, *27,* 313–328.

Davidson, D. Belief and the basis of meaning. *Synthese,* 1974, *27,* 309–323.

Davidson, D. Semantics for natural language. In D. Davidson and G. Harman (Eds.), *The logic of grammar.* Encino, California: Dickenson, 1975. Pp. 18–24.

Dummett, M. Truth. *Proceedings of the Aristotelian Society,* 1958–1959, *59,* 141–162.

Dummett, M. What is a theory of meaning? (I). In S. Guttenplain (Ed.), *Mind and language.* Oxford: Clarendon, 1975. Pp. 97–138.

Dummett, M. What is a theory of meaning? (II). In G. Evans and J. McDowell (Eds.), *Truth and Meaning: Essays in semantics.* Oxford: Clarendon, 1976. Pp. 67–137.

Dummett, M. *Truth and other enigmas.* Cambridge: Harvard University Press, 1978.

Gazdar, G. Formal pragmatics for natural language implicature, presupposition, and logical form." Unpublished doctoral dessertation, University of Reading, 1976.

Grice, H. P. Logic and conversation. In D. Davidson and G. Harman (Eds.), *The logic of grammar.* Encino, California: Dickenson, 1975. Pp. 64–75.

Grice, H. P. Further notes on logic and conversation. In P. Cole (Ed.), *Syntax and semantics 9: Pragmatics.* New York: Academic Press, 1978. Pp. 113–127.

Harman, G. H. Deep structure as logical form. In D. Davidson and G. Harman (Eds.), *Semantics of Natural Language.* Dordrecht: Reidel, 1972. Pp. 25–47.

Harman, G. H. Logical form. In D. Davidson and G. Harman (Eds.), *The logic of grammar.* Encino, California: Dickenson, 1975. Pp. 283–307.

Horn, L. R. Remarks on Neg-Raising. In P. Cole (Ed.), *Syntax and Semantics 9: Pragmatics.* New York: Academic Press, 1978. Pp. 129–220.

Kaplan, D. Demonstratives. Unpublished ms. Department of Philosophy, University of California, Los Angeles, 1977.

Katz, J. J., and Langendoen, D. T. Pragmatics and presupposition. *Language,* 1976, 52, 1–17.

Kempson, R. *Presupposition and the delimitation of semantics.* Cambridge: Cambridge University Press, 1975.

Lakoff, G. A note on ambiguity and vagueness. *Linguistic Inquiry,* 1970, *1,* 357–359.

Lakoff, G. Linguistics and natural logic. In D. Davidson and G. Harman (Eds.), *Semantics of natural language.* Dordrecht: Reidel, 1972. Pp. 545–665.

Lakoff, G. Linguistic gestalts. *Proceedings of the Chicago Linguistics Society,* 1977, *13,* 236–287.

Lewis, D. General semantics. In G. Harman and D. Davidson (Eds.), *Semantics of natural language.* Dordrecht: Reidel, 1972. Pp. 169–218.

McCawley, J. D. Conversational implicature and the lexicon. In P. Cole (Ed.), *Syntax and Semantics 9: Pragmatics.* New York: Academic Press, 1978. Pp. 245–259.

Putnam, H. Meaning and reference. *Journal of Philosophy,* 1973, *70,* 699–710.

Putnam, H. *Meaning and the moral sciences.* London: Routledge and Kegan Paul, 1978.

Quine, W. V. O. *From a logical point of view.* Cambridge, Massachusetts: Harvard University Press, 1953.

Quine, W. V. O. *Word and object.* Cambridge, Massachusetts: MIT Press, 1960.

Quine, W. V. O. *Ontological relativity and other essays.* New York: Columbia University Press, 1969.
Rorty, R. Review of *Why Does Language Matter to Philosophy?* Ian Hacking. New York: Cambridge University Press, 1975. *Journal of Philosophy,* 1977, *74,* 416–432.
Russell, B.A.W. On denoting. *Mind,* 1905, *14,* 479–493.
Russell, B.A.W. *Our knowledge of the external world.* London: Allen and Unwin, 1914.
Russell, B.A.W. Descriptions. *Introduction to mathematical philosophy.* London: Allen and Unwin, 1919. Pp. 167–180.
Russell, B.A.W. *An inquiry into meaning and truth.* London: Allen and Unwin, 1940.
Sadock, J. M. Larry Scores a Point. *Pragmatics Microfiche,* 1975, *1.4,* G10–G13.
Sadock, J. M. On testing for conversational implicature. In P. Cole (ed.), *Syntax and semantics 9: Pragmatics.* New York: Academic Press, 1978. Pp. 281–197.
Schwarz, D. S. On pragmatic presupposition. *Linguistics and Philosophy,* 1977, *1,* 247–258.
Scott, D. S. Does many-valued logic have any use? In S. Körner (Ed.), *Philosophy of logic.* Berkeley: University of California Press, 1976. Pp. 64–74.
Stalnaker, R. Pragmatics. In D. Davidson and G. Harman (Eds.), *Semantics of natural language.* Dordrecht: Reidel, 1972. Pp. 380–397.
Stalnaker, R. Presuppositions. *Journal of Philosophical Logic* 1973, 2, 447–457.
Stalnaker, R. Pragmatic presuppositions. In M. Munitz and P. Unger (Eds.), *Semantics and philosophy.* New York: New York University Press, 1974. Pp. 197–214.
Stoy, J. E. *Denotational semantics: The Scott–Strachey approach to programming language theory.* Cambridge: MIT Press, 1977.
Strawson, P. F. On referring. *Mind,* 1950, *59,* 320–344.
Strawson, P. F. *Subject and predicate in logic and grammar.* London: Methuen, 1974.
Wilson, D. *Presuppositions and Non-truth-conditional semantics.* New York: Academic Press, 1975.
Zwicky, A. and Sadock, J. Ambiguity tests and how to fail them. In J. P. Kimball (Ed.), *Syntax and Semantics 4.* New York: Academic Press, 1975. Pp. 1–36.

PRESUPPOSITION, OPACITY, AND AMBIGUITY

RUTH M. KEMPSON
School of Oriental and African Studies
University of London

Until recently it was widely assumed that in the sentence triplets (1)–(4), the sentences (a) and (b) of each triplet presupposed the sentence (c); and correspondingly that the presuppositions of a sentence were those conditions which had to be met not only in order for the sentence to be true—since this is the defining condition of entailment—but also in order for the sentence to be false (and its negation true).

(1) a. *The gypsy regretted that the captain was in prison.*
b. *The gypsy didn't regret that the captain was in prison.*
c. *The captain was in prison.*

(2) a. *The bishop of Avebury visited Enid's art gallery.*
b. *The bishop of Avebury did not visit Enid's art gallery.*
c. *There is a bishop of Avebury.*

(3) a. *The detective in charge of the operation bribed the witnesses.*
b. *The detective in charge of the operation did not bribe the witnesses.*
c. *There was a detective in charge of the operation.*

(4) a. *The secretary of the Fine Arts Committee ran the art exhibition in 1935.*

Syntax and Semantics, Volume 11: Presupposition

ISBN 0-12-613511-8

b. *The secretary of the Fine Arts Committee did not run the art exhibition in 1935.*
c. *There was a secretary of the Fine Arts Committee in 1935.*

One standard problem for the presupposition account is the existence of conditions under which the presuppositions can be suspended, and, more specifically, the existence of negative sentences in which supposed presuppositions of the sentence in question are suspended.

(5) *The gypsy did not regret that the captain was in prison because she knew that he had in fact escaped.*

(6) *The bishop of Avebury did not visit Enid's art gallery—there is no bishop of Avebury.*

(7) *The detective in charge of the operation did not bribe the witnesses as there was no one in charge of the operation.*

(8) *The secretary of the Fine Arts Committee did not run the art exhibition in 1935 as the Fine Arts Committee had not been set up then.*

Insofar as this problem is treated within the pro-presupposition lobby,[1] it is dismissed as a matter of ambiguity, involving a quite different sense of the negative sentence in question. Accordingly, negative sentences have been said to be ambiguous between a sense in which the presuppositions are preserved and a sense in which they are suspended. Furthermore, in the case of definite noun phrases at least, this view coincides with the Russellian analysis of negative existential sentences as being ambiguous between external negation, in which the falsity operator is external to the existential quantifier and includes it within its scope, and internal negation, in which the falsity operator is internal to the existential quantifier and is included within the quantifier's scope. Consider, for example, a sentence such as *The king of France is wise* with a logical form.[2]

$$(\exists x)(Kx \mathbin{\&} Wx \mathbin{\&} (y)(Ky \supset y = x))$$

[1] See, for example, the brief mention in the Kiparsky and Kiparsky article which started the recent controversy (Kiparsky and Kiparsky, 1971, p. 351).

[2] The predicate letters K and W represent the property of being king of France and wise, respectively.

Russell's view was that there were two analyses of the negative sentence *The king of France is not wise:*

$$-(\exists x)(Kx \;\&\; Wx \;\&\; (y)(Ky \supset y = x))$$
$$(\exists x)(Kx \;\&\; (y)(Ky \supset y = x) \;\&\; -Wx)$$

I have criticized this distinction between internal negation and external negation in some detail elsewhere (Kempson, 1975), but there is an additional aspect to the problem which has broader implications for the general concept of ambiguity. The two concepts of negation are not independent, as we shall shortly see, and all purported cases of ambiguity where there is a logical dependence between the interpretations in question are problematic. This was first noticed by Zwicky and Sadock who pointed out (1975) that there is no available test for cases such as these. Their principle criterion for ambiguity concerned verb phrase pro-forms. Whenever a sentence containing an ambiguous verb phrase is conjoined to a second sentence containing a verb phrase pro-form (requiring an interpretation of identity to the antecedent verb phrase), then, in virtue of that antecedent sentence string's being ambiguous and corresponding to two different derivations in the grammar, the only possible interpretation of the following verb phrase pro-form is that it be identical to the interpretation of its antecedent. In other words, there is no possibility of crossed interpretations; the first sentence having one of its interpretations, the second, with the verb phrase pro-form, having the other of its interpretations. This prediction is indeed correct for all clear cases. Sentences (9) and (10) have no more than two interpretations each.

(9) *John saw her duck and so did little Billy.*

(10) *Maisy likes visiting relatives and so does Mary-Anne.*

This restriction is in contrast to sentences which are not ambiguous but merely unspecified with respect to some contrast. Thus, a sentence such as (11),

(11) *I have five neighbors and so does Margaret.*

allows interpretations in which the specification of the neighbors can vary across the two conjuncts of the sentence without contradiction, precisely because the semantic interpretation of *neighbor* does not include any specification of sex, age, nationality, etc. Zwicky and Sadock pointed out that any case of ambiguity where one reading is more general than the second reading will always fail the ambiguity test by default, since crossed interpretations (suggesting nonambiguity) will always be available on the more general reading. These are the cases where one reading of the sentence in question (the more specific one) entails the second reading of the sentence. Thus any purported ambiguity involving two interpretations where one entails the other cannot be tested by this criterion. Moreover there is no other means of testing such ambiguities.

The examples that Zwicky and Sadock discussed in this connection were cases such as *dog* which is used not only sex-neutrally to denote the entire class of dogs but also to denote the class of male dogs. This problem in fact applies to all cases of lexical extension, often referred to traditionally as polysemy. However the problem is not restricted to lexical ambiguity. The majority of cases of scope ambiguity in opaque contexts involve just such a dependence between the interpretations. Scope ambiguity almost invariably involves a more general reading and a more specific reading. Moreover, as the extent of claimed scope ambiguities mushrooms (cf. Hall–Partee, 1972, 1974), it becomes all the more critical that such claims be testable. I wish to claim here that it is no coincidence that such purported scope ambiguities invariably fail the available ambiguity tests, since they are indeed unambiguous.[3] If this is so, then the Wilson–Kempson view of presupposition[4] receives further confirmation, since the invocation of an internal–external negation ambiguity to preserve the case for presuppositions will no longer be a possible move to make.

Though I wish to consider opaque environments generally in due course, my argument initially concerns the purported ambiguity of negative sentences; and by way of preliminary, we must first consider a definition of the two proposed types of negation. Internal negation involves an interpretation of negative sentences consistent with a presuppositional analysis. That is, certain conditions are necessary for the truth of the negative sentence just as they are for the positive sentence, and if these conditions are not met the sentence is said to be

[3] This idea is originally due to Deirdre Wilson, without whom this article could never have been written. I am very grateful to her, and to Peter Cannings and Annabel Cormack, for their comments on this chapter. However no one but myself can be held responsible for the final version and the mistakes that remain in it.

[4] See Wilson (1975) and Kempson (1975).

odd and neither true nor false, just as in the case of the positive sentence—hence the truth table definition of internal negation:

P	−P
T	F
F	T
−(T ∨ F)	−(T ∨ F)

In the case of external negation, the negative sentence is said to be true if the corresponding positive sentence is not true without regard to whether that positive sentence is false or neither true nor false[5]—hence the truth table definition of external negation:

P	¬P
T	F
F	T
−(T ∨ F)	T

The postulated distinction in these two truth tables is an attempt to capture the dual facts that, under most normal circumstances, asserting (being committed to the truth of) sentences (1b), (2b), (3b) and (4b) appears to commit the speaker to the truth of sentences (1c), (2c), (3c), (4c), respectively—this corresponding to the first truth table; but that, under certain circumstances, being committed to the truth of sentences (1b), (2b), (3b) and (4b) can be compatible with denying the truth of (1c), (2c), (3c) and (4c), respectively, as in (5)–(9).

This presuppositional approach invoking the ambiguity of negation, is in contrast to an entailment based approach to the same implications. On this latter view, the logical dependence between a sentence and its entailments holds only if the sentence is true. If it is false, and its corresponding negative congener is therefore true, there is no logical dependence between that sentence and the sentences it entails. Hence for an entailment relation to hold between two sentences S_1 and S_2, the truth of S_2 must follow from the truth of S_1 but there is no such consequence if S_1 is false. The assertion that S_1 is false is compatible either with S_2 being true or with S_2 being false. The existence of sentences such as (5)–(9) is consistent with this view and poses no

[5] This is the definition given in Herzberger (1970). See Kempson (1975, pp. 95–96) for an argument that this is the only plausible definition. The symbol ¬ is used for convenience to distinguish external from internal negation.

problems for it: Under an entailment analysis accordingly, no ambiguity of negative sentences need be invoked.

With these definitions in mind, let us turn to a detailed analysis of the sentence pair (4a) and (4b) to see why the putative ambiguity of negative sentences such as (4b) falls into the category of sentences which are not amenable to any known ambiguity test.

[4a] *The secretary of the Fine Arts Committee ran the art exhibition in 1935.*

[4b] *The secretary of the Fine Arts Committee did not run the art exhibition in 1935.*

According to a presuppositional analysis, (4a) presumably entails at least the following set of sentences,

(12) *The secretary of the Fine Arts Committee organized the art exhibition in 1935.* (hereafter S_1)

(13) *The secretary of the Fine Arts Committee ran an art exhibition in 1935.* (hereafter S_2)

(14) *The secretary of the Fine Arts Committee ran an exhibition in 1935.* (hereafter S_3)

(15) *It was the art exhibition that the secretary of the Fine Arts Committee ran in 1935.* (hereafter S_4)

(16) *It was an art exhibition that the secretary of the Fine Arts Committee ran in 1935.* (hereafter S_5)

and it presupposes each of sentences (17)–(20).

(17) *There was a secretary of the Fine Arts Committee in 1935.* (hereafter S_6)

(18) *There was a Fine Arts Committee in 1935.* (hereafter S_7)

(19) *There was an art exhibition in 1935.* (hereafter S_8)

(20) *There was an exhibition in 1935.* (hereafter S_9)

Sentence (4b) is then on this view ambiguous between an internal negation reading in which the presuppositions are preserved, and an external negation reading in which they fall within the scope of negation. Correspondingly a truth-conditional specification of the logical form of (4b) must be of the order:

Internal negation

$$S_6 \,\&\, S_7 \,\&\, S_8 \,\&\, S_9 \,\&\, -(S_1 \,\&\, S_2 \,\&\, S_3 \,\&\, S_4 \,\&\, S_5)$$

External negation

$$-(S_1 \,\&\, S_2 \,\&\, S_3 \,\&\, S_4 \,\&\, S_5 \,\&\, S_6 \,\&\, S_7 \,\&\, S_8 \,\&\, S_9)$$

According to an entailment-based analysis of existence implications, the sole reading of (4b) is that corresponding to the reading of external negation (except that the values "neither true nor false" and "false" would fall under the same value, namely "false"). By de Morgan's equivalence that

$$-(P \,\&\, Q) \equiv -P \vee -Q$$

it follows that the logical form of (4b) corresponding to external negation is equivalent to

$$-S_1 \vee -S_2 \vee -S_3 \vee -S_4 \vee -S_5 \vee -S_6 \vee -S_7 \vee -S_8 \vee -S_9$$

The interpretation of v is of course inclusive, (4b) thus being true if any one or more of the conjuncts of the preceding specified logical form are true. There are undoubtedly dependencies between many of the conjuncts: It is for example impossible for S_8 to be false and any one of S_1, S_2, S_4 or S_5 to be true. To this extent this specification is simplistic. However it is uncontentious that the logical form of such a sentence under the so-called external interpretation involves a disjunction of the negation of each of the entailments of the corresponding positive sentence. Such a disjunctive logical form captures the compatibility of the sentence with a number of different possibilities without this being grounds for ambiguity (just as *or* in this inclusive sense[6] is not ambiguous according as each of its conjuncts is or is not true). Now among these possibilities is the possibility that S_6, S_7, S_8 and S_9 are true but S_1, S_2, S_3, S_4 and S_5 are false. But this possibility corresponds to internal negation.[7] Hence external negation allows for and is compatible with a number of cases including precisely those cases with which internal negation is said to be compatible. In other words, external negation is more general than internal negation. This being

[6] If my arguments in this article prove correct, *or* will, of course, present another example where ambiguity (between inclusive and exclusive or) has been mistakenly invoked, as has already been argued by Barrett and Stenner (1971).

[7] Internal negation itself involves a disjunction, but this further problem does not affect the point at issue.

so, we should expect, conversely, that the internal negation interpretation of the sentence entails the external negation interpretation of the sentence. And indeed it does: $P \& Q \& -(R \& S)$ entails $-(P \& Q \& R \& S)$; for when the former is true so, necessarily, is the latter. And internal negation has the logical form $P \& Q \& -(R \& S)$, external negation the logical form $-(P \& Q \& R \& S)$. Hence for any negative sentence, the internal negation interpretation entails the external negation interpretation.

Suppose then that we relinquish the claim of ambiguity in negative sentences: The question arises as to which interpretation of negation under the ambiguity analysis should be said to be the logical form of negative sentences. It is clear that it is the broad scope of negation, external negation, which must be adopted as the logical form, since it is only this interpretation that predicts that the string is compatible with the denial of the existence of the objects referred to by the noun phrases in that sentence.

What grounds might there be for making this move, for saying—despite the ease with which a relatively standard logic can capture the difference between the two types of interpretation—that negative sentences are not ambiguous in this way? The standard reason for invoking ambiguity has been that ambiguity in sentences is a datum about which speakers (can be led to) have intuitions. Accordingly the grammar must be designed to make the correct predictions vis-à-vis these intuitions. However this assumption is altruistic. This has been most convincingly argued by Reeves (1975), but it is in any case easily demonstrated by giving a set of sentences each of which has been argued to be (truth-conditionally) ambiguous (Partee, 1972, 1974).

(21) *John would like to marry a girl his parents don't approve of.*

(22) *John married a girl his parents don't approve of.*

(23) *Bill caught a snipe.*

(24) *The man who murdered Bill is insane.*

(25) *Mary believes that the man who lives upstairs is insane.*

(26) *Smith's murderer is probably insane.*

(27) *Sam is afraid to talk to a professor in the department.*

(28) *Big Mack intentionally shot a student.*

(29) *Mary reluctantly bet on the best horse.*

One of the few things these sentences have in common is that it is not at all clear whether or not they are ambiguous. Ambiguity, except in the clearest cases, is simply not a matter that can be decided by mere intuition alone. The decision as to whether to analyze a sentence as ambiguous is theoretical, and it is based not on the possibility of ambiguity itself but on the range of entailments and corresponding contradictions that the grammar must predict for any sentence. This is the standard motivation for a specific truth-conditional analysis of all sentences: The precise set of truth conditions for any individual sentence is determined by the set of contradictory sentences which result from conjoining the sentence in question with other sentences. Where the incompatibilities in question bear no relation to each other, then it is necessary to invoke ambiguity. Thus the defining condition for ambiguity is that the sets of truth conditions be logically independent.

In the case of the often invoked ambiguities of *John saw her duck* and *Visiting relatives can be a nuisance* these conditions are indeed logically independent.[8] The motivation for invoking ambiguity in the former case, for example, lies in the set of contradictory sentences (30)–(36).

(30) *John saw her duck but he didn't see her move.*

(31) *John saw her duck but she didn't move.*

(32) *John saw her duck but she didn't lower herself at all.*

(33) *John saw her duck but she was at that moment stretching up to the light switch.*

(34) *John saw her duck but she hasn't got a duck.*

(35) *John saw her duck though she hasn't got any animals.*

[8] It has been suggested by Lakoff (at the Cambridge Colloquium on Formal Semantics of Natural Language, April 1973) that in the related example *They will be visiting relatives,* the two readings are not logically independent, but mutually entail each other. This claim is, however, false. There are contexts in which the sentence is true on one reading but false on another—contexts in which either the people being visited are all relatives but are not related to their visitors, or the people who are visiting are all related to each other but are not visiting their relatives. Lakoff failed to notice that there is nothing in either interpretation of the sentence which requires that the visitors are related to the people being visited.

(36) *John saw her duck but she hasn't got any possessions.*

It is sentences such as these that must, by an assignment of logical form to the sentence, be predicted by the grammar to have a contradictory interpretation. But there is no way of devising a unitary logical form to capture this set of contradictions. Moreover, there is no independent motivation for setting up a single disjunctive semantic representation. In other words, the interpretation of *John saw her duck* involves two sets of truth conditions which are logically independent: hence the invocation of ambiguity.

In the case of internal and external negation, the sets of truth conditions are not logically independent. If we consider the sentence string (4b) in a pretheoretic way prior to specifying its logical form within a grammar, the datum we are faced with is that the string is compatible with the truth of the sentences (17)–(20), and with their falsity—of which sentence (8) gives partial demonstration. As a string, there is therefore no inference that can be made between it and the sentences (17)–(20). Accordingly, there is no justification for invoking ambiguity. From this argument, it follows that all cases of ambiguity where one reading is logically dependent on another will be excluded by fiat.[9]

There are two further arguments which lead to this conclusion. First it is plausible to argue that such ambiguities are unnecessary. It is widely agreed that for any individual language, the goal of semantics is to provide for every sentence a specification (logical form) from which the semantic relations which that sentence bears to others in the language—such as entailment and contradiction—can be predicted by general rule.[10] For any case of purported ambiguity where one reading includes the other, it follows from this goal that it is simply unnecessary to invoke ambiguity since, by judicious selection of one of those readings, one is able to make all the required predictions of sentence-relatedness. As was demonstrated in the case of external and internal negation, the latter is invariably a proper subset of the

[9] It might be argued that this conclusion cannot be correct since it would necessitate the prediction that any two sentences where one entails the other would be synonymous, with the interpretation of the entailed sentence. But such a consequence does not follow. The claim is only that a single sentence with putative logically dependent interpretations is not ambiguous. Nothing follows from this about two distinct sentences.

[10] I have assumed throughout this chapter that semantics is truth-conditional, and that the specification of semantic representations is identical to the specification of logical forms. See Kempson (1977, Chapter 3) for detailed arguments for this position.

former. Hence in specifying external negation as an interpretation of a negative sentence, it is always redundant to add a specification of internal negation.

For the second argument, suppose we assume—counterfactually—that there is no ambiguity in natural languages. Accordingly we assign to each sentence string a single logical form to capture the set of contradictions which can be formed by conjoining that sentence with others in the language (argued previously to be the standard motivation for a specific truth-conditional analysis of a given sentence). In many cases, the unambiguous ones, there will of course be no problem. But consider again the case of *John saw her duck*. Since the sentences (30)–(36) are not in fact contradictions but only contradictions upon one interpretation, the analyst has no option but to agree that sentences (37)–(42) are not entailments of that sentence.

(37) *John saw her move.*

(38) *She moved.*

(39) *She lowered herself.*

(40) *She has a duck.*

(41) *She has an animal.*

(42) *She has some possessions.*

The only sentences which are entailments of this sentence, if we maintain this assumption of no ambiguity, are assertions relating to the existence implications concerning *they* and *her* and to the predicate *saw*.

(43) *John exists.*

(44) *She exists.*

(45) *John saw something.*

The analyst has two alternatives: He could restrict the logical form he devises for *John saw her duck* to match only the three entailments (43)–(45). Alternatively, he could set up a disjunctive semantic representation, the two disjuncts corresponding to the two interpretations with which we are familiar. The significance of this latter move is that the logical form of the sentence will be of the form $P \vee Q$ and from this no inferences can be drawn directly: $P \vee Q$ does not entail either P or Q. As anyone familiar with the rule of Vel-elimination knows, the only inferences that can be deduced from a sentence of the form $P \vee Q$ are those which can be drawn from *P* and, separately, from *Q*. Hence assigning a logical form of this type to *John saw her duck* will indeed capture the fact that the only entailments of this sentence are (43)–(45).

Similar alternatives will be open to the analyst in the case of negative sentences such as (1b), (2b), (3b), and (4b). Either he must submit that such sentences have no logical form at all, since no inferences can be drawn from them, or he can specify their logical form as a disjunction in the manner of the logical form assigned to external negation interpretation (see p. 289). Parallel problems, and a parallel choice of solutions, will arise with all opaque contexts. Take one of the simpler cases:

(46) *John wants a car.*

The only inferences, if we exclude the possibility of ambiguity, are (47)–(49).

(47) *There is an individual called John.*

(48) *John wants something.*

(49) *John wants something which has the properties that cars have.*

Crucially, there is no implication of the existence of a car. The analyst accordingly has a choice. Either the logical form he assigns to this sentence corresponds solely to the entailments (47)–(49), with no disjunction (and no specification allowing the inference of the existence of a car corresponding to the object of *wants*), or the logical form he assigns to (46) must contain a disjunction incorporating the existence implication of there being an individual corresponding to the expression *a car*. In neither choice of logical form will there follow the implication of existence for the expression *a car*.

Now in the case of true ambiguities such as *John saw her duck*, the two solutions possible with an assumption of no ambiguity are both extremely implausible. A logical form matching only the entailments (43)–(45) is quite insufficient as a characterization of the sentence. But the alternative solution, postulating a disjunctive semantic representation, is no more plausible. It is not the case that the interpretation of the sentence is unspecified as to which of its two possibilities holds, which is what is implicit in a single disjunctive specification of logical form. On the contrary, a speaker uttering the sentence *John saw her duck* commits himself either to the set of entailments (37)–(39) together with (43)–(45), or to the entailments (40)–(45), but not to both.

A speaker cannot utter the sentence believing both disjuncts to be true and intending the sentence to be understood that way. However in the case of negative sentences, a logical form in the form of a disjunction (equivalently, $-(P \& Q \& R \& S)$ is precisely what I have argued is required. And in the case of *John wants a car,* neither of the two solutions postulated under the assumption of no ambiguity are a priori implausible. Thus it transpires that making the false assumption that ambiguity does not exist in natural languages only leads to a contradiction in cases such as *John saw her duck* and not in the case of negative sentences, and not—more generally—in other opaque environments. These arguments, by the principle of Occam's Razor alone, strongly suggest that neither negative sentences nor sentences containing other opaque contexts should be analyzed as ambiguous.

In the cases of both negation and opaque environments in general, purported ambiguities are not amenable to known available ambiguity tests. I have argued that, despite this, there are good reasons for not invoking ambiguity in these cases. For anyone so arguing, it is of course incumbent upon them to provide an alternative analysis. In the case of negative sentences, I pointed out initially that it was only under a presupposition based analysis that the ambiguity of negation need be invoked, and that the prediction of nonambiguity of negative sentences is consonant with an entailment based analysis of what have been referred to as presuppositions. This analysis has been spelled out in detail elsewhere (Kempson, 1975; Wilson, 1975). But what of the more general problem of opaque contexts as exemplified by sentences (21), (25), (27), and (46)?

(21) *John would like to marry a girl his parents don't approve of.*

(25) *Mary believes that the man who lives upstairs is insane.*

(26) *Sam is afraid to talk to a professor in the department.*

(46) *John wants a car.*

I suggested two alternative solutions earlier. On the one hand, the logical form of such sentences might contain no specification of the possible implication of existence of the object denoted by the noun phrase contained in the opaque context. I suggested, however, that an alternative was to specify such an implication (in the normal way, let us assume, with an existential quantifier format) as one element of a disjunction. The problem is to what might it be disjoined? The only plausible answer is to a specification of the nonexistence of that same individual. According to this analysis, the logical form of (46) would therefore include a specification along the following lines:

$$(\exists x)([CAR]x) \vee -(\exists x)([CAR]x)$$

But such a specification is entirely otiose. For a representation which does NOT include a proposition P as part of its logical form itself guarantees that the sentence in question is compatible with both P and $-P$.[11] Thus it appears that the only specification of such opaque contexts is the intensional reading, for this is compatible with both the existence and the nonexistence of the objects in question.

There is an interesting side effect to this conclusion. It has often been pointed out (Montague, 1974, Partee, 1974, 1975) that the ambiguity arising in opaque contexts can only be handled naturally within a Montague grammar framework, and that it cannot be satisfactorily handled within the domain of standard predicate calculus. It therefore might seem that my arguments against invoking ambiguity in opaque contexts could be used to erode one of the central arguments in favor of Montague grammar. However quite the reverse is true. For as Partee points out (1974), it is only the intensional reading of such sentences which cannot be handled within a standard logic: The extensional reading provides no problem. And if my arguments are correct, it is a specification of the intensional interpretation which we require for the logical form of these sentences. It is these interpretations which only the more sophisticated machinery of Montague grammar appears to be able to handle at all satisfactorily. Thus if my arguments are correct, the evidence remains in favor of a Montague grammar analysis of opaque contexts, despite their lack of ambiguity.[12]

REFERENCES

Barrett, R., and Stenner, A. (1971) On the myth of the exclusive "or". *Mind*, 1971, 79, 116–121.

Herzberger, H. Truth and modality in semantically closed languages. In R. Martin (Ed.), *The paradox of the liar*. New Haven: Yale University Press, 1970. Pp. 25–46.

Kempson, R. M. *Presupposition and the delimitation of semantics*. Cambridge: Cambridge University Press, 1975.

[11] Unless of course P (or $-P$) is independently entailed by that logical form. This possibility does not arise in the case in question.

[12] For detailed suggestions as to the formalization of opaque contexts within a Montague framework, see Montague (1974) and Partee (1974).

Kempson, R. M. Semantic theory. Cambridge: Cambridge University Press, 1977.

Kiparsky, P. and Kiparsky, C. Fact. In D. Steinberg and L. Jakobovits (Eds.), *Semantics.* Cambridge: Cambridge University Press.

Montague, R. Quantification in ordinary English. In Thomason, R. (Ed.), *Formal philosophy: Selected papers of Richard Montague.* New Haven: Yale University Press, 1974. Pp. 247–270.

Partee, B. H. Opacity, coreference and pronouns. In G. Harman, and D. Davidson, (Eds.), *Semantics of natural language.* Dordrecht: Reidel, 1972. Pp. 415–441.

Partee, B. H. Opacity and scope. In M. Munitz, and P. Unger, (Eds.), *Semantics and philosophy.* New York: New York University Press, 1974. Pp. 81–102.

Partee, B. H. Montague grammar and transformational grammar. *Linguistic Inquiry,* 1975, *6,* 203–300.

Reeves, A. Ambiguity and indifference. *Australasian Journal of Philosophy,* 1975, *53,* 220–237.

Wilson, D. *Presuppositions and non-truth-conditional semantics.* New York: Academic Press.

Zwicky, A. and Sadock, J. Ambiguity tests and how to fail them. In J. Kimball (Ed.) *Syntax and Semantics 4.* New York: Academic Press, 1975.

ORDERED ENTAILMENTS: AN ALTERNATIVE TO PRESUPPOSITIONAL THEORIES

DEIRDRE WILSON
University College of London

and

DAN SPERBER
CNRS and Université de Paris X

In the last few years, the theoretical status of presuppositions has become increasingly unclear. On the one hand, those who want to distinguish semantics from pragmatics have generally concluded that there can be no coherent semantic account of presuppositions. On the other hand, attempts to explain presuppositional phenomena on the basis of purely pragmatic rules, with no appeal to semantic presuppositions, have largely failed. What remains is an undeniable set of facts about presuppositional behavior, which are very amenable to observation and classification, but which seem to resist satisfactory explanation in any well established framework. In this chapter we propose a new framework and a new approach. The new framework is, surprisingly, semantic; the new approach involves a series of novel claims about the nature of semantic description. Given these, a natural solution to the presupposition problem follows automatically.

1. THE PRESUPPOSITION PROBLEM

Most theories of presupposition, whether semantic or pragmatic, have been responses to a range of judgments which are instantly com-

Syntax and Semantics, Volume 11: Presupposition

ISBN 0-12-613511-8

pelling.[1] For example, the following sentences seem to convey the same information, but to convey it in different ways:

(1) *It is Peter who is married to Sarah.*

(2) *It is Sarah that Peter is married to.*

Both (1) and (2) entail (3a) and (3b), in the sense that if (1) or (2) is true, (3a) and (3b) must also be true:

(3) a. *Someone is married to Sarah.*
b. *Peter is married to someone.*

More generally, any proposition entailed by (1) is entailed by (2), and vice versa. However, someone who asserts (1) is felt to have taken (3a), but not (3b), for granted, whereas someone who asserts (2) is felt to have taken (3b), but not (3a), for granted. This difference between (1) and (2) is normally preserved under denial and questioning: Thus someone who denies or questions (1) will normally be seen as taking (3a) for granted, while someone who denies or questions (2) will be seen as taking (3b) for granted. There is a very wide range of similar, well established facts.

These facts are problematic for those who advocate a standard truth-conditional semantics, recognizing only a single formal type of truth condition or entailment. For these people, since (1) and (2) have exactly the same set of entailments, they must be treated as semantically identical. But if they are semantically identical, there can be no semantic basis for the obvious differences in behavior of (1) and (2) under assertion, questioning or denial. These differences, for standard truth-conditional semanticists, must therefore have a purely pragmatic explanation. Many attempts have been made to provide such purely pragmatic accounts, mainly within a Gricean framework.[2] However, although certain aspects of presuppositional behavior do seem to have some suitable account in Gricean terms, we do not believe that any GENERAL account of presuppositional behavior can be formulated exclusively in these terms.

Someone who believes that presuppositions can be identified with Gricean conversational implicatures would have to show that (1) and

[1] The Fregean presuppositions advocated by Katz (1972, Sections 4-2, 8-4) concern a much narrower range of facts. Although we shall maintain that a linguistic ordering of entailments should replace all presuppositional devices, the weaker claim that linguistic ordering as described here should complement rather than replace Fregean conditions of referentiality would still be quite substantial.

[2] An excellent treatment is given in Gazdar (1976).

denials of (1), for example, conversationally implicate (3a) and not (3b), whereas (2) and denials of (2) implicate (3b) and not (3a). A conversational implicature in turn depends on the prima facie violation of one of Grice's conversational maxims concerning relevance, informativeness, brevity and ease of comprehension.[3] As long as (1) and (2) are treated as semantically identical, it is hard to see how they could bring about different violations of the maxims of relevance and informativeness. Indeed, for Grice, two semantically identical sentences must always give rise to identical conversational implicatures unless they differ rather dramatically in length or ease of comprehension, so that they differ in their violations of the two other maxims concerning brevity and perspicuity. There is no such difference between (1) and (2), which are not only truth-conditional equivalents, but are also built on the same syntactic pattern, and contain the same lexical items. It seems, then, that the obvious pragmatic differences between (1) and (2) can never be attributed to Gricean conversational implicatures.

A different problem confronts those who want to account for presuppositional behavior in terms of Gricean conventional implicatures.[4] In the first place, the status of conventional implicatures seems just as unclear as that of presuppositions themselves. If they are treated as part of semantics, then they will have to have the same formal properties as semantic presuppositions, since they will be used to predict the same range of behavior: They will then be subject to all the criticisms leveled against the semantic presuppositional approach. Moreover, conventional implicatures as Grice defined them were not truth conditions at all, being logically independent of the truth of the sentence which carried them. It is hard to see how the obvious truth-conditional properties of semantic presuppositions could be explained in terms of Gricean conventional implicatures. On the other hand, if they are treated as purely pragmatic, we are left with no explanation at all of why they exist. Conversational implicatures are squarely based on undeniable pragmatic considerations (relevance, informativeness, and so on). Conventional implicatures cannot be traced back to independent pragmatic principles in this way. It seems, then, that to claim that pragmatic presuppositions are really conventional implicatures involves no more than a change in terminology, with no resulting clarification of their status. The same seems to be true of pragmatic approaches in terms of appropriateness conditions on utterances, as has been amply demonstrated elsewhere.[5]

[3] See Grice (1975).

[4] See for example Karttunen and Peters (1975).

[5] See Wilson (1975b).

Failing a purely pragmatic account of the differences in presuppositional behavior of sentences such as (1) and (2), one is naturally led to consider whether these sentences do not perhaps, after all, differ in their semantics, and whether the standard truth-conditional approach to semantics should not be rejected. For those who want to provide a semantic account of the differences between (1) and (2), there has long seemed no alternative but to set up a new type of truth condition, formally distinct from standard entailments, and to distinguish (1) and (2) on the basis of these two different formal types of truth condition. Thus, (1) could be treated as entailing (3b) but presupposing (3a), while (2) could be treated as entailing (3a) but presupposing (3b). The formal differences between presuppositions and entailments—for example that presuppositions were preserved under questioning and negation while entailments were not—could then be used to explain the pragmatic differences between (1) and (2). Exactly parallel considerations would lead to the setting up of semantic presuppositional analyses in a very wide range of well known cases.

In the last few years, the semantic approach to presuppositions has been severely, and in our view justifiably, criticized. We do not intend to review these criticisms here.[6] However, one obvious point against the semantic presuppositional approach is that it does not seem well equipped to handle the fact that (4), in which (1) occurs embedded, shares most of the presuppositional characteristics of (1):

(4) *Bob says it is Peter who is married to Sarah.*

As with (1), someone who asserts, questions or denies (4) will generally be taken as assuming (3a), rather then asserting, questioning or denying it himself. Yet the formal properties of semantic presuppositions are such that (3a) cannot be treated as a semantic presupposition of (4) without making grossly false predictions about the truth conditions for sentences conveying reported speech. In particular, if (3a) turns out to be false, none of the predicted effects of semantic presupposition failure would follow. Thus, even apart from the internal incoherence of the semantic presuppositonal approach, it can never account for the presuppositional behavior of sentences like (4).[7]

The issue is now clear. There is no denying the existence of what

[6] See for example Wilson (1975a), Kempson (1975), Karttunen (1973), and Boër and Lycan (1976).

[7] Karttunen (1973) treats *say* as a plug, blocking off the presuppositions of its complement. This treatment provides no explanation for the obvious presuppositional behavior of sentences like (4), behavior which is also extremely hard to account for on Gricean lines.

we have been calling presuppositional behavior, and no denying the fact that it needs to be explained. But there seems to be no entirely satisfactory explanation for this behavior, either in semantic or in pragmatic terms. The existence of presuppositional behavior is unassailable: Its theoretical status is increasingly puzzling.

We will argue that there is a semantic explanation after all.[8] It seems that presuppositional behavior cannot be explained by postulating two different TYPES of truth condition: presuppositions and entailments. However, before concluding that sentences with the same truth conditions must therefore be semantically identical, we should investigate another possible source of semantic differences. Semantic differences might result, not from differences in TYPES of truth condition, but from differences in the organization of truth conditions of a SINGLE formal type. This is not a possibility that has generally been considered. It is usually assumed that the entailments of a sentence constitute an unordered set (or that any ordering the set may have—for example, a logically determined one—is semantically irrelevant) and that the semantic representation of a sentence either just is that set of entailments or is a logical form which would specify it. We shall try to show, on the contrary, that the entailments of a sentence constitute an ORDERED (or partially ordered) set, with considerable internal structure.[9] On the basis of this internal structure, we think we can distinguish, for a given utterance, those entailments which are centrally important, or focalized, from those which are peripheral, and, among the focalized ones, those which are in the foreground of attention from those which are in the background. Using these linguistically determined distinctions we can predict a wide range of facts about the pragmatic behavior of utterances. Thus, if semantics is done along the lines we suggest, we think we can provide a satisfactory semantically based solution to most of the problems presuppositional theories were intended—but failed—to solve.

2. PRELIMINARY REMARKS ON LINGUISTIC ORDERING

In this section, we give an intuitive characterization of the kind of facts that might be best understood in terms of a claim that entail-

[8] Semantic in the sense that it is part of grammar and concerns meaning. Katz (1972) would call it stylistic or rhetorical; no substantive issue need be involved here.

[9] This possibility was first put forward in Wilson (1970). A development was attempted in Sperber (1975).

ments are linguistically ordered. In doing this, we shall make two assumptions: one semantic, the other pragmatic.

On the semantic level we assume that the basis for semantic description is provided by a standard truth-conditional approach: An adequate semantic description will specify or give a means of specifying all the entailments (in the case of a declarative, truth conditions) of the sentence being described. Thus, among the entailments of (5) will be (6a)–(6f):

(5) *Bill's father writes books.*

(6) a. *Bill exists.*
b. *Bill has a father.*
c. *Someone writes books.*
d. *A parent of Bill's writes books.*
e. *Someone's father does something.*
f. *Someone does something.*

Someone who asserts (5) will, logically speaking, commit himself to the truth of all of (6a)–(6f), and all other such entailments of (5).

On the pragmatic level, we shall assume that a crucial part of understanding an utterance consists in establishing its relevance as intended by the speaker. This will involve computing the (nontrivial) consequences that follow when it is added to the set of previously held assumptions. Here only shared assumptions are taken into account.[10] Clearly, not all the entailments of an utterance contribute equally to establishing its relevance. For instance, (7) entails both (8a) and (8b), but under circumstances that are fairly easy to grasp, (8b) would carry the main consequences and give the whole utterance most of its relevance:

(7) *There's a funny smell—your coat's on fire!*

(8) a. *There is a funny smell.*
b. *Your coat is on fire.*

The interpretation of an utterance will thus involve some method of picking out and bringing to the forefront of attention the pragmatically most important entailments, on which the general relevance of the utterance depends.

An assumption we shall not take for granted, but rather wish to prepose and develop, is that a speaker may use linguistic means to indi-

[10] For detailed discussion of the notion of relevance, and an attempted definition, see Sperber and Wilson (forthcoming).

cate the pragmatically most important entailments of his utterance. More precisely, he may place them in the foreground of the ordered set of entailments carried by his utterance. The general line of argument for this claim is that truth-conditionally equivalent sentences such as (1) and (2) will in fact be given different pragmatic interpretations in the same circumstances, or will be appropriate to different circumstances. As we have shown, this fact cannot be accounted for either in purely pragmatic terms or purely truth-conditional terms. It suggests a non-truth-conditional dimension to semantic description. The way that we propose to introduce this dimension is as follows: A sentence will be analyzed semantically into a set of entailments; simultaneously, the syntactic, lexical or phonological form of the sentence will impose an ordering on these entailments. Thus sentences like (1) and (2), which differ in their linguistic form, may also differ in the degrees of importance they assign to their common set of entailments, marking different members of this set as semantically the most salient.

As a case where syntactic differences affect the linguistic ordering of entailments, consider the following. A speaker who wants to express two logically independent propositions may express them as two syntactically independent (or coordinate) main clauses, or as a main-clause–subordinate-clause structure. If he chooses the syntactically independent structure, as in (7) or (9), it is obvious that, linguistically speaking, both propositions entailed by his utterance are equally important. If in the end one is considered more relevant than the other, it will be for purely pragmatic reasons, and with no linguistic guidance on the part of the speaker. However, when the same two propositions are expressed, one as a main clause and the other as a subordinate clause, as in (10), there are clearly perceivable differences in the order of importance assigned to them:

(9) *I admire Bergstrom, and I have invited him to give the opening address.*

(10) *I have invited Bergstrom, who I admire, to give the opening address.*

Both (9) and (10) entail (11a) and (11b):

(11) a. *I admire Bergstrom.*
b. *I have invited Bergstrom to give the opening address.*

In (9), (11a) and (11b) are both expressed as main clauses, which suggests that each has a pragmatic importance of its own. No pragmatic difference between (11a) and (11b) is linguistically determined. In (10), however, (11a) is expressed as a subordinate clause and (11b) as a main clause. This syntactic difference is automatically interpreted as suggesting a pragmatic difference in the importance of the two entailments: (11a) is ordered lower than (11b). This in turn suggests that the most relevant part of the content of (10) lies in (11b). Note that this pragmatic difference, although perfectly noticeable, is too slight to be accounted for in presuppositional terms: A questioning or denial of (10) could well involve a questioning or denial of (11a). A presuppositional theory establishes only two levels of conditions associated with a given utterance. Examples such as (10) tend to show that there is an indefinite number of levels of prominence among the entailments of a sentence, depending on its complexity, and that even if presuppositional theories were justified, they would still have to be complemented by some subtler ordering device.

A similar, and if anything stronger, effect is achieved when a logically independent entailment is expressed by a phrase rather than a main clause, as illustrated in the following pairs:

(12) *This book is boring, and it is expensive.*

(13) *This boring book is expensive.*

(14) *This is a beautiful tree, and Herb has planted it.*

(15) *Herb has planted this beautiful tree.*

Because of their syntactic form, (12) and (14) are naturally interpreted as if the speaker was trying to make two separate but equal pragmatic points, one for each main clause. In (13) and (15) two separate points can still be discerned, but the one expressed as a phrase is clearly subordinate to the one expressed as a main clause.

It can be seen from cases (9)–(15) that syntactic form may impose an ordering on two logically independent entailments. What is the effect of syntactic form upon entailments that are logically ordered, in the sense that one entails the other? Consider the following:

(16) *Peter is married, and he is married to Sarah.*

(17) *Peter is married to Sarah.*

(18) *It is Sarah that Peter is married to.* [= (2)]

All three of these entail (19a) and (19b), and (19a) itself entails (19b):

(19) a. *Peter is married to Sarah.*
b. *Peter is married to someone.* [= (3b)]

Sentence (16) expresses the two logically related entailments given in (19) as two coordinate clauses. Someone who utters it thus suggests that (19a) has some relevance of its own, and that the information that (19b) contains over and above (19a) also has some relevance of its own. In other words, in (16) the syntactic form cancels the pragmatic effect that the logical ordering between (19a) and (19b) might otherwise have had.

In the case of (17), its syntactic form does not strictly determine its pragmatically most important point. Yet on a preferred interpretation of (17), (19a) would be taken for granted, and the fact that it is Sarah rather than someone else that Peter is married to would be the relevant part of its content. On this interpretation, (19b) would be in the background, as suggested by the logical ordering. However, this is not the only possible interpretation, and the relevant part of its content might in the appropriate circumstances be that Peter is the one, or that marriage is the relationship: The syntactic form suggests no more than an order of preference among these interpretations.

In (18), on the other hand, the syntactic form compellingly indicates that (19b) is to be taken for granted, and that the relevance of the utterance lies in the information conveyed by (19a) over and above (19b). Thus, in the case of logically ordered entailments, syntactic form may cancel, confirm or strengthen this logical ordering, and determine certain aspects of its pragmatic interpretation. As before, we find that an entailment directly expressed by a main clause will tend to be ordered above one expressed by a subordinate clause. A similar or stronger effect will be achieved when an entailment is expressed by a phrase as opposed to a clause, as in (20):

(20) *Peter's spouse is Sarah.*

Note again that in (16)–(18) and (20), (19b) is placed in four different positions on some intuitively grasped ordering scale, a fact which could hardly be accounted for in terms of a simple distinction between two levels: entailments and presuppositions. Syntactic form appears as a subtle means of imposing an order on the entailments carried by a sentence.

Lexical choice, on the other hand, can be a means of NOT ordering entailments. Compare the following:

(21) *Mike killed the man; he did so willfully and illegally.*

(22) *Mike, who killed the man, did so willfully and illegally.*

(23) *Mike willfully and illegally killed the man.*

(24) *Mike murdered the man.*

All of these entail (25a) and (25b):

(25) a. *Mike killed the man.*
b. *Mike acted willfully and illegally.*

As we have already seen, both these entailments will be prominent in (21). Example (25a) will be ordered below (25b) in (22), and above it in (23). In (24), where both entailments are determined by the same lexical item, pragmatic considerations may give more importance to one or the other; for general empirical reasons (25a) is likely to be more relevant, but this need by no means always be the case. We would like to argue that when two logically independent entailments such as (25a) and (25b) are determined by the same lexical item, whatever pragmatic difference they may occasionally or regularly present will be due to strictly pragmatic reasons: No linguistic ordering ever takes place between such entailments, and neither of them is brought into special prominence. Obviously there is room for conflicting intuitions on this point: It has often been argued that part of the meaning of certain lexical items such as *bachelor* and *spinster,* or *regret* and *realize,* determines not an entailment but a presupposition. Strong evidence for such a view would be given, on a presuppositional account, by a pair of words where the presupposition determined by one would be the entailment determined by the other, and vice versa; on a linguistic ordering account, by a pair of truth-conditionally equivalent words having reverse effects in terms of suggested pragmatic importance of entailments. The fact that (to our knowledge) there is no such pair of words is evidence for the view that when two logically independent entailments are determined by the meaning of a single lexical item, no linguistic guidance is given as to which, if any, is pragmatically the more important.[11] Conversely, expressing by a phrase, as in (23), or a subordinate clause, as in (22), a meaning that could be expressed by a single lexical item is a way of suggesting linguistically

[11] The one pair standardly cited in the literature is *accuse–criticize,* one of which would presuppose that an action was bad and assert that a certain person had done it, the other of which would make the reverse presupposition and assertion (see Fillmore, 1972). Although detailed discussion of the meanings of these words would take us out of our way, we do not believe that anything like this account can be maintained; indeed, it would be surprising if it COULD be maintained, since we should then expect to find large numbers of similar pairs making use of the same possibilities of lexical contrast, and this expectation is not borne out at all. For further remarks on factive and other lexically determined entailments, see pages 320–321.

that some aspects of this meaning are more important than others. Expressing each aspect by a main clause, as in (21), is a way of suggesting linguistically that each aspect is pragmatically important in its own right.

This approach would explain both why it is sometimes appropriate to spell out one's meaning, as in (21)–(23), and why it is sometimes most inappropriate, as in (27) compared to the truth-conditionally equivalent (26)[12]:

(26) *My God, the baby has just fallen down the stairs!*

(27) *My God, the baby has just fallen down the series of steps for passing from one level to another!*

The complex clausal phrase of (27) in lieu of *stairs* in (26) should be interpreted as a suggestion that some aspects of the meaning of *stairs* should have special attention paid to them, a most incongruous suggestion in the context.

Notice, incidentally, that this approach would render useless the Gricean maxim of brevity: A pragmatic concern for relevance, combined with a linguistic ordering used to indicate the most relevant entailments, would make cases such as (27) violations of a (somewhat revised) maxim of relevance; it would also, and correctly we think, predict that examples such as (21)–(23) need not violate any maxim or carry any conversational implicature although, given their truth-conditional equivalence to the much shorter (24), they would certainly violate any maxim of brevity.

It might be tempting at this stage to propose a generalization and claim that the position occupied by a given entailment in an ordering of entailments depends on which kind of syntactic constituent determines this entailment: whether a main clause, a subordinate clause, a clausal phrase, a simple phrase, or a simple lexical item. These types of determinants would correspond, in that order, to lower and lower orderings.[13]

[12] This pair of sentences was first used in Chomsky (1966) to make a similar point about the pragmatic nonequivalence of synonyms.

[13] One might also incorporate into this generalization the effects of free deletion rules, contrasting (i) and (ii):

(i) *Bill picked up the book and read something from it.*

(ii) *Bill picked up the book and read* $\emptyset$ *from it.*

Example (i), unlike (ii), might be seen as an invitation to speculate about exactly what Bill read from the book. By providing for differences in the ordering of entailments between (i) and (ii), one might make it possible to account for such pragmatic differences.

However, while some such principle might clearly be used to make a wide range of correct predictions about the linguistic ordering of entailments and consequent presuppositional behavior, there are reasons for not adopting it. The most important is that the syntactic and lexical aspects of ordering either correspond to those predicted by phonological stress or are overridden by them: This suggests that syntax and lexicon affect the semantic ordering not directly, but through their interaction with stress assignment.

That stress, when contrastive, can override any syntactic or lexical effect is shown by (28a)–(28d):

(28)
a. *BILL'S father writes books.*
b. *Bill's FATHER writes books.*
c. *Bill's father* WRITES *books.*
d. *Bill's father writes BOOKS.*

Although these sentences all entail the same set of propositions, they each draw attention to different members of this set; in our terms, they order them differently. For instance, though all four sentences entail that someone's father writes books, the only sentence where this proposition plays a direct part in interpretation is (28a), where it exhibits standard presuppositional behavior. Similarly, all four sentences entail that Bill's father does something regarding books, but only in (28c) does this entailment play a direct part in the interpretation; and so on. Since these examples differ neither syntactically nor lexically, it is clear that we need some ordering principle sensitive to stress. In

---

In fact, the effects of free deletion rules are often of considerable pragmatic significance. Thus, though (iii) is semantically related to (iv), it would normally be interpreted as conveying (v):

(iii) *Socrates picked up the hemlock and drank ∅.*

(iv) *Socretes picked up the hemlock and drank something.*

(v) *Socrates picked up the hemlock and drank it.*

One might argue that the effect of free deletion is to induce very low ordering of the propositions containing the deleted element, and go on to argue that low ordered propositions will be interpreted as pragmatically irrelevant. There are two ways that pragmatic irrelevance can arise: either because the content of the propositions concerned is essentially trivial, as in (ii), or because it is recoverable from the context, as in (iii). Another type of recoverability from context is, of course, in the case of propositions already known to the hearer. Thus, assigning a low order to a given proposition in the semantic analysis of a sentence can have a number of quite different, though related, pragmatic effects.

Section 3 we propose such a principle: As will be seen, most of the ordering predictions made on the basis of syntactic and lexical considerations follow automatically from this new principle which we hope, when fully explicated, might turn out to be adequate on its own.

3. VARIABLE SUBSTITUTION, STRESS, AND THE ORDERING OF ENTAILMENTS

Among the set of entailments carried by a given sentence, there is a subset in which we are interested. For (29), this subset is listed in (30a)–(30j):

(29) *You've eaten all my apples.*

(30)
a. *You've eaten all my apples.*
b. *You've eaten all someone's apples.*
c. *You've eaten all of something.*
d. *You've eaten something.*
e. *You've done something.*
f. *You've done something to all my apples.*
g. *You've eaten some quantity of my apples.*
h. *You've eaten all of something of mine.*
i. *Someone's eaten all my apples.*
j. *Something's happened.*

The list in (30) by no means exhausts the entailments of (29): For example, it includes no lexically determined entailments. However, those listed in (30) have two interesting properties. First, they possess a logical structure: Each either entails, or is entailed by, one or more other members of the set. This logical structure is brought out in diagram (31) overleaf, where downward arrows link entailing sentences with the sentences they entail, and thus each downward path through the diagram (31) defines a series in which each sentence entails its successor and is entailed by its predecessor.

The second interesting property of the entailments listed in (30) is that each of them is the result of substituting a variable (represented here for convenience by an indefinite phrase: *someone, something, do something*) for a particular syntactic constituent in (29), and that all such truth preserving substitutions have been listed in (30). Thus (30b), for example, is the result of substituting a variable for the determiner *my*; (30d) is the result of substituting a variable for the NP *all my apples;* (30e) of substituting a variable for the VP *eaten all my apples;* (30f) of substituting a variable for the verb *eaten,* and so on.

(31)

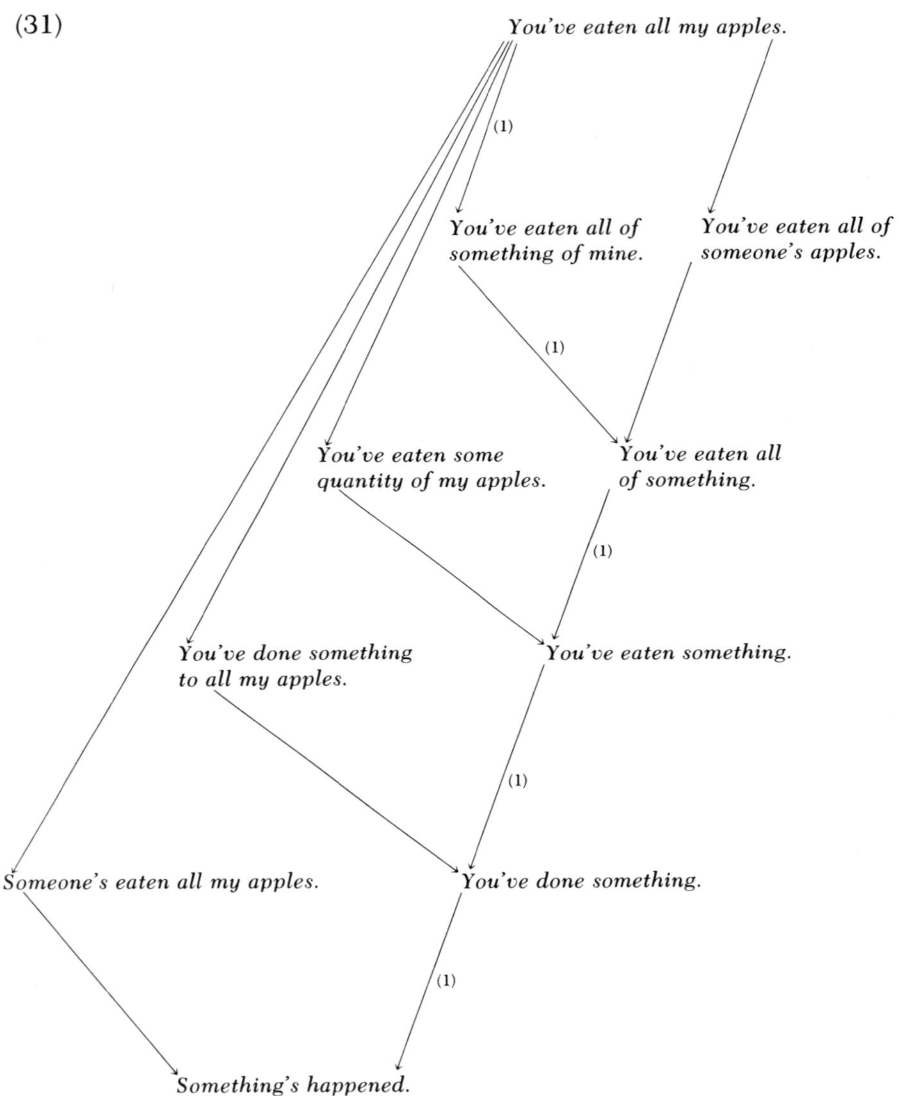

For each of the entailments in (30), then, there is a particular surface syntactic constituent to which it is linked by variable substitution. The possibility of such links was first noticed by Chomsky (1972), to whom we are heavily indebted for this aspect of our treatment.

Notice that an explication of such a variable-substitution mechanism would raise nontrivial questions regarding the domain of the variables. For instance, simply substituting a variable *someone* for the NP *no one* in (32) would yield (33), which is not entailed by (32) but rather contradicts it:

(32) *He saw no one.*

(33) *He saw someone.*

However, the issue thus raised relates closely to the interpretation of interrogatives. An interrogative such as (34) is often described as presupposing (33) and expressing a request for the actual value of the variable *someone:*

(34) *Who did he see?*

The fact that (32) is a possible answer to (34) belies that description and suggests that the domain of the variable to be substituted for *no one* in (32) is the very domain of possible answers to (34). More generally, for each constituent in a sentence there is an associated question to which this constituent provides an answer, and an associated variable which, by substitution, determines an entailment which is also involved in the interpretation of the question. Thus, explicating the variable-substitution mechanism which we are positing need raise no question not already raised independently, and may even shed light on some such questions. Pending an explication, we have chosen not to formalize our account in terms of the existential variables of the predicate calculus, which would be misleading in the light of (32)–(34).

Introducing some terminology, we shall call the set of entailments linked to surface structure by variable substitution the GRAMMATICALLY SPECIFIED ENTAILMENTS, or FOCAL RANGE, of a sentence. Thus the grammatically specified entailments of (29) are listed in (30), and their internal logical structure is shown in (31).

Our first substantive claim is that the only entailments of a sentence to which attention can be drawn as a direct effect of linguistic form are grammatically specified entailments. To make this claim more explicit, let us further define a notion of direct entailment. A grammatically specified entailment *P* DIRECTLY ENTAILS its entailment *Q* iff there is no other grammatically specified entailment *R* which is entailed by *P* and which entails *Q*. Our claim is that if two grammatically specified entailments are both directly entailed by a third—as, for instance, (30b) and (30g) are both directly entailed by (30a)—their relative order (and therefore their suggested pragmatic importance relative to each other) is a function of linguistic form; whereas if two grammatically UNspecified entailments are both directly entailed by the same grammatically specified entailment, there can be no linguistically determined order between them, and if they differ in pragmatic importance, it must be for purely pragmatic reasons.

Our second substantive claim is that when a sentence is uttered on a given occasion, only a subset of its focal range is considered in establishing its relevance, and that an order of preference among possible subsets is determined by stress assignment. To make this claim more explicit, we define for each stressed item in the sentence a series of possible FOCI: Any syntactic constituent containing the stressed item is a possible focus. Thus in (35) the focus associated with the stressed item *apples* may be either the N *apples*, the NP *my apples*, the NP *all my apples*, the VP *eaten all my apples*, or the sentence as a whole:

(35) *You've eaten all my APPLES.*

Variable substitution on each of these constituents will yield the series of entailments linked by the downward arrows labeled (1) in (31). As already noted, this series has an internal logical structure, each member entailing its successor and being entailed by its predecessor. We shall call this series the FOCAL SCALE associated with the stressed item *apples* in (35). More technically, the possible focal scales in a focal range are its maximal, strictly ordered subsets. We claim that the pragmatic interpretation of a simple sentence normally involves the selection of a single focal scale, and that the stress pattern determines an order of preference among possible focal scales (in an obvious way), so that the focal scale just listed for (35) will be its preferred scale when it is uttered with normal stress. Further, it seems that in the case of contrastive stress, the scale associated with that stress is not preferred but rather prescribed. If pragmatic considerations should override this linguistic indication, with the result that the relevance of the utterance is established on the basis of a grammatically specified entailment not included in the prescribed focal scale, a highly perceptible infelicity will occur.

Each focal scale is compatible with a number of possible choices of focus. The actual association of a given focus with that focal scale will determine a partition of the scale into two distinct subsets, which we claim play different and complementary roles in the interpretation of utterances. Suppose for instance that we choose as focal scale for (35) the one determined by the stressed item *apples*, and as focus the NP *all my apples*. By variable substitution on the focused NP we obtain entailment (30d): *You've eaten something*. We shall call the entailment obtained from a sentence by variable substitution on its focus the FIRST BACKGROUND ENTAILMENT, or for short and when no confusion would arise, the BACKGROUND of the sentence with that focus: Thus (30d) is the background of (35) with focus *all my apples;* and the background will vary as the choice of focus changes. The proposition or propositions above the background on the focal scale—the set of propositions in the scale which entail the background—we shall call the FOREGROUND. Briefly, we claim that whatever information the foreground contains that is not also contained in the background will determine the relevance of the utterance. This claim will be developed in the next section. However, even this brief characterization of the role of focus in determining a background and a foreground is enough to suggest a fourth substantive claim: that the distinction between normal and contrastive stress affects the choice of focus. For instance, if (35) is assigned normal sentence stress, with the heaviest stress falling on the noun *apples,* it seems that the hearer is steered towards selection of one of the larger possible constituents as focus: essentially the largest NP, or the VP, or even the S. On the other hand, use of heavy or contrastive stress on *apples* seems to steer the hearer towards selection of one of the *smaller* possible constituents as focus: in this case the noun *apples* or the NP *my apples.* Here again, contrastive stress seems to be generally more compelling in its effects than normal stress.

To conclude this section: The assumption, following Chomsky (1972), that there is a variable-substitution mechanism based on surface constituent structure yields a series of conceptual distinctions and empirical hypotheses which we shall examine more closely in the next section. Grammatically specified entailments, generated by variable substitution, are set apart from other entailments, and may turn out to play a different and more important role in interpretation. The set of these grammatically specified entailments—the focal range—has an internal logical structure, a partial ordering which may turn out to be given a pragmatic interpretation. Strictly ordered focal scales can be naturally defined over the focal range; they can further be associated with stressed minimal constituents. It may turn out that the interpretation of utterances involves the selection of a focal scale, and that the stress pattern determines an order of preference among alternative scales. Each surface constituent can be chosen as focus and can, together with the variable-substitution mechanism, determine a partition of a focal scale into a foreground and a background, which may turn out to play different roles in interpretation. The nature of the stress—contrastive or normal—may contribute to the selection of the focus. In other words, a rather simple initial assumption has a wide range of consequences which are well worth investigating. In particular, this assumption provides a means by which sentences with the same propositional content may be distinguished semantically, a preliminary condition for a satisfactory treatment of presuppositional behavior.

4. PRAGMATIC INTERPRETATION

We have now provided a secure linguistic basis for the pragmatic rules to work on. A subset of the entailments of a sentence is grammatically specified and ordered. We propose that this ordering is pragmatically interpreted in terms of relevance: The higher ordered entailments are assumed to be the most relevant, to contain the point of the utterance. Of course this assumption may be falsified by the context, but then the utterance will be perceived as inappropriate or infelicitous (or, under certain conditions, as figurative).[14]

The specific proposal we want to make is the following. The general point of the utterance will be seen as lying in the increment of information which has to be added to the background to obtain the proposition as a whole. The point will be structured by the order of entailments in the foreground. The increment of information needed to obtain a foreground proposition from the one immediately below it in the scale will be a distinct part of the point. In other words, each proposition in the foreground will have to be more relevant (that is, bring about more consequences when added to shared assumptions) than the one immediately below it. Returning to (35), with focus *all my apples* and background (36):

(35) *You've eaten* ***all my*** *APPLES.*

(36) *You've eaten something.*

The general point of the utterance will be seen as lying not in the fact that you've eaten *something,* but in exactly what it is that you've eaten. In other words, the general point of (35) will be the same as the one (37) would normally have:

(37) *What you've eaten is all my apples.*

Furthermore, the foreground of (35) is composed of (38a)–(38c):

(38) a. *You've eaten all my apples.*
b. *You've eaten all of something of mine.*
c. *You've eaten all of something.*

[14] For further discussion, see Sperber and Wilson (forthcoming).

We claim that the general point of (35) is analyzable into three subparts, each relevant in its own right: the fact that what you've eaten was all of something, the fact that this something was something of mine, and that fact that this something of mine was apples. On the other hand, the fact that you've eaten all of somebody's apples is not a distinct, linguistically determined part of the point on this interpretation, although it would be if the stressed item determining the focal scale were *my* rather than *apples*, with the focus remaining the same —in this case (30b) would be in the focal scale and in the foreground.

With a different stress assignment and a different focus, the general point of the utterance would be completely different. Consider (39) with background (40):

(39) *YOU'VE eaten all my apples.*

(40) *Someone's eaten all my apples.*

Here the point of the utterance will be seen as lying in the increment of information which has to be added to (40) to obtain (39): not in the fact that someone's eaten all my apples, but in the fact that you're the one who has done it. In other words, (39) will be interpreted pragmatically as similar to (41):

(41) *The person who's eaten all my apples is you.*

Within this framework, the background of an utterance with a given focal scale and a given focus will exhibit typical presuppositional behavior. Without being relevant itself, it will be a necessary condition for establishing relevance. Without knowing that (40) is the background of (39), one will have no way of determining the increments of information in terms of which the intended point of the utterance is discovered. Also, in a typical presuppositional manner, the background propositions will normally be preserved under denial or questioning. Denying or questioning the background would amount to denying the relevance of the whole utterance. However, this notion of background differs from usual notions of presupposition in that it is both linguistically determined and not logically distinct from a standard entailment. Most previous accounts could achieve only one of these effects: If presuppositions were treated as having the formal properties of entailments, then they had to be seen as identifiable on a purely pragmatic basis, while if they were treated as linguistically determined, then they had to be seen as differing in formal properties from standard entailments.

Thus, at least where entailments in the focal scale are concerned, linguistic ordering provides an alternative to presuppositional theories, whether semantic or pragmatic, in dealing with presuppositional behavior.

What predictions does our framework suggest or permit as regards entailments not included in the focal scale? In particular, how does it deal with grammatically unspecified entailments, which are of course the vast majority of the entailments of any given sentence? Depending on their logical relation to the foreground and background, entailments not included in the focal scale fall naturally into three categories: (*a*) those which are entailed by the background, (*b*) those which entail the background, (*c*) those which neither entail nor are entailed by the background. If these three categories turned out to exhibit different pragmatic potentialities, this would of course vindicate our proposed framework. And indeed they do seem to differ from each other in important respects.

Consider (42a)–(42c) as entailed by (35):

(42) a. *You've eaten some fruit.*
b. *You've swallowed something.*
c. *Someone has eaten some apples.*

Example (42a) is an entailment of the first category: It entails the background (36), *You've eaten something.* Example (42b) is entailed by the background, and is thus in the second category, while (42c) neither entails nor is entailed by the background, and is therefore in the third category.

We would argue that these three entailments of (35) exhibit quite different pragmatic potentialities. Here we want to consider two different aspects of pragmatic behavior: first, what happens under normal interpretation, where speakers make correct estimations of the assumptions they share with their hearers; second, what happens under nonideal interpretation, where speakers' estimations about the assumptions they share with their hearers are incorrect.

Under normal interpretation, (42a) might, without inappropriateness or infelicity, contribute to the relevance of the utterance. Imagine for instance that the hearer is allergic to fruit; then (35) could quite naturally be uttered and stressed as indicated, and the grammatically unspecified entailment (42a) would play an obvious role in establishing its relevance. More generally, we want to claim that grammatically unspecified entailments which themselves entail the background may felicitously be involved in establishing the relevance of the utterance, as long as they are pragmatic reasons indicating their involvement. However, there is no LINGUISTIC indication that they should be so involved, nor are they linguistically ordered otherwise than through the ordering of their directly entailing grammatically specified entailments. In other words, unspecified entailments which entail the background may be, but do not have to be, part of the point of an utterance.

It is for this reason that when the hearer in fact assumes that (42a) is NOT true, he can deny or question it without thereby denying or questioning the relevance or appropriateness of (35): What he will be denying or questioning is part of the point of (35), and it is this point that the hearer will be rejecting. In standard presuppositional terms, then, (42a) need exhibit no presuppositional behavior, and may naturally fall within the scope of denials or questionings of (35).

Just as entailments which entail the background are potential, but not necessary parts of the point of the utterance, entailments like (42b), which are entailed by the background, are potential, but not necessary parts of the effective presupposition. Example (42b) differs from the first background entailment (36) in that only the latter HAS to be considered in order to establish the intended point of the utterance. However, suppose that (42b) is false, or assumed by the hearer to be false. Denying or questioning it will amount to a denial or questioning of (36), and hence to a denial or questioning of the relevance or appropriateness of (35) itself. Thus under nonideal conditions, where speaker and hearer disagree about the truth of (42b), it will exhibit standard presuppositional behavior, while under normal conditions, where speaker and hearer agree that (42b) is true, it may, but need not, be actively considered in establishing the intended point of the utterance of (35).

Entailment (42c) behaves like neither (42a) nor (42b). Under normal conditions, it stays completely out of the picture in the interpretation of (35), contributing neither to the point nor to the background. If there are pragmatic reasons for considering it particularly relevant, either the preferred interpretation of (35) would have to be replaced by some other—for example that of (39)—or a high degree of infelicity would be perceived. In the case where (42c) is false, or believed by the hearer to be false, a denial of it (*Nobody has eaten any apples*) would constitute a very strong denial of (35), and would maybe suggest that it was infelicitous though not irrelevant. Generally, we claim that entailments which are neither entailed by, nor entail the background should normally play no part in the interpretation of an utterance; if they do, some infelicity, which may be intentional on stylistic grounds, may result; but it will not be the kind of inappropriateness caused by standard presupposition failure.

Using this framework, we can now provide solutions to two particular problems about presuppositional behavior that have often been noted. The first is to do with the "presupposition cancelling" effects of heavy stress. Consider (43), for example, with background (44):

(43) *My BROTHER wants to meet you.*

(44) *Someone wants to meet you.*

Among the grammatically unspecified entailments of (43) will be (45):

(45) *I have a brother.*

Furthermore, (45) falls into the third category of entailments defined earlier: It neither entails nor is entailed by the background, and should therefore, under normal circumstances, contribute nothing to the interpretation of (43). However, notice also that (45) forms part of the increments of information which have to be added to the background (44) to obtain (43) itself, and thus, by our earlier definitions, might play some part in establishing the general relevance of (43). It cannot, of course, constitute the main point of (43): To utter (43) with the sole purpose of informing someone that one has a brother would clearly be infelicitous. Nonetheless, there are obvious circumstances in which it could be a subsidiary point (with slight figurative overtones), and because of this, as predicted by our framework, (45) should exhibit no presuppositional behavior with respect to (43).

On the other hand, consider (46), with background (47):

(46) *My brother wants to MEET you.*

(47) *My brother wants to do something.*

Sentence (46) still has (45) as a grammatically unspecified entailment, but this time (45) falls into the second category of entailments defined earlier: It is entailed by the background (47). It should thus be capable of exhibiting standard presuppositional behavior, as provided for by our definitions, and denying it would amount to denying the appropriateness of (46). More generally, then, we are predicting that existential "presuppositions" will lose their presuppositional qualities when they form part of the increments of information that have to be added to the background to obtain the foreground, and that heavy or contrastive stress will under the circumstances described contribute to this loss of presuppositional qualities.

The second problem we shall mention is one of even longer standing. Why is it that factive verbs are felt to presuppose, rather than assert their complements? In other words, why is someone who utters (48), with background (49), felt to have taken (50) for granted?

(48) *Susan regrets* ***that she*** *LEFT.*

(49) *Susan regrets something.*

(50) *Susan left.*

We have already dismissed one possible solution to this problem: In claiming that lexically determined entailments cannot be directly ordered, we have argued against any decision to account for the presuppositional qualities of factives by direct ordering of their entailments. Nonetheless, our present framework provides for these presuppositional qualities in the following way. Entailment (50), for example, is a grammatically unspecified entailment of (48), and falls into our third category of entailments: It neither entails, nor is entailed by, the background (49). We will thus predict that it should play no part in the normal interpretation of (48), and in particular that (48) could not be used to make the primary point that Susan left. It is for this reason that (50) is generally felt to be presupposed by someone who utters (48). Nonetheless, (50) also forms part of the increments of information that have to be added to the background to obtain (48) itself: It is thus in the same category of entailments as the existential entailment (45) with respect to (43). Under special circumstances, then, and again with slight figurative overtones, it could be used to make a subsidiary point in the utterance of (48). We are thus claiming that it does not behave like a standard presupposition, but that denying it will nonetheless amount to a denial of the appropriateness of (48).

In conclusion, the mechanism of variable substitution brings with it a distinction between five groups of entailments, which indeed behave differently in pragmatic interpretation:

1. Foreground entailments, each of which must be relevant in its own right
2. The first background entailment, which acts as a presupposition, and which is crucially used in establishing the point of the utterance
3. Entailments which themselves entail the background, which may be—but do not have to be—relevant in their own right
4. Entailments which are themselves entailed by the background, which may—but do not have to—exhibit presuppositional behavior
5. Entailments which neither entail nor are entailed by the background, which should not be involved in normal interpretation, and can be so involved only at the cost of some (possibly intentional) infelicity.

Furthermore, foreground and background entailments are ordered, while other entailments are indirectly ordered through the grammatically specified entailments that entail them, and an order of preference is given for alternative foreground–background pairs. All these complex distinctions which correspond to, and may account for, intuitively perceived differences follow naturally from quite simple initial assumptions which, we have claimed, may find an independent justification in the description of interrogatives. Clearly this theoretical framework, if valid, could account for a much wider range of linguistic and pragmatic facts than could presuppositional theories, with their simple, two-level distinction. It is possible, of course, that some facts naturally accountable for in a presuppositional framework cannot be accounted for in our terms; if this turned out to be true, then we would argue that our framework should at least complement presuppositional theories. However, since we are not aware of any such facts, we should like to make the stronger proposal that presuppositional theories should be abandoned, and replaced by the theory of ordered entailments that we have outlined here.[15]

ACKNOWLEDGMENTS

We would like to thank Gerald Gazdar, Judy Klavans-Rekosh, John Lyons, Geoff Pullum and Neil Smith for a number of helpful comments on an earlier version.

REFERENCES

Boër, S. and W. Lycan The myth of semantic presupposition. *Ohio State University Working Papers in Linguistics*, 1976, no. 21, 1–90.

Chomsky, N. *Topics in the theory of generative grammar.* The Hague: Mouton, 1966.

Chomsky, N. Deep structure, surface structure and semantic interpretation. In N. Chomsky, (Ed.), *Studies on semantics in generative grammar.* The Hague: Mouton,

Fillmore, C. Verbs of judging: An exercise in semantic description. In C. Fillmore and D. T. Langendoen (Eds), *Studies in linguistic semantics.* New York: Holt, 1971. Pp. 273–290.

Gazdar, G. Formal pragmatics for natural language: Implicature, presupposition and logical form. Unpublished doctoral dissertation. University of Reading, 1976.

Grice, H. P. Logic and conversation. In P. Cole and J. Morgan (Eds), *Syntax and Semantics 3: Speech Acts.* New York: Academic Press, 1975. Pp. 41–58.

Karttunen, L. Presuppositions of compound sentences. *Linguistic Inquiry,* 1973, *4,* 169–193.

[15] For a general account of many of the issues raised in this chapter, see Sperber and Wilson (forthcoming).

Karttunen, L., and Peters, S. Conventional implicature in Montague grammar. *Proceedings of the 1st Annual Meeting of the Berkeley Linguistic Society*. Berkeley: University of California Press, 1975. Pp. 266–278.

Katz, J. J. *Semantic theory*. New York: Harper and Row, 1972.

Kempson, Ruth *Presupposition and the delimitation of semantics*. Cambridge: Cambridge University Press, 1975.

Sperber, D. Rudiments de rhétorique cognitive. *Poétique*, 1975, *23*, 389–415.

Sperber, D. and Wilson, D. *The interpretation of utterances: Semantics, pragmatics and rhetoric*. (Forthcoming)

Wilson, D. Presuppositions II. Unpublished mimeo, MIT, 1970.

Wilson, D. *Presuppositions and non-truth-conditional semantics*. New York: Academic Press, 1975. (a)

Wilson, D. Presupposition, assertion and lexical items. *Linguistic Inquiry*, 1975, *6*, 95–114. (b)

ON REPRESENTING EVENT REFERENCE

PHILIP L. PETERSON
Syracuse University

1. SYNOPSIS

The presupposition expressed by a factive clause in a sentence with a factive predicate (e.g., that Mary refused the offer *vis-à-vis John realized that Mary refused the offer*) appears to be sufficiently similar to the presupposition that a unique referent exists in a use of a definite description (e.g., that there is one and only one King of France *vis-à-vis The King of France is bald*) to suggest that the same concept of presupposition (no matter what its ultimate analysis) is at work. Presuming that it is the same concept of presupposition then makes it plausible to propose that phrases referring to events (or to processes, actions, activities, or states) be analyzed as factive clauses and predicates taking event phrases in the subject or object position are a subspecies of factives. I argue against this conclusion by showing (*a*) that reference to events and reference to individuals can be fruitfully represented in the same way; and (*b*) that event phrases are not factive clauses and so are to be associated not with factive predicates but with EVENTIVES.

Syntactic and semantic phenomena concerning specificness (± Specific, grammatically) motivate a distinction between subject-specificness and speaker-specificness (e.g., *John wants to find a woman* can be either nonspecific with respect to *a woman*, subject-specific, or

Syntax and Semantics, Volume 11: Presupposition

ISBN 0-12-613511-8

speaker-specific). To represent the varieties of specificness by using a Russellian uniqueness clause requires not only scope variation but also a Strawsonian-inspired representation of underlying referential presupposition—especially in light of the one less specificness alternative for *I want to find a woman* vis-à-vis *John wants to find a woman. Mary's refusal of the offer* in *John wants to watch Mary's refusal of the offer* has the same ambiguities. Therefore, representing the reference to an event requires representing the unique occurrence of it (parallel to the unique existence of the individual referred to by a definite or specific indefinite description) in an exactly similar way.

Grammatical support for representing event reference in the same way as individual reference (via specific noun phrases) is represented results from a Vendler-inspired approach to factives. A new definition for factives is, roughly, that factive predicates are those which take factive clauses, where factive clauses are all and only those noun phrases which are not indirect questions but which permit substitution of a corresponding indirect question (*wh*-nominalization) preserving grammaticality. This syntactic test for factive clauses and factives (a transderivational constraint) predicts those predicates to be factives which pass the semantic test (of preservation of presupposition through negation), which Kiparsky and Kiparsky's syntactic tests fail to predict (making *know* a nonfactive syntactically, for example). Some communication verbs and some conjecture verbs seem to be counter-examples to the test: Both types prove HALF FACTIVE, (significantly ambiguous between factive and nonfactive uses). But when the nonfactive uses of communication and conjecture verbs appear to take indirect questions, they are really only taking indirect quotations of questions and so produce no genuine counterexamples. However, emotive factives which take factive clauses in the object (not the subject) do provide recalcitrant cases, but cases deemed too singular as grounds for rejecting the new syntactic test for factives.

If the test for factive clausehood is carelessly applied, some event phrases fall into the category of nonfactive clauses (phrases for propositions). Explicitly distinguishing event phrases and EVENTIVES from factive clauses and factives clarifies the test. Two tests for event phrases are, roughly, that a noun phrase refers to an event if and only if a corresponding full-sentence structure cannot be substituted preserving grammaticality and that a noun phrase NP_j refers not to an event (but to a fact or a proposition) if *that* NP_j *occurs* can be substituted for it preserving grammaticality.

Given that event phrases are not factive clauses and event phrases can be represented parallel to phrases referring to individuals, it might still be proposed that factive clauses themselves be represented in the same way. This proposal proves implausible. Not only must the notion of facts OBTAINING be introduced (like individuals existing and events occurring), but also two abstract predicates, *is true* and *makes true*, must be utilized to pursue the parallel in an increasingly complicated semantic representation. The analysis strongly suggests that facts should not be considered to be referred to in any way parallel to individual or event references.

Among the implications for Montague Grammar (see Appendix) is the proposal for distinguishing between two types of conventional implicatures in an extension of Montague Grammar.

2. REFERENTIAL PRESUPPOSITION AND FACTIVES

I shall show in this section that a Strawsonian approach to representing reference to objects (reference through appropriate uses of definite descriptions and specific indefinite NPs) applies equally well to representing reference to events. Consider (1), (2), and (3).

(1) *The King of France is bald.*

(2) *The King of France is not bald.*

(3) *There is one and only one King of France.*

In a typical declarative use of (1), the subject NP is used to REFER to a particular object that the speaker PRESUPPOSES exists. That is, (3) is genuinely presupposed by (1), not implied or entailed by (1), as Russell would have it. The referent's existence and uniqueness is said to be presupposed because denial of the proposition presupposed to be true (that the referent uniquely exists) does not imply or entail that (1) is false (or that the proposition expressed by (2) is true). If (1) entailed its presupposition (3), then the presupposition's denial would imply the denial of (1), that is, (2) by *modus tollens*. But *modus tollens* does not apply in the Strawsonian approach. Rather, the use of (1) is said to be not suitable for successfully expressing either a truth or falsehood when the presupposition fails.[1]

[1] This is sometimes expressed by saying that (1) is neither true nor false if the presupposition fails. I resist that way of describing the matter because it misleadingly suggests that (1) does express a proposition when the referential presupposition fails. However, I think (1) in that case expresses no proposition at all—though, of course, it comes very close. Also, by *entails* in this discussion, I mean the relation between propositions defined as follows: "p entails q" =df. "$\Box(p \supset q)$."

Another way of putting it is that both the assertion of (1) and the assertion of (2) presuppose the unique existence of the referent—each separately presupposes (3). [If (1) and (2) each entailed (3), where (1) iff not-(2), then (3) would be a tautology because not-(3) entails a contradiction.] This statement permits an easy comparison of Strawsonian referential presupposition with the presuppositions used to characterize so-called factive predicates (Kirpasky and Kiparsky, 1971). For JUST AS typical declarative uses of (1) and (2) each presuppose the truth of (3), SO typical declarative uses of (4) and (5) presuppose the truth of (6).

(4) *John realized that Mary refused the offer.*

(5) *John didn't realize that Mary refused the offer.*

(6) *Mary refused the offer.*

Furthermore, in line with the first method of characterizing referential presupposition, (4) does not imply or entail (6). If (4) did entail (6) and (6) were false (i.e., a use of it expressed a false proposition), then (4) via *modus tollens* would be false. But (4) is neither true nor false—or rather, it expresses neither a true nor a false proposition—when (6) is false. Rather (4) fails to express a proposition that could be true or false when its presupposition fails. (For example, one might say that John neither realized nor failed to realize that Mary refused the offer, because she didn't refuse it at all.) So, both kinds of examples—reference via definite descriptions and presupposition of truths in factive sentences (those expressed in factive clauses)—seemingly permit the application of a Strawsonian concept of presupposition.

Grammarians and others might question whether facts are REFERRED TO in (4) and (5). Indeed, there is a difference between the presupposition in factive cases and the presupposition in definite description cases. The latter are REFERENTIAL presuppositions and the former are another sort—perhaps FACTIVE PRESUPPOSITIONS. There is some point to this objection (which I will explore later), but I want to point out now that the concept of presupposition in both kinds of cases—(1) presupposing (3) and (4) presupposing (6)—is, or can be considered, the same concept.[2]

[2] A useful paper that corrects some mistaken ideas of grammarians on presupposition (a suitably Strawsonian concept pertaining to reference in light of distinguishing presuppositions from entailment) is Katz, 1973. Although I generally agree with all of Katz's explanations, there is a slight difference in our uses of PROPOSITION that may prove more than merely an innocent terminological variation. In any case, I would pre-

I believe that one very plausible approach to considering the reference to events, and the presuppositions involved in using event phrases, is to subsume them under the concept of factive clause (or some extension of factive clause). That is, predicates that take event phrases (in the subject or object, ignoring other positions here and elsewhere in this chapter) either are (*a*) just factive predicates or (*b*) belong with them in a generic category or a reasonable extension of the category of factives. That is, just as (4) presupposes (6) [that is, a use of (4) presupposes but does not entail the truth of (6)], so

(7) *John watched Mary refuse the offer.*

presupposes (and does not entail) (6). For the denial of (7), particularly in the form

(8) *John didn't watch Mary refuse the offer.*

also presupposes the truth of (6). In this way, predicates that take event phrases, such as

(9) a. Predicates taking event phrases in the subject:
occur, take place, begin, last, end, happen, sudden, gradual, violent, prolonged, cause(?), *a cause of, an occurrence, a happening*
b. Predicates taking event phrases in the object:
watch, hear, follow, observe, cause(?)

are also factives (or an extension of factives, or in the same genus as factives). Then also, event phrases would be a new species of factive clause (or an extension of them, or in the same genus). Plausible as this approach may be, I believe it is a mistake! I will show this by (*a*) illustrating the ease with which event phrases can be assimilated to phrases for objects (such as definite descriptions and specific indefinite NPs) with respect to faithful semantic representation of sentences in which they occur; and (*b*) explaining the syntactic (and further se-

---

fer a speech act theoretic development of presupposition (and of propositions) such that reference failure (via failure of the referential presupposition to be true) is a failure of locutionary act. Thus, achievement of an illocutionary act is barred (since the locutionary act is a necessary condition) and it is only the successful achievement of certain (not all) illocutionary acts that can express a proposition that can be true or false. This makes my sort of PROPOSITION rather more abstract than Katz's, his being (so far as I can tell) just the meaning of a declarative sentence. However, though I do institute a speech act approach in this chapter, I do not think that bars either a syntactic account (via abstract syntax or generative semantics) or an interpretive semantics account of these presuppositions (of factives and other predicates) even though there are well known difficulties.

mantic) differences between event phrases and factive clauses, differences that motivate a new category of predicates deemed EVENTIVES, for example, those predicates of (9).

3. REFERENCES TO INDIVIDUALS AND EVENTS

I have proposed in Peterson (1975) that an adequate semantic representation of phrases making SPECIFIC references (such as in grammatically specific indefinite NPs) not only must include a Russellian uniqueness clause in order to represent the referential presupposition but also must contain another source for scope variation.[3] The new source of scope variation is to be found in representing underlying speech act structure, analogous to Ross's introduction of abstract formatives for a generic illocutionary force of declaratives, his *say* (Ross, 1970). (There is a multitude of species of declaratives, so Ross's *say* is rather generic; cf. Vendler, 1972, Chapter 1.) The need for speech act representation comes to light as a result of distinguishing speaker-specificness from subject-specificness. Consider, for example (typical felicitous uses of) (10) and (11):

(10) *John wants to find a woman.*

(11) *I want to find a woman.*

wherein *a woman* is ±Specific. (11) has one less specificness alternative than (10). For *a woman* in (10) can be (*a*) specific for John (subject-specific) but not for the speaker or (*b*) specific for the speaker as well as John.[4] However, (11) can only be specific for the speaker. Of course, both (10) and (11) permit the nonspecific use of *a woman*. Thus, with respect to ±Specific of *a woman*, (10) has three alternatives (nonspecific, subject-specific, and speaker-specific) and (11) has two (nonspecific and speaker-specific). If we use a Russellian sort of approach to semantic representation, then the alternatives of (10) could be represented as (12).

(12) a. Nonspecific: *John wants* (E*x*)(*x is a woman* & *John finds x*)
b. Subject-specific: *John wants* (E*x*)(*Woman*(*x*) & (*y*)(*Woman*(*y*) $\supset x = y$) & *John finds x*)

[3] Some think scope variation alone is sufficient. (Cf. Peterson, 1975, 1976a, and 1976b for additional related discussion.)

[4] The alternative of being speaker-specific and not subject-specific does not seem to exist in the data (cf. Palacas).

c. Speaker-specific: (Ex)(*Woman*(x) & (y)(*Woman*(y) $\supset x = y$) & *John wants*(*John finds x*))

That is, the existence of the uniqueness clause in the scope of *John wants* in (12b) represents the subject-speciffiicness of *a woman;* whereas, the uniqueness clause outside the scope of *John wants* in (12c) represents speaker-specificness. (Sufficient determinateness of the predicate *woman* must also be presumed.)[5] But this Russellian approach will not work since substituting *I* for *John* throughout (12) gives the same number of alternatives rather than one less. The answer I proposed is the introduction of abstract formatives ***presuppose*** and ***assert.*** Then (12) is replaced by (13) as representing the specificness alternatives of (10).[6]

(13) a. ***I assert*** (*John* ***presupposes*** (Ex)(Wx & *John wants* (*John finds x*)))
b. ***I assert*** (*John* ***presupposes*** (Ex)(Wx & (y)(Wy $\supset x = y$) & *John wants* (*John finds x*)))
c. ***I presuppose*** (Ex)(Wx & (y)(Wy $\supset x = y$) & I ***assert*** (*John wants* (*John finds x*)))

Again *I* could be substituted throughout (13) to allegedly represent the alternatives of (11), but the one less alternative representation would not be achieved for (11). To resolve the problem note that (14), the correlate of (13b) for the *I* cases—i.e., for (11)—would be CONCEPTUALLY ill-formed.

[5] For example, replace *a woman* by *a woman he had lunch with last week.* Only by also presuming determinateness (i.e., that all women who ate lunch with him last week are identical to the one presupposed to exist) is the uniqueness clause a plausible representation of specificness. I will represent the presumption of sufficient determinateness in the predicate hereafter by using a fully formalized predicate in the representation rather than the unformalized ones as in (12); that is, Wx is a determinate form of *x is a woman.*

[6] (13b) does not represent *John presupposes that there is a unique woman he wants to find.* That sentence would have an ordinary *presuppose* in its underlying structure. ***Presuppose*** (so emphasized) represents not the ordinary one, but the existential presupposition of reference—that presupposition of existence involved when one refers to something, that which cannot be missing if genuine reference is intended. However, (13b) might be taken to represent *John, presupposing there is a unique woman* (*of a certain determinate type*), *wants to find her.* Since this sentence is nearly synonymous with the subject-specific reading or use of (10), I can speculate that this special ***presuppose*** (referential) possibly surfaces sometimes, though not typically. That the scopes of presupposition, assertion, and existential quantifiers cross in this approach to semantic representation is, though curious, no ultimate difficulty and even a virtue.

(14) Supposedly subject- but not speaker-specific: ***I* ***assert*** (*I* ***presuppose*** (Ex)(Wx & (y)(W$y \supset x = y$) & *I want* (*I find* x))).

This is conceptually ill-formed because ***presuppose*** is stipulated to represent the referential presupposition IN an assertion (and in other analogous illocutionary acts and in mental acts and states). This is further stipulated to BE represented when ***presuppose*** has an ***assert*** within its scope—not vice versa. [(13b) is not a counterexample, since its ***presuppose*** goes with *John* and is connected to *John wants.*][7]

This approach applies perfectly well to references to events. (See Peterson, 1975, 1976a, and 1976b, for additional discussion of the approach.) First, the presupposition of (7) was stated to be (6). But that presupposition can be *re*stated, apparently without change in sense, by

(16) *Mary's refusing the offer occurred.*

This restatement is advisable in order to keep the SAME phrase for an event in both (7) and (16). I choose the word *occur* somewhat arbitrarily. *Happened* would do as well. Also, I use *events* to cover not only events, but processes, activities, actions, and states (e.g., statewise: *Mary's being drunk* (*Mary's drunkenness*) *caused John to be annoyed*). Now if we permit the symbolized existential quantifier (Ex) to represent not only the existence but also the occurrence of something (objects, of course, exist and only events occur), or if permit (Ex) to represent a genus to which both *exists* and *occurs* (in the intended senses) belong, then the same formats for specific and nonspecific ref-

[7] The only thing that (14) might be a candidate for representing would be (15).

(15) *I presuppose that there exists one and only one woman that John wants to find* (*or, . . . and John wants to find her*).

But (15) is not synonymous with (11), simply because the making of a presupposition is distinct from the stating of it. Strawsonian referential presuppositions are, in fact, destroyed when they are expressed. Presupposing in the Strawsonian sense, I submit, is part of a locutionary act, not what comes later (logically) in the illocutionary act of predication. In (15) I predicate a presupposition of myself and do not simply make it (reference-wise). In fact, I find (15) slightly odd, like saying *I command you to shut the door* rather than simply *Shut the door.* Is *I command you to shut the door* a genuine command (outside of special contexts such as the Military) or simply a quasi-report? The parallel is further illuminating, for *I commanded you to shut the door* is completely unobjectionable, just as is *I presupposed that there was one and only one particular woman that John wants* (*wanted*) *to find.* Also note that (14) with ***I assert*** deleted would represent the mental act of my wanting to find a specific woman and could be conceptually well-formed. However, that would not be the representation of a speech act or anything said, but only of something thought.

erence to objects can be utilized. Formula (17b), then is an appropriate semantic representation (speech-act-wise) of (7).

(17) a. (Nonspecific: ***I presuppose*** (Ex) (Rx & ***I assert*** (*John watched* x))
b. (Specific: ***I presuppose*** (Ex)(Rx & (y)(R$y \supset x = y$) & ***I assert*** (*John watched* x))

where Rx = "x is a refusal by Mary of the offer" and is represented to be sufficiently determinate via R (cf. footnote 5 and footnote 8).

Formula (17b) contains a representation of the presupposition of event occurrence, the same presupposition that can be independently expressed by a use of (16). Example (17a) would be more appropriate as a representation (nonspecific event reference) of

(18) *John watched a refusal or refusals* [i.e., one or more such refusals] *by Mary of the offer.*

Also, the representations proposed in (17) might also seem to represent

(19) *John watched Mary's refusal of the offer.*

instead of (7). Derived nominals are very good event phrases (often seemingly the least equivocal phrases possible). The special predicate "Rx," however, is not intended to be limited to representing derived nominals. Rather, derived nominals, gerundives, mixed cases, certain infinitives and possibly even whole sentence clauses (though they raise important problems to be considered) can in certain contexts be used to refer to events (or actions, activities, processes, or states). "Rx" could be defined as (20).

(20) "Rx" = df. "x is an event (process, action, activity, or state) of Mary's refusing (of) the offer (or refusal of it, or what occurs if and only it is true that Mary refuses the offer)."

That is, Rx represents a predicate for a kind of event. The uniqueness clause in (17b) represents specificness or uniqueness. If only one such event is referred to (presupposed to exist as the referent), then that must be contained in the full semantic representation.[8]

[8] The uniqueness clause represents event specificness in exactly the same way it does for referent specificness in the object reference cases; namely, the predicate of the clause (the event predicate Rx above, for example) must be determinate enough to make it plausible that there is only one such. This determinateness is present for a case like

Therefore, for many cases wherein a gerundive, a derived nominal, a mixed case, or some infinitives occur, there is reference to an event. And such reference can be contained in semantic representations that are exactly like representations of references to objects. Some typical varieties are (21)–(24). The event reference alternatives (as a function of specificness alternatives) of (21) are portrayed in (22), and those of (23) are portrayed in (24).

(21) *Harry wanted John's protests to cause* { *Mary's refusal of the offer* / *Mary's refusing the offer* / *Mary's refusing of the offer* / *Mary to refuse the offer* / *(*that*) *Mary refused the offer* }

(22) a. Nonspecific: ***I assert*** (*Harry* ***presupposed*** (Ex)(Rx & *Harry wanted* (*John's protests cause* x)))

Mary's refusal of the offer. A *refusal of something by someone* (*or other*) would be rather indeterminate, the same as *a refusal*. But does not the predicate become not just determinate, but absolutely specific with the addition of it's being Mary's refusal of the offer? (And if not, then do not some additional components or other (e.g., specifying time and place) make the determinate predicate absolutely specific?) I think not. No matter how determinate a predicate (e.g., an event predicate like *a refusal of Gerald Ford's offer of a job that Ford made on July 1, 1976, and which was by Mary on July 4, 1976* [*at noon, in the White House, etc.*]), the presupposition of the existence of such a very determinate event is still not in itself the presupposition that the event is singular (specific, unique) unless that proviso is added. That is what interpolating a uniqueness clause in the semantic representation achieves. It is needed for the very determinate predicate just mentioned above (parenthetically), since it is still logically possible, no matter how unlikely, that there were two or more refusals of Ford's offer at the same time and place.

Also, not making a distinction between subject and speaker specificness for *watch* in (17), as I have not, amounts to (or at least closely relates to) treating *watch* extensionally. If Mary's refusal of the offer is identical (by some event identity criterion) to her turning down the job, then if John watched the former he watched the latter whether he knows it or not. On the other hand, if *watch* is thought to be nonextensional in the object, then a speaker-specific versus subject-specific representation such as (17b)′ and (17b)″ would seem required.

(17) b′ Subject-specific: ***I assert*** (*John* ***presupposed*** (Ex)(Rx & (y)(R$y \supset x = y$) & *John watched* x)

(17) b″ Speaker-specific: same representation as (17b) in the text

That is, relative to me, the speaker, what John saw is represented as opaque in (17b)′, but not in (17b)″. In (17b)′, it may or may not be that I take what I claim he watched to be a refusal of the offer by Mary (or that such an event even occurred). In (17b)″, however, I am represented as committed to what John watched being a refusal by Mary.

b. Subject-specific: *I* ***assert*** (*Harry* ***presupposed*** (E*x*)(R*x* & (*y*)(R*y* ⊃ *x* = *y*) & *Harry wanted* (*John's protests cause x*)))

c. Speaker-specific: *I* ***presuppose*** (E*x*)(R*x* & (*y*)(R*y* ⊃ *x* = *y*) & *I* ***assert*** (*Harry wanted* (*John's protests cause x*)))

where "R*x*" is defined as in (20).[9]

(23) *Harry wanted* { *Mary's refusal of the offer* / *Mary's refusing the offer* / *Mary's refusing of the offer* / **Mary to refuse the offer.* / ?(*that*) *Mary refused the offer* } *to cause John to leave.*

(24) a. Nonspecific: *I* ***assert*** (*Harry* ***presupposed*** (E*x*)(R*x* & *Harry wanted* (*x causes John to leave*)))

b. Subject-specific: *I* ***assert*** (*Harry* ***presupposed*** (E*x*)(R*x* & (*y*)(R*y* ⊃ *x* = *y*) & *Harry wanted* (*x causes John to leave*)))

c. Speaker-specific: *I* ***presuppose*** (E*x*)(R*x* & (*y*)(R*y*

[9] Some comments:

1. I omit analogous details about the event or state referred to by *John's protests.*

2. In (22a) and (22b) the so-called opaque reading of *want* is presumed. This may appear not true because the existence and uniqueness clauses are outside the scope of *wants.* However, ***presuppose*** is itself opaque and ***presuppose*** and *wants* work as a unit —representing the referential presupposition of or in a wanting (by Harry, which because he makes it does not necessarily imply it's truth).

3. The alternative where a use of (21) does not referentially presuppose Mary's refusal occurred on anyone's part (speaker or subject) would be like (22a), but would be without a ***presuppose*** and with the existential quantifier within the scope of *wants;* that is,

I ***assert*** (*Harry wanted* (Ex)(Rx & *John protests cause x*))

4. It seems to me that (21) is less likely to have a nonopaque reading with respect to the object of *cause* [as in (c) or in nonspecific but transparent *wants*] than (23) is with respect to the subject of *cause.* This fact (if it is one) seems also related to (or just a part of) the fact that *cause* more readily takes event phrases (where occurrence of the event is presupposed through negation) in the subject than in the object. That is, it is not so clear that *John's protests didn't cause Mary's refusal of the offer* (*Mary to refuse the offer*) does presuppose that the refusal occurred.

$\supset x = y$) & *I* ***assert*** (*Harry wanted* (*x causes John to leave*)))

where Rx is defined as in (20).[10]

So what? Is this not only (at best) a virtuoso performance in manipulating logical notation (and, at worst, a threshold-of-frustration test for grammarians)? It would be if there were nothing in which to ground event phrases.[11] The independent support for this approach resides in the syntactic tests for segregating event phrases (i.e., phrases that do presuppose the occurrence of the event they introduce as a function of the meanings of their components).

4. THE GRAMMAR OF FACTS AND EVENTS

One way to begin to extract the relevant syntactic distinctions is to notice that there are some complicated NPs—some derived nominals, gerundives, and mixed cases—that, in abstraction from their typical contexts, can be three ways referentially ambiguous, referring to facts, to propostions, or to events. Only careful attention to their linguistic contexts can help specify reference. Let NP_i be defined as the following alternatives:

$$\underbrace{\left\{\begin{matrix} \textit{Mary's refusal of the offer} \\ \textit{Mary's refusing the offer} \\ \textit{Mary's refusing of the offer} \end{matrix}\right\}}_{NP_i}$$

Then note that NP_i can occur in any of the following:

(26) a. Factives $NP_i \left\{\begin{matrix} \textit{was significant} \\ \textit{was discovered by John} \\ \textit{was known by John} \end{matrix}\right\}$

$$\textit{John} \left\{\begin{matrix} \textit{forgot} \\ \textit{discovered} \end{matrix}\right\} NP_i$$

[10] Comments:

1. Note 9 comments apply.

2. The fifth alternative to (23)—with the relevant NP being (*that*) *Mary refused the offer*—is very questionable I think. I include it to try to find a case where an unnominalized sentence clause can occur. Notice that it is less questionable in the simpler *That Mary refused the offer caused John to leave.* That full sentences (unnominalized) occur only rarely and/or awkwardly will turn out to be a symptom of the difference between factive clauses and event phrases.

[11] I do not acquiesce entirely, however, to these objections prior to independent grounding. For I think the linguistic data do provide modest support for applying the distinctions about specificness to phrases referring to events.

b. Nonfactives $\mathrm{NP}_i \left\{\begin{matrix} \textit{was unlikely} \\ \textit{was feared by John} \\ \textit{was possible} \end{matrix}\right\}$

John $\left\{\begin{matrix} \textit{assumed} \\ \textit{feared} \end{matrix}\right\} \mathrm{NP}_i$

c. Eventives $\mathrm{NP}_i \left\{\begin{matrix} \textit{was sudden} \\ \textit{caused John to leave} \\ \textit{began before lunch} \end{matrix}\right\}$

John $\left\{\begin{matrix} \textit{heard } \mathrm{NP}_i \\ \textit{followed } \mathrm{NP}_i \textit{ with great interest} \end{matrix}\right\}$

In (26a), NP_i refers to a fact (or, presupposes the truth of a proposition or is a factive clause). In (26b), NP_i does not refer to a fact (or, presuppose the truth of a proposition, or constitute a factive clause), but to a proposition (a proposition that may be true but which is neither asserted, implied, or presupposed to be by using such sentences). In (26c), it refers to an event. But, how can it be said that in (26a) and (26b), NP_i refers to **different** things? It appears that NP_i can (maybe not always, but nevertheless sometimes) refer to the same thing in both (26a) and (26b) type cases. One reason for saying this is that one person can, for example, know, discover, or forget that Mary refused the offer (Mary's refusal be known, discovered, or forgotten by him) and another person can merely believe, charge, or fear it (Mary's refusal be believed, charged, or feared by him). That is, the same thing —Mary's refusal of the offer—can be the subject or object of both factive and nonfactive predicates. Zeno Vendler (1972, Chapter V) argues against this (and actually suggests the approach I adopt and extend herein). Vendler does not develop the approach for factives and nonfactives in general, but works mainly with *know* and *believe*. Also, he does not consider any NPs other than whole sentence clauses and indirect questions. (Complex NPs with embedded sentences that are only relative clauses are beside the point here, though that is sometimes hard to see; cf. Vendler, 1972, pp. 94–99, and Peterson, 1977a,b.) However, adopting his approach, and considering these other nominalizations (inspired by Chomsky, 1970) and the wider classes of factives and nonfactives (Kiparsky and Kiparsky), does produce a syntactic test for the fact–proposition distinction.

Ignoring temporarily event phrases, cases like (26c), and concentrating only on cases like (26a) and (26b) yields the following test. The idea of the test is to substitute for a complicated NP in question an indirect question that CORRESPONDS to a full sentence from which the NP is transformationally derived (though in the derived nominal cases a pretense is required). If the substitution preserves grammaticality, then the original reference of the NP was to a fact (or, the NP was a genuine factive clause). More exactly stated:

(*F*/*P*) A. A noun phrase NP_i refers to a **fact** if and only if (i) there is a full-sentence structure S_i embedded in the deep structure (or one nearly identical to it) of the sentence NP_i occurs in and S_i is the *de*-vendlerization of NP_i, and (ii) S_i can be replaced by at least one CORRESPONDING indirect question structure S_i' preserving grammaticality in the ultimate surface form based on this revised deep structure.

B. If NP_i satisfies (i), or (A), but fails the test in (ii), then the referent of NP_i is a PROPOSITION.[12]

Two things are central to understanding (*F*/*P*), vendlerization and CORRESPONDING indirect questions. The latter is the easiest to understand. (28a) through (28e) are some CORRESPONDING indirect questions for the forms (respectively) of (27a) through (27e).

(27)
a. *Mary left the meeting.*
b. *Mary left the meeting at noon.*
c. *Mary left by the backdoor.*
d. *Mary left because she was bored.*
e. *Mary attended the meeting at the hotel.*

(28)
a. *who left the meeting; what Mary left*
b. *when Mary left the meeting*

[12] (*F*/*P*) is (3)″ of Peterson, 1977a (see for a fuller discussion and development of Vendler's distinction). It seems to me possible that the approach I have adopted from Vendler is what Kiparsky and Kiparsky were vaguely thinking of when they said, "The studies of Lees (1960) and Vendler (1964), however, contain many interesting semantic observations on sentential complementation and nominalization which still await formal description and explanation." (footnote p. 365). Also, there is an important qualification (or clarification) to be made about (*F*/*P*); namely, any NP_i to which (*F*/*P*) is applied must be a full-sentence clause, a derived nominal, gerundive, or mixed case (or be a subsurface NP for certain infinitives). Indirect questions per se are inappropriate. The test does not apply vacuously to them. The REFERENCE (or factive clausehood) of NPs that are not indirect questions is tested via indirect question substitution preserving grammaticality. I take no stand on whether some or all indirect questions REFER to facts or are full fledged factive clauses. One might claim that by analogy they are factive clauses, but that is not shown by (*F*/*P*). By this qualification, the question of whether inquisitive verbs (*ask, wonder, investigate, etc.*) are factives (because they take factive clauses) can be answered negatively.

c. *how Mary left the meeting*
d. *why Mary left*
e. *where Mary attended the meeting*

Vendlerization is a pseudotransformation. Pretend—contra Chomsky, 1970 (who is probably right)—that all nominals are derived by syntactic transformations from underlying full-sentence structures (although derived nominals probably are not so derived). Call this pretended generic nominalization (there would be several species of it) "vendlerization." Then *de*-vendlerization would be reversing the (pretended) transformation to obtain its underived underlying full-sentence structure. How both of these details work into the application of (*F*/*P*) can be seen most easily in examples (29) through (38).

Successful tests that satisfy A(ii) of (*F*/*P*) are as follows (original NPs occur in a and products of the test in b):

(29) Gerundives:
a. *Mary's refusing the offer surprised no one.*
b. What Mary refused surprised no one.

(30) Derived nominals:
a. *John discovered Mary's refusal of the offer.*
b. *John discovered who refused the offer.*

(31) Mixed cases:
a. *Mary's refusing of the offer was significant.*
b. *It was significant who refused the offer.*

(32) Infinitives:[13]
a. *Mary is known to have left.*
b. *It's known who left.*

(33) Full clauses:
a. *John knew (forgot, realized, . . .) that Mary refused the offer.*
b. *John knew (forgot, realized, . . .) who refused the offer.*

The following examples fail test A(ii) of (*F*/*P*), satisfying B and so refer to propositions:

[13] Note that cases like (32) do not have a relevant NP in surface structure that supposedly refers to a fact or a proposition. Yet there is nevertheless something about uses of such sentences that somehow refers to a fact (or to a proposition). So, strictly speaking, the NP_i of such infinitive cases must occur in a subsurface structure.

(34) Gerundives:
a. *Mary's having refused the offer was unlikely.*
b. **Who refused the offer was unlikely.*

(35) Derived nominals:
a. *John fears Mary's refusal of the offer.*
b. **John fears who refused the offer.*[14]

(36) Mixed cases:
a. *Mary's refusing of the offer was believed by no one.*
b. **Who refused the offer was believed by no one.*

(37) Infinitives:
a. *Mary is likely to have refused it.*
b. **It's likely who refused it.*

(38) Full clauses:
a. *John suspected that Mary refused the offer.*
b. **John suspected who refused the offer.*

In addition to this extension of Vendler's idea, I have also proposed that Kiparsky and Kiparsky's concept of factive predicate be syntactically defined utilizing (*F/P*) as follows:

(*DEF*) a. A predicate is a factive predicate if and only if it takes factive clauses in either its subject or object.

b. A noun phrase is a factive clause if and only if it satisfies A(ii) of (*F/P*) (i.e., refers to a fact).[15]

This syntactic test should segregate all and only those predicates that are specified by the usual semantic test (the test which is, I think, the main characterization motivating the study of these constructions);

[14] In (35), (36), and (38) care must be taken not to interpret the *who . . .* phrases as free relatives (synonymous with *the one who . . .*). With free relative interpretations, the sentences are grammatical. Ungrammaticality occurs when the phrases are interpreted as genuine indirect questions.

[15] I use *refer* loosely here and in (*F/P*) to mean *refer, presuppose, introduce, and/or express*. Those who cannot accept even such a loose use vis-à-vis facts (since *inter alia* it suggests that factive clauses are singular terms denoting facts which I agree is at best a very misleading proposal), can simply omit the final phrase of (*DEF*) so that only being a factive clause is thereby defined (not REFERENCE to facts). Also, make a similar adjustment in (*F/P*).

namely, a predicate is a factive if the truth of the proposition expressed by its subject or object NP is preserved through negation of the predicate. (Call this the NEGATION TEST. It permits the assimilation to Strawsonian approaches as sketched previously.) One virtue of this (*DEF*) is that it does not classify *know* as a nonfactive syntactically (as Kiparsky and Kiparsky classify it).

Candidates for counterexamples to (*F/P*) are not hard to find. Alleged exceptions to the sufficiency condition (a NP is a factive clause if appropriate substitution preserves grammaticality) are communication verbs (*say, tell, show, indicate,* etc.) and conjecture verbs (*guess, predict, estimate,* etc.).[16] All communication verbs are ambiguous between a factive use and a nonfactive use.[17] In any particular kind of occasion or interpretation (discourse context), a communication verb must be taken one way or the other. *Say* is the easiest verb to examine. If *say* is not followed by a direct quotation, then it is ambiguous between an indirect quotation sense (nonfactive) and a factive sense. For example,

(39) *John said that Mary refused the offer.*

typically has a preferred reading of indirect quotation. True or false, John communicated a claim that Mary refused the offer. But *say* admits another (perhaps rarer) reading such that, for example, (39) presupposes that Mary did refuse the offer and merely expresses the proposition that John said so. Substitute *didn't say* for *said* in (39) and observe that there is a use of that sentence in which it is presupposed that Mary refused the offer.[18]

[16] Prior to considering these counterexamples, it might be proposed that inquisitive verbs (*ask, wonder, etc.*) ought to be factives since they take indirect questions and, apparently, indirect questions REFER to facts also. I warned against this in Note 12. Indirect question substitution preserving grammaticality is a test for the substituend's identity. The substituend itself is never an indirect question.

[17] Vendler calls these HALF FACTIVE (personal communication). Note that even if neither communication verbs nor conjecture verbs are HALF FACTIVE (ambiguous between factive and nonfactive uses), that will cause no problem since if they are not ambiguous then they are all nonfactive and the solution I give will still apply.

[18] A legitimate objection to HALF FACTIVES is that there is no difference between HALF FACTIVES and nonfactives. If John believes Mary refused the offer, then that Mary refused it can be either true or false. Isn't claiming HALF FACTIVITY (or ambiguity) the same thing? I think not, though I need not prove the point here, since my main problem concerns the nonfactive uses of HALF FACTIVES. Let it suffice here to say that it appears to me that in

(1) *John didn't believe that Mary refused the offer.*

(2) *John didn't say that Mary refused the offer.*

The problem, however, is that these communication verbs do permit grammatical substitution of indirect questions even on their nonfactive uses. My solution to this problem is to introduce a distinction between genuine indirect questions and merely apparent ones that are actually indirect quotations of questions.[19] Thus, when a nonfactive use of a communication verb appears to satisfy A(ii) and so violates the sufficiency condition, it really does not since the alleged indirect question that preserved grammaticality in applying the test was spurious. It was the indirect quotation of a question.

Conjecture verbs (*guess, predict,* etc.) seem worse. They are also ambiguous between factive and nonfactive uses, but even so the nonfactive uses permit indirect questions that do not seem to be indirect quotations of questions. Still, my answer stands. These verbs take either a new kind of indirect quotation of questions or, at the very least, a direct analogue of indirect quotation. Typically, predictions, estimates, and guesses are spoken (or are presumed to have been when reported, as opposed to beliefs, fears, *etc.*) When they have not been spoken, I claim that reports of them are still indirect quotations, though only indirect quotations of what was thought (perhaps, quasi-indirect-quotations).[20]

---

(2) has an extra kind of use that (1) does not. Granted, in the nonfactive use of either (1) or (2), it can be either true or false that Mary refused the offer. Yet, (2) can be used in a sense wherein it is presupposed she refused the offer, whereas (1) does not seem to have such a use (merely retaining the **possibility** of the complement being either true or false).

[19] Vendler's terminology shows its strength here. He resisted calling the relevant *wh*-nominals *indirect questions* (though that is what they are traditionally called), preferring a new term—INDIRECT CLAIMS. That is the point, I think. The substitution of indirect questions preserving grammaticality is only a test for factive clausehood when the indirect questions are indirect claims. When they are indirect quotations of questions—which they all are on the nonfactive uses of communication verbs—they are not indirect questions in the relevant sense.

[20] We can now question why the complements of all nonfactives (wherein only a proposition is REFERRED to) cannot be taken to be indirect quotations (like communication and conjecture verb complements), for they are all thoughts (mental acts and/or states paralleling speech acts). Of course, nonfactives could be viewed that way, but differ remember in that the nonfactive conjecture and communication verbs **do** take seemingly relevant *wh*-nominals. The question was why they do [in the face of (*F*/*P*) and (*DEF*)]. (There simply is no such problem for the other nonfactives.) The answer that indirect quotation is involved makes perfectly good sense for communication verbs and extends by analogy to conjecture verbs. Such further extension is not needed for the other nonfactives. (If it were, then indeed (*F*/*P*) and (DEF) would be rather ad hoc, stipulative, and trivial.)

The most troublesome counterexamples are emotive predicates that are factives. Since some do not seem to permit indirect question substitution preserving grammaticality, the necessity condition (an NP is a factive clause only if the substitution goes through) is apparently violated. Consider *regret* (like *resent* and *deplore*). The following are ungrammatical for some English speakers (and at best only borderline grammatical for others):

(40) **I regret (it) who left the meeting early.*
**John regretted how Mary wrote the letter.*
**Mary regretted when John refused the offer.*

Yet *regret* is one of the prime examples of factive verbs and is constantly used as a perfect example for the semantic negation test. But also notice that emotive factives taking factive clauses in the subject (*important, crazy, odd,* etc.) **do** take indirect questions grammatically. I conclude that emotive factives taking factive clauses in the object are the sole genuine counterexamples to (*F/P*) and (*DEF*). Since this small class is such a singular exception, I am inclined to live with it and just hope that some fuller account of emotives will eventually explain why this subclass does not succumb.[21]

Another matter concerns circularity. In these paragraphs on communication and conjecture verbs, a certain air of circularity might seem to arise. For I defend (*F/P*) by saying that some indirect questions are not genuine or the relevant type on the nonfactive reading of certain kinds of verbs. So, evidently one must already be able to tell whether the verb in question is nonfactive to find out whether the indirect question is genuine or spurious. But indirect questions have to be used to find out if a verb (or use of a verb) is factive or nonfactive. So, we are in a circle. It can be avoided, I think, by just starting with the notion of a genuine indirect question (indirect claim) which must be distinguished from a spurious one like indirect quotation of a question. This distinction stands on its own, as grounded in the most simple examples with *say* (prior to questioning its factivity or HALF FACTIVITY). Then only genuine indirect questions (claims) are to be used in the test for factive clausehood and, subsequently, for predicate factivity. Extending the genuine–spurious indirect question distinction to conjecture verbs is somewhat strained I admit, but it is not entirely implausible.

[21] I am grateful to Kashi Wali for her persistence in pressing this counterexample. Kashi Wali has also suggested that my revision of factives is intimately connected with assertiveness (see Hooper, 1975). Maybe; but right now I think assertiveness, like emotiveness, just crossclassifies with factivity. Further, I recommend taking everything I say herein about assertives to apply to their nonparenthetical uses—uses that all assertives must have if something like Hooper's double assertion theory (p. 95) is true. For if a parenthetical use of an assertive amounts to two assertions, then the one of them which again has the assertive in it must be a nonparenthetical use (on pain of infinite regress).

The question of **event reference** and EVENTIVES arises by noting that some NPs would be apparently **mis**classified by (*F*/*P*). Although some NPs occurring with EVENTIVES—those predicates of (9)—pass test A(ii) of (*F*/*P*), others do not, but seem to pass test B. And the latter eventuality conflicts with the semantic data I believe. For example, (7) would pass test A(ii) if the indirect question replacement were, for example, *what Mary did.* Therefore, *Mary refuse the offer* would (when used in such a linguistic context) refer to a fact and, further, *watch* would be a factive. (This kind of result is what would motivate treating reference to events like reference to facts, rather than like reference to objects as I have sketched it.) However, some other indirect questions replacing *Mary refuse the offer* in (7), or *Mary's refusal of the offer* in *John watched Mary's refusal of the offer* (to mollify those who object that *Mary refuse the offer* in (7) is not an NP), would lead to ungrammatical surface forms. Consider (7)′.

(7)′ **John watched* {*who refused the offer* / *what Mary refused* / *when Mary refused the offer*}.

These are all ungrammatical when the verb objects are genuine indirect questions (indirect claims), not free relatives. (Of course, on the free relative uses of these strings, grammatical interpretations can be found. For example, *John watched the one who refused the offer* (*the thing which was refused*) [(?) *the time at which Mary refused the offer*].) So, it is possible to conclude that certain NPs fail test A(ii) and satisfy B and, as a consequence, conclude that they refer to propositions.

A modification of B of (*F*/*P*) partially resolves the problem. If some (or many) candidate indirect questions are tried as substitutions, as directed by A(ii) and none of them preserve grammaticality, then it would appear that B would be satisfied (or probably satisfied); that is, a proposition is referred to. But to block the mistaken (empirically undesired) attribution of reference to a proposition in some cases, a further elaboration of the proposition–reference condition B is needed. The elaboration that works is that it must be possible to substitute a full-sentence clause (a *that-p* clause, logically) in the same context while preserving grammaticality. That is, replace B of (*F*/*P*) with

B′ NP_i refers to a PROPOSITION if and only if

a. It satisfies A(i) but fails test A(ii), and
b. The deep structure containing the *de*vendlerized NP can generate a surface structure containing a

full-sentence clause (a *that-p* clause) where the resulting sentence is grammatical.

B′b is, again, a preservation-of-grammaticality test. Full-sentence substitution must preserve grammaticality in order to confirm reference to propositions rather than to facts.[22]

This leaves out certain complicated NPs such as those that refer to events (actions, activities, processes, and states). Another test, (E), clears up some of the rough edges.

(*E*) For an NP_i that is a gerundive, mixed case, or derived nominal in surface structure (or for which there is an analogous NP in near-surface structure, as with certain infinitives)

f. If replacing NP_i with *that* NP_i *occurs* (*occurred*) (or *that* NP_i *obtains* [*obtained*] for states) preserves grammaticality, NP_i refers to a fact or proposition

e. If grammaticality is not preserved in this substitution, then NP_i in its original context refers to an event (process, etc.).

Thus, we have two tests for event reference—failure of fact and proposition reference (through failure to preserve grammaticality through full-sentence substitution), and failure to preserve grammati-

[22] This may not seem so completely to nail down (7) as involving an event reference as it does *John followed Mary's acceptance of the offer with a lengthy speech* or *Mary's refusing the offer preceded the timely conviction of the worthy lawyers*. Substituting (*that*) *Mary refused the offer* in the latter two cases yields ungrammaticality, but it may be thought that (7) already contains such a substitution. Actually, it does not—at least not of the right type. The right type is one that permits *that* interpolation. That is, use *that* interpolation as a test of full-sentence clausehood—as in *John fears* (*believes, claimed,* etc.) *that Mary refused the offer* and *It's unlikely* (*probable*) *that Mary refused the offer*. Interesting questions arise with *cause,* for even though **John watched that Mary refused the offer* is ungrammatical, still *That Mary refused the offer caused John to be annoyed* might be all right. Yet, **Mary's acceptance caused that John was annoyed* is ungrammatical. I want to claim at the present time that the tests for event reference work well for all the eventives except *cause*. Indeed, the structure of *cause* (or of *causes*) is a topic for a large and complex study, for which the investigations reported herein should be regarded as necessary preliminaries.

A related matter is that *what . . . did* (*is*) phrases as in *what Mary did* (e.g., refuse the offer) or *what Mary is* (e.g., dead serious) might be considered indirect questions. Then, given the fact that (*F/P*) requires only some indirect question (not all or just one certain type), it could be thought that the eventives of (9) were nearly all factives since they all take phrases like *what Mary did* (*is*). This would be a mistake, for such phrases are not indirect questions, but free relatives; for example, *John watched what Mary did* paraphrases *John watched the action that Mary performed* (*or activity or process she was engaged in*).

cality through the addition of *occurs* (*occurred*) or *obtains* (*obtained*).[23] Some examples of event reference are (41) and (42).

(41) *Mary's refusal of the offer was followed by silence.*
B′ result:
(That) Mary refused the offer was followed by silence.
E result:
That Mary's refusal of the offer occurred was followed by silence.

(42) *Mary's refusal of the offer was tragic.*
B′ result:
That Mary refused the offer was tragic.
E result:
That Mary's refusal of the offer occurred was tragic.

The subject of (41), therefore, refers to an event and *was followed by* is an EVENTIVE (since presupposition of the event's occurrence remains through negation of the predicate). The subject of (42), however, is not referring to an event. Of course, the subject of (42) ought to have previously passed the A(ii) test of (*F*/*P*) to show it to be a factive clause and *tragic* a factive (the fact referred to remaining through predicate negation).

The idea behind E can be extended to problematic clauses like *what Mary did* (concerning whether it is a genuine indirect question). For example, applying E to

(43) *What Mary did happened before lunch.*

(counting *what Mary did* as a relevant NP_i even though it is not a derived nominal, gerundive, or mixed case) yields

(44) **That what Mary did occurred happened before lunch.*

[23] *Obtain* is not wholly satisfactory here, but something similar is needed. For with states, it is awkward (at the least) to conclude *Mary's fatigue* in *John discovered Mary's fatigue* refers to a fact because *John discovered that Mary's fatigue occurred* is all right. *John discovered that Mary's fatigue obtained* is not much better. Yet, something like it seems required in order to conclude that *Mary's fatigue* in *Mary's fatigue lasted two days* refers to an event (an extended sense of *event*, that is, because it is an occurrent state) since **That Mary's fatigue obtained* (?*occurred*) *lasted two days* is ungrammatical. (A generic word for the existence of states like *occurs* is for the existence of events, processes, actions, and activities is seemingly hard to come by.)

This shows that the subject NP of (43) refers to an event.[24] Some readers might notice, however, that full sentences sometimes seem grammatical (or very nearly so) in the event phrase position. Consider (45) for example.

(45) a. *That Mary refused the offer caused John's strange behavior.*
b. *That Mary refused the offer was the cause of John's behavior.*
c. *That Mary refused the offer was the reason for John's behavior.*

I think a and b are rather questionable. But those who find all of (45) acceptable might also find (46) grammatically acceptable.

(46) *That Mary's refusal of the offer occurred caused John's behavior.*

I believe there is a resolution of these supposedly troublesome cases (along the line of a more complicated analysis utilizing free relatives, cf. Peterson, 1977a) and will here presume that qualms based on (45) are insufficient to disconfirm the general characterization of event phrases and, thereby, of EVENTIVES that I have achieved. (Also, cf. Peterson, 1978.)

5. ON REPRESENTING FACT REFERENCE

Therefore, event phrases are syntactically and semantically distinct (at least in English) from phrases for facts (factive clauses) and phrases for propositions (factive clause candidates that fail). In fact, the syntactical tests give some ground for the difference (fine, perhaps) I have incorporated in my articulation of the semantic tests. The semantic tests are both preservation-of-presupposition-through-negation tests. However, with factives I have said that the fact presupposed with a use of a sentence containing a factive predicate remains presupposed through negation, whereas with eventives I have said the occurrence of the event remains presupposed through negation. An objection could be that this is only a verbal difference in stating the semantic characterizations. One could just as well put both tests in exactly the same form by introducing the concept of a fact obtaining. (This use of

[24] Also, remembering (B)′ and again permitting the alleged indirect question *what Mary did* to count as a relevant NP_i still produces an ungrammatical result—namely, **That Mary refused the offer happened before lunch.*

obtain must be distinct from states obtaining in parallel with events occurring and also be distinct from states-of-affairs obtaining.) Facts do not occur or exist (properly speaking), but do obtain. That is, actual facts obtain and merely potential and nonactual facts do not obtain. So, we could make the semantic negation tests exactly parallel each other by stating them as follows:

Factive: A predicate is a factive if and only if the presupposition that a fact obtains (the one referred to by a factive clause in the context) remains presupposed through negation of the predicate.

Eventive: A predicate is an eventive if and only if the presupposition that an event occurs (the one referred to by an event phrase in the context) remains presupposed through negation of the predicate.

I believe this is a legitimate, and not too misleading, paraphrase of the main semantic characterizations. Still, I insist there is a difference worth respecting due to the syntactic differences just revealed. Also, it is worth remembering to respect the difference by not introducing the close parallel that results from utilizing *obtains.* I believe, as I will argue, that the noted differences are sufficient to give some independent syntactic support for marking a difference in semantic representation (as well as in the informal semantic characterizations eschewing the new *obtains*).

In light of the semantic representation speculations I began with (concerning specific reference and event phrases), one might suppose that the same approach ought to be utilized for fact references and presuppositions. Thus, one might propose (47) as a representation of (4) to parallel (17b) as a representation of (7).

(47) ***I assert*** (***John presupposed*** $(\mathrm{E}x)(\mathrm{F}x \;\&\; (y)(\mathrm{F}y \supset x = y) \;\&$ *John realized* x))

where "Fx" =df. "x is the (or a) fact of Mary refusing the offer"

(which, if the distinction between facts and events is to be respected as I have argued, must be a distinct predicate from "Rx," the event predicate used above). I have many qualms about this, principally, about the quantification over positions other than that of logical subject. For even though verb objects can certainly be logical subjects—for example, as in *John saw Mary* (and so John saw someone) and *John watched Mary's refusal* (and so John watched something, an event)—verb objects that are neither objects nor events but facts and propositions (such as some objects of *forget* and *fear*) may still seem to be as suspicious for quantification over as are predicates. (E.g., should we permit "(EF)(F(John))" as a representation of *John is (or does) something*"?) To avoid straightforward and primitive quantification over facts, however, is not easy and requires more virtuoso (or frustrating) notational manipulation than that in which I have already engaged. I will sketch it in conclusion to demonstrate that treating fact (and proposition) reference as parallel to object and event reference is in any case tortuous and therefore suspicious.

I postulated event predicates like "Rx" above, being a notational abbreviation for *x is **an** event of Mary refusing the offer*. With such a predicate, the specific event of Mary refusing the offer could be abbreviated by "$(\iota x)(Rx)$."

(48) "$(\iota x)(Rx)$" =df. "***the*** event of Mary refusing the offer"

What this definite description for a specific event refers to can be identified with a particular occurrence and, as a result, related to the proposition that Mary refuses the offer as in (49).

(49) $$(\iota x)(Rx) = (\iota y)(y \text{ occurs iff } p)$$

Where "p" =df. "Mary refuses the offer."[25] The identity of (49) amounts to something very like (or exactly the same as) event abstraction. For it should be read *The event of Mary refusing the offer is the same thing as that which occurs if and only if Mary refuses the offer.* This enables us to obtain a logical subject position for quantification over events through a definition that (*a*) mentions propositions (i.e., the final clause after iff mentions a proposition, cf. footnote 28); but (*b*) does not quantify over them (since a position for quantifying over them is not yet specified, quantification over positions flanking logical connectives not being orthodox).[26] The same procedure can be fol-

[25] The *iff* (*if and only if*) is not, of course, simply material equivalence. But neither is it mutual entailment (necessary equivalence). I suspect it must be (here and elsewhere following) something like analytical equivalence of a species stronger than mutual logical entailment. The details of this stronger equivalence—which is also needed to defend Peterson, 1971—are very important to work out. But not in this paper.

[26] If some way were devised to incorporate the substitution of the right side of (49) into the deepest possible (logical and/or semantic–syntactic) structure for every sentence containing an expression referring to an event, then there would be (I would guess now) a logically oriented development of motivations very like or the same as those for generative semantics and/or abstract syntax (i.e., events would be "eliminated" transformationally). I suspect that such an approach is not very promising and that the prudent course is to suppose that (49) would be incorporated in the semantic component of a grammar as a sort of semantic equivalence rule (meaning postulate).

lowed to derive analogous formulas for quantification over facts and propositions.

To represent reference to facts and propositions, first define two special predicates:

(50) $$\text{“}\mathcal{M}(u, v)\text{”} = \text{df. “}u \text{ makes } v \text{ true”}$$
$$\text{“}\mathcal{T}(u)\text{”} = \text{df. “}u \text{ is true”}$$

The idea here is that facts make propositions true, and that propositions alone are said to be true, to bear truth values.[27] A definite description for use in referring to a specific proposition can be defined then

(51) "the proposition that p" =df. "$(\imath y)(\mathcal{T}(y) \text{ iff } p)$"

where p is filled by a declarative sentence such as *Mary refused the offer*. (As should be obvious now, care should be taken not to jump to conclusions about what a sentence clause is or refers to.) That is, propositions are those THINGS which are true or false. A definite description for use in referring to a specific fact can be defined

(52) "The fact that p = df. "$(\imath x)(\mathcal{M}(x, (\imath y)(\mathcal{T}(y) \text{ iff } p)))$"

where again "p" is filled by some declarative sentence such as *Mary refused the offer*. That is, facts are those THINGS which make a proposition true.[28] Consider, for example, the proposition that Mary refused the offer.

[27] The predicate "$\mathcal{T}$" is eliminable, though I will not carry out the elimination. For example:

$$\text{“}\mathcal{T}\text{”}(u)\text{”} = \text{df. “}(\mathrm{E}x)\mathcal{M}(x,u)\text{”}$$

The reverse, elimination "$\mathcal{M}$" in favor of "$\mathcal{T}$", is also possible. For example,

$$\text{“}\mathcal{M}(u, v)\text{”} = \text{df. “Makes }(u, \mathcal{T}(v))\text{”}$$

The latter may be much more interesting grammatically, especially if the *Makes* predicate is syntactically and semantically fundamental in other ways (a fundamental species of *cause*, for instance).

[28] I said that "p" mentioned a proposition in (50). One might wonder what "p" mentions (loosely, what it REFERS to) in (51) and (52). Is it still a proposition? Or a fact for (52) and a proposition for (51)? First, if we apply (*F*/*P*) to such formulas (or to the stilted English they directly generate), then both are propositions. (I.e., *if and only if* cannot be grammatically followed by indirect questions.) But, secondly, does (*F*/*P*) show the position of "u" in "$\mathcal{M}(u, v)$" to be a factive clause (a position for expressions REFERRING to facts). I think it might. But discovering whether it does or not must await further investigations of *make* and *causes*.

(53) a. "The proposition that Mary refused the offer" =df. "$(\imath y)(\mathcal{T}(y)$ iff Mary refused the offer))"
b. "the fact that Mary refused the offer" =df. $(\imath x)(\mathcal{M}(x, (\imath y)(\mathcal{T}(y)$ iff Mary refused the offer)))"

The definiens of (53b) can be stated (in admittedly awkward English): *That* [fact] *which makes true that* [proposition] *which is true if and only if Mary refused the offer.*

With these incredible notational devices, we can design a format sufficiently similar to those representations for references to objects and events which respects the real linguistic differences between objects and events on the one hand and facts and propositions on the other. One simple example to suggest how this is to be done is (54), a representation of (4) (wherein fact reference is subject-specific).

(54) ***I assert*** (*John* ***presupposed*** $(Ex)(\mathcal{M}(x, (\imath y)(\mathcal{T}(y)$ *iff Mary refused the offer*) & $(w)((\mathcal{M}(w, (\imath y)(\mathcal{T}(y)$ *iff Mary refused the offer*) $\supset w = x)$ & *John realized* x))

It is not at all clear that such a representation is a good candidate for being the genuine (legitimate, revealing, and/or logically adequate) semantic representation (or a guide to it) for a particular use of (4). Perhaps it only represents some use of a sentence that expresses a proposition which is logically equivalent to what (4) can be used to express. I would prefer to investigate other ways of representing straightforward factives (and related nonfactives) before accepting this tortuous method of emulating the representations of references to objects and events.

APPENDIX: IMPLICATIONS FOR MONTAGUE GRAMMAR

Because there is considerable interest today in utilizing Montague's approach to semantic representation (via extensions and modifications of his ideas particularly as they are expressed in "The Proper Treatment of Quantification in Ordinary English" [PTQ], Montague, 1974), it may be useful to outline some implications of what I have shown for Montague Grammar. The following remarks should be understood to be preliminary speculations providing, at best, some hypotheses for investigations.

Sentences like *The King of France is bald* are semantically represented in Montage Grammar by translations into formulas of his particular brand of intensional logic. In the interesting intensional contexts, *The King of France is bald* is represented by a formula expressing a membership relation; for example, some formula roughly tantamount to (A_1).[29]

(A_1) *The property of being bald is a member of the set of properties of an existing and unique King of France.*

Since my preceding arguments have shown that event reference should be treated as similar to reference to objects, *Mary's refusal of the offer happened before lunch* ought to be represented semantically (i.e., translated into appropriate notations of intensional logic) in a directly analogous way by a formula also expressing a membership relation, one roughly tantamount to (A_2).

(A_2) *The property of happening-before-lunch is a member of the set of properties of an event of Mary refusing the offer.*

That is, event occurrence ought to be (*a*) paralleled to unique existence of determinate kinds of objects; and (*b*) contrasted with the treatment of factive presuppositions. (Also, it is not clear that events need to be entirely new kinds of basic entities. It seems likely that on Montague's, or almost any other, approach they can be defined as derived entities (e.g., meaning postulates formulated which define events in terms of objects, properties, relations, etc.)

How should factive presuppositions be represented in Montague Grammar terms in order to establish a contrast? The easiest way is simply to adopt the extension of Montague Grammar (proposed by Karttunen and Peters) of representing conventional implicatures. That is, permit a conventional implicature representation to represent the presuppositions relating to factives and prohibit that for referential presuppositions. For example, for *It's significant that Mary refused the offer*, represent it in a formula like (A_3).

(A_3)
a. *The property of being-significant is a member of the set of properties of a unique fact of Mary refusing the offer.*
b. *The property of refusing the offer is a member of the set of properties of Mary.*

[29] For the sake of clarity as well as brevity I eschew Montague's notations and discuss what typical Montague notations would be aimed at representing informally and without giving any details.

where (A_3a) is to capture the meaning of (proposition expressed or assertion made by) *It's significant that Mary refused the offer* and (A_3b) is to capture the conventional implicature. (Further, it can be left open which failures of conventional implicature result in truth-valuelessness and which do not.) (Again, a derived entity, a fact, must be utilized, but it is also probably definable via appropriate meaning postulates.)

This approach to marking a difference between referential and factive presuppositions amounts to adopting Russell's theory within intensional contexts for referential presuppositions (intensionalizing Russell, which Montague has already done in PTQ) and adopting a descendent of Grice's theory for factive presuppositions. I do not find this minimal strategy very exciting. Some other alternative(s) ought to be devisable which utilize(s) more of the details of the results reported herein. What I believe to be especially significant in my suggestions for semantic representations for referential presuppositions is the QUANTIFYING OUT of presuppositions into proposition asserted (a kind of scope crossing that can seem misleading if not perverse at first, but which proves harmless). That is, some object or event is presupposed to uniquely exist in the assertion about it to the effect that it has some property or stands in some relation. The same thing, I suggest, should **not** be thought to occur with factive presuppositions (no QUANTIFYING OUT). How could this be captured in a further extension or modification of Montague Grammar? I suggest speculatively that the following ought to be one candidate for approaching a suitable extension (hopefully, there will be others).

First, let both kinds of presuppositions (referential and factive) be represented as conventional implicatures à la Karttunen and Peters. That is, add to (A_1) a conventional implicature representation (A_4).

(A_4) *The properties of a unique King of France are instantiated.*

But this appears to make the Montaguesque representations [which, remember, I have only described, not actually given in (A_1) through (A_3)] directly analogous in the two cases. Actually, they would not be tightly analogous, for (A_1) needs a further detail that (A_3) does not. For it must also be clearly shown that what is represented as instantiating the properties in question by (A_4) is the same entity (an object or event as the case may be) that (A_1) mentions; that is, the revised (A_1) ought to represent something like (A_1)′.

(A_1') a. *The property of being bald is a member of the set of properties of an existing unique King of France, k.*
b. *The properties of a unique king of France are instantiated in k.*

where *k* denotes a unique object. Alternatively, consider (A_1)″ which I prefer because of the explicit display of a variable-binding operation form (A_1b)″ to (A_1a)″.

a. *The property of being bald is a member of the set of properties of an existing, unique King of France,* x_i ←
b. *The properties of a unique King of France are instantiated in some entity* x_i ——

where the arrow represents the QUANTIFYING OUT more clearly represented in formulas like (13b) and (17b) in this chapter.

The point is that factive presuppositions will not require such intimate connection (QUANTIFYING OUT) between proposition representation and conventional implicature representation. Perhaps it is on the basis of such a contrast that factive presuppositions and any other nonreferential presuppositions might be proposed to not create truth-valuelessness when the presupposition is not satisfied. They need not create Russellianly false propositions either, but often simply true ones with mistaken presuppositions; for example, (*a*) a use of *Tarski lived in Princeton* is true, even though one presupposition of its past tense is false, namely, that Tarski died; or (*b*) a use of *The American spaceship failed to land on Venus* is true even though the conventional implicature (presupposition) that the spaceship was intended to land there is false. That is, some kinds of false presuppositions do not cause the assertion involved to be Russellianly false, Strawsonianaly truth-valueless, or even Austinianly infelicitous at the rhetic act stage (Though I do not think all assertions with false nonreferential presuppositions can be true, for example, some of the most straightforward factives.)

In sum, when QUANTIFYING OUT of a conventional implicature (because it is a referential presupposition), truth-valuelessness (or, failure to express a proposition that could be true or false) does occur when the implicature is false, but truth-valuelessness need not occur in the other (nonreferential, non-QUANTIFYING OUT) cases of conventional implicature failure.

REFERENCES

Chomsky, N. Remarks on Nominalization. In R. Jacobs and J. Rosenbaum (Eds.), *Readings in English transformational grammar.* Boston: Ginn, 1970).

Hooper, J. On assertive predicates. In J. Kimball (ed.), *Syntax and Semantics* 4. New York: Academic Press, 1975. Pp. 91–124.

Karttunen, L., & Peters, S. What indirect questions conventionally implicate. In *Papers from the 12th Regional Meeting of the Chicago Linguistic Society.* Chicago: University of Chicago Press, 1976.

Katz, J. On defining "presupposition." *Linguistic Inquiry,* 1973, *4,* 256–260.

Kiparsky, P., & Kiparsky, C. Fact. In D. Steinberg & L. Jakobvits (Eds.), *Semantics.* Cambridge: Cambridge University Press, 1971.

Montague, R. The Proper Treatment of Quantification in Ordinary English. In R. Thomason (Ed.), *Formal philosophy: Selected papers of Richard Montague.* New Haven: Yale University Press, 1974.

Palacas, A. Specificness in generative grammar. Forthcoming in a *Festschrift* for W. P. Lehmann.

Peterson, P. L. Grelling's paradox: Some remarks on the grammar of its logic. Paper presented at the 4th International Congress on Logic, Methodology, and the Philosophy of Science, Bucharest, 1971.

Peterson, P. L., On the logical representation of specific noun phrases. In *Proceedings of the 5th International Congress on Logic, Methodology, and the Philosophy of Science.* Preprinted volume, pp. XI 23–24, University of Western Ontario, 1975.

Peterson, P. L. An abuse of terminology: Donnellan's distinction in recent grammar. *Foundations of Language,* 1976, *14,* 239–242. (a)

Peterson, P. L. On specific reference. *Semantikos,* 1976, *1* (3), 63–81.(b)

Peterson, P. L. Facts and Propositions. Paper presented at the Conference on Philosophy of Language, N.Y. State University College at Buffalo, February 26, 1977.(a)

Peterson, P. L. How to infer belief from knowledge. *Philosophical Studies,* 1977, *32,* 203–209.(b)

Peterson, P. L. What causes effects? Unpublished manuscript, 1978.

Ross, J. R. On Declarative Sentences. In R. Jacobs and J. Rosenbaum (Eds.), *Readings in English transformational grammar.* Boston: Ginn, 1970.

Vendler, Z. *Res cogitans: An essay in rational psychology.* Ithaca, New York: Cornell University Press, 1972.

TRUTH-VALUE GAPS, MANY TRUTH VALUES, AND POSSIBLE WORLDS[1]

S. K. THOMASON

Simon Fraser University

The topic of this chapter is mathematical models for presupposition. I will suggest some particular models of my own, but the main point I want to make is that there are two quite different things for such models to do, and that it is unreasonable to expect any one model to do both.

1. MODELS FOR IMPLICATION

Let me first illustrate with a simpler problem, that of implication. One thing a model can do is specify an implication relation between sentences of a suitable formal object language. This formally defined relation should be transparently analogous to our intuitive notion of implication, so the apparatus of the model should not include anything ontologically dubious, like "possible worlds" or "intermediate truth values."

Classical logic supplies such a model, as follows. The object language L is that of first-order predicate logic, with an identity symbol $=$, a set Pred_m of m-place predicate symbols for each $m \geqslant 1$, and a set Const of constant symbols. A STRUCTURE is a triple $\mathscr{A} = (D, f, g)$,

[1] This work was supported in part by the National Research Council of Canada.

Syntax and Semantics, Volume 11: Presupposition

ISBN 0-12-613511-8

where D is a nonempty set, f assigns to each m-place predicate symbol an m-ary relation on D, and g assigns to each constant symbol an element of D:

$$f(P) \subseteq D^m = \{(d_1, \ldots, d_m): d_1, \ldots, d_m \in D\} \quad \text{if } P \in \text{Pred}_m,$$
$$g(a) \in D \quad \text{if } a \in \text{Const}.$$

A VALUATION for $\mathscr{A}$ is a pair (V, W) of functions, such that W assigns to each term a member of D

$$W: \text{Term} \longrightarrow D$$

and V assigns to each formula either 1 ("True") or 0 ("False")

$$V: \text{Fla} \longrightarrow \{0, 1\}$$

satisfying (1)–(8):

(1) $W(a) = g(a)$, if $a \in \text{Const}$,

(2) $V(Pt_1 \ldots t_m) = 1$ iff $(W(t_1), \ldots, W(t_m)) \in f(P)$, if $t_1, \ldots, t_m \in \text{Term}$ and $P \in \text{Pred}_m$,

(3) $V(t_1 = t_2) = 1$ iff $W(t_1) = W(t_2)$, if $t_1, t_2 \in \text{Term}$,

(4) $V(\neg\phi) = 1$ iff $V(\phi) \neq 1$,

(5) $V(\phi \vee \psi) = 1$ iff $V(\phi) = 1$ or $V(\psi) = 1$,

(6) $V(\phi \wedge \psi) = 1$ iff $V(\phi) = 1$ and $V(\psi) = 1$,

(7) $V(\exists x\phi) = 1$ iff $V'(\phi) = 1$ for some $(V', W') \approx_x (V, W)$,

(8) $V(\forall x\phi) = 1$ iff $V'(\phi) = 1$ for all $(V', W') \approx_x (V, W)$,

(where $(V', W') \approx_x (V, W)$ means that $W'(y) = W(y)$ for every variable y other than x).

If ϕ is a sentence, that is, a formula without free variables, then $V(\phi)$ is independent of (V, W) and we write $\mathscr{A}(\phi)$ for $V(\phi)$. Finally, we define ϕ IMPLIES ψ if whenever ϕ is true then ψ is true:

$$\phi \text{ implies } \psi \quad \text{iff} \quad (\forall \mathscr{A})(\mathscr{A}(\phi) = 1 \Rightarrow \mathscr{A}(\psi) = 1),$$

and, incidentally, ϕ is LOGICALLY TRUE if ϕ is always true:

$$\phi \text{ is logically true} \quad \text{iff} \quad (\forall \mathscr{A})(\mathscr{A}(\phi) = 1).$$

Now, on what basis is this accepted as a good model of implication? The reasons are intuitive, and not subject to mathematical proof. We perceive that statements in English can be "formalized" in L, so that one statement implies another, according to our intuitive understanding of implication, if and only if the sentence of L which formalizes the one implies, according to the formal definition, the sentence of L which formalizes the other.

The model just described I will call a METALANGUAGE model of implication, since it introduces an implication relation into the metalanguage. The other sort of model introduces an implication CONNECTIVE, $\longrightarrow$, into an object language, so I shall call it an OBJECT-LANGUAGE model. Its purpose is not to define a formal notion of implication—that was done already by the metalanguage model—but to display perspicuously some properties of that notion.

What sort of properties? Let $D_{\mathcal{M}}$ be the set of sentences of L. Sentences can be combined by negation, disjunction, and conjunction, so introduce corresponding operations $f^{\neg}_{\mathcal{M}}, f^{\vee}_{\mathcal{M}}$, and $f^{\wedge}_{\mathcal{M}}$ on $D_{\mathcal{M}}$. Now introduce the relation $I_{\mathcal{M}}$, to hold of two members of $D_{\mathcal{M}}$ just when the first implies the second (according to the metalanguage model). I have just defined a structure $\mathcal{M}$ for the first order language $L_{\mathcal{M}}$ having a relation symbol I and operation symbols $f^{\neg}, f^{\vee}$, and $f^{\wedge}$. I have in mind the sort of properties expressed by sentences of $L_{\mathcal{M}}$; for example, the sentences

$$\forall x \forall y (Ixy \vee Iyx)$$
$$\forall x \forall y (I(x, f^{\vee}(f^{\neg})(y), y)).$$

The first sentence is false in $\mathcal{M}$, since neither Pa nor Pb implies the other, and the second is true in $\mathcal{M}$ since ϕ implies $\psi \vee \neg\psi$ for any sentences ϕ and ψ.

Thus, the duty of an object-language model is to indicate which sentences of $L_{\mathcal{M}}$ are true in $\mathcal{M}$. But perspicuity is important, so a SIMPLE model which works for, say, the universal sentences (like the previous examples), might be as useful as a more complicated one which works for all sentences.

In fact, this is just what happens. Propositional modal logic, with $\longrightarrow$ treated as strict implication (in any normal system no stronger than S5) works for the universal sentences of $L_{\mathcal{M}}$. Add propositional quantifiers (and stick to S5), and it works for all sentences. I will not bother to state these claims precisely now. I will just ask you to realize that it is mathematically provable that strict implication is, in a precisely specifiable sense, a correct representation of the implication relation defined by the metalanguage model. So the object-language model can be judged by comparison with the metalanguage model, and there is no need for the object-language model to correspond transparently to our intuitions or to be ontologically modest.

2. A METALANGUAGE MODEL FOR PRESUPPOSITION

Now let us turn to the problem of presupposition, using the previous work on implication as a guide. Bas C. van Fraassen's discussions of presupposition (1968, 1969) sacrifice precision for the sake of generality, but we can reconstruct a plausible metalanguage model of presupposition from his work on truth-value gaps (1966, 1968). The object language is that of first-order predicate logic, augmented by an existence predicate E. Such a language is capable of accounting for presuppositions occasioned by nonreferring proper names, as *Pegasus has a white hind leg*, and (which seems to have been van Fraassen's main concern) of differentiating between implication and presupposition: Pa implies, but does not presuppose, itself, and presupposes, but does not imply, Ea.

However, this object language is not really rich enough for a metalanguage model of presupposition. It OUGHT to be rich enough that EVERY genuine instance of presupposition is formalizable. I will not pretend to do that, but will make my object language rich enough to formalize Strawson's examples (1952) concerning the king of France and all John's children. Let L' then be L augmented by an existence predicate, a definite description operator, and a restricted generalization operator:

$$\begin{array}{ll} Et \in \text{Fla} & \text{If } t \in \text{Term}, \\ ix\phi \in \text{Term} & \text{if } \phi \in \text{Fla} \quad \text{and} \quad x \in \text{Var}, \\ (\forall x|\phi)\psi \in \text{Fla} & \text{if } \phi, \psi \in \text{Fla} \quad \text{and} \quad x \in \text{Var}. \end{array}$$

The definition of structure is almost the same as before, only now we permit $g(a)$ to be undefined for some (or all) constants a. I will soon define VALUATION (V, W) for a structure $\mathscr{A}$; define ϕ PRESUPPOSES ψ if whenever ϕ is either true or false then ψ is true, and also define LOGICALLY TRUE, IMPLIES, and NECESSITATES:

$$\begin{array}{lll} \phi \text{ presupposes } \psi & \text{iff} & (\forall\mathscr{A})(\mathscr{A}(\phi) \in \{0, 1\} \Rightarrow \mathscr{A}(\psi) = 1), \\ \phi \text{ is logically true} & \text{iff} & (\forall\mathscr{A})(\mathscr{A}(\phi) = 1), \\ \phi \text{ implies } \psi & \text{iff} & (\forall\mathscr{A})(\mathscr{A}(\phi) = 1 \Rightarrow \mathscr{A}(\psi) = 1 \\ & & \qquad \& \ \mathscr{A}(\psi) = 0 \Rightarrow \mathscr{A}(\phi) = 0), \\ \phi \text{ necessitates } \psi & \text{iff} & (\forall\mathscr{A})(\mathscr{A}(\phi) = 1 \Rightarrow \mathscr{A}(\psi) = 1). \end{array}$$

Obviously, we cannot have V:Fla $\longrightarrow \{0, 1\}$ as before; V must be permitted either to take on values other than 0 and 1 or to be undefined for some formulas. That is, we must admit either many truth values or truth-value gaps. Like van Fraassen, I will use truth-value gaps; but unlike him, I will use them in an inessential way. My model will require only trivial modifications to fit a three-valued framework —for an arbitrary finite number of truth values, change "trivial" to "minor."

A valuation (V, W) then, for a structure $\mathscr{A} = (D, f, g)$, is a pair of partially defined functions V:Fla $\longrightarrow \{0, 1\}$ and W:Term $\longrightarrow D$, satisfying certain conditions. The first 19 conditions I take to be uncontentious:

(9) $W(x) \in D$ if $x \in$ Var,

(10) $W(a) = g(a)$ if $g(a)$ is defined,

(11) $W(a)$ is undefined if $g(a)$ is undefined,

(12) $V(\neg\phi) = 1$ iff it is not the case that $V(\phi) = 1$,

(13) $V(\neg\phi) = 0$ iff $V(\phi) = 1$,

(14) $V(\phi \vee \psi) = 1$ iff $V(\phi) = 1$ or $V(\psi) = 1$,

(15) $V(\phi \vee \psi) = 0$ iff $V(\phi) = V(\psi) = 0$,

(16) $V(\phi \wedge \psi) = 1$ iff $V(\phi) = V(\psi) = 1$,

(17) $V(\phi \wedge \psi) = 0$ iff $V(\phi) = 0$ or $V(\psi) = 0$,

(18) $V(\forall x\phi) = 1$ iff $V'(\phi) = 1$ for all $(V', W') \approx_x (V, W)$,

(19) $V(\forall x\phi) = 0$ iff $V'(\phi) = 0$ for some $(V', W') \approx_x (V, W)$,

(20) $V(\exists x\phi) = 1$ iff $V'(\phi) = 1$ for some $(V', W') \approx_x (V, W)$,

(21) $V(\exists x\phi) = 0$ iff $V'(\phi) = 0$ for all $(V', W') \approx_x (V, W)$,

(22) $V((\forall x|\phi)\psi) = 1$ iff $V(\exists x\phi) = 1$ and, for every $(V', W') \approx_x (V, W)$, if $V'(\phi) = 1$ then $V'(\psi) = 1$,

(23) $V((\forall x|\phi)\psi) = 0$ iff $V(\exists x\phi) = 1$ and,
for some $(V', W') \approx_x (V, W)$,
$V'(\phi) = 1$ and $V'(\psi) = 0$,

(24) $V(Et) = 1$ iff $W(t)$ is defined,

(25) $V(Et) = 0$ iff $W(t)$ is undefined,

(26) if $W(t_1), \ldots, W(t_m)$ are all defined, then
$V(Pt_1 \ldots t_m) = 1$ iff $(W(t_1), \ldots, W(t_m)) \in f(P)$,
$V(Pt_1 \ldots t_m) = 0$ iff $(W(t_1), \ldots, W(t_m)) \notin f(P)$,

(27) if $W(t_1)$ and $W(t_2)$ are both defined, then
$V(t_1 = t_2) = 1$ iff $W(t_1) = W(t_2)$,
$V(t_1 = t_2) = 0$ iff $W(t_1) \neq W(t_2)$,

(28) $W(ix\phi) = d$ iff, for all $(V', W') \approx_x (V, W)$,
$V'(\phi) = 1$ iff $W'(x) = d$.

According to (12) and (13), the negation of a statement is true if and only if the statement is not true, and false if and only if the statement is true. A disjunction, by (14) and (15), is true just when at least one disjunct is true, false just when both disjuncts are false (and, consequently, lacking truth value in the remaining cases). According to (22) and (23), *All John's children are asleep* is true exactly if John has at least one child and all his children are asleep, false exactly if John has at least one child who is not asleep, and lacking truth value if John is childless. A definite description, according to (28), refers to the unique object satisfying the description, if there is a unique such object, and otherwise fails to refer.

The conditions (10), and (12)–(21) are just an elaboration of the classical (1)–(8), elaboration being necessary because V and W may now be undefined for some arguments. If ϕ is a formula of L (the classical language) and $g(a)$ is defined for every constant a occurring in ϕ, then the calculation of $V(\phi)$ using these conditions is exactly the same as the calculation using (1)–(8). Therefore, in particular, a sentence of L having no constant symbols is logically true in the present sense if and only if it is in the classical sense.

It remains to be decided what to do with $Pt_1 \ldots t_m$ and $t_1 = t_2$ when one of the terms fails to refer. With van Fraassen, I will require that $Pt_1 \ldots t_m$ lack truth value in that event:

(29) If any of $W(t_1), \ldots, W(t_m)$ is undefined,
then $V(Pt_1 \ldots t_m)$ is undefined.

I think this is probably an oversimplification, that some predicates (for example, *was worshipped by*) CAN be truly or falsely asserted of nonreferring terms in some argument places. It would complicate things only technically to avoid the oversimplification by equipping each predicate symbol with some numerical superscripts, so I will not bother. Understand the predicate symbols as representing, not arbitrary predicates, but arbitrary existence-presupposing predicates.

Unlike van Fraassen, I will treat identity as existence-presupposing:

(30) If either or both of $W(t_1)$ and $W(t_2)$ is undefined, then $V(t_1 = t_2)$ is undefined.

My reasons are three. First, I cannot decide whether *Santa Claus is the president of the United States* asserts that Santa is identical to Jimmy Carter (and so, according to van Fraassen, is false) or that he has the property of president-of-the-United-States-ness (and so is lacking truth-value). So I would like to minimize the formal significance of the distinction. Second, I suspect that one reason for declaring an identity statement to be false when one term refers and the other does not is to permit the eliminability of the existence predicate in favor of the identity predicate. Contrary to what might be supposed, such an elimination is permitted by (9)–(30): Et and $\neg\neg(\exists x)(x = t)$ are logically equivalent in the strongest sense—if either of $V(Et)$ and $V(\neg\neg(\exists x)(x = t))$ is defined, then they both are, and they are equal. Finally, the view that $t = t$ should be logically true, even though t may fail to refer, leads to some difficulties in a language admitting definite descriptions. If $ixPx = ixPx$ is to be logically true, then probably so also should be $ixPx = ix((Qx \vee \neg Qx) \wedge Px)$ and even $ix(Rx \wedge \neg Rx) = ix(Qx \wedge \neg Qx)$. But there seems to be no natural way of specifying $V(t_1 = t_2)$ which accomplishes this, short of setting $V(t_1 = t_2) = 1$ whenever both $W(t_1)$ and $W(t_2)$ are undefined. It would not bother me too much to have *Santa Claus is the president of the United States* be false, but I cannot accept that *the square circle* = *the greatest prime* is true-as-a-matter-of-logic.

It may be instructive to compare the notions of logical truth as defined classically (c-logical truth), by van Fraassen's metalanguage model for presupposition (v-logical truth), and by the present model (p-logical truth), for sentences of L. If no constants occur in such a sentence, then the three notions coincide.

Suppose though that constants are allowed to occur (but the identity symbol is not). Every structure in the classical sense (c-structure) is a structure in the sense of the present model (p-structure), and every c-valuation is a p-valuation, and $V(\phi)$ is the same by (1)–(8) as by (9)–(30). So every sentence which is p-logically true is c-logically true. The converse fails, since $\neg Pa \supset \exists x \neg Px$ is c-logically true but not p-logically true—consider a structure in which $f(P) = D$ but $g(a)$ is undefined. Similarly, as van Fraassen shows, every v-logically true sentence is c-logically true, but not conversely.

Actually, van Fraassen shows that ϕ is v-logically true if and only if, for every p-structure $\mathscr{A}$ and "classical valuation" (V, W) for $\mathscr{A}$, $V(\phi) = 1$. A "classical valuation" (restricted to formulas of L without the identity symbol) is like a p-valuation, except that if any of $W(t_1), \ldots, W(t_m)$ is undefined then $V(Pt_1 \ldots t_m)$ is arbitrarily either 0 or 1.

If (V, W) is a p-valuation for $\mathscr{A}$, let (V', W') be the "classical valuation" which is like (V,W) except that $V'(Pt_1 \ldots t_m) = 0$ when $V(Pt_1 \ldots t_m)$ is undefined. Then $V'(\phi) = 1$ if and only if $V(\phi) = 1$ (by induction on the length of ϕ). This shows that every v-logical truth is a p-logical truth. The converse is not true, since $Pa \supset \exists x Px$ is p-logically true. Thus, for formulas of L without equality, van Fraassen's logical truths are properly contained in mine, which in turn are properly contained in those of classical logic.

How is it that I have come even closer to classical logic than van Fraassen, without resort to such contrivances as "classical valuations" and "supervaluations"? It is simple—I used the sort of negation which naturally preserves classical tautologies, even in the presence of truth-value gaps (or intermediate truth-values), while van Fraassen's negation does not. My negation is the sort exemplified by *It is not the case that Pegasus has a white hind leg* (a true statement), and van Fraassen's is found in *Pegasus does not have a white hind leg* (which is neither true nor false).

"Aha!" you say, "Wonderful new connectives." I think not. Both negations are truth functional, and easily expressible, in fact commonly expressed, in English. They were both there all the time. Classical logic has no need to differentiate them, but we are going beyond (not against!) classical logic, and have to give up some classically innocuous oversimplifications.

But can my object language really be "rich enough" without the other negation? Certainly not—let us add it. If you have any other pet connectives, add them too—so long as they are truth-functional. I am not being entirely facetious here—there ARE other important connectives, for example, the sort of conjunction which is true if both conjuncts are true, false if the first is false or if the first is true and the second false, and lacking truth value otherwise. Peters (1977) takes this as the prototypical *and*, which may be correct. At any rate, it does occur in English, and sometimes very usefully so.

Let L^* then be L', augmented by a new connective $\sim$, and add to the defining conditions for valuations

(31) $$V(\sim\phi) = 1 \text{ iff } V(\phi) = 0,$$

(32) $$V(\sim\phi) = 0 \text{ iff } V(\phi) = 1.$$

From now on, by the "metalanguage model for presupposition," I shall mean the model based on L^* and (9)–(32).

As promised, it is trivial to modify this model to accommodate a third truth value instead of truth-value gaps: in (29) and (30) replace the last *is undefined* by $\notin \{0, 1\}$. For more than three truth values, it would be necessary to expand upon (9)–(32) to specify the conditions under which $V(\phi)$ takes on the various intermediate values. Provided this is done in a way which does not contradict (9)–(32), the definitions of PRESUPPOSES and LOGICALLY TRUE will not be affected. (Also, technically, if there are to be more than three truth values, then the definition of $(V, W) \approx_x (V', W')$ must be modified.)

I believe that this metalanguage model for presupposition formalizes a reasonably clear informal notion of LOGICAL PRESUPPOSITION in about the same way that the standard metalanguage model for implication formalizes LOGICAL IMPLICATION. Or at least that such a model can be obtained by elaborating on mine, without discarding any of its essential features. (I have already suggested one such elaboration, in connection with (29). Another would be to account for truth-value gaps resulting from category mismatch: A structure would designate a collection $\mathscr{C}$ (categories) of subsets of D, and each $f(P)$ would be a function from some $C_1 \times \cdots \times C_m$ [where each $C_i \in \mathscr{C}$) into $\{0, 1\}$, and $V(Pt_1 \ldots t_m)$ would be undefined if $(W(t_1), \ldots, W(t_m)) \notin C_1 \times \cdots \times C_m$]. In any case, my model is adequate to account for the most famous examples *Pegasus has a white hind leg, The king of France is wise*, and *All John's children are asleep*. And very importantly, it does not utilize any artifices (such as "classical valuations," supervaluations, intermediate truth values, possible individuals, possible worlds, or inexpressible connectives) not found in the standard model for implication. Nor does it preclude at least some such devices, for example, intermediate truth values and/or funny connectives, should anyone feel an explanation involving them more natural.

A "material presupposition" connective (the term is due to Woodruff (1970)) is definable in L^*: $\phi \supset_p \psi =_{df} (\phi \vee \sim\phi) \supset \psi$. This connective is related to the presupposition relation in the same way that (classically) material implication is related to the implication relation. That is, $\phi \supset_p \phi$ is logically true if and only if ϕ presupposes ψ. (While we are on the subject, ϕ implies ψ—in the sense of the present model —if and only if $(\phi \supset \psi) \wedge (\sim \psi \supset \sim \phi)$ is logically true, and ϕ necessitates ψ if and only if $\phi \supset \psi$ is logically true.)

Moreover, L^* (but not L') is STANDARD in approximately the sense of Rosser and Turquette (1952), so presumably L^* is axiomatizable in a fairly routine way.

3. AN OBJECT-LANGUAGE MODEL FOR PRESUPPOSITION

Now let us turn to the construction of object-language models for presupposition. As with implication, the function of an object-language model is perspicuously to exhibit the behavior of a presupposition connective $\longrightarrow$ compatible with the defined presupposition relation. I will be more careful this time, and state exactly how formulas of propositional logic, with the connective $\longrightarrow$, are to be understood as expressing properties of the presupposition relation. Let $L_{\mathcal{M}}$ now be the first-order language having a binary predicate symbol P, and function symbols $f^{\neg}_{\mathcal{M}}$, $f^{\sim}$, $f^{\vee}$, and $f^{\wedge}$. The metalanguage model defines a structure $\mathcal{M}$ for $L_{\mathcal{M}}$: $D_{\mathcal{M}}$ is the set of sentences of L^*, $P_{\mathcal{M}}(\phi, \psi)$ holds if and only if ϕ presupposes ψ, $f^{\neg}_{\mathcal{M}}(\phi) = \neg\phi$, etc.

A TERM of $L_{\mathcal{M}}$ is obtained from variables via the function symbols. An ATOMIC FORMULA of $L_{\mathcal{M}}$ is of the form $P(t_1, t_2)$, where t_1 and t_2 are terms of $L_{\mathcal{M}}$. An OPEN FORMULA of $L_{\mathcal{M}}$ is a Boolean combination of atomic formulas (that is, it is built up via $\neg$, $\vee$, $\wedge$ from atomic formulas). A UNIVERSAL sentence of $L_{\mathcal{M}}$ is one of the form $\forall x_1 \ldots \forall x_m A$, where A is open. A PRENEX sentence of $L_{\mathcal{M}}$ is one of the form $Q_1 x_1 \ldots Q_m x_m A$, where A is open and each Q_i is either $\forall$ or $\exists$.

The THEORY of $\mathcal{M}$ is the set of all sentences of $L_{\mathcal{M}}$ which are true in $\mathcal{M}$; the UNIVERSAL THEORY is the subset comprising the UNIVERSAL sentences true in $\mathcal{M}$. For example, $\forall x P(x, f^{\vee}(x, f^{\sim}(x)))$ is in the universal theory of $\mathcal{M}$, because ϕ presupposes $\phi \vee \sim\phi$ for every sentence ϕ of L^*. Also, $\forall x \forall y [\exists z (P(x, z) \wedge P(z, y)) \equiv P(x, y)]$ is in the theory of $\mathcal{M}$, because if ϕ presupposes χ and χ presupposes ψ then ϕ presupposes ψ, and conversely, if ϕ presupposes ψ then ϕ presupposes $\phi \vee \sim\phi$ and $\phi \vee \sim\phi$ presupposes ψ.

Now let L_0 be the propositional language with connectives $\neg$, $\sim$, $\vee$, $\wedge$, and $\longrightarrow$. Let a SIMPLE formula of L_0 be a Boolean combination of subformulas $\delta \longrightarrow \epsilon$, where no $\longrightarrow$ occurs in δ or ϵ. Each formula δ in which no $\longrightarrow$ occurs corresponds to a term $t(\delta)$ of $L_{\mathcal{M}}$, obtained by replacing the connectives by the corresponding function symbols, and the propositional variables of L_0 by variables of $L_{\mathcal{M}}$:

$$\begin{aligned} t(p_i) &= x_i, \\ t(\neg\epsilon) &= f^{\neg}(t(\epsilon)), \\ t(\sim\epsilon) &= f^{\sim}(t(\epsilon)), \\ t(\delta\vee\epsilon) &= f^{\vee}(t(\delta),t(\epsilon)), \\ t(\delta\wedge\epsilon) &= f^{\wedge}(t(\delta),t(\epsilon)). \end{aligned}$$

So each formula $\delta \longrightarrow \epsilon$, where no $\longrightarrow$ occurs in δ or ϵ, corresponds to an atomic formula $T(\delta \longrightarrow \epsilon)$ of $L_{\mathcal{M}}$, namely, $T(\delta \longrightarrow \epsilon) = P(t(\delta), t(\epsilon))$. And each simple formula α corresponds to an open formula $T(\alpha)$ of $L_{\mathcal{M}}$, the same Boolean combination of the $T(\delta \longrightarrow \epsilon)$s as α is of the $(\delta \longrightarrow \epsilon)$s:

$$\begin{aligned} T(\neg\alpha) &= \neg T(\alpha), \\ T(\alpha\vee\beta) &= T(\alpha)\vee T(\beta), \\ T(\alpha\wedge\beta) &= \mathrm{T}(\alpha)\wedge T(\beta). \end{aligned}$$

So a simple formula of L_0 can be understood as expressing the same fact about the structure $\mathcal{M}$—that is, about the presupposition relation —as the universal sentence $T^*(\alpha) = \forall x_1 \ldots \forall x_m T(\alpha)$. For example, $p \longrightarrow (p\vee \sim p)$ corresponds to $\forall x P(x, f^{\vee}(x, f^{\sim}(x)))$, which is true in $\mathcal{M}$, and $p \longrightarrow p$ corresponds to $\forall x P(x, x)$, which is false in $\mathcal{M}$. Moreover, every universal sentence of $L_{\mathcal{M}}$ is of the form $T^*(\alpha)$, for some simple formula α of L_0; so the whole of the universal theory of $\mathcal{M}$ is expressed in L_0.

Now to construct a correct object-language model based on L_0 is simply to define logical truth for L_0 in such a way that if α is a simple formula then α is logically true if and only if $T^*(\alpha)$ is true in $\mathcal{M}$.

This can be done by treating $\longrightarrow$ as "strict presupposition" in a version of S5 admitting truth-value gaps: a **FRAME** is a nonempty set W (of "possible worlds"), and a **VALUATION** v for W assigns to each propositional variable p a pair (S, T) of disjoint subsets of W. (Think of S and T as the sets of possible worlds in which p is true and false, respectively.) Then v is extended to assign such a pair (S, T) to every formula of L_0: If $v(\alpha) = (S^{\alpha}, T^{\alpha})$ and $v(\beta) = (S^{\beta}, T^{\beta})$ then

$$\begin{aligned} v(\sim\alpha) &= (T^{\alpha}, S^{\alpha}), \\ v(\neg\alpha) &= (W - S^{\alpha}, S^{\alpha}), \\ v(\alpha \vee \beta) &= (S^{\alpha} \cup S^{\beta}, T^{\alpha} \cap T^{\beta}), \\ v(\alpha \wedge \beta) &= (S^{\alpha} \cap S^{\beta}, T^{\alpha} \cup T^{\beta}), \\ v(\alpha \longrightarrow \beta) &= \begin{cases} (W, \phi) & \text{if } S^{\alpha} \cup T^{\alpha} \subseteq S^{\beta} \\ (\phi, W) & \text{otherwise.} \end{cases} \end{aligned}$$

(The last clause is equivalent to defining

$$\alpha \longrightarrow \beta =_{\mathrm{df}} \Box((\alpha \vee \sim \alpha) \supset \beta),$$

where

$$v(\Box\alpha) = \begin{cases} (W, \phi) & \text{if } v(\alpha) = (W, \phi) \\ (\phi, W) & \text{otherwise.)} \end{cases}$$

Finally, α is LOGICALLY TRUE if, for every frame W and valuation v for W, $v(\alpha) = (W, \phi)$, that is, α is true in every world.

This is not the ONLY correct way of defining logical truth for L_0. We could have used a weaker modal logic than S5; or we could have had many truth values and possibly more connectives; or we could have used different truth conditions for $\Box$, for example,

$$v(\Box\alpha) = \begin{cases} (W, \phi) & \text{if } v(\alpha) = (W, \phi) \\ (\phi, W) & \text{if } v(\alpha) = (S, T), T \neq \phi \\ (\phi, \phi) & \text{otherwise.} \end{cases}$$

Or we could have combined these variations. I will not go into detail, but I have to include a plug for my forthcoming paper, which has theorems roughly to the effect that everything we know about ordinary two-valued modal logic can be transferred in a routine way to any such system.

We have seen that the universal theory of $\mathcal{M}$ can be embedded in L_0. By adding propositional quantifiers to L_0, call the new system QL_0, we can capture the whole of the theory of $\mathcal{M}$. For every sentence of $L_{\mathcal{M}}$ is equivalent to a prenex sentence, which is of the form $Q_1x_1 \ldots Q_mx_mT(\alpha)$ for α a simple formula of L_0. The corresponding formula of QL_0 is of course $Q_1P_1 \cdots Q_mp_m\alpha$. We define logical truth for QL_0 approximately as for L_0—a frame now is a pair (W, π) where W is a nonempty set and π is a nonempty collection of pairs of disjoint subsets of W, closed under the operations corresponding to the connectives $\sim$, $\neg$, $\vee$, and $\wedge$, and in addition satisfying the condition that if $(S, T) \in \pi$ and $S \neq \phi$ then $(S', T) \in \pi$ for some $S' \subseteq S$ with $\phi \neq S' \neq S$. In other words, QL_0 is analogous to S5 with propositional quantifiers, with the condition that π be atomless (cf. Fine, 1970).

It can be proved that $Q_1x_1 \ldots Q_mx_mT(\alpha)$ is true in $\mathcal{M}$ if and only if $Q_1p_1 \ldots Q_mp_m\alpha$ is logically true as a formula of QL_0. So this object-language model faithfully reflects the metalanguage model.

I will conclude with an example which shows that the study of the object-language model can produce information about presupposition which is not readily obtained by direct examination of the metalanguage model. It can be shown that QL_0 is decidable; that is, there is an algorithm which determines, of any given formula of QL_0, whether or not it is logically true. (The essential reason for this is the $\aleph_0$-categoricity of atomless Boolean algebras.) Because QL_0 faithfully interprets the theory of $\mathcal{M}$, this provides an algorithm for determining the truth or falsity of any first-order statement about the presupposition relation defined by the metalanguage model.

4. ADDENDUM

This chapter is very nearly a transcription of my remarks at the Lawrence conference. I decided not to add mathematical proofs of my claims concerning the interpretability of the theory of $\mathcal{M}$ in L_0 and QL_0, since a mathematically viable presentation would digress too far from the principal concerns of this chapter.

After the conference, Stanley Peters sent me a reprint of his paper (1977), of which I wish I had known before. Peters has recognized that presupposition has something to do with MODAL logic with truth-value gaps. But his presupposition relation is relative to a given assignment of intentions to the morphemes of the object language: Whether *Mary realizes that John sings* presupposes *John slouches* depends upon whether John slouches in every possible world in which he sings. At least from the standpoint of logic, a presupposition relation between sentences of an uninterpreted language seems more useful.

REFERENCES

Fine, K. Propositional quantifiers in modal logic. *Theoria*, 1970, *36*, 336–346.

Peters, S. A truth-conditional formulation of Karttunen's account of presupposition. *Texas Linguistic Forum*, 1977, *6*, 137–149.

Rosser, J. B. and Turquette, A. R. *Many-valued logics*. Amsterdam: North-Holland, 1952.

Strawson, P. F. *Introduction to logical theory*. London: Methuen, 1952.

Thomason, S. K. Possible worlds and many truth values. *Studia Logica*, forthcoming.

van Fraassen, B. Singular terms, truth-value gaps, and free logic. *The Journal of Philosophy*, 1966, *63*, 481–495.

van Fraassen, B. Presupposition, implication, and self-reference. *The Journal of Philosophy*, 1968, *65*, 136–152.

van Fraassen, B. Presuppositions, supervaluations, and free logic. In K. Lambert (Ed.), *The logical way of doing things*. New Haven: Yale University Press 1969. Pp. 67–91.

Woodruff, W. Logic and truth value gaps. In K. Lambert (Ed.), *Philosophical problems in logic*, Dordrecht: Reidel, 1970. Pp. 121–142.

PRESUPPOSITION AND DISCOURSE STRUCTURE

JAMES D. McCAWLEY

University of Chicago

1. PRAGMATIC PRESUPPOSITION

In this chapter, I will attempt to solve certain puzzles about the interpretation of definite NPs by putting together ideas that were first developed in two papers by Lauri Karttunen (1969, 1974). I will accordingly begin by sketching the major contribution of one of those papers, Karttunen's (1974) treatment of pragmatic presupposition.

In his 1974 paper, Karttunen departs from his earlier treatments of presupposition by attempting to solve the 'projection problem' for presuppositions of compound sentences in pragmatic rather than semantic terms. Karttunen's earlier papers (1973, 1977)[1] attempted to extend the notion of semantic presupposition to sentences such as (1), in which the presupposition of the second conjunct may (1a) or may not (1b) be "canceled" or "filtered out" by the first conjunct, depending on what the first conjunct happens to be:

(1) a. *Humphrey is incompetent, and Johnson realizes that Humphrey is incompetent.*
b. *Rusk is irresponsible, and Johnson realizes that Humphrey is incompetent.*

[1] In speaking of "earlier papers," I refer to the date of writing, not to the date of publication.

Syntax and Semantics, Volume 11: Presupposition

ISBN 0-12-613511-8

Thus, in some sense (1a) does not presuppose that Humphrey is incompetent but (1b) does. Karttunen at first (1973) gave an analysis of presupposition in which (1a) would come out false and (1b) lacking a truth value in a situation in which Humphrey is not incompetent and Rusk is not irresponsible.[2] Two major problems quickly arose which cast serious doubt on Karttunen's 1973 proposals. First, they did not account for all instances of compound propositions embedded within compound propositions, failing, for example, to account for the fact that the presupposition of the *regret* clause in (2) is filtered out by the rest of the sentence:

(2) *If Nixon is Jewish, then he loves his mother and he regrets that he is Jewish and loves his mother.*

Second, they could account for the filtering of presuppositions that occurs in such sentences as (3), in which the filtering must be based on factors external to the sentence, only by in effect removing the account from the realm of semantic presupposition:

(3) *If Carter has appointed Milton Friedman secretary of labor, he regrets that he has named an opponent of big government to the cabinet.*

Karttunen (1974) avoided the problems raised by (2) and (3) by recasting in terms of a novel conception of pragmatic presupposition his 1973 treatment, which had recognized only semantic presupposition (that is, the notion of presupposition as a relation $A \gg B$ between propositions, which holds when B must be true in order for A to have a truth value at all). Karttunen's notion of pragmatic presupposition is based on a notion of CONTEXT as the set of propositions that the speaker and addressee(s) can take for granted at the given point of the discourse (that is, the propositions that either have been "established" already in the discourse or can be taken as common knowledge of the participants) and a notion of acceptability relative to a context: A sentence S pragmatically presupposes a proposition A if A must be entailed by a context X for S to be acceptable relative to X. Karttunen accordingly was able to reformulate his 1973 rules in terms of

[2] This makes *and* non-truth-functional: The conjuncts in (1a) have the same truthvalues as their counterparts in (1b) but the compound propositions differ in truth value. Truth-functionality in a system that allows truthvalue gaps appears to be attainable only at the price of gross arbitrariness. Under the best known alternative system of assigning truth values to compound propositions, namely van Fraassen's system of supervaluations (1969, 1971), $\wedge$, $\vee$, and $\supset$ are non-truth-functional, though the non-truth-functionality arises in different cases than in Karttunen's 1973 system.

the notion "*S* is acceptable relative to *X*" (abbreviated S/X). For example, his 1973 rule for the presuppositions of conjoined sentences (4a) took the revised form (4b), and his rule (5a) for conditional sentences was recast as (5b):

(4) a. $A \wedge B \gg C$ if $A \gg C$, and
$A \wedge B \gg C$ if $B \gg C$ and A does not entail C.
b. $A \wedge B/X$ if and only if A/X and $B/X \cup \{A\}$.

(5) a. $A \supset B \gg C$ if $A \gg C$, and
$A \supset B \gg C$ if $B \gg C$ and A does not entail C.
b. $A \supset B/X$ if and only if A/X and $B/X \cup \{A\}$.

Under the new treatment, the account of the filtering of the presupposition of the second conjunct of (3) is as follows: *x regrets S* will be acceptable relative to a context that entails *S*. Sentence (3) will be acceptable relative to a context *X* if and only if *Carter has appointed Milton Friedman secretary of labor* is acceptable relative to *X* (this might require, say, that *X* entail that Carter exists, that Milton Friedman exists, and that the position of secretary of labor exists; let us assume that our *X* meets those conditions) and *Carter regrets that he has appointed an opponent of big government to the cabinet* is acceptable relative to $X \cup$ {*Carter has appointed Milton Friedman secretary of labor*}. The last condition will be met if and only if this incremented context entails that Carter has appointed an opponent of big government to the cabinet. This condition will be met if *X* includes the propositions that secretary of labor is a Cabinet post and that Milton Friedman is an opponent of big government. The normalness of (3) results from the fact that those propositions are reasonable pieces of common knowledge for the participants in a discourse to assume as background knowledge.

Karttunen's 1973 rules do not account for the filtering in (2) (that is, they incorrectly imply that (2) presupposes that Nixon is Jewish and loves his mother) because they provide no way for the antecedent of the conditional and the first conjunct of the conjunction to join forces: By (4a), *Nixon loves his mother and he regrets that he is Jewish and loves his mother* presupposes that Nixon is Jewish and loves his mother, since *Nixon loves his mother* does not entail *Nixon is Jewish and loves his mother*. Then By (5a), (2) will then presuppose that Nixon is Jewish and loves his mother, since the antecedent (*Nixon is Jewish*) does not entail the presupposition of the consequent (*Nixon is Jewish and loves his mother*). In terms of the 1974 analysis, this problem disappears. Representing (2) as $A \supset (B \wedge C)$, (2) will be acceptable relative to a context *X* if and only if A/X and $(B \wedge C)/X \cup \{A\}$;

that is, if and only if A/X, $B/X \cup \{A\}$, and $C/X \cup \{A, B\}$. Let us assume that X contains the propositions that Nixon exists and that Nixon has a mother. Then A/X and $B/X \cup \{A\}$, since the demands that A and B makes on a context are already met by X. The demand that C imposes on a context is that the context entail C's complement clause, which happens to be $A \wedge B$; but $X \cup \{A, B\}$ trivially entails $A \wedge B$: Any set of propositions entails a conjunction of members of that set. Thus (2) is acceptable relative to any context that includes the propositions that Nixon exists and that Nixon has a mother; that is, Karttunen's revised treatment shows how the constituents of (2) filter out the presupposition of the *regret* clause.

Karttunen's 1974 approach has some interesting characteristics that have not received adequate attention. First, his treatment is completely neutral as to what the semantic presuppositions of compound sentences are, and indeed, as to whether it even makes sense to speak of semantic presuppositions of compound sentences: It allows one to assign truthvalues to compound sentences in accordance with van Fraassen's system of supervaluations, or to treat them as not having determinate truthvalues (not even determinately having a truthvalue gap). It allows a variety of possible relationships between semantic and pragmatic presupposition; for example, one could maintain that all pragmatic presuppositions, even if not themselves semantic presuppositions, are always derived from semantic presuppositions by rules such as (4b) and (5b). Secondly, it does not include all of the things ever referred to as "pragmatic presuppositions;" thus it enriches the typology of presupposition by subdividing what has previously been treated as a uniform domain. For example, the information on which the choice among *he*, *she*, and *it* is based has occasionally been said to be presupposed by sentences containing pronouns (McCawley, 1968). That information is clearly not a semantic presupposition, since (6) will not lack a truthvalue merely because the neighbor is really a male transvestite:

(6) *My neighbor loves her mother.*

Independently of the neighbor's actual sex, (6) expresses a true or a false proposition depending only on whether the neighbor loves his or her mother. But the "presupposition" embodied in (6) is not a pragmatic presupposition in Karttunen's sense either. To use *she* one need not have already established in the discourse that the referent is female, nor need one take it as common background knowledge of speaker and addressee: One can utter (6) even if one believes that the addressee has no information as to the neighbor's sex. Third, Karttunen's notion of "context" allows one to separate the notions of presupposition from notions that they have erroneously been associated with, for example, the notion of belief on the part of the speaker, and to describe what an utterance accomplishes in terms of its effect on the CONTEXT rather than in terms of such notions as the knowledge and beliefs of the speaker and addressee.

Stalnaker (1978) has in fact given an analysis of assertion essentially in terms of the effect an assertion has on the context: That an assertion, unless challenged or retracted, caused the proposition asserted to be added to the context. Thus, if X is the context when a speaker utters a sentence by which he asserts the proposition p, then $X \cup \{p\}$ is the context for the immediately following utterance unless the addressee challenges the assertion or the speaker withdraws it.[3] Stalnaker's approach renders more tractable some of the puzzles discussed by Grice (1967, lecture V). When a teacher asks a pupil when the battle of Waterloo was fought, the pupil's reply that it was fought in 1815 is not supposed to cause the teacher to know or to believe that it was fought in 1815 (presumably the pupil assumes that the teacher knows the answer and that nothing the pupil says will sway the teacher's position as to what the right answer is). However, the pupil's answer DOES cause the proposition that Waterloo was fought in 1815 to become part of the context (unless it is challenged by the teacher or is withdrawn by the pupil), since until that point in the proceedings, the teacher does not take the proposition for granted IN THAT DISCOURSE, whereas from that point on he may. (Of course, the situation is somewhat odd in that the teacher may decide arbitrarily how much of the material that the pupil is responsible for will count as context, and may tacitly revise that decision if, for example, the pupil does especially well with the first few questions. However, that is not very different from the more normal situation in which a person is explaining something that he is not sure his addressee has any knowledge of, discovers from the addressee's responses that the addressee is indeed well informed about it, and accordingly starts taking much more for

[3] I ignore here the fact that the context is incremented in additional ways. For example, it will be incremented by the proposition that the speaker uttered the sentence that he did, regardless of whether the addressee challenges the content of that sentence, and it will be incremented by any propositions that the speaker and addressee learn through obvious experience in the course of the interchange, for example, the proposition that there has just been a loud scream from the next room.

granted than he had originally.) A similar situation is found with another interchange discussed by Grice:

(7) MOTHER: *It's no good denying it: You broke the window, didn't you?*
CHILD: *Yes, I did.*

Here the mother's purpose is not to inform the child that he broke the window or to cause the child to believe that he broke the window, or even necessarily to determine whether he broke it (she and he may know perfectly well that he broke it, and each may know perfectly well that the other knows). The mother's purpose is to cause the child to make the proposition that he broke the window become part of the context, which she may desire to do in order that she may then felitcitously ask him whether he is sorry that he broke the window.

A proposition that is known by the speaker, is known by the addressee, is known by the speaker to be known by the addressee, and is known by the addressee to be known by the speaker, still need not be part of the CONTEXT. Moreover, the context may include propositions known by both participants to be false and known by each of the participants to be known by the other to be false. Suppose that a district director of the IRS decides to harass publishers of pornography by ordering audits of their income tax returns. Suppose, however, that the IRS has assigned Al Goldstein's audit to an agent who, unbeknown to his superiors, disapproves of IRS tactics and thinks Goldstein has every right to continue to publish *Screw* without government interference. In his interview with Goldstein, the agent, by avoiding things that the IRS could easily challenge, lets Goldstein know he is on Goldstein's side, though for his own protection he maintains the posture of a tough interrogator. It may be that Goldstein has deducted twice as much for depreciation on his house as the IRS code allows him to, that the agent knows that, and that Goldstein knows that the agent knows that, but neither raises that matter, and the proposition that Goldstein deducted more for depreciation than the IRS allows does not become part of the context. Near the end of the interview, Goldstein may say "It's a pleasure to pay taxes that support our boys in Taiwan and Angola," and the proposition that it is a pleasure becomes part of the context even though Goldstein knows it is not a pleasure, the agent knows it is not a pleasure, and each knows that the other knows it is not a pleasure. Much the same can be said about Christmastime conversations between parents and children, in which the proposition that there is a Santa Claus is part of the context and Billy utters sentences whose acceptability depends on that proposition being part of the context, even though Billy no longer believes in Santa Claus, his parents know he no longer believes in Santa Claus, and he knows his parents know that.

2. DEFINITE DESCRIPTIONS

Much of the huge literature on the analysis of definite description deals with the question of whether the existence proposition embodied in Russell's analysis belongs where Russell has it or is rather a presupposition. Thus, Strawson (1950) contests Russell's analysis of (8a) as (8b) on the grounds that Russell's analysis makes (8a) false when there is no king of France, whereas (according to Strawson, 1950; partially retracted in Strawson, 1964), it is neither true nor false in that case:

(8) a. *The king of France is bald.*
b. $(\exists x)(\mathrm{KF}x \wedge (\forall y)(y \neq x \supset \sim\mathrm{KF}y) \wedge \mathrm{B}x)$

Curiously, virtually no attention has been given to the other proposition embodied in (8a), the uniqueness proposition (that is, that no one other than x is king of France). Kempson (1975, p. 110) is to my knowledge alone in having given serious consideration to the uniqueness proposition and having argued that it has a different status from the existence proposition: While Kempson finds the existence proposition a simple entailment and not a semantic presupposition—that is, with Russell, she takes (8a) to express a false proposition when there is no king of France—she takes the uniqueness proposition not to be an entailment of (8a) but a condition on its normal use. The existence of more than one king of France does not make (8a) express a false proposition—it merely makes it unclear what proposition (8a) expresses. Equally curiously, discussion of definite descriptions has been almost exclusively confined to the case of singular definite descriptions and no real attempt has been made to develop an analysis that covers plural definite NPs as well as singular ones. In the pages that follow, I will attempt to redress these imbalances in the existing literature.

Let us begin by considering definite NPs in which the uniqueness condition appears to be grossly violated:

(9) a. *The dog is hungry.*
b. *The dogs are hungry.*

The fact that (9a) does not commit the speaker to there being only one dog in the world (and can express a true proposition in a world containing millions of dogs) has generally been accommodated within the Russellian analysis by treating it as referring to a limited universe of discourse—a universe of discourse containing not all of the objects that exist or have existed but only a selection that are relevant to the current purposes, with only one of them being a dog. That proposal has the fatal defect of being unable to cope with sentences such as (10a) and (10b), which make reference to dogs other than the one to which *the dog* is supposed to refer:

(10) a. *The dog likes all dogs.*
a′. *The dog likes himself.*
b. *The dog had a fight with another dog yesterday.*

If the standard proposal were correct, (10a) ought to convey the same thing as (10a′) (since in a universe of discourse containing only one dog, that dog is all the dogs there are) and (10b) ought to be self-contradictory. The plural definite NP in (9b) presents a similar problem: Whatever analysis one gives to plural definite descriptions, (9b) cannot involve restricting the universe of discourse to the dogs referred to as *the dogs,* since then (11a) ought to convey something along the lines of (11a′) and (11b) ought to be contradictory:[4]

(11) a. *The dogs like all dogs.*
a′. *The dogs like each other.*
b. *The dogs had a fight with three other dogs yesterday.*

I propose that the individuals or sets referred to by definite descriptions stand in the same relationship to the whole universe of discourse as does the context in Karttunen's sense to the whole set of true propositions (or perhaps, the set of propositions known to be true). Suppose that to each utterance of a discourse there corresponds not merely a set X of propositions that have been "established" up to that point of the discourse but also a set Y of objects that have been "identified" up to that point of the discourse. I will refer to this set as the CONTEX-

[4] A similar point can be made about proper names on the basis of examples like

Schwartz admires all persons called Schwartz.
The Schwartzes admire all persons called Schwartz.

The last example is not completely parallel to (11a), since the circumstances under which a group of persons can be referred to as *the Schwartzes* are more restricted than those under which a group of dogs can be referred to as *the dogs.*

TUAL DOMAIN. The interpretation of a definite description relates to the contextual domain rather than to the universe of discourse. As a first approximation, to be modified later, $(\iota x : Fx)Gx$ is evaluated by determining whether exactly one member of the contextual domain has the property F; if so, $(\iota x : Fx)Gx$ is true if G is true of that element and is false if G is false of it. It will have no truth value if the contextual domain has no member with the property F or if it has more than one. Plural definite descriptions can easily be accommodated within this framework: The members of the contextual domain need not all be individuals—they can also be sets—and the definite description can be interpreted as $(\iota x : x$ is a set of dogs), and so on. Note that a set can belong to the contextual domain without its members belonging to it. For example, you may take for granted the identity of the set of your neighbor's dogs without taking for granted the identity of each dog of your neighbor's—you may not be able to tell one of his dogs from another nor even know how many dogs he has.

Just as the context will include both propositions that are taken as common knowledge and propositions that have been established by things said earlier in the discourse, the contextual domain will include both objects whose identities are taken as common knowledge of the participants and objects whose identities have been established by things said earlier in the discourse. Thus, the contextual domain, like the context, is incremented as the discourse proceeds. In an earlier paper, Karttunen (1969) sketched a mechanism by which the contextual domain is incremented: Existentially quantified propositions serve not only to assert that there is an individual (or a set) with the property in question but also to create a referential constant that can figure in subsequent discourse. Moreover, just as the context can be TEMPORARILY incremented, so can the contextual domain. Recall (5b), Karttunen's rule for determining the acceptability of a conditional sentence relative to a context. The acceptability of $A \supset B$ relative to a context X depends on the acceptability of B relative to an enlarged context, namely $X \cup \{A\}$. However, this incrementation of the context is only temporary: A figures as part of the context only in testing the acceptability of the consequent of the conditional and is no longer part of the context when the next utterance is produced.

There is a similar temporary incrementation of the contextual domain with individuals whose existence follows from the antecedent. The remainder of this chapter will be devoted to application of analyses involving temporary incrementation of the contextual domain in making sense out of sentences that would otherwise be highly problematic. I will lead up to these analyses, however, by dealing with some sentences that are not particularly problematic under standard treatments of quantification but which allow an alternative analysis based on Karttunen's proposals that is supported over the standard analysis by linguistic facts.

There are two popular analyses of sentences like (12), in which *any* occurs in the antecedent of a conditional: Either the *any* is interpreted as a universal quantifier with wide scope, as in Quine (1960), that is, (12) is taken as a universal quantification of *If x fails the exam, I'll be disappointed;* or it is interpreted as an existential quantifier that is in the scope of some element (such as *if* or *not*) that triggers a transformation of "*some–any* conversion" (Klima, 1964; Horn, 1972):

(12) *If any student fails the exam, I'll be disappointed.*
a. ($\forall x$: student x)(x *fails the exam* $\supset$ *I'll be disappointed*).
b.(($\exists x$: student x)(x *fails the exam*) $\supset$ *I'll be disappointed*).

Sentences like (13), in which a pronoun in the consequent refers back to the *any* expression in the antecedent, look at first as if they force one to accept the analysis of *any* as a wide scope universal and reject the analysis as a narrow scope existential:

(13) *If any student asks me, I'll tell him the answer.*
a. ($\forall x$: student x)(x *asks me* $\supset$ *I tell* x *the answer*).
b. *(($\exists x$: student x)(x *asks me*) $\supset$ *I tell* x *the answer*).

Under the narrow-scope existential analysis, the pronoun is outside the scope of the quantifier. Thus, if the pronoun were simply a repetition of the bound variable, the putative logical structure would be the incoherent expression (13b). There is, however, linguistic evidence favoring an analysis with an existential quantifier in the antecedent over an analysis with a wide scope universal quantifier, namely the possibility of the ellipses in (14):

(14) a. *If any student asks me, I'll tell him the answer, but if not, I'll assume that my explanation has been sufficient.*
b. *If you find a copy of* Principia Mathematica, *I'll pay you $10 for it. If not, would you please get me a copy of* War and Peace?

If not is derived through deletion of the clause that the *not* negates. Under the analysis with an existential quantifier in the antecedent of the conditional, both (14a) and (14b) involve repeated existential clauses, namely ($\exists x$: student x)(x *asks me*) in (14a) and ($\exists x$: *x is a copy of* War and Peace)(*you find* x) in (14b), and the deletion of the second occurrence of the existential clause under identity with the first yields the desired output. An analysis with a wide-scope universal quantifier is not available in (14b), which consists of two separate sentences, thus of more than could be the scope of a quantifier, and is semantically unsatisfactory in the case of (14a): If (14a) were a universal quantification of *If x asks me, I'll tell x the answer, but if x doesn't ask me, I'll assume my explanation was sufficient*, (14a) would imply that if at least one student does not ask me, I will assume that my explanation has been sufficient, whereas (14a) does not imply that—it only implies that if no student asks me, I will assume the explanation was sufficient.

An analysis in terms of a temporarily incremented contextual domain allows (13b) to be resurrected. The analysis is based on the following two observations. First, existential propositions add to the contextual domain constants corresponding to the variables bound by the existential quantifiers. Building this observation into a theory of logical form amounts to giving official sanction to the informal notational practise of mathematicians, who will give axioms for the notion "group" in the form (15), with the postulate that every element has an inverse involving the same symbol e that figures as a bound variable in the axiom that there is an identity lement, even though it is outside the scope of the quantifier binding that variable:

(15) . . .

$$(\exists e)(\forall x)(xe = ex = x)$$
$$(\forall x)(\exists \bar{x})(x\bar{x} = \bar{x}x = e)$$

Mathematicians of course generally proceed to show that there can be only one identity element and thus to justify the use of a constant referring to "the identity element" in the last axiom. However, they do not interrupt their presentation of the axioms to do that, and thus at least briefly they use a variable that appears bound in one axiom as a constant in subsequent axioms and proofs.

Under Karttunen's 1969 proposals, existential quantifiers in natural language behave as in the mathematicians' informal usage: The existential quantifier serves both to bind a variable and to make available a constant (what Karttunen calls a DISCOURSE REFERENT) that instantiates the existential proposition. Using primes to indicate the discourse referents corresponding to given existentially quantified variables, we can then take the axiom that there is an identity element as adding to the contextual domain a discourse referent e' and adding to the context the proposition $(\forall x)(xe' = e'x = x)$. The postulate that every element has an inverse should then strictly speaking be formulated with an e' instead of an e. Semantics for expressions involving discourse referents can be provided along the lines of van Fraassen's (1969) definition of supervaluation: If in a given model an expression φ involving a discourse referent c' corresponding to an existential proposition $(\exists x)\psi$ has the same truthvalue no matter what element instantiating $(\exists x)\psi$ is substituted for c', then φ has that truthvalue in the model. Otherwise, that is, if different assignments of c' differ as to the truthvalue they yeild for φ, φ has no truthvalue in the model.

The second consideration on which the following analyses are based is that the termporary incrementation of the context Karttunen embodied in (5b) is exactly paralleled by an incrementation of the contextual domain. That is, those propositions and constants that would be added permanently to the context and contextual domain if a given proposition is asserted are instead added to it temporarily when that proposition is used as the antecedent of a conditional. The relationship of (13) to a context and contextual domain is then given by the following arrangement:

(16) ((∃*x*: student *x*)(*x asks me*) ⊃ (*I tell x' the answer*))
X $X \cup \{$*x' asks me*, student $x'\}$
Y $Y \cup \{x'\}$

X and *Y* here are the context and contextual domain for the whole utterance. The antecedent is interpreted relative to that context and that contextual domain. The consequent is interpreted relative to the enlarged context and contextual domain given below it.

Consider now the definite articles in (17):

(17) a. *When a motorcycle collides with a truck, the motorcycle is generally damaged worse than the truck.*
b. *When a Honda collides with a three-axle semi, the motorcycle is generally damaged worse than the truck.*

The sketched framework allows one to take these occurrences of *the* in under the same analysis that applies to sentences such as (9). The interpretation of the definite articles in the consequent of (17a) will be relative to a contextual domain to which have been added discourse referents corresponding to the existentially quantified NPs of the antecedent and a context to which have been added the propositions *x' is a motorcycle*, *y' is a truck*, and *x' collides with y'*, where *x'* and *y'* are the two discourse referents. The search through the contextual domain will yield at least one motorcycle, namely x', and at least one truck, namely y'. Assuming for the moment that it yields no other motorcycles or trucks, that is, assuming that no motorcycle or truck had been in Y to begin with; (I will discuss shortly the case where Y does contain motorcycles and/or trucks), x' and y' will then be picked as the referents of the two definite descriptions, yielding what is evidently the correct truth conditions for (17a). Sentence (17c) is analyzed similarly, except that the normal interpretation depends on the context containing certain information, namely that Hondas are motorcycles and that three-axle semis are trucks. The enlarged contextual domain relative to which the consequent is interpreted would then contain two objects that the enlarged context would allow one to identify as a motorcycle and a truck. Those two objects would be picked as the referents for the two definite descriptions.

The following sentences present great difficulties with regard to determining how the quantifiers fit into the logical structures and over what domains the quantifiers range:

(18) a. *If a war breaks out in Uganda, it will spread to Tanzania.*
b. *If we have a son, we'll name him Oscar.*
c. *Whenever I have a headache, I lie down until it goes away.*
d. *If blisters develop on the patient's body, you should bandage them.*

However, whatever the solution is to those problems, Karttunen's proposals provide a way of accounting for the pronouns. Specifically, the contextual domain will be supplemented by discourse referents corresponding to the war, the son, the headache, and the blisters, and those discourse referents figure in the respective consequents. The problem that these sentences pose for the standard quantificational analysis, in which there is a universal quantifier with wide scope (for example, *for every blister x, if x develops on the patient's body, you should bandage x*), is that they force one to recognize a universe of discourse containing not only persons, places, things, and times, but also disembodied blisters and temporally unanchored wars. This oddity can be reduced by taking the universe of discourse to be time-dependent (that is, different objects exist at different times, and a blister that I developed in the last hour cannot be a value of a variable that ranges over the objects of 4:00 PM yesterday) and to be timebranch-dependent (that is, one must allow alternative future lines of development, and these will differ as to what blisters and wars exist, as well as what persons and objects). But a standard analysis would then render the antecedent of the conditional nearly vacuous: *For all times t, for all sons of ours x at t, if we have x, we'll name x Oscar.* Your son cannot be your son without your having had him. I submit that the right analysis in each of these cases must have an antecedent that says that a war breaks out in Uganda, that you have a son, and so on, with that clause causing the temporary addition of corresponding discourse referents to the contextual domain. However, I do not yet have a way that I am satisfied with of deploying quantifiers in such an analysis. In (19) I present an analysis for (18c), which is the least problematic of these examples, since it does not involve coming into being:

(19) $(\forall t)((\exists x)\text{headache}(x, \text{I}, t) \supset \textit{I lie}_t \textit{ down until } x' \textit{ goes away}).$
$X \qquad\qquad X \cup \{\text{headache}(x', \text{I}, t)\}$
$Y \qquad\qquad Y \cup \{x'\}$

I will conclude by discussing two important issues that I have avoided so far. First, some of the sentences that I wish to analyze with existential quantifiers in the antecedents of conditionals are given more general interpretations than are others. For example, the first half of (14a) could be taken as implying that if several students ask the speaker, he will tell each the answer, whereas the first half of (14b) cannot be taken as implying that the speaker will pay $10 for each copy of *Principia Mathematica* that the addressee finds. This difference cannot be ascribed simply to the difference between *any* in (14a) and *a* in (14b), since there are sentences with *a* that are given an interpretation as broad as is (14a):

(20) *If a student is caught cheating, he will be expelled from the university.*

I am inclined to believe that the generality of the interpretation given to these sentences depends not only on their logical form but also on considerations of cooperativity. For example, (18b) is not interpreted as expressing a commitment to name all sons Oscar—but only as a commitment to naming the next son Oscar. The reason for this is that since sons come one at a time and there is a custom of giving each child a different name, the strongest commitment consistent with prevailing customs one could make would be to name the next son Oscar. The commitment would not be taken as applying to subsequent sons unless the speaker provided warning that he was violating the conventions for naming children. A similar consideration would apply to

(14b): Readers, as opposed to book dealers, normally need only one copy of a book and not an unlimited supply.

The second issue that I glossed over arose in the discussion of (17), where I suggested that the definite articles were acceptable because the enlarged contextual domain would contain exactly one motorcycle and exactly one truck. But (17a) is perfectly acceptable at a point in the discourse where one is already talking about three specific motorcycles and four specific trucks, in which case the enlarged contextual domain will contain four trucks and five motorcycles and thus there should be no referent for the two definite descriptions. The solution to this problem is identical to the solution of another problem that I have avoided, namely that it is possible to use a singular definite NP such as *the dog* even after NPs have been used that will introduce additional dogs to the contextual domain as discourse referents:

(21) *Yesterday* ***the dog*** *got into a fight with* ***a dog. The dogs*** *were snarling and snapping at each other for half an hour. I'll have to see to it that* ***the dog*** *doesn't get near* ***that dog*** *again.*

The possibility of discourses like (21) shows that the contextual domain cannot be simply the unstructured set that I have taken it to be so far. Rather, there must be a hierarchy of successively broader domains, with those elements that are most "prominent" at the given point in the discourse being in the first level of the hierarchy. Suppose that we make the following stipulations: First, the temporary additions to the contextual domain are added at the top of the hierarchy as a new first level. Second, in interpreting a definite description, one starts at the first level of the hierarchy and searches until one reaches a level containing an item of the type in question. If there is only one such element on that level, that element is the referent of the definite description. If there is more than one such element on that level, the definite description is rejected as unacceptable and the sentence is not interpreted. If no level of the hierarchy contains an element of the type in question, the definite description is rejected as unacceptable. In the case of (17a), the search for referents for *the motorcycle* and *the truck* will be relative to a contextual domain whose first level contains exactly one motorcycle and one truck, namely, the temporary additions, even if lower levels in the contextual domain contain several motorcycles and trucks. Thus, the temporary discourse referents are the referents of the two definite descriptions. Permanent additions to the contextual domain, such as the second dog in (21), can be added at either a higher or a lower level of the hierarchy than other items (it is up to the speaker to determine which items are to be "more prominent"). In (21), the second dog has been added at a lower level than the first one (which continues to be called *the dog*). A search for a referent for *the dog* will find it in the first level, and a search for a referent for *the dogs* will find it in the second level, namely, the set consisting of your dog and the other dog.

What is one then to do with the definite descriptions that hitherto have been taken as the paradigm case—those such as (21), which require no prior knowledge by anyone of the identity of the object referred to and can be analyzed quite comfortably according to Russell's proposal?

(22) a. *The solution to this equation, whatever it is, is between 43 and 947.*
b. *The person who killed this child is insane.*

The analysis of these sentences can be integrated with the treatment of definite descriptions previously sketched by making the universe of discourse the bottom level of the contextual domain. The search for a referent for the definite descriptions in (22) will then exhaust the contextual domain as hitherto understood and will continue in the new bottom level of the contextual domain and, if there is exactly one member of that level (the universe of discourse) fitting the definite description, will pick that element as the referent.

There is one major respect in which this last modification in my treatment of definite descriptions conflicts with the notion of contextual domain that I have been developing, namely, that the universe of discourse is not shared by the parties to the discourse the way that the context and contextual domain proper are. One can assert that all politicians are corrupt and obtain assent to that assertion without agreeing with one's interlocutors as to what individuals there are and which are politicians—even as to what possible individuals there are and which are (possible) politicians—and without assuming that such agreement prevails. Moreover, as Hawkins (1976, 1977) has pointed out, definite NPs can serve to add to the addressee's universe of discourse individuals of whose existence he was previously unaware. For example, when one utters (23), one does not assume prior knowledge by the addressee that there is a dog on the land in question:

(23) *Don't go through that gate, or the dog will bite you.*

Hawkins notes also that definite NPs are used in informing the addressee of the identity of the parts of an unfamiliar object, even if one knows that the addressee has no prior knowledge of the existence of those parts, let alone their uniqueness as parts of the given whole:

(24) *This is the frammis, this is the external effluent-collector, and this is one of the lateral lypto-graphs.*

Note that the existence and uniqueness of the items in question are conveyed rather than presupposed in both (23) and (24): One can utter (23) in order to inform the addressee that there is a dog attached to the land beyond the gate (whereas *a dog* would not convey that—perhaps the land beyond the gate is covered with a substance whose odor sends dogs into a rage and the speaker is afraid the addressee will get some on his shoes). Also, (24) can be used in instructing the addressee about not only what sorts of objects the various items are but also their relation to the larger structure to which they belong (as opposed to *This is a frammis*).

I conjecture that the way to reconcile the analysis of examples (21)–(24) with the earlier examples is to describe the goal of the search in terms of the contextual domain not at the outset of the search but at the conclusion, and to allow the interpretation of the definite description to involve either locating items already in the contextual domain or adding new items to the contextual domain, whichever will produce a resulting contextual domain such that there is at least one item of the type in question and that in the first level of the contextual domain that contains such items there is exactly one.

I remark in conclusion that the treatment of definite descriptions sketched in this chapter has a lot in common with work done in artificial intelligence under the rubric of "procedural semantics.,"[5] in which the meanings of expressions are given as algorithms for determining a referent or a truthvalue for the expression, where the algorithm typically involves searches through structured domains.

REFERENCES

Grice, H. P. Logic and conversation. Unpublished William James lectures, Harvard University, 1967.

Hawkins, J. A. On explaining some ungrammatical sequences of article + modifier in English. *Papers from the twelfth regional meeting, Chicago Linguistic Society.* Chicago: Chicago Linguistic Society, 1976. Pp. 287–301.

[5] A good account of procedural semantics, with stimulating suggestions for its employment in the analysis of natural language, is given in Miller and Johnson–Laird (1976).

Hawkins, J. A. The pragmatics of definites, I. *Linguistische Berichte,* 1977, *47,* 1–27.
Horn, L. R. *On the semantic properties of logical operators in English.* Unpublished Doctoral thesis, University of California at Los Angeles, 1972.
Karttunen, L. Discourse referents. Paper presented at the International Conference on Computational Linguistics, Sånga-Säby, Sweden, 1969. [Now in J. McCawley (Ed.), *Syntax and Semantics, 7, Notes from the linguistic underground.* New York: Academic Press, 1976. Pp. 363–385.]
Karttunen, Lauri. Presuppositions of compound sentences. *Linguistic Inquiry,* 1973, *4,* 169–193.
Karttunen, L. Presupposition and linguistic context. *Theoretical Linguistics,* 1974, *1,* 181–194.
Karttunen, L. Remarks on presuppositions. In A. Rogers, J. Murphy, and R. Wall (Eds.), *Performatives, presuppositions, and implicatures.* Washington: Center for Applied Linguistics, 1977.
Klima, E. S. Negation in English. In J. S. Fodor and J. J. Katz (Eds.), *The structure of language.* Englewood Cliffs, New Jersey: Prentice-Hall, 1964. Pp. 246–323.
McCawley, J. D. The role of semantics in a grammar. In E. Bach and R. Harms (Eds.), *Universals in linguistic theory.* New York: Holt, Rinehart, and Winston, 1968. Pp. 124–169. Reprinted with notes in J. D. McCawley, *Grammar and Meaning,* New York: Academic Press, 1976. Pp. 59–98.
Miller, G. A., and Johnson-Laird, P. *Language and perception.* Cambridge, Massachusetts: Harvard University Press, 1976.
Stalnaker, R. Assertion. In P. Cole (Ed.), *Syntax and semantics, 9, Pragmatics.* New York: Academic Press, 1978. Pp. 315–332.
Strawson, P. F. On referring. *Mind,* 1950, *59,* 320–344. [Also in Strawson, 1971, pp. 1–27.]
Strawson, P. F. Identifying reference and truth values. *Theoria,* 1964, *30,* 96–118. [Also in Strawson, 1971, pp. 75–95.]
Strawson, P. F. *Logico-linguistic papers.* London: Methuen, 1971.
van Fraassen, B. Presuppositions, supervaluations, and free logic. In K. Lambert (Ed.), *The logical way of doing things.* New Haven: Yale University Press, 1969. Pp. 67–91.
van Fraassen, B. *Formal semantics and logic.* New York: Macmillan, 1971.

BIBLIOGRAPHY OF WORKS DEALING WITH PRESUPPOSITION

IVAN A. SAG AND ELLEN F. PRINCE
University of Pennsylvania

Adams, D., M. Campbell, V. Cohen, J. Lovins, E. Maxwell, C. Nygren, and J. Reighard, eds. (1971) *Papers from the Seventh Regional Meeting of the Chicago Linguistic Society,* University of Chicago Department of Linguistics.

Allwood, J. (1972) "Negation and the Strength of Presuppositions, or There Is More to Speaking than Words," *Gothenburg Logical Grammar Report* 2.

Allwood, J. (1975) "Conventional and Nonconventional Presupposition," in E. Hovdhaugen, ed., *Papers from the Second Scandinavian Conference of Linguistics,* Department of Linguistics, University of Oslo. Pp. 1–14.

Allwood, J. (1977) "Truth, Appropriateness and Focus," *Pragmatics Microfiche* 2.5, A2-B2.

Anderson, S. R. (1972) "How to Get *even,*" *Language* 48, 893–906.

Andersson, L.-G. (1973) "Presuppositional Structures in Temporal Clauses," *Gothenburg Logical Grammar Report* 3.

Antley, K. (1974) "McCawley's Theory of Selectional Restriction," *Foundations of Language* 11, 257–272.

Åqvist, L. (1965) "A New Approach to the Logical Theory of Interrogatives," *Philosophical Studies,* University of Uppsala.

Atlas, J. D. (1975a) "Frege's Polymorphous Concept of Presupposition and Its Role in a Theory of Meaning," *Semantikos* 1.1, 29–44.

Atlas, J. D. (1975b) "Presuppositions: A Semanticopragmatic Account," *Pragmatics Microfiche* 1.4, D13-G14.

Atlas, J. D. (1977a) "Negation, Ambiguity, and Presupposition," *Linguistics and Philosophy* 1.3, 321–336.

Atlas, J. D. (1977b) "Presupposition Revisited," *Pragmatics Microfiche* 2.5, D5-D11.

Atlas, J. D. (1979) "Presupposition, Negation, and the Anti-Realist Theory of Meaning," in C.-K. Oh and D. Dinneen, eds. (1979) Pp. 265–281.

Austin, J. L. (1962) *How to Do Things with Words,* Oxford University Press, New York.

Baker, A. (1956) "Presupposition and Types of Clause," *Mind* 65, 368–378.

Baker, C. L. (1970) "Double Negation," *Linguistic Inquiry* 1, 169–187.

Ball, C. N. and E. F. Prince (1977) "A Note on Stress and Presupposition," *Linguistic Inquiry* 8, 585.

Bar-Lev, Z. (1975) "Presupposition as a Semantic Constituent," *Glossa* 9, 123–138.

Beach, W., S. Fox, and S. Philosoph, eds. (1977) *Papers from the Thirteenth Regional Meeting of the Chicago Linguistic Society,* University of Chicago Department of Linguistics.

Bellert, I. (1974) "On Inferences and Interpretation of Natural Language Sentences," *Theoretical Linguistics* 1, 215–231.

Belnap, N. (1963) "An Analysis of Questions," Systems Development Corporation, TM-1287/000/00, Santa Monica, California.

Belnap, N. (1966) "Questions, Answers, and Presuppositions," *Journal of Philosophy,* 63, 609.

Belnap, N. (1969) "Questions: Their Presuppositions and How They Can Arise," in K. Lambert, ed., 1969.

Belnap, N. D. Jr. and T. B. Steel, Jr. (1976) *The Logic of Questions and Answers*, Yale University Press, New Haven, Connecticut.

Bhatia, T. K. (1974) "The Coexisting Answering Systems and the Role of Presuppositions, Implications and Expectations in Hindi Simplex Yes/No Questions," in M. LaGaly, R. Fox, and A. Bruck, eds. (1974) Pp. 47–61.

Bickerton, D. (1975a) "Reference in Natural Semantax," *Pragmatics Microfiche* 1.1, D1-G8.

Bickerton, D. (1975b) "Some Assertions about Presuppositions about Pronominalization," in R. Grossman, J. San, and T. Vance, eds. (1975b) Pp. 24–35.

Bickerton, D. (1975c) "Two Levels of Logical Presupposition," in R. Grossman, J. San, and T. Vance, eds. (1975a) Pp. 48–59.

Bickerton, D. (1979) "Where Presuppositions Come From," in C.-K. Oh and D. Dinneen, eds. (1979) Pp. 235–248.

Binnick, R., A. Davison, G. Green, and J. Morgan, eds. (1969) *Papers from the Fifth Regional Meeting of the Chicago Linguistic Society*, University of Chicago Department of Linguistics.

Black, M. (1952) "Definition, Presupposition and Assertion." *Philosophical Review* LXI, 532–550. Reprinted in M. Black (1954) *Problems of Analysis*, Cornell University Press, Ithaca, New York. Pp. 24–45.

Black, M. (1958) "Presupposition and Implication," in S. Uyeda, ed. (1958) *A Way to the Philosophy of Science*, Waseda University Press, Tokyo. Reprinted in M. Black (1962) *Models and Metaphors*, Cornell University Press, Ithaca, New York. Pp. 48–63.

Böer, S, S. and W. Lycan (1974) "Invited Inferences and Other Unwelcome Guests," *Papers in Linguistics* 6, 483–505.

Böer, S. and W. Lycan (1976) "The Myth of Semantic Presupposition," *OSU Working Papers in Linguistics* 21. Also available from Indiana University Linguistics Club.

Bolinger, D. (1976) "Gradience in Entailment," *Language Sciences* 41, 1–13.

Brodda, B. (1976) "Presuppositions in Text and the Filter Concept," in F. Karlsson, ed., *Papers from the Third Scandinavian Conference of Linguistics,* Text Linguistic Research Group, Academy of Finland, Turku. Pp. 71–80.

Cantrall, W. R. (1971) "Comparison and Presupposition," *Linguistic Inquiry* 2, 573–574.

Carden, G. (1977) "Comparatives and Factives," *Linguistic Inquiry* 8, 586–589.

Caton, C. (1959) "Mr. Strawson on Referring," *Mind* LXVII, 539–544.

Caton, C. (1966) "Epistemic Qualification of Things Said in English," *Foundations of Language* 2, 37–66.

Chafe, W. (1976) "Givenness, Contrastiveness, Definiteness, Subjects and Topics," in C. N. Li, ed. (1976) Pp. 25–56.

Chomsky, N. (1971) "Deep Structure, Surface Structure and Semantic Interpretation," in D. Steinberg and L. Jakobovits, eds. (1971) Pp. 183–216. Also in N. Chomsky (1972b). Pp. 62–119.

Chomsky, N. (1972a) "Some Empirical Issues in the Theory of Transformational Grammar," in S. Peters, ed., *Goals of Linguistic Theory*, Prentice-Hall, Englewood Cliffs, New Jersey. Pp. 60–130. Also in Chomsky (1972b). Pp. 120–202.

Chomsky, N. (1972b) *Studies on Semantics in Generative Grammar*, The Hague, Mouton.

Chvany, C. V. (1973) "On the Role of Presuppositions in Russian Existential Sentences," in C. Corum, T. C. Smith-Stark, and A. Weiser, eds. (1973) Pp. 68–77.

Clark, H. H. (1977) "Inferences in Comprehension," in D. LaBerge and S. J. Samuels, eds. *Basic Processes in Reading*," Erlbaum, Hillsdale, New Jersey. Pp. 243–263.

Clark, H. H., and S. E. Haviland (1977) "Comprehension and the Given-New Contract," in R. O. Freedle, ed., *Discourse Production and Comprehension*, Ablex, Norwood, New Jersey. Pp. 1–40.

Cohen, D. (1973) "On the Mis-Representation of Presuppositions," *Glossa* 7, 21–38.

Cole, P., ed. (1978) *Syntax and Semantics 9: Pragmatics*, Academic Press, New York.

Cole, P., and J. Morgan, eds. (1975) *Syntax and Semantics 3: Speech Acts*, Academic Press, New York.

Coleman, L. (1975) "The Case of the Vanishing Presupposition," in *BLSI, Proceedings of the First Annual Meeting of the Berkeley Linguistics Society*, Berkeley, California.

Cooper, D. (1974) *Presupposition*, The Hague, Mouton.

Corum, C., T. C. Smith-Stark, and A. Weiser, eds. (1973) *Papers from the Ninth Regional Meeting of the Chicago Linguistic Society*, University of Chicago Department of Linguistics.

Cresswell, M. (1965) "The Logic of Interrogatives," in J. Crossley and M. Dummett, eds. (1965), *Formal Systems and the Recursive Functions*, North-Holland, Amsterdam.

Dahlgren, K. (1974) "The Pragmatics of Presupposition," *UCLA Papers in Syntax* 5, 1–17.

Dale, P. S. *et al.* (1976) "The Influence of the Form of the Question on Eyewitness Testimony of Preschool Children," *Stanford University, Papers and Reports on Child Language Development* 12, 89–96.

Darden, B., C.-J. Bailey, and A. Davison, eds. (1968) *Papers from the Fourth Regional Meeting of the Chicago Linguistic Society*, University of Chicago Department of Linguistics.

Dascal, M. and M. Avishai (1974) "A New 'Revolution' in Linguistics?—'Text-Grammars' vs. 'Sentence-Grammars'," *Theoretical Linguistics* 1, 195–213.

Davidson, D. and G. Harman, eds. (1972) *Semantics of Natural Language*, D. Reidel, Dordrecht.

Davidson, D. and G. Harman, eds. (1975) *The Logic of Grammar*, Dickenson, Encino, California.

Delacruz, E. B. (1976) "Factives and Proposition Level Constructions in Montague Grammar," in B. Partee, ed. (1976), *Montague Grammar*, Academic Press, New York. Pp. 177–200.

Delisle, G. L. (1972) "Syntactic Feature Switching: Two Cases," *Stanford Working Papers on Language Universals* 10.

De Rijk, R. P. G. (1974) "A Note on Prelexical Predicate Raising," in P. Seuren, ed. (1974) *Semantic Syntax*, Oxford University Press, London. Pp. 43–74.

DiSciullo, A.-M. (1976) "*Sémantique et Pragmatique*," in *Papers from the Sixth Annual Meeting, North Eastern Linguistics Society*. Pp. 75–86.

Doherty, Monika. (1973) " 'Noch' and 'schon' and their presuppositions," in F. Kiefer and N. Ruwet, eds., *Generative Grammar in Europe, FL Supp. Series 13*, Reidel, Dordrecht. Pp. 154–177.

Donaldson, S. K. (1973) "On the (Possibly) Presuppositional Nature of *when*-Clauses in Hindi," *Studies in the Linguistic Sciences* 3.2, 28–42.

Donnellan, K. S. (1966) "Reference and Definite Descriptions," *Philosophical Review* 75, 281–304. Reprinted in D. Steinberg and L. Jakobovits, eds. (1971) Pp. 100–114. Also in J. Petöfi and D. Franck, eds. (1973). Also in J. Rosenberg and C. Travis, eds. (1971). Pp. 195–211.

Ducrot, O. (1966) " 'Le Roi de France est sage': Implication logique et présupposition linguistique," *Etudes de Linguistique Applique* 4, 39–47.

Ducrot, O. (1971) *Les présupposés. Condition d'emploi ou éléments du contenu?*, Arbeitspapier, Paris.

Ducrot, O. (1972) *Dire et ne pas dire: Principes de sémantique linguistique*, Paris.

Ducrot, O. (1975) "Je trouve que," *Semantikos* 1.1, 62–88.

Ebert, K. (1973) "Präsuppositionen in Sprechakt," in J. Petöfi and D. Franck, eds. (1973).

Egli, U. (1971) "Zweiwertigkeit und Präsuppositionen," *L.inguistische Berichte* 13, 74–77.

Emonds, J. (1970) *Root and Structure Preserving Transformations*. Doctoral dissertation, MIT. Available from Indiana University Linguistics Club.

Emonds, J. (1976) *A Transformational Approach to Syntax: Root, Structure-Preserving, and Local Transformations*, Academic Press, New York.

Farkas, D., W. Jakobsen, and K. Bloom, eds. (1978) *Papers from the Fourteenth Regional Meeting of the Chicago Linguistic Society*, University of Chicago Department of Linguistics.

Fauconnier, G. (1975a) "Polarity and the Scale Principle," in R. Grossman, J. San, and T. Vance, eds. (1975a) Pp. 188–199.

Fauconnier, G. (1975b) "Pragmatic Scales and Logical Structures," *Linguistic Inquiry* 6, 353–376.

Fillmore, C. (1965) "Entailment Rules in a Semantic Theory," *Project on Linguistic Analysis*, Report #10, Ohio State University.

Fillmore, C. (1969) "Types of Lexical Information," in F. Kiefer, ed., *Studies in Syntax and Semantics*, Humanities Press, New York, Pp. 109–137. Also in D. Steinberg and L. Jakobovits, eds. (1971) Pp. 273–289.

Fillmore, C. (1971) "Verbs of Judging: An Exercise in Semantic Description," in Fillmore, C. and D. T. Langendown, eds. (1971) Pp. 273–289. Also in Petöfi and Franck, eds. (1973).

Fillmore, C., G. Lakoff, and R. Lakoff, eds. (1974) *Berkeley Studies in Syntax and Semantics, Volume 1*, Institute of Human Learning, Department of Linguistics, University of California, Berkeley.

Fillmore, C. and D. T. Langendoen, eds. (1971) *Studies in Linguistic Semantics*, Holt, New York.

Fodor, J. D. (1970) "*The Linguistic Description of Opaque Contexts.*" Doctoral dissertation, MIT. Available from Indiana University Linguistics Club.

Fraser, B. (1971) An Analysis of *even* in English," in C. Fillmore and D. T. Langendoen, eds. (1971). Pp. 151–178.

Frege, G. (1892) "Über Sinn und Bedeutung," *Zeitschrift f. Philosophie und philosoph. Kritik* 100, 25–50. English Translation: "On Sense and Reference," in P. Geach and M. Black, eds. (1952) *Translations from the Philosophical Writings of Gottlob Frege*, New York, Philosophical Library. Pp. 56–78. Also in F. Zabeeh, E. Klemke, and A. Jacobson, eds. (1974) Pp. 112–140. Also in H. Feigl and W. Sellars, eds. (1949) *Readings in Philosophical Analysis*, New York: Appleton-Century-Crofts. Also in J. Moravcsik, ed. (1974) Pp. 13–32. Also reprinted elsewhere.

Grabirel, G. (1971) "Kennzeichnung und präsupposition," *Linguistische Berichte* 15, 27–31.

Garner, R. (1971) " 'Presupposition' in Philosophy and Linguistics," in C. Fillmore and D. T. Langendoen, eds. (1971). Pp. 22–42.

Gazdar, G. (1976) *Formal Pragmatics for Natural Language: Implicature, Presupposition and Logical Form*. Doctoral dissertation, University of Reading. Available from Indiana University Linguistics Club.

Gazdar, G. (1977a) "Plumbing beyond Repair: Leaking Plugs and Faulty Filters," Unpublished paper, University of Sussex.

Gazdar, G. (1977b) "Implicature, Presupposition and Logical Form," Available from Indiana University Linguistics Club.

Gazdar, G. (1978) "Heavy Parentheses Wipe-Out Rules, Okay?" *Linguistics and Philosophy* 2(2), 281–289.

Gazdar, G. (1979) "A Solution to the Projection Problem," in C.-K. Oh and D. Dinneen, eds. (1979) Pp. 57–89.

Gazdar, G. (In preparation) *Pragmatics*, Academic Press, New York.

Gazdar, G., E. Klein, and G. K. Pullum (1977) *A Bibliography of Contemporary Linguistic Research*. Garland, New York.

Geach, P. (1965) "Assertion," *The Philosophical Review* LXXIV 4, 449–465. Also in Rosenberg and Travis, eds. (1971) Pp. 250–261.

Geis, M. and A. M. Zwicky. (1971) "On Invited Inference," *Linguistic Inquiry* 2, 561–566.

Givón, T. (1972) "Forward Implications, Backward Presuppositions, and the Time Axis of Verbs," in J. Kimball, ed., *Syntax and Semantics 1*, Seminar Press, New York. Pp. 20–50.

Givón, T. (1973) "The Time-Axis Phenomenon," *Language* 49, 890–925.

Grant, C. K. (1958) "Pragmatic Implication," *Philosophy* XXXIII, 303–324.

Green, G. (1968) "On *too* and *either*, and Not Just *too* and *either*, Either," in B. Darden, C.-J. Bailey, and A. Davison, eds. (1968) Pp. 22–39.

Grice, H. P. (1968) "Logic and Conversation (unabridged version)," Unpublished manuscript; text of Grice's William James Lectures at Harvard University.

Grice, H. P. (1968)"Logic and Conversation," Unpublished manuscript; text of Grice's William James Lectures at Harvard University. Excerpted in D. Davison and G. Harman, eds. (1975) Pp. 64–75. Also excerpted in P. Cole and J. Morgan, eds. (1975) Pp. 4–58.

Gross, M. (1977) "Une analyse non-présuppositionelle de l'extraction dans *c'est . . . qu . . . ,*" *Lingvisticae Investigationes* I. 1, 39–62.

Grossman, R., L. San, and T. Vance, eds. (1975a) *Papers from the Eleventh Regional Meeting of the Chicago Linguistic Society*, University of Chicago Department of Linguistics.

Grossman, R., L. San, and T. Vance, eds. (1975b) *Papers from the Parasession on Functionalism*, Chicago Linguistic Society.

Gundel, J. (1974) *The Role of Topic and Comment in Linguistic Theory,* Doctoral dissertation, University of Texas at Austin.

Haiman, J. (1976) "Presuppositions in Hua," in S. Mufwene, C. Walker, and S. Steever, eds. (1976) Pp. 258–270.

Hajičová, E. (1974) "Meaning, presupposition and allegation," *Philologica Pragensia* 17, 18–25. Reprinted in W. Klein and A. von Stechon, eds. (1974), *Functional Generative Grammar in Prague,* Scriptor. Pp. 160–172.

Hajičová, E. (1976) "Some Remarks on Presuppositions," Read at the International Conference of Computational Linguistics, Debrecen, 1971. Printed in F. Papp and G. Szepe, eds., *Papers in Computational Linguistics,* Akademiai Kiado, Budapest. Pp. 189–197.

Hall, R. (1958) "Assuming—One Set of Positing Words," *Philosophical Review* LXVII, 52–75.

Hall, R. (1961) "Presuming," *Philosophical Quarterly* 11, 10–21.

Halvorsen, P.-K. (1976) "Syntax and Semantics of Cleft-Sentences," in S. Mufwene, C. Walker, and S. Steever, eds. (1976) Pp. 271–286.

Hamblin, C. L. (1966) "Review of Åkvist, 1965," *Australasian Journal of Philosophy* 44, 385–390.

Hamblin, C. L. (1971) "Mathematical Models of Dialogue," *Theoria* 37, 130–155.

Hancock, R. (1960) "Presuppositions," *The Philosophical Quarterly* 10, 73–78.

Harder, P. and C. Kock (1976) "The Theory of Presupposition Failure," *Travaux du Cercle Linguistique de Copenhague* XVII, Akademisk Forlag, Copenhagen.

Harnish, R. M. (1972) *Studies in Logic and Language*, Doctoral dissertation, M.I.T.

Hasegawa, K. (1972) "Transformations and Semantic Interpretation," *Linguistic Inquiry* 3, 141–159.

Hausser, R. (1973) "Presuppositions and Quantifiers," in C. Corum, T. C. Smith-Stark, and A. Weiser, eds. (1973) Pp. 192–204.

Hausser, R. (1976a) "Presupposition in Montague Grammar," *Theoretical Linguistics* 3.3, 245–280.

Hausser, R. (1976b) "Scope Ambiguity and Scope Restrictions in Montague Grammar," *Amsterdam Papers in Formal Grammar* 1, 95–131.

Heinämäki, O. (1972) "Before," in P. Peranteau, J. Levi, and G. Phares, eds. (1972) Pp. 139–151.

Heringer, J. T. (1972) "Some Grammatical Correlates of Felicity Conditions and Presuppositions," *OSU Working Papers in Linguistics* 11. Also available from Indiana University Linguistics Club.

Herzberger, H. G. (1973) "Dimensions of Truth," *Journal of Philosophical Logic* 2.4, 535–556.

Herzberger, H. G. (1976) "Presuppositional Policies," in A. Kasher, ed. (1976), *Language in Focus: Foundations, Methods and Systems*, Reidel, Dordrecht. Pp. 139–164.

Hintikka, J. (1959) "Existential Presuppositions and Existential Commitments," *Journal of Philosophy* 56, 125–137.

Hintikka, J. (1962) *Knowledge and Belief,* Cornell University Press, Ithaca, New York.

Hintikka, J. (1969a) "Existential Presuppositions and Their Elimination," in J. Hintikka, ed. (1969c) Pp. 23–44.

Hintikka, J. (1969b) "Existential Presuppositions and Uniqueness Presuppositions," in J. Hintikka (1969c) Pp. 112–147. Also in K. Lambert, ed. (1970) Pp. 20–55.

Hintikka, J. (1969c) *Models for Modalities: Selected Essays*, Reidel, Dordrecht.

Hiz, H., ed. (1977) *Questions*, Reidel, Dordrecht. (See, in particular, papers by Malone, Karttunen, and Hintikka.)

Hooper, J. (1975) "On Assertive Predicates," in J. Kimball, ed., *Syntax and Semantics, Vol. 4*. Academic Press, New York. Pp. 91–124.

Hooper, J. and S. A. Thompson (1973) "On the Applicability of Root Transformations," *Linguistic Inquiry* 4, 465–498.

Horn, L. R. (1969) "A Presuppositional Analysis of *only* and *even*," in R. Binnick, A. Davison, G. Green, and J. Morgan, eds. (1969) Pp. 98–107.

Horn, L. R. (1970) "Ain't It Hard (Anymore)," in *Papers from the Sixth Regional Meeting of the Chicago Linguistic Society*, University of Chicago Department of Linguistics.

Horn, L. R. (1972) *On the Semantic Properties of Logical Operators in English,* Doctoral dissertation, UCLA. Available from Indiana University Linguistics Club.

Hornby, P. A. (1971) "The Role of Topic-Comment in the Recall of Cleft and Pseudo-cleft Sentences," in D. Adams, M. Campbell, V. Cohen, J. Lovins, E. Maxwell, C. Nygren, and J. Reighard, eds. (1971) Pp. 445–453.

Hornby, P. A. (1974) "Surface Structure and Presupposition," *Journal of Verbal Learning and Verbal Behavior* 13, 530–538.

Hull, R. D. (1974) *A Logical Analysis of Questions and Answers*, Doctoral dissertation, Cambridge University.

Hull, R. D. (1975) "A Semantics for Superficial and Embedded Questions in Natural Language," in E. L. Keenan, ed. (1975). Pp. 35–45.

Hungerland, I. C. (1960) "Contextual Implication," *Inquiry* III, 86–89.

Huntley, M. (1976) "Presupposition and Implicature," *Semantikos* 1.2, 67–88.

Hurford, J. R. (1972) "The Diachronic Reordering of Phonological Rules," *Journal of Linguistics* 8, 293–295.

Hutchinson, L. G. (1971) "Presupposition and Belief Inferences," in D. Adams, M. Campbell, V. Cohen, J. Lovins, E. Maxwell, C. Nygren, and J. Reighard, eds. (1971) Pp. 134–141.

Jackendoff, R. S. (1972) *Semantic Interpretation in Generative Grammar (Chapter 6)*, M.I.T. Press, Cambridge, Massachusetts.

Jake, J. (1977) "Gapping, Pragmatics and Factivity," in W. Beach, S. Fox, and S. Philosoph, eds. (1977) Pp. 165–172.

Joshi, A. K. and S. J. Rosenschein (1976) "Some Problems of Inferencing to Decomposition of Predicates," Paper presented at the International Conference of Computational Linguistics, Ottawa, June, 1976.

Joshi, A. K. and R. M. Weischedel (1976) *Some Frills for Modal Tic-Tac-Toe: Semantics of Predicate Complement Constructions*, IEEZ Computer Society (special issue of *Artificial Intelligence*).

Joshi, A. K. and R. M. Weischedel (1977) "Computation of a Subclass of Inferences: Presupposition and Entailment," *American Journal of Computational Linguistics*, January, 1977.

Just, M. A., and H. H. Clark (1973) "Drawing Inferences from the Presuppositions and Implications of Affirmative and Negative Sentences," *Journal of Verbal Learning and Verbal Behavior* 12, 21–31.

Kaplan, S. J. (1977) *Cooperative Responses from a Natural Language Data Base Query System: Preliminary Report*, Moore School of Electrical Engineering, The University of Pennsylvania.

Karttunen, F. and L. Karttunen (1977) "*Even* Questions," in J. Kegl, D. Nash, and A. Zaenen, eds. (1977) Pp. 115–134.

Karttunen, L. (1970) "On the Semantics of Complement Sentences," in *Papers from the Sixth Regional Meeting of the Chicago Linguistic Society*, University of Chicago Department of Linguistics. Pp. 115–134.

Karttunen, L. (1971a) "Discourse Referents," Indiana University Linguistics Club.
Karttunen, L. (1971b) "The Logic of English Predicate Complement Constructions," Indiana University Linguistics Club.
Karttunen, L. (1971c) "Some Observations on Factivity," *Papers in Linguistics* 4, 55–69.
Karttunen, L. (1971d) "Counterfactual Conditionals," *Linguistic Inquiry* 7, 566–567.
Karttunen, L. (1971e) "Implicative Verbs," *Language* 47.2. Reprinted in J. Petöfi and D. Franck, eds. (1973).
Karttunen, L. (1973) "Presuppositions of Compound Sentences," *Linguistic Inquiry*, 4.2, 167–193.
Karttunen, L. (1974) "Presupposition and Linguistic Context," *Theoretical Linguistics* 1, 181–194. Also in A. Rogers, B. Wall, and J. Murphy, eds. (1977) Pp. 149–160.
Karttunen, L. and S. Peters (1975) "Conventional Implicature in Montague Grammar," in *BLSI, Proceedings of the First Annual Meeting of the Berkeley Linguistics Society*, Berkeley, California. Pp. 266–278.
Karttunen, L. and S. Peters (1976) "What Indirect Questions Conventionally Implicate," in S. Mufwene, C. Walker, and S. Steever, eds. (1976) Pp. 351–368.
Karttunen, L. and S. Peters (1977) "Requiem for Presupposition," in *BLS 3, Proceedings of the Third Annual Meeting of the Berkeley Linguistics Society*. Pp. 360–371.
Karttunen, L. and S. Peters (1979) "Conventional Implicature," in C.-K. Oh and D. Dinneen, eds. (1979) Pp. 1–56.
Kasher, A. (1974) "Mood Implicatures: A Logical Way of Doing Generative Pragmatics," *Theoretical Linguistics* 1, 6–38.
Katz, J. J. (1972a) "Interpretive Semantics Meets the Zombies: A Discussion of the Controversy about Deep Structure," *Foundations of Language* 9, 549–596.
Katz, J. J. (1972b) *Semantic Theory*, Harper and Row, New York.
Katz, J. J. (1973) "On Defining Presupposition," *Linguistic Inquiry* 4, 256–260.
Katz, J. J. (1977) "Propositional Structure and Illocutionary Force (Chapter 3)," Crowell, New York.
Katz, J. J. (1979) "A Solution to the Projection Problem for Presupposition," in C.-K. Oh and D. Dinneen, eds. (1979) Pp. 91–126.
Katz, J. J. and D. T. Langendoen (1976) "Pragmatics and Presupposition," *Language* 52, 1–17.
Katz, J. J. and P. Postal (1964) *An Integrated Theory of Linguistic Description*, MIT Press, Cambridge, Massachusetts.
Keefe, R. (1977) "Thoughts on How Not to Delimit Semantics," *York Papers in Linguistics* 7, 181–186.
Keenan, E. L. (1971a) "Two Kinds of Presupposition in Natural Language," in C. Fillmore and D. T. Langendoen, eds. (1971) Pp. 44–52.
Keenan, E. L. (1971b) "Names, Quantifiers and the Sloppy Identity Problem," *Papers in Linguistics* 4, 211–232.
Keenan, E. L. (1972) "On Semantically Based Grammar," *Linguistic Inquiry* 3, 413–461.
Keenan, E. L. (1974) "Logical Presupposition in Natural Language," in C. H. Heidrich, ed., *Semantics and Communication*, North-Holland, Amsterdam. Pp. 229–250.
Keenan, E. L., ed. (1975) *Formal Semantics of Natural Language*, Cambridge University Press, Cambridge.
Keenan, E. L. and R. D. Hull (1973) "The Logical Presuppositions of Questions and Answers," in J. Petöfi and D. Franck, eds. (1973). Pp. 441–466.
Kegl, J., D. Nash, and A. Zaenen, eds. (1977) *Proceedings of the Seventh Annual Meeting of the North Eastern Linguistic Society*. MIT Press, Cambridge, Massachusetts.

Kempson, R. M. (1973a) "Review of C. Fillmore and D. T. Langendoen, eds. (1971)," *Journal of Linguistics* 9, 120–140.
Kempson, R. M. (1973b) "Presupposition: A Problem for Linguistic Theory," in *Transactions of the Philological Society*, 29–54.
Kempson, R. M. (1975) "Presupposition and the Delimitation of Semantics," Cambridge University Press, Cambridge.
Kempson, R. M. (1979) "Presupposition, Opacity, and Ambiguity," in C. K. Oh and D. Dinneen, eds. (1979) Pp. 283–297.
Kiefer, F. (1972) "Über Präsuppositionen," in F. Kiefer, ed. (1972). Pp. 275–304.
Kiefer, F., ed. (1972) *Semantik und generative Grammatik*, Frankfurt/Main.
Kiparsky, P. and C. Kiparsky (1970) "Fact," in M. Bierwissch and K. Heidolph, eds. (1970) *Progress in Linguistics*. The Hague: Mouton. Pp. 143–173. Also in D. Steinberg and L. Jakobovits, eds. (1971) Pp. 345–369. Also in J. Petöfi and D. Franck, eds. (1973) Pp. 315–374.
Klein, E. H. (1975) "Two Sorts of Factive Predicate," *Pragmatics Microfiche* 1.1, B5-C14.
Klemke, E., ed. (1970) *Essays on Bertrand Russell*. University of Illinois Press, Urbana, Illinois.
Kock, C. (1976) "Presupposition and the Linguistics of Literature," in F. Karlsson, ed., *Papers from the Third Scandinavian Conference on Linguistics*, Text Linguistic Research Group, Academy of Finland, Turku. Pp. 245–252.
Kotschi, T. (To appear) "On the Distinction between Presuppositions and Conversational Implicatures," *Journal of Pragmatics*'
Kummer, W. (1973) "Pragmatic Implication," in J. Petöfi and H. Rieser, eds. (1973).
Kuroda, S. Y. (1969) "Remarks on Selectional Restrictions and Presuppositions," in F. Kiefer, ed. (1969), *Studies in Syntax and Semantics*, Reidel, Dordrecht. Pp. 138–167.
Kuroda, S. Y. (1974) "Geach and Katz on Presupposition," *Foundations of Language* 12, 177–199.
Kuroda, S.-Y. (1977) "Description of Presuppositional Phenomena from a Non-Presuppositional Point of View," *Lingvisticae Investigationes*, 1. 63–162.
Kuroda, S.-Y. (1979) "Katz and Langendoen on Presupposition," in C.-K. Oh and D. Dinneen, eds. (1979) Pp. 183–198.
Kutschera, F. V. (1974) "Indicative Conditionals," *Theoretical Linguistics* 1, 257–269.
Kutschera, F. V. (1975) "Partial Interpretations," in E. L. Keenan, ed. (1975). Pp. 156–174.
La Galy, M., R. Fox, and A. Bruck, eds. (1974) *Papers from the 10th Regional Meeting of the Chicago Linguistic Society*, University of Chicago Department of Linguistics.
Lakoff, G. (1970) "Linguistics and Natural Logic," *Synthese* 22½, 151–271. Reprinted in Davidson and Harman, eds. (1972). Pp. 545–665.
Lakoff, G. (1971a) "Presupposition and Relative Well-Formedness," in D. Steinberg and L. Jakobovits, eds. (1971) Pp. 329–340.
Lakoff, G. (1971b) "The Role of Deduction in Grammar," in C. J. Fillmore and D. T. Langendoen, eds. (1971) Pp. 63–72.
Lakoff, G. (1975) "Pragmatics in Natural Logic," in E. L. Keenan, ed. (1975). Pp. 283–286.
Lakoff, G. (1977) "Pragmatics in Natural Logic," in A. Rogers, B. Wall, and J. Murphy, eds. (1977) Pp. 107–134.
Lakoff, R. (1971) "If's, And's, and But's about Conjunction," in C. Fillmore and D. T. Langendoen, eds. (1971) Pp. 115–150.
Lambert, K. ed. (1969) *The Logical Way of Doing Things*, Yale University Press, New Haven, Connecticut.

Lambert, K. ed. (1970) *Philosophical Problems in Logic*, Reidel, Dordrecht.

Landsman, C. (1972) *Discourse and Its Presuppositions*, Yale University Press, New Haven, Connecticut.

Langendoen, D. T. (1971) "Presupposition and Assertion in the Semantic Analysis of Nouns and Verbs in English," in D. Steinberg and L. Jakobovits, eds. (1971) Pp. 341–344.

Langendoen, D. T. and H. Savin (1971) "The Projection Problem for Presuppositions," in C. Fillmore and D. T. Langendoen, eds. (1971) Pp. 55–62. Also in J. Petöfi and D. Franck, eds. (1973) Pp. 365–372.

Lee, C. (1972) "Presupposition of Existence of Theme for Verbs of Change (in Korean and English)," *Foundations of Language* 9, 384–391.

Lemmon, E. J. (1966) "Sentences, Statements, and Propositions," in B. Williams and A. Montefiore, eds. (1966) *British Analytical Philosophy*, Routledge and Kegan Paul, London. Pp. 87–107. Also in J. Rosenberg and C. Travis, eds. (1971) Pp. 233–249.

Leonard, H. S. (1959) "Interrogatives, Imperatives, Truth, Falsity, and Lies," *Philosophy of Science* 26, 172–186.

Lewis, D. (1969) *Convention: A Philosophical Study*, Harvard University Press, Cambridge, Massachusetts.

Lewis, D. (1973) *Counterfactuals*, Harvard University Press, Cambridge, Massachusetts.

Lewis, D. (1978) "Truth in Fiction," *American Philosophical Quarterly* 15.1.

Li, C. N., ed. (1976) *Subject and Topic*, Academic Press, New York.

Liberman, M. (1973) "Alternatives," in C. Corum, T. C. Smith-Stark, and A. Weiser, eds. (1973) Pp. 346–355.

Liberman, M. and I. A. Sag. (1974) "Prosodic Form and Discourse Functions," in M. La Galy, R. Fox, and A. Bruck, eds. (1974) Pp. 416–427.

Lightfoot, D. (1973) "Présuppositions dans la grammaire transformationelle," *Lingua* 31, 177–199.

Linsky, L. (1967) "Reference and Referents," in L. Linsky (1967) *Referring*. Routledge and Kegan Paul, London. Pp. 116–131. Reprinted in D. Steinberg and L. Jakobovits, eds. (1971) Pp. 76–85.

Linsky, L., ed. (1952) *Semantics and the Philosophy of Language*, University of Illinois Press, Urbana, Illinois.

Llewelyn, J. (1961) "Collingwood's Doctrine of Absolute Presupposition," *The Philosophical Quarterly* II, 42/43, 49–60.

Llewelyn, J. (1962) "Presuppositions, Assumptions, and Assertions," *Theoria* 158–172.

Lutzeier, P. (1976) "The Counterfactual Reading of *before*," *Amsterdam Papers in Formal Grammar* 1, 170–193.

Manor, R. (1974) "A Semantic Analysis of Conditional Assertion," *Journal of Philosophical Logic* 3, 37–52.

Martin, J. (1975a) "A Many-Valued Semantics for Category Mistakes," *Synthese* 31, 63–83.

Martin, J. (1975b) "Karttunen on Possibility," *Linguistic Inquiry* 6, 339–341.

McCawley, J. D. (1970) "Where Do Noun Phrases Come From?" in R. Jacobs and P. Rosenbaum, eds. (1970) *Readings in English Transformational Grammar*. Waltham, Massachusetts. Pp. 166–183. Reprinted in revised form in D. Steinberg and L. Jakobovits, eds. (1971) Pp. 217–231.

McCawley, J. D. (1974) "*If* and *only if*," *Linguistic Inquiry* 5, 632–635.

McCawley, J. D. (1979) "Presupposition and Discourse Structure," in C.-K. Oh and D. Dinneen, eds. (1979) Pp. 371–388.

McCawley, J. D. (ms.) "Everything that Linguists Have Always Wanted to Know about Logic* . . . . .*But Were Ashamed to Ask," Unpublished manuscript, University of Chicago. Chapter 9: Presupposition.

McCawley, J. D., ed. (1976) "*Syntax and Semantics 7: Notes from the Linguistic Underground*," Academic Press, New York.

Meisel, J. M. (1973) "Presuppositions in Object and Adverbial Constructions," *Lingua* 31, 213–236.

Montague, R. (1969) "Presupposing," *The Philosophical Quarterly* 19, 98–110.

Moore, T. (1973) "Focus, Presupposition, and Deep Structure," in M. Gross, M. Halle, and M.-P. Schützenberger, eds. (1973) *The Formal Analysis of Natural Languages*. The Hague, Mouton. Pp. 88–99.

Moravcsik, J., ed. (1974) *Logic and Philosophy for Linguists: A Book of Readings*. Mouton, The Hague and Humanities Press, Atlantic Highlands, New Jersey.

Morgan, J. L. (1969) "On the Treatment of Presupposition in Transformational Grammar," in E. Binnick, A. Davison, G. Green, and J. Morgan, eds. (1969) Pp. 167–177.

Morgan, J. L. (1973a) "How Can You Be in Two Places at Once, When You're Not Anywhere at All?" in C. Corum, T. C. Smith-Stark, and A. Weiser, eds. (1973) Pp. 410–427.

Morgan, J. L. (1973b) *Presupposition and the Representation of Meaning: Prolegomena*, Doctoral dissertation, University of Chicago.

Mufwene, S., C. Walker, and S. Steever, eds. (1976) *Papers from the 12th Regional Meeting of the Chicago Linguistic Society*, University of Chicago Department of Linguistics.

Muraki, M. (1970) *Presupposition, Pseudo Clefting, and Thematization*, Doctoral dissertation, University of Texas.

Muraki, M. (1972) "Discourse Presupposition," *Papers in Linguistics* 5.2.

Muraki, M. (1974) "Presupposition in Cyclic Lexical Insertion," *Foundations of Language* 11, 187–214'

Nelson, E. J. (1946) "Contradiction and the Presupposition of Existence," *Mind* 55, 318–327.

Nerlich, G. (1965) "Presupposition and Entailment," *American Philosophical Quarterly* 2, 33–42.

Neubauer, P. (1976) "The 2^3 Verbs Pretend," in J. D. McCawley, ed. (1976) Pp. 399–408'

Oh, C'-K. (1974a) "More on Degree of Factivity," in M. La Galy, R. Fox, and A. Bruck, eds. (1974) Pp. 517–527.

Oh, C.-K. (1974b) "Presupposition and Meaning Change by Transformational Rules," in R. W. Shuy and C.-J. Bailey, eds., *Towards Tomorrow's Linguistics*, Georgetown University Press, Washington, D.C. Pp. 1–11'

Oh, C.-K. and D. Dinneen, eds. (1979) *Syntax and Semantics* 11: *Presupposition*, Academic Press, New York.

Oh, C.-K. and K. Godden (1979) "Presuppositional Grammar," in C.-K. Oh and D. Dinneen, eds. (1979) Pp. 225–234.

Õim, H. (1973) "Presuppositions and the Ordering of Messages," in F. Kiefer, ed. (1973) *Trends in Theoretical Linguistics in the Soviet Union*, Reidel, Dordrecht. Pp. 1123–1134'

Olshewsky, T., ed. (1969) *Problems in the Philosophy of Language*. Holt, Rinehart, and Winston; New York.

Osgood, C. E. (1971) "Where Do Sentences Come From?" in D. Steinberg and L. Jakobovits, eds. (1971) Pp. 497–529.

Pak, T. (1974) "The Fictivity of Kiparskian Factivity," *Studia Linguistica* 28, 1–6.

Peranteau, P., J. Levi, and G. Phares, eds. (1972) *Papers from the Eighth Regional Meeting of the Chicago Linguistic Society*, University of Chicago Department of Linguistics.

Peters, S. (1975a) "Presupposition and Logical Form," *Texas Linguistic Forum* 122–133.

Peters, S. (1975b) "Presuppositions and Conversation," *Texas Linguistic Forum* 2, 122–134.

Peters, S. (1977) "A Truth Conditional Formulation of Karttunen's Account of Presupposition," *Texas Linguistic Forum* 137–149.

Peterson, P. L. (1979) "On Representing Event Reference," in C.-K. Oh and D. Dinneen, eds. (1979) Pp. 324–355.

Petöfi, J. and D. Franck, eds. (1973) *Präsupposition in der Linguistik und der Philosophie*, Athenäum, Frankfurt/Main.

Petöfi J. and H. Reiser (1973) "Präsuppositionen und Folgerungen in der Textgrammatik," in Petöfi and Franck, eds. (1973) Pp. 485–594.

Petöfi J. and H. Reiser, eds. (1973) *Studies in Text Grammar*, Reidel, Dordrecht.

Postal, P. (1972) "A Few Factive Facts," *Linguistic Inquiry* 3, 396–400.

Prince, E. F. (1978a) "A Comparison of *wh*-Clefts and *it*-Clefts in Discourse," *Language* 54.4, 893–906'

Prince, E. F. (1978b) "On the Function of Existential Presupposition in Discourse," in D. Farkas, W. Jakobsen, and K. Bloom, eds. (1978). Pp. 362–376. Also in J. Petöfi, ed. (1979) *Text vs. Sentence*, Buske Verlag, Hamburg.

Prince, G. (1973) "Presupposition and Narrative Strategy," *Centrum* 1.1, 23–31.

Prior, A. and M. Prior (1955) "Erotetic Logic," *Philosophical Logic* 64, 43–59.

Reis, M. (1973) "Entanglement on Factives," *Linguistic Inquiry* 4, 261–271.

Reis, M. (1974a) "Further *ands* and *buts* about Conjunction." in M. La Galy, R. Fox, and A. Bruck, eds. (1974) Pp. 539–550.

Reis, M. (1974b) "Präsuppositionen und Syntax: Eine Vorstudie," Habil-Schrift, University of Munich.

Rescher, N. (1967) "On the Logic of Presupposition," *Philosophy and Phenomenological Research* 21, 521–527.

Rivero, M. L. (1971) "Mood and Presupposition in Spanish," *Foundations of Language* 7, 305–336.

Rivero, M.-L. (1972) "Remarks on Operators and Modalities," *Foundations of Language* 9, 209–241.

Roberts, G. (1969) "A Problem about Presuppositions," *Mind* 78, 270–271.

Rodman, R., R. Nolan, and S. Munsat (1977) "Some Remarks on Pragmatics and Presupposition," Unpublished paper, University of North Carolina at Chapel Hill.

Rogers, A., B. Wall, and J. Murphy, eds. (1977) *Proceedings of the Texas Conference on Performatives, Presuppositions and Implicatures*, Center for Applied Linguistics, Arlington, Virginia.

Rosenbaum, H. (1975) "Some Steps in the Acquisition of Factive and Implicative Sentences," in *BLS 1, Proceedings of the First Annual Meeting of the Berkeley Linguistic Society*, Berkeley, California. Pp. 475–485.

Rosenberg, J. and C. Travis, eds. (1971) *Readings in the Philosophy of Language*, Prentice-Hall, Englewood Cliffs, New Jersey'

Rosenberg, M. S. (1975a) "Factives That Aren't So," in R. Grossman, L. San, and T. Vance, eds. (1975a) Pp. 475–476.

Rosenberg, M. S. (1975b) "Why Negation Would Wreck Havoc with Counterfactive Verbs, If There Were Any," *Papers in Linguistics* 8, 89–100.

Ross, J. R. (1975) "Clausematiness," in E. L. Keenan, ed. (1975) Pp. 422–475.

Russell, B. (1905) "On Denoting," *Mind* 14, 479–493. Also in D. Davidson and G. Harman, eds. (1975) Pp. 184–192. Also in F. Zabeeh, E. Klemke, and A. Jacobsen, eds. (1974) Pp. 141–158. Also in T. Olshewsky, ed. (1969) Pp. 300–311. Also reprinted elsewhere.

Russell, B. (1920) "Descriptions," in B. Russell (1920) *Introduction to Mathematical Philosophy, 2nd edition*, London. Pp. 167–180. Also in L. Linsky, ed. (1952) Pp. 95–110. Also in J. Rosenberg and C. Travis, eds. (1971) Pp. 166–174.

Russell, B. (1957) "Mr. Strawson on Referring," *Mind* LXVI. Also in B. Russell (1959) *My Philosophical Development*. Allen and Unwin, London. Pp. 238–245. Also in I. Copi and J. Gould, eds. (1967) *Contemporary Readings in Logical Theory*. MacMillan, New York. Pp. 127–132. Also in T. Olshewsky, ed. (1969) Pp. 333–338.

Rutherford, W. (1970) "Some Observations Concerning Subordinate Clauses in English," *Language* 46.1, 97–115.

Sag, I. A. and E. F. Prince (1979) "Bibliography of Works Dealing with Presupposition," in C.-K. Oh and D. Dinneen, eds. (1979) Pp. 389–402.

Schacter, J. (1971) *Presupposition and Counterfactual Conditional Sentences*, Doctoral dissertation, UCLA.

Schacter, P. (1973) "Focus and Relativization," *Language* 49.1, 19–46.

Schiebe, T. (1975) *Über Präsuppositionen zusammengesetzer Sätze im Deutschen*, Almqvist and Wiksell, Stockholm.

Schiebe, T. (1979) "On Presupposition in Complex Sentences," in C.-K. Oh and D. Dinneen, eds. (1979) Pp. 127–154.

Schiebe, T. (To appear) "Review of D. Wilson (1975), *Presuppositions and Non-Truth-Conditional Semantics*," *Studies in Language*.

Schmerling, S. (1971) "Presupposition and the Notion of Normal Stress," in D. Adams, M. Campbell, V. Cohen, J. Lovins, E. Maxwell, C. Nygren, and J. Reighard, eds. (1971) pp. 242–253.

Schmerling, S. (1974) "A Reexamination of Normal Stress," *Language* 50.1, 66–73.

Schnitzer, M. (1971) "Presupposition, Entailment and Russell's Theory of Descriptions," *Foundations of Language* 7, 297–299.

Schwarz, D. S. (1976) "Notes from the Pragmatic Wastebasket: On a Gricean Explanation of the Preferred Interpretation of Negative Sentences," *Pragmatics Microfiche* 2.1, E4-F10.

Schwarz, D. S. (1977) "On Pragmatic Presupposition," *Linguistics and Philosophy* 1.2, 247–258.

Searle, J. (1969) "Proper Names," in J. Searle (1969) *Speech Acts*. Cambridge University Press, Cambridge. Pp. 162–174. Also in J. Petöfi and D. Franck, eds. (1973) Pp. 159–172. Also in D. Steinberg and L. Jakobovits, eds. (1971) Pp. 134–141.

Sellars, W. (1954) "Presupposing," *Philosophical Review* 63, 197–215. Also in E. Klemke, ed. (1970) Pp. 173–189.

Sgall, P. (1975) "Conditions of the Use of Sentences and a Semantic Representation of Topic and Focus," in E. L. Keenan, ed. (1975) Pp. 297–312.

Shenaut, G. (1975) "Valves: Plumbing the Presuppositional Depths (Or, What's a Plug like You Doing in a Hole like This?)," in R. Grossman, L. J. San, and T. Vance, eds. (1975) Pp. 498–513.

Sinha, A. K. (1973) "Factivity and Relations between Main and Subordinate Clauses in Hindi," in C. Corum, T. C. Smith-Stark, and A. Weiser, eds. (1973) *You Take the High Node and I'll Take the Low Node: Papers from the Comparative Syntax Festival*. Chicago Linguistic Society, Chicago. Pp. 155–163.

Snyder, L. S. (1976) "The Early Presuppositions and Performatives of Normal and

Language Disabled Children," *Stanford University Papers and Reports on Child Language Development* 12, 221–229.

Soames, S. (1976) *A Critical Examination of Frege's Theory of Presupposition and Contemporary Alternatives*, Doctoral dissertation, MIT.

Spears, A. K. (1973) "Complements of Significant-Class Predicates: A Study in the Semantics of Complementation," in C. Corum, T. D. Smith-Stark, and A. Weiser, eds. (1973) Pp. 627–638.

Stalnaker, R. (1970) "Pragmatics," *Synthese* 22, 272–289. Also in D. Davidson and G. Harman, eds. (1972) Pp. 380–397. Also in J. Petöfi and D. Franck, eds. (1973) Pp. 389–408.

Stalnaker, R. C. (1973) "Presuppositions," *Journal of Philosophical Logic* 2, 447–457.

Stalnaker, R. C. (1974) "Pragmatic Presuppositions," in M. Munitz and P. Unger, eds. (1974) *Semantics and Philosophy*. New York University Press, New York. Pp. 197–214. Also in A. Rogers, B. Wall, and J. Murphy, eds. (1977) Pp. 135–148.

Stalnaker, R. (1975) "Presuppositions," in D. Hockney, W. Harper, and B. Freed, eds. (1975) *Contemporary Research in Philosophical Logic and Linguistic Semantics*. Dordrecht, Reidel. Pp. 31–41.

Stalnaker, R. (1978) "Assertion," in P. Cole, ed. (1978). Pp. 315–332.

Steinberg, D. and L. Jakobovits, eds. (1971) *Semantics: An Interdisciplinary Reader*, Cambridge University Press, Cambridge.

Strawson, P. (1950) "On Referring," *Mind* 59, 320–344. Also in F. Zabeeh, E. Klemke, and A. Jacobson, eds. (1974) Pp. 159–192. Also in J. Petöfi and D. Franck, eds. (1973) Pp. 193–220. Also in J. Rosenberg and C. Travis, eds. (1970) Pp. 147–172. Also in T. Olshewsky, ed. (1969) Pp. 312–333. Also reprinted elsewhere.

Strawson, P. (1952) *Introduction to Logical Theory*, Methuen.

Strawson, P. (1954) "A Reply to Mr. Sellars," *Philosophical Review* 63, 216–231. Also in E. Klemke, ed. (1970) Pp. 190–204.

Strawson, P. (1964) "Identifying Reference and Truth Values," *Theoria* 30, 96–118. Also in D. Steinberg and L. Jakobovits, eds. (1971) Pp. 86–99. Also in E. Klemke, ed. (1970) Pp. 236–255.

Thomason, R. H. (1977) "Where Pragmatics Fits In," in A. Rogers, B. Wall, and J. Murphy, eds. (1977) Pp. 161–166.

Thomason, S. K. (1979) "Truth-Value Gaps, Many Truth Values, and Possible Worlds," in C.-K. Oh and D. Dinneen, eds. (1979) Pp. 357–369.

Van der Auwera, J. (1979) "Pragmatic Presupposition: Shared Beliefs in a Theory of Irrefutable Meaning," in C.-K. Oh and D. Dinneen, eds. (1979) Pp. 249–264.

Van Fraassen, B. C. (1966) "Singular Terms, Truth Value Gaps, and Free Logic," *Journal of Philosophy* LXIII.17, 481–495.

Van Fraassen, B. C. (1968) "Presupposition, Implication and Self-Reference," *Journal of Philosophy* 65, 136–152.

Van Fraassen, B. C. (1969) "Presuppositions, Supervaluations and Free Logic," in K. Lambert, ed. (1969) Pp. 67–91.

Veltman, F. (1976) "Prejudices, Presuppositions and the Theory of Conditionals," *Amsterdam Papers in Formal Grammar* 1, 248–281.

Vennemann, T. (1973) "Explanation in Syntax," in J. Kimball, ed. (1973) *Syntax and Semantics 2*, Seminar Press, New York. Pp. 1–50.

Vennemann, T. (1975) "Topics, Sentence Accent, Ellipsis: A Proposal for Their Formal Treatment," in E. L. Keenan, ed. (1975) Pp. 313–328.

Verschueren, J. F. (1977) "Reflections on Presupposition Failure: A Contribution to an Integrated Theory of Pragmatics," *Journal of Pragmatics* 2, 107–152.

Vlach, F. (1974) "Factives and Negatives," in C. Fillmore, G. Lakoff, and R. Lakoff, eds. (1974) Section XXI.

Weischedel, R. M. (1975) *Computation of a Unique Class of Inferences: Presupposition and Entailment*, Doctoral dissertation, University of Pennsylvania.

Weischedel, R. M. (1979) "A New Semantic Computation while Parsing: Presupposition and Entailment," in C.-K. Oh and D. Dinneen, eds. (1979) Pp. 155–182.

Wilkinson, R. W. (1970) "Factive Complements and Action Complements," in *Papers from the 6th Regional Meeting of the Chicago Linguistic Society*, University of Chicago Department of Linguistics. Pp. 425–446.

Wilson, D. M. (1972) "Presuppositions on Factives," *Linguistic Inquiry* 3, 405–410.

Wilson, D. M. (1975a) "Presupposition, Assertion, and Lexical Items," *Linguistic Inquiry* 6, 95–114.

Wilson, D. M. (1975b) *Presupposition and Non-Truth-Conditional Semantics*, Academic Press, New York.

Wilson, D. M. and D. Sperber (1977) "A New Approach to Presuppositions," *Pragmatics Microfiche* 2.5, B3-D4.

Wilson D. and D. Sperber (1979) "Ordered Entailments: An Alternative to Presuppositional Theories," in C.-K. Oh and D. Dinneen, eds. (1979) Pp. 299–323.

Woodruff, P. (1970) "Logic and Truth-Value Gaps," in K. Lambert, ed. (1970) Pp. 121–142.

Wunderlich, D. (1973) "Präsupposition in der Linguistik," in J. Petöfi and D. Franck, eds. (1973) Pp. 467–484.

Zabeeh, F., E. Klemke, and A. Jacobson, eds. (1974) *Readings in Semantics*, University of Illinois Press, Urbana.

Zuber, R. (1972) *Structure presuppositionelle du langage*, Dunod, Paris.

Zuber, R. (1975) "On the Semantics of Complex Sentences," Indiana University Linguistics Club.

Zwicky, A. M. (1971) "On Reported Speech," in C. Fillmore and D. T. Langendoen, eds. (1971) Pp. 73–77.

Zwicky, A. M. (1973) "Bibliography I: Coivs.," *OSU Working Papers in Linguistics* 16, 99–106.

AUTHOR INDEX

SUBJECT INDEX

WORD (AND EXPRESSION) INDEX

N

O

P

R

S

T

CONTENTS OF PREVIOUS VOLUMES

Hedged Performatives, *Bruce Fraser*
Asymmetric Conjunction and Rules of Conversation, *Susan F. Schmerling*
Where to Do Things with Words, *John Robert Ross*
The Synchronic and Diachronic Status of Conversational Implicature, *Peter Cole*
Some Interactions of Syntax and Pragmatics, *J. L. Morgan*
'Meaning', *Richard T. Garner*
Meaning$_{nn}$ and Conversational Implicature, *Richard A. Wright*
The Soft, Interpretive Underbelly of Generative Semantics, *Jerrold M. Sadock*

Volume 4

Ambiguity Tests and How to Fail Them, *Arnold M. Zwicky and Jerrold M. Sadock*
Some Universals for Quantifier Scope, *Georgette Ioup*
Cause and Control: On the Semantics of Interpersonal Manipulation, *Talmy Givon*
On Assertive Predicates, *Joan B. Hooper*
Verbs of Hedging, *Per Lysvag*
Predictive Analysis and Over-the-Top Parsing, *John P. Kimball*
Semantics and Syntax of Motion, *Leonard Talmy*
Bully for Us, *John Grinder and Suzette Haden Elgin*
Small Clauses in English, *Edwin S. Williams*

Volume 5

Subject, *S.-Y. Kuroda*
Subject Raising, *Susumu Kuno*
Reflexivization: A Transformational Approach, *Noriko Akatsuka McCawley*
Reflexivization: An Interpretative Approach, *Kazuko Inoue*
Passivization, *Irwin Howard and Agnes M. Niyekawa-Howard*
Causativization, *Masayoshi Shibatani*
Relativization, *James D. McCawley*
Complementation, *Lewis S. Josephs*
Negation, *Naomi Hanaoka McGloin*
Tense, Aspect, and Modality, *Minoru Nakau*
Nominal Compounds, *Seiichi Makino*
Honorifics, *S. I. Harada*

Volume 6

The Grammar of Causative Constructions: A Conspectus, *Masayoshi Shibatani*
PART 1: THEORETICAL FOUNDATIONS
Semantic Causative Types, *Leonard Talmy*
Remarks on What Can Cause What, *James D. McCawley*
The Precyclic Nature of Predicate Raising, *Frederick J. Newmeyer*
Where Do Instrumental NPs Come from?, *Richard H. Wojcik*
On Experiencer Causatives, *Noriko A. McCawley*
Idioms and Lexicalization in English, *James T. Heringer*
The Iffyness of Transitive Verbs, *Robert Binnick*
On Composite Predication in English, *Michael B. Kac*
PART 2: UNIVERSALS AND LANGUAGE PARTICULAR STUDIES
The Syntax of Causative Constructions: Cross-Language Similarities and Divergences, *Bernard Comrie*
Lexical and Nonlexical Causatives in Bantu, *Robin Cooper*
Some Constraints on Bantu Causativization, *Talmy Givon*
On the Semantics of Causative Construction in Hindi-Urdu, *Yamuna Kachru*
On the Hungarian Causative Verb and Its Syntax, *Robert Hetzron*
Some Constraints on Turkish Causativization, *Karl E. Zimmer*
Lahu Causative Constructions: Case Hierarchies and the Morphology/Syntax Cycle in a Tibeto–Burman Perspective, *James A. Matisoff*

Contents of Previous Volumes

Volume 10